HIS SECOND SELF

The Bio-Bibliography of
Victor Rousseau Emanuel

OTHER SPECTRE BOOKS

HIS SECOND SELF

The Bio-Bibliography of Victor Rousseau Emanuel

Compiled by
Morgan A. Wallace

The Spectre Library
2011

DEDICATIONS AND ACKNOWLEDGMENTS

To the memory of the late Virgil Utter, for without his words of encouragement, none of these strange adventures in publishing would have occurred.

Foremost, my wife, Barbara, while none may know her, most have an understanding spouse. Trust me; nobody has more patience.

For unlimited graciousness, assistance, and patience, I am grateful to Victor Rousseau Emanuel's extended family. Thank you for sharing memories of your grandfather, the many photographs and letters, and kind words along the way.

For allowing entry and access to the archival records and letters of the International Press Bureau, I wish to heartily thank the librarians at the University of Waterloo Library.

A gargantuan debt of gratitude to the wonderful staff in the Reference Department at the Jean Rhein Central Branch library in Casselberry, Florida. In particular, to Marie, Nancy, and Guy, whom tirelessly and adroitly fulfilled my interlibrary loan requests.

To all of the universities and colleges across the globe that individually filled requests or answered questions, providing photocopies of archived documents.

And, to all of the other researchers and collectors in the field, including Michael Ashley, Victor Berch, Fred Cleaver, Richard Polt, Arthur Hackathorn, Will Murray, Olivier Raynaud, Phil Stephensen-Payne, Richard Robinson, Richard Simms, and the late Forrest J. Ackerman…and everyone else I failed to note.

CONTENTS

INTRODUCTION

Victor Rousseau Emanuel: A Search for Self-Identity

Originally named Avigdor Rousseau Emanuel (2 January 1879), Avigdor likely became Victor at his Bar Mitzvah. Sired by Joel Emanuel and Georgiana Rousseau, he had three siblings; Montague Rousseau Emanuel was six years his senior, while Phyllis Elizabeth Emanuel and Dorothy Margaret Emanuel were six and eight years his junior. The Emanuel family lived near Hyde Park and Notting Hill. The children were cared for by various nannies over the years and rarely interacted with their parents, creating a sterile, unloving family environment.

From age 8 to 13, he attended the Warlingham School for boys, living primarily on bread and butter. The young Emanuel was horrified by meat that oozed its own bloody juices his whole life. Education was excellent; he was grateful for his tutelage in French, German, Greek and Latin, English histories, and various works of literature. His last year was marred by personal horror at the hands of one of his teachers, whom physically and mentally assaulted him.

Emanuel enrolled at Harrow on May of 1892 and resided at The Knoll until Christmas 1895. He enrolled a month later than all the other boys. Emanuel had undergone an operation—due to an abdominal "rupture"—at home. Furthermore, Harrow had offered a full scholarship that his father fully expected him to win. He did not. The failure led to a schism between he and his father, whom felt that Emanuel should readily have achieved the scholarship. Childhood memories—before Warlingham—of his father were of love and adoration. Harrow wiped that slate clean for the rest of his life. Emanuel had become an embarrassment not only to his father, but to the entire family.

Entering Harrow a month late also barred Emanuel from the then already established cricket team. Although he loved cricket, he was never were permitted to play, unlike football, which was mandatory. Bullying and harassment—due to his Judaic heritage—followed Emanuel throughout his years at Harrow. Damaging to the character and morale of the young man, the hazing later served as a model for many of Emanuel's early manlier works of fiction, in which the weaker man pits himself against seemingly insurmountable odds. Further humiliation occurred when Emanuel was the only lad to attend the three days' holiday that Harrow allowed for the Harrow and Eton cricket-match. Neither of his parents accompanied him to London, while every boy he knew had a parent with them. Emanuel took the bus, alone, to the cricket-grounds.

Come the Summer of 1895, two books came into Emanuel's hands. The first came from his older brother, surprising him. Being years older, Montague rarely crossed trails with Emanuel, yet handed him a book on Browning. The second book was *The Story of an African Farm* by Olive Schreiner, published originally under the pseudonym of Ralph Iron. After reading the novel, he wanted that world for his own. That Fall, he became an associate—or, subscriber—to the *Journal of the Incorporated Society for Psychical Research*, per the October 1895 edition. The Society's original goals investigated thought-transference, mesmerism, mediumship, Reichenbach Phenomena, apparitions and haunted houses, séances, and the history of all the aforementioned phenomena. Other early members included Arthur Conan Doyle, William Butler Yeats, Carl Gustav Jung, and Alfred Russel Wallace. Member and poet Frederic Myers was responsible for coining the term "telepathy" which later came to replace "thought-transference."

In 1896, Emanuel attended the Balliol College Oxford. To further his embarrassment, he failed to obtain the history scholarship. His father was not amused. The question of a career was something of a mystery to him. He had had no prior direction in life. His brother became a barrister, though had relinquished his desire to be a doctor per his father's interests. Was Emanuel to pursue the same tact?

Law was not for him. He chanced to study medicine, but failed miserably in the preliminaries. His failure in school, monetary debts, and a horrific home life offset by the potential romantic beauty of South Africa…there seemed one logical choice. He embarked for South Africa with about fifty pounds shortly before Queen Victoria's Diamond Jubilee in 1897.

What Emanuel did for the next four years would be entirely unknown if not for his unpublished semi-autobiographical texts as a reference.

> I made the acquaintance of a major on board, a wealthy man who took a fancy to me. He invited me to be his guest at the hotel in Cape Town, where we spent a week together, drinking, and studying the night life. I loved this beautiful city at the base of the majestic Table Mountain, from whose flat top the clouds would roll down like a tablecloth. I was enraptured by the cosmopolitan crowds, Dutch, native, and Malay.

After a week, the unnamed major took him to Bulawayo, a town that only a year earlier had been under intense siege. He was introduced to a surveyor whom was mapping the lands near the Shangani River in Matabeleland. Emanuel signed on as his assistant, to which he admits to being the most "useless assistant." Before long, Emanuel's skin began showing signs of scurvy. Eventually they reached Gwelo (now called Gweru). Next was the town Enkeldoorn (now Chivhu) in which he was hired on as a

schoolmaster to a Boer family. He wrote home and received a harsh letter, followed swiftly by a second, containing a five-pound note. With the newly acquired funds, he quit his job, and caught a ride into Salisbury (now Harare). He obtained a job as "copying clerk" for a firm of lawyers. He lost the job three months later, not due to inefficiency, but an inability to bring in clients. Jobless, he walked the distance back to Bulawayo. The journey took nearly three weeks, and he learned to balance his sole possessions upon his head, just as was local custom. Application to police posts obtained him minor food provisions in the way of a can of bullybeef and a pound of flour. At some point along his journey he learned of America's victories against Spain in Santiago and Manila. He applied to the Mounted Police, but was turned away due to an apparent heart condition. Emanuel was briefly a restaurant cashier then an assistant selling secondhand clothes in Bechuanaland (now Botswana). The railway was finally constructed, linking Bulawayo to Cape Town. With cash in hand from his father again, late in 1898, he arrived in Johannesburg.

> Even in the year 1898 Johannesburg was a city of considerable size. In the center was the inevitable market-square, filled at night with covered wagons and recumbent oxen, a sight that must long ago have disappeared, I suppose, with the arrival of motor transportation. Extending through the heart of the town, following the line of the gold reef, were the enormous white mounds of chemical refuse, "tailings," on which no blade of grass would grow.

It is in Johannesburg that Emanuel's life made the proverbial pivotal turning point. He landed a job with the *Standard and Diggers' News* and immediately swapped that for a better job on the *Transvaal Leader*. Despite being a horrible reporter, the editors recognized an education about the man and made him sub-editor. When the second Boer War developed, Emanuel enlisted with Bethune's Mounted Infantry but was only with the outfit from 19 October 1899 to 25 November 1899. He confesses to being "a bullet-shy young recruit" and was dismissed from the outfit. He re-enlisted with the irregular Colonial Scouts at Pietermaritzburg on 20 December 1899, after some mules he was handling were annexed by another major. He took up residence in the town of Potchefstroom. The British troops had abandoned the town and Emanuel learned that it was to be overrun by bloodthirsty Boers.

> I now realized that my position was not a pleasant one, for I was in an enemy town, wearing civilian clothes...so I walked over to the local pub, which was kept by an Englishman and his wife, to seek their advice. The lady told me that the Boers had taken her husband away that morning.

Mrs. Trevor already had a "British agent" hiding in a cellar barrel. Emanuel slipped under a parlor sofa. This lasted a few days before the pair agreed to escape separately through enemy lines. Emanuel took to the railroad line and arrived at a British outpost. Rumor held that the other fellow had been caught, and shot.

Discharged 4 April 1900, he made his way back to Johannesburg and performed the unthinkable. He went into business for himself, after obtaining additional funds from his father...as a grocer. A couple of weeks later the funds had dried up. The business was a failure.

Realization dawned upon him that his future resided in being a newspaperman. With the war now over, those of English birth were given free passage back to England.

> I went to Cape Town and secured passage aboard a transport, to eat salt horse, as they termed the pickled beef, and to learn the art and comfort of sleeping in a hammock aboard a rolling ship. It was strange to get off the boat at Tilbury, on the lower Thames, and see the white faces, in such contrast to the bronzed ones of South Africa.

While he had been in Johannesburg, Emanuel wrote a novel about his military experiences and posted it back home to a London publisher. Now home, he was delighted to have found that Methuen was to publish *Derwent's Horse*. The novel is dedicated "In Gratitude To Mrs. Trevor, of Potchefstroom, Who Hid Me In Strange Places When The Boers Came In, August, 1900."

The novel opens with an inept soldier named "Lowndes" whom is almost certainly a mirror image of Emanuel during his enlistment. Lowndes reads like the proverbial ass, constantly making mistakes and is the "regimental butt." He is given to be the son of a plantation owner, a well-educated gentleman whom believes he should have been "given" rather than "earned" a commission. The story immediately shifts to two other enlisted men; they behave like idiots throughout the novel. Their outfit—Derwent's Horse—is given two weeks' leave, and the pair involve themselves in idiotic escapades. Upon returning to camp, they head off in the final chapter to battle the Boers. The primary idiot of the pair loses his life, after clearly foreshadowing that he is tired of life, and his mate cries over the loss briefly, then ditches his slow horse and takes his dead mate's horse. Lowndes rebounds in the end and is somewhat straightened out; he kills the enemy, and Derwent's Horse mounts up, moves on, leaving the dead. A weak plot and abysmal characterization make for a less than memorable read.

It was a very bad book, and I don't remember getting any money for it, but now my career seemed definitely marked out for me. I was to be a newspaperman, and write novels on the side. And of course I must go to the land of Hearst and Pulitzer. Life in Johannesburg just before the outbreak of the war had been thrilling, and I envisaged America as an enlarged Johannesburg, and the life of an American reporter as something romantic. Those few months that I spent in London in 1901 were the only time when I felt something of a home life. But I was eager to be gone. Of course there were no passports or immigration restrictions in those days. In the month of June, 1901, I sailed from Southampton to embark on my chosen career.

A Study in Trial and Error: 1901—1908

New York City and Emanuel's beautiful memories of Johannesburg were in fact in stark contrast.

The New York of 1901 was something almost unimaginable today. It was the flood-time of venal politics and a corrupt police force, the day of Big Bill Devery, the police commissioner, and of Richard Croker of Tammany Hall. There were telephone poles all the way down Broadway to the Battery, and the tallest skyscraper was the World Building, on Park Row. However, the first of the modern skyscrapers was in course of construction, the so-called Flatiron Building, where the winds swirled about the intersection of Broadway and Fifth Avenue, and loafers used to assemble to watch the ladies' skirts blown about their ankles. I was, of course, attracted to the Tenderloin, below Thirty-fourth Street,

the heart of the theatrical district and the night life of the city. New York was what is called "wide open." It was like a frontier town, with dance-halls and amusement places, every corner saloon a brothel, and as many prostitutes swarming on the streets as in Piccadilly Circus. Gamblers sat on chairs in the middle of Twenty-ninth Street, transacting their business.

He met with Hearst's *New York Journal* managing editor, Arthur Brisbane, and secured a staff position. A few days later he resigned, dazed, confused, and overwhelmed. Next he sought out Mr. Wright, editor of the oldest continuously running New York paper, the *Commercial Advertiser*. Emanuel settled in with the staff, more at ease, and earned about 10 to 12 dollars per week. Here he met two gentlemen. Walter Durrant, a young reporter and graduate of Cornell; he resided in a garret on the south side of Washington Square. The other was Joseph Jacobs, author of numerous books. Emanuel found in Jacobs a local father figure and occasional source of monetary loans. Less than a year passed and Emanuel severed connections with the paper, about the Summer of 1902, for he made a horrible reporter.

Not in the least dismayed over the loss of his occupation, he set forth writing his second novel—*Spartacus*—concerning ancient Rome, along the lines of Gustave Flaubert's novel, *Salammbo*.

More importantly, Emanuel came to be employed as "Pussyfoot" Johnson's assistant in the construction of an encyclopedia concerning temperance and prohibition. Lacking a job, chum Joseph Jacobs learned of the position and Emanuel moved into Johnson's home in Laurel, Maryland. He earned $16 per week.

I look back upon my life with the Johnsons with deep nostalgia. They were simple, natural, kindly people, a typical fine American family. There were no reservations, no nuances, no nicknames, and there was normal family affection. There were none of the inhibitions and complexes of my own home life…I had been with the Johnsons some eighteen months, I think, when the Chicago firm that was responsible for financing the encyclopedia decided to discontinue, owing to lack of funds, although the work was almost completed. I had been living with people I loved, and had been more content than at any time in my life. I had been away from England for a second period of four years.

Emanuel was also involved to some degree with the temperance movement, as illustrated by an undated [circa 1904—1905] pamphlet circulated by The New Voice Press of Chicago entitled "The World's Consumption of Liquors" by Victor R. Emanuel. The New Voice Press, established 25 September 1884, published weekly 16-page booklets concerning the temperance or prohibition movement using worldwide facts to support their efforts. Contributors included lead editor John G. Woolley, E. J. Wheeler, T. E. Stephens, Bernie Babcock, J. Burritt Smith, and the renown William E. Johnson alias "Pussyfoot," among numerous others. They also issued their own temperance novels. It is possible that Emanuel applied himself to other temperance documents; a family letter written to his brother in 1904 implies a heated discussion on alcoholism, moderation, and medicinal uses.

Emanuel also contributed to the *Jewish Encyclopedia*, published by Funk & Wagnalls, in the 1905 and 1906 editions, under his full name. He may well have contributed to earlier and later editions as well. Emanuel's residence is listed as being in Laurel, Maryland, clearly indicating that he was working from Johnson's home.

Desiring a loving home life resplendent of the joy and happiness he felt while residing with the Johnsons, Emanuel set sail for England, early in 1905. Moving in with his family, he spent long hours pounding his fingers away on a Blickensderfer typewriter, presented to him by Mr. Johnson. Cyril Pearson offered him a job with the *Daily Express*, which he accepted. He was at home amongst his own countrymen, his brief journalism experience in America was invaluable, and yet, he was homesick for America. Family surliness, pettiness, and the dissolution of a friendship with his brother settled things.

It was an intolerable situation, but still I should have stuck to my job until I was earning enough money to live by myself. My decision turned on a trifle, as most decisions do. I reached it after reading a few lines of poetry. The Longfellow centenary was approaching, and I was planning an article, which was later rejected, as had all the stories that I had written…The efficient cause of my decision to return to America was a few lines from Longfellow's "Building of the Ship":

Thou too sail on, O Ship of State,
Sail on, O Union, grand and great.

I sent a message to my father through my mother, saying that I thought I could do better in America. He was more than glad to give me fifty pounds to be rid of me.

He departed the third day of June from Southampton and arrived 11 June 1905 at Ellis Island. Again.

Ellis Island documents suggest that Emanuel provided multiple destinations. He planned to visit the Johnson family, hit Washington D. C., perhaps to try journalism in the nation's capital, with a final address given as 45 Washington Square, New York City.

A career in journalism eluded him. Emanuel landed a job addressing envelopes for a firm, and found the job enjoyable. It required no brains; he earned about eighty-cents a day. His nights were spent at Mills Hotel on Bleecker Street.

Three years after beginning his second novel attempt were spent revising *Spartacus* along Flaubert's masterpiece and only once was it sent to a publisher, in September 1905. Emanuel had shot for the stars. Rejection. And while he consigned the manuscript to the garbage-can, Houghton-Mifflin maintained the practice of noting the receipt of every single manuscript and wrote a detailed record concerning the plot and a decision as to why the novel was accepted or rejected. In short, while Emanuel clearly had a firm grasp of Roman history, *Spartacus* was a weak novel with poor characterization.

Toward the end of 1905 Emanuel wrote a half-dozen vignettes for the nationally syndicated children's pages. Chum Ryan Walker, a cartoonist, suggested Emanuel should relocate to St. Petersburg, Florida, as a change in perspective and enlightenment. He resided on an orange grove operated and farmed by an elderly gentleman. His experiences in the South led to various Florida-oriented special articles being published in the "Magazine Section" of the *Baltimore American* in 1907. They were subsequently syndicated. Three other syndicated "special" articles have thus far been discovered in early 1906, but the paper of origin is unknown.

He returned to New York and set sail again for England, aboard a cattle-boat. While again residing with his parents, Emanuel attended speed classes, learned the Isaac Pitman system of shorthand, and learned Spanish to a fair degree, all with the resolve to tackle America's journalism field again.

William Whiteley, the department-store proprietor, had been murdered by his illegitimate son, and of course all of us, to whom Whiteley's had been an institution since childhood, were greatly shocked. My mother came to me, and said: "I'll get you the money to go to America. I'm afraid of your doing something like that to your father." It was a shocking thing to say. What my mother had been telling me was that my father's attitude toward me had been so bad that I might reasonably harbor thoughts of parricide. My mother sold a diamond brooch, and gave me the fare to America.

Emanuel departed from Liverpool two months after Whiteley's murder, and on 9 March 1907, he arrived at Ellis Island. Destination: 207 14th Street, New York City.

He obtained a job with the New York telephone directory but resigned to obtain a job paying $20 per week, editing Will Carleton's *Every Where* magazine, in mid-1907. The job lasted only two or three months. Two articles appearing under the alias Egbert Prentice beyond a doubt came from Emanuel's hand. They represent the highest quality that Emanuel yearned to create.

His first noteworthy sale of fiction appears in the September 1907 issue of *The Munsey* magazine, printing "The Last Cartridge." It is a tale about one woman's love and deceit in the oblique Northern wilderness.

Through a lady on the staff of *Harper's Magazine*, I obtained a job in one of the departments of Harper & Brothers, at ten dollars a week. I was a kind of office boy—that is to say, I had to clean up and sweep out the litter. After a while I was inspired to write a letter to the firm, asking to be transferred to a literary department, and detailing my qualifications. To my amazement—for I don't know how it happened—I was taken on the staff of the famous old *Harper's Weekly*. Within two weeks of my arrival I was the work-horse of the *Weekly* staff. I passed on manuscripts, edited copy, and fulfilled the other duties of an associate editor. My salary was quickly raised to fifteen dollars, the next year to twenty-five, and then to thirty, where it remained for three years.

While working for *Harper's Weekly,* he whipped up numerous specialty articles and short stories. He befriended Charles and Vera Johnston; she was of Russian aristocracy and niece to Madame Blavatsky. Edith Thomas was a poet and a reader for *Harper's Magazine.* An extremely close relationship developed with Herman Scheffauer, poet and author, whose literary works Emanuel published in *Harper's Weekly.* Herman eventually abandoned America for England and loosely represented Emanuel's future quality-written short stories overseas, selling them to some of England's leading magazines during the early part of the next decade.

Stories unfit for *HW* earned Emanuel $25/per with the *Illustrated Sunday Magazine* supplement. Based out of Buffalo, NY, the *ISM* was operated by *Buffalo Times'* fiction editor Samuel W. Hippler, and syndicated throughout America in major US city papers. Emanuel was able to offer the *ISM* colorful fiction full of regional ethnicity.

Another Sunday supplement that Emanuel briefly entered before its own demise was the *Literary Magazine.* John Judson Hamilton, editor of the *Des Moines Daily News*, purchased the doomed Chicago supplement in January 1909. Under the Chicago owners, it claimed to have had a circulation around 200,000. May 1909, the *Literary Magazine* was back in existence, appearing likely in the *Des Moines Daily News*, as well as in the *Pittsburgh Dispatch*, the *Washington Herald*, the *Colorado Springs Gazette* and countless others. By September, circulation was at 117,000, and was listed as being carried in Washington, Pittsburgh, Lowville, Omaha, and others. The *Literary Magazine* suspended business mid-1910. Liabilities were announced at $17,000 while assets were listed at $15,000.

The earliest known application of Emanuel's alias—H. M. Egbert—is attributed to *Harper's Weekly* (26 December 1908) article "Helping the Filipinos to Fight Disease." Why it was employed is a complete mystery, as Emanuel utilized it here only the one time. Additionally, the alias has only been applied to non-fiction only the one known instance, although it had appeared earlier as "Egbert Prentice" twice in *Every Where* magazine. The non-de-plume "H. M. Egbert" translated is "His Majesty Egbert," after King Egbert, one of the earliest rulers of Britain.

The Early Years With the IPB: 1908—1912
November 1908 ought to be etched in stone. While residing at 97 Clark Street, in Brooklyn, Emanuel replied to an advertisement placed in a literary journal by the International Press Bureau of Chicago, asking what sort of fiction they require. Supervised by William Gerard Chapman and seconded by George T. Pardy, Emanuel participated in a chaotic relationship with the IPB for the next 35 years, one that would cultivate his skills, teach him how to work the market, and earn him many critics. This relationship between Chapman and Emanuel would be an unofficial one of gentlemanly understanding: Emanuel sent in fiction, Chapman bought and placed them. There were no royalties, except on novels. This was a syndication bureau. No contract existed between the pair ... until 1919.

In spite of the many gaping holes present in the files of the International Press Bureau—held by the University of Waterloo—a good deal of detail is present. Large gaps in the files exist from late 1912 through all of 1917, however, there are enough scant details to reconstruct some of what transpired during the interim. The dating of stories during this period of 1912—1917 is construed from their numerous rejection slips.

The files take up again in January 1918, but the friendly relations between Emanuel and Chapman are tenuous at best. Emanuel was threatening to sue Chapman for various breach of permission; the latter was purportedly offering novels to publishers without Emanuel's consent.

Despite two years of bickering, they maintained cordial business relations through-out the entire fiasco, Emanuel continuously turning in stories and Chapman making the effort to place them. Either one could easily have severed all relations at any time, as there was no legal contract between the pair, only an outstanding debt. One thing was clear: Chapman was no longer Emanuel's agent. The field was clear for Emanuel to place literature directly. All his pulp thrillers were sent to Mr. Davis at *Munsey/Argosy* first, then forwarded to Chapman to place on a commission basis. This relationship perished upon Chapman's death in 1945.

In December 1908, Emanuel submitted the vignette "Brandy and Soda" and the short "The Jam God." The IPB paid $5 and $10 for the pair. "The Jam God" readily sold, cut-down, to *Short Stories* magazine (May 1909). The former was nationally syndicated. Emanuel churned out vignettes thereafter for many years with the IPB. With Chapman invading Emanuel's literary markets, he allowed Chapman access only to the nomenclature 'H. M. Egbert,' along with a biography only to be attached to that name, never to his own 'Victor Rousseau' alias. With so many vignettes pouring in Chapman requested another pseudonym, to which Emanuel noted in March 1910 that he often utilized 'Harold Carter' on vignettes. This was no bold claim. The name often appears in the

national newspapers as early as April 1908. In July 1912, Emanuel laid claim that he had sold over 90% of the 70 storiettes he submitted to the defunct N.E.A. (Newspaper Enterprise Association, of Cleveland, OH) for more than two years. The N.E.A. was owned by the Scripps group, and handled the *Detroit Evening News*, *Cleveland [Penny] Press*, *Denver Express*, *Pueblo Sun*, *Dallas Dispatch*, *Memphis Press*, *Nashville Times*, *Oklahoma News*, and *Evansville Press*.

After eight months of churning out humorous and romantic vignettes for the syndication service, Emanuel wanted to turn his hand to writing a series. He had a specific one in mind—dealing with haunted houses, demoniacal possession, etc—after having read a series of stories in *Pearson's* a decade earlier. The series was to run under the title *The Surgeon of Souls*.

After receiving the first two installments in the planned series, Chapman requested that Emanuel construct a synopsis of the remaining titles. Chapman wanted to develop a circular to send out to prospective clients. Remarkably the IPB retained Emanuel's original synopsis for the series, dated 27 October 1909, noting the third through twelfth planned stories. The synopsis is interesting for a variety of reasons. Emanuel had never constructed a plot in advance before, and in reading the below entry, anyone that has read the series may note that he did not strictly adhere to the plot outlines. Further, one must wonder: What became of the tales below that never were printed?

3. THE BROKEN SCROLL. A semi-humorous story of white magic, dealing with the methods adopted against one another by two rival Jewish co-workers, and Brodsky's solution.
4. THE TENTH COMMANDMENT. The mystery of a haunted house which is coveted by a neighbor, and the unexpected solution which "lays" the

spirit and incidentally explains the meaning of the much-discussed last commandment of the Decalogue.

5. THE VAMPIRE. A weird story of maternal love extending beyond the grave, showing the interdependence of spirit and flesh, and the dead mother's attempt to pull her children across the boundary of life.

6. THE SECRET SHRINE. A pathetic story of a bereaved father who seeks to enter into communication with his dead child, demonstrating the evil that results from meddling with the occult.

7. THE LEGACY OF HATE. A story dealing with the terrible penalty and retribution that follow hatred, showing how the antagonism of two brothers worked itself out in suffering until the lesson was learned.

8. THE BRAND OF BIRTH. This story takes up the mystery of reincarnation, showing how one born under conditions of adversity was enabled to recognize and understand the conditions that had brought about his misfortunes.

9. HOMO HOMUNCULUS. A weird experiment in the creation of a living man and its consequences.

10. IN MORTAL SIN. The battle with the hosts of evil for the possession of the soul of a man who died in mortal sin.

11. THE DREAM THAT CAME TRUE. A love story that transends mortality teaching the eternity of love and the nothingness of life.

12. THE TREE OF KNOWLEDGE. Ivan Brodsky's attempt to solve the mysteries that were denied him, and the culminating tragedy.

A number of the plots were deemed unsuitable for the newsprint market or not a proper fit for the series, including "The Broken Scroll," which involved Dr. Ivan Brodsky solving a humorous case rather than a serious episode of ghosts and ghouls. Chapman paid $17 for the story separately, to hold for special sale. Another, "The Vampire," was simply too "gruesome," as Chapman put it. The tale was returned to Emanuel and destroyed. Despite his keen interest and abilities to intelligently write upon the subject of the soul and supernatural affairs, the series sold poorly, effecting only three city sales. Eleven tales in the series were later resuscitated in *Weird Tales* magazine (September 1926—July 1927); a twelfth story —"Homo Homunculus"— was accidentally destroyed by the IPB years earlier. Though initially a loss, the IPB sixteen years later had recovered their lost $200 investment.

The basis for *The Surgeon of Souls* stems from his influential teenage years when he subscribed to the Society for Psychical Research in England and also in Emanuel's religious beliefs. He was a regular attendee of the Washington Avenue Baptist Church, listening to the preaching of Reverend Dr. Robert MacDonald, a graduate of Harvard University with degrees in philosophy. He was far from your regular sermon-reading clergyman. MacDonald preached the beliefs of the Emmanuel Movement. He believed that faith and hypnotism would "cure hysteria, insomnia, neurasthenia, drunkenness, religious melancholia and suicidal mania." MacDonald had received his instruction from Reverend Dr. Elwood Worcester, one of the original founders (with McComb) at the Emmanuel Episcopal Church of Boston. He used as his guide Worcester's *Religion and Medicine: The Moral Control of Nervous Disorders*, a work that referred to clergyman as "physician to the soul." Sound familiar? Emanuel mentions in "The Case of the Jailer's Daughter" that Dr. Ivan Brodsky "was an expert hypnotist and received delicate cases from all parts of the country; lost and multiple personality, amnesia, agraphia, aboulia, all the odds and ends of neuroses…" Emanuel also utilized as his springboard a book written by his own clergyman, entitled *Mind, Religion and Health*, released in 1908 by Funk & Wagnalls. MacDonald also married Emanuel in 1912 to Elva Baker; this is somewhat surprising as her uncle—Edwin Richmond—was a reverend of the Baptist faith and resided in New York City, too. He met her via his close friend, Walter Durrant. About this time, Emanuel also underwent a transformation. He became a Christian.

Believing that he had unlimited abilities at hand to write stories with more of an international flair, Emanuel turned in early 1910 to writing *A King's Courier*. In this, Captain Adams, discharged by the foreign office secretary, finds a new position as one of the king's diplomats, often carrying secret notes, performing as a spy, and countering the actions of foreign spies. The series is brilliant. Acquired for $200, it sold generously amongst the national city papers and sold abroad to Cassell & Co., courtesy of Chapman's English agents, Curtis Brown, managed by Mrs. Hanshew. First-world appearances of each tale in the series is complicated, as America and England ran the series simultaneously. An additional story was written at Chapman's request to replace another in the series, but the replacement story was not up to par; "The Flights of Abdul Hamid" was purchased separately and held pending an opening in a special market. National small-town papers also gobbled up the series, often printing it as *Detective-Diplomat: Narrative of Captain Adams*.

While asking Chapman for notes on his syndicates' better selling stories, Chapman, recognizing in Emanuel a unique writing ability, posted him an excerpted article and picture of a gyroscope. The idea of writing a fantastic tale entirely around one central object and maintaining interest for 12 consecutive installments seemed impossible to Emanuel at the time, but the gyroscope would not be entirely forgotten.

Upon the successful sale of *A King's Courier*, Emanuel became interested in writing along similar plots, turning to an international-adventure on the high seas. Written June 1910, *Under the Black Flag* was to be a story from the criminal point-of-view, a man-without-a-country sailing with worldwide adventures. Unacceptable in the newspaper field, Chapman sent the story out to the magazine and pulpwood markets, where it met with stern criticism and denouncing H. M. Egbert as utilizing too much blood-n-thunder, sensationalism, etc. The story suffered many revisions and was enhanced from a six-part 27,000-word story to double the parts and word count before selling nine years later for $60 in the original form to the *Chicago Ledger* as *Under the Striped Man's Flag*. An unconfirmed Cassell & Co publication in 1913 reportedly published the condensed version, possibly released as *The Freebooter*. Confirmed is its UK appearance in Cassell's *The Corner* magazine, seventeen years later. It ran in five complete installments, and *The Corner* printed the serial under the original title. Overall, the serial was a monetary loss to Chapman.

Determined to write three to four series per year, Emanuel wrote two months later another international spy series and added some blood-n-thunder flavoring, resulting in *The King of Knaves*. Although Chapman was wary about handling another blood-thirsty series, it landed to his immense relief locally with *The Blue Book Magazine*, running monthly March 1911 through February 1912. Moreover, with the international element, they were acceptable in the English trade. While notes suggest a sale was cemented, the source is unknown. The series also syndicated in American and Canadian newspapers under the helm of a lengthier title, being *An Audacious Hazard of Nikolai, Independent Agent, as Related by His Lieutenant, Summers*.

In October, Chapman requisitioned a series of 12 true crime tales involving detectives. This concept was beyond Emanuel's personal abilities, resulting in his having to visit the New York Public Library to perform research on possible subjects. In addition, the detective market was already well-covered. Instead, Emanuel churned out 12 stories involving worldwide murders handled by the police, resulting in the *World-Famous Police Mysteries*. The series took three months to complete and sold moderately, syndicating in such papers as the *Washington Post*, the *Buffalo Sunday Times*, etc. Additionally, it sold in England. More attractive, the stories, being true in nature, would be forever saleable, reappearing in *Detective Story Magazine* in 1919 under the byline of George Munson, a few in *Clues* magazine a decade later, and later yet in the 1940s via the rare Canadian Superior pulp publications. The continual sales were wonderful to the IPB's pocketbook, but Emanuel never saw a dime of it. An additional thirteenth tale was supplied and paid for with the original twelve. It was eventually printed under the byline of George Munson, as a stand-alone true crime title in the 23 September 1919 issue of *Detective Story Magazine* as "Detective Anchisi and the Fort Wayne Gang."

Having promised earlier this year a detective series, Emanuel launched that December into outlining a new series based on the infamous investigator William P. Sheridan. Sheridan's uncanny "eye" for detail aroused the interest of Inspector Thomas Byrnes, aka the Tsar of Mulberry Street. It soon developed that anything or anyone Sheridan ever laid his eyes on were forever burned into his memory! Facts, figures, places people were sighted, a chance glance, passersby on trains, at depots, subways, nothing escaped the uncanny eye of Sheridan. Upon reading an article in the paper—where Emanuel frequently drafted many of his storylines—he embraced Sheridan to the point of stealing his nickname for the

title, *The Man With the Camera Eyes*. Due to a glut on the market of Egbert series, these were uniquely bylined as by Harold Carter. They were mundane tales, and Peter Crewe, the investigator, always got his man, but the "eye" was hardly played up to a Sherlock Holmes status, as originally intended. Further damage resulted with the series lacking any romantic elements. Consequently, the series sold barely better than *The Surgeon of Souls*, failing to reach the magazine market entirely or the English markets.

Despondent that a number of series had failed to create a wonderful sales-sensation for Chapman's IPB, Emanuel wondered what flaws existed in his various series. The answer was "romance." There lacked in all of them the romantic angle, no central heroine. By March 1911, Emanuel settled on a series of hopeless-romantic tales involving the formerly wealthy Englishman named Lord Jocelyn searching America for a wife with money to replenish the family funds back in England. The *Quest of Gentle Hazard* was finished by the end of April, and met with Chapman's satisfaction. In this series was the romantic angle necessitated by American newspaper editors and sporting the international appeal necessary to produce the English sale. Chapman was very keen on this series having worldwide appeal. And yet, it sold poorly, effecting in a quarter-year two city-paper sales, and one mail-order magazine sale, this reportedly to *New Idea Woman's Magazine*.

About May 1911, his address changed to 83 Pleasant Avenue, Montclair, New Jersey, near Cornell University. The reason for the move is unknown, but by April 1912, he was back in Brooklyn, a half-mile south of his old Clark Street address, now at 166 State Street.

Realizing the feminine aspect was a strong motivator in acquiring a sale, Emanuel from July to September 1911 wrote a romantic serial, featuring a charming Brooklyn schoolgirl on her way overseas to witness the coronation of King George in England. First rights were sold cheap to the small *Canada West* (Oct 1911—Apr 1912) outfit as a favor, serializing as *Aviator No. 6*. Before it was permissible to execute a sale in the United States, Chapman had to sit on the serial a full year. It circulated serially in *The People's Popular Monthly* under its original title of *Anne Ives, Mascot*. Chapman more than recouped his initial losses, and was later able to sell the serial abroad and to the small town presses via the Western Newspaper Union (WNU), making this one of his better commercial successes.

For the next couple of months Emanuel floundered about, aimlessly attempting to conceive of a fresh plot, concocting ridiculous heroine leads such as a cab driver, before settling in November on a journalist. *Isabel Marston, Star Reporter*, was born, and yet, despite Emanuel's personal experiences in the field of journalism and his ability to play up the international angles, it was rejected by *The Blue Book Magazine* initially and every other American magazine, before finally effecting a partial sale in England's *Cassell's Magazine of Fiction* (September 1912—February 1913). This led to yet another notch in a line of literary failures.

Despite the apparent disappointments, Chapman was still coming out slightly ahead and willing to continue their unofficial relationship. In addition, Emanuel was to wed on the 25th of March to Elva Baker, a schoolteacher. With marriage on the horizon, Emanuel had long-range plans to devote himself full-time writing rather than eke out a living as an editor at *Harper's Weekly*. His plans were rushed into fruition ahead of schedule. Emanuel unofficially represented chum Herman Scheffauer, and Hippler had not paid for a story recently printed in the *ISM*. Rapid-fire scathing letters to the editor sealed Emanuel's fate, eliminating a source of income at a crucial time. However, the IPB's short story service has assumed shape. Could Emanuel supply a steady weekly supply of storiettes to meet their demand? Yes; three shorts at 1200 words each for $12 or one long and one short story for $10 per week. Before he was through, Emanuel wrote over 1000 romance storiettes for the service, writing under many confirmed pseudonyms such as H. M. Egbert, Harold Carter, Frank Filson, George Munson, Emanuel Radcliffe and Emanuel Redcliffe, John Edgerton, and possibly Percy Keble, E. R. Moon, Egbert Warring, and others. While the latter three are questionable, Frank Filson is irrefutable. On the 1910 Census, Emanuel was a boarder in Harris Filson's home. Several Frank Filson stories are foreign war-thriller vignettes. A worthwhile note is that another occupant in Harris Filson's home, by the name of Otto Schmidt, worked as a painter, and was the inspiration for Emanuel's classic weird tale "Jackson's Wife," in *The Smart Set* (May 1909). One story exists by John Edgerton— "The Man in the Swamp"—is a direct condensed version of Emanuel's "The Man of Pelican Key," appearing in *Ainslee's* (July 1912). This was not the first time that Emanuel had reworked a story as a storiette.

While the vignettes landed in various newspapers, one of the best on-going sources for bibliographic reference is Chicago's *The Day Book*, a digest-sized journal of the day's events sans fanfare that insisted on not relying on advertising as a means of financial support or political control. The paper lasted from 28 November 1911 through 6 July 1917. Running daily, excluding Sundays, New Year's Day, Fourth of July, Thanksgiving, and Christmas, and being based in Chapman's own literary playground, *The Day Book* provides an excellent chronological database. However, there are drawbacks. The first year of its existence provided non-bylined vignettes. Stories based on title and plots have been confirmed to match those from the defunct NEA syndicate. Many of these were written by Emanuel under his Harold Carter alias. Whom had sold these old vignettes to *The Day Book*?

Despite this mystery, on 29 July 1912, the daily short story service provided by Chapman officially commenced, complete with bylines. Some older material initially appeared, before the newer stock took over. An index to Emanuel's tales in *The Day Book*, as complete as possible, and courtesy of the Library of Congress, is also included in this volume.

The idea of using a gyroscope in a series of fantastic adventures again resurfaced. Emanuel had grasped upon an idea and constructed them with an aim toward effecting a sale with *The Blue Book Magazine*, but when a friend pointed out that he was celebrating the adventures of a criminal, Emanuel scrapped the manuscripts and began anew. By mid-February 1912, a number of stories were finished and sent in to Chapman for his approval. A month later, the stories were all to-hand, and Chapman was ecstatic. *The Devil Chair*, carrying the H. M. Egbert byline, was a startlingly fresh series, rife with action, psychological revenge, romance, heartache and raw emotion with a stunning climax. He rushed them to *The Blue Book Magazine* immediately. Refused! *The Devil Chair* faced many criticisms, ranging from their blood-n-thunder sensationalism to the fact that they were not twelve independent stories. Chapman's foolish demand that the stories be written to conform to two markets had once again handicapped Emanuel's abilities. The pulps wanted serials. *The Devil Chair* met its demise finally after being tied up at *The Readers' Magazine* before being unloaded into the newspaper syndicates in the Fall of 1913. Remarkably, *The Devil Chair* did effect a sale in England, to *The News of the World*, reportedly printed in 1913.

By April, a crossover between hopeless romantic and diplomatic fiction was created. *The League of Lost Causes* provided an intriguing situation, in which a love-struck millionaire succumbs to offering his millions for a cause and a woman, only to learn that he has been deceived into aiding the enemy all along. In an effort to rectify the situation, he switches sides while pursuing the love interest, in a fruitless effort to learn whether she ever truly loved him. The series failed to strike the magazines, circulating from mid-1912 to as late as February 1915 down at *Holland's* before eventually landing in the US syndicate market. The series first debuts as a partial sale of seven tales, to begin in the Fall of 1912 in an unknown Cassell & Co publication.

The Ambiguous Years With the IPB: Fall 1912—December 1917

One of the nation's greatest literary journals expired soon after the death of J. P. Morgan in 31 March 1913. Emanuel and nearly all of the staff in-the-know firmly believed that Morgan and other financiers were secretly funding *Harper's Weekly*. The publication had only one rule: Do not print anything about Wall Street. Emanuel was among the first to be discharged; he was given pay for ten days and "a letter of praise." Most notably, this was the last job Emanuel ever held.

With his salaried income annihilated, Emanuel and Elva were in a financial crisis. They moved somewhere near the McDowell Colony of Peterborough, New Hampshire, and applied for a bungalow. This met with a letter of rejection, so they accepted the invitation of a friend in Maine. While there, tragedy beset the Emanuel couple. They were cursed with the birth of a stillborn daughter, their first baby. The pair eventually found living arrangements in Quebec.

> In the summer we stayed at French country hotels, where I was very happy, and always at home with the French people. Once we rented a cottage on the north shore of the St. Lawrence, almost at the edge of civilization…. The scenery was superb, the gaunt hills towering above the mighty river.

They moved again to Long Island and after a year, back to Quebec, residing on 170 Grande Allcc.

While hunting another job, he was contracted by the Lowell Observatory to write special articles, to appear in *World's Work* sometime after September 1913. However, in December, astronomer Percival Lowell had scrapped the entire project.

With *Harper's Weekly* out of the picture, the road was clear for Chapman to finally utilize the more prestigious Victor Rousseau alias on higher quality fiction. A plot involving the use of the divining rod was improbable. Another proposed story turned down was too burlesque. He inquired of Chapman again: what stories sold well in the syndicate? The answer was mystery, true crime, and an original series dealing with reincarnation that had sold relatively well by Fredric Reddale, *The Man Who Remembered*. With Emanuel's interest in the paranormal, Chapman re-quisitioned a fresh series on reincarnation, *The Tracer of Egos*, carrying the Victor Rousseau byline. Nine of the original twelve sold to *Holland's* (June 1913—February 1914), a magazine of the South with an immense circulation and a decent subscription-base. A year later they were printed in the syndicates and elsewhere via the WNU, but like *The Surgeon of Souls*, failed to sell in England.

Between projects, Emanuel continued to directly sell short stories, such as to *Young's Magazine*. For example, in "The Return of Ephraim" (January 1913), a Negro criminal is sent to Sing-Sing by his own gang leader and openly ridiculed by his lover in court. Two years in prison has transformed him into a muscle-bound maniac, bent on meting out physical vengeance about the leader and reacquiring the tittering girl. This tale is subsequently rewritten, eliminating offensive Negro elements, names are altered, the violence is toned down, and the tale is now set in England. It ran a few months later in

England's *The Novel* magazine, as "The Return of Bill."

Emanuel had frequented the northern reaches of Canada as a favorite vacation destination, away from the noise and filth of New York City. These travels inspired him to write early in 1913 the first of many Canadian wilderness serial novels. *Jacqueline of Golden River* made the rounds heavily before landing in March 1914 with the Munsey editors, whom paid $600 for the novel. It languished another year before serializing with *All-Story Cavalier Weekly* in four installments (13 February—6 March 1915). The serial syndicated in many national papers, making it an extremely profitable serial for the IPB. A 1920 novelization effected a decent distribution of 1500 copies by June 1921.

Soon after, Emanuel dived into a series dealing with the *habitants*, a term referring to the French settlers of the St. Lawrence River and Gulf region. Bandied about as "habitant" stories among magazine editors, *The Blue Book Magazine* purchased 9 of the original 12, and cast them as *Tales of the St. Lawrence Riverway* (September 1914—May 1915). The title was unofficial, and the stories had no particular sequential order nor precisely referred to the riverway region. The tales actually occur in and around the village of St. Jean, Quebec. The basis for the stories was lifted from an earlier story Emanuel had written for *Harper's Weekly* (10 December 1910) entitled "The Keeper of the Light." In fact, the lighthouse in that story was also reused in "The Lie of Pere Sebastian." The stories were constructed around mid-1913, each featuring *le curé*—translated means "priest"—and were all good, clean stories with morals. They represented the best of Emanuel's abilities when he strived for quality. The other three habitants stories not featuring *le curé* were printed in *The Red Book Magazine* (May 1914, October 1914, and January 1915). All 12 stories sold for $30 each, but the IPB syndicated the stories many times over, even as late as 1933 with the *Toronto Star*. He continued to occasionally write more short stories involving the adventures of *le curé*, although not all were published.

Not all ventures panned out for the IPB; when they acquired a series of twelve stories late in 1913 entitled *Adventures of Venus*, it was an abysmal failure. Relatively little is known about this series, save that it was littered with cockney dialect, making it undesirable amongst the magazines and newspaper editors, ranked as Emanuel's first definite literary flop. It circulated heavily among *Popular*, *People's*, *Holland's*, both the *Associated* and *Illustrated Sunday Magazine* supplements, then *Ainslee's*, *Pearson's*, *Top-Notch*, and finally with *Snappy Stories* in May 1915 before being pigeon-holed until a market made itself available. *Top-Notch* had offered in March 1915 to buy the series at 1 cent per word, but Chapman wanted double that figure, declining the offer. Despite an inability to effect a sale, Chapman continued to ask more money for unsold original stories, erroneously believing that even an unsalable story's value appreciably increased over the years. By 1922, Chapman was asking $1200 for the dozen, more than double the original offer price.

The Messiah of the Cylinder
Spring 1914, Emanuel turned to writing his magnum opus, *The Messiah of the Cylinder*. Discussing *The Messiah of the Cylinder* requires a greater depth of coverage as the novel is heralded by many science fiction enthusiasts as Emanuel's greatest literary achievement. *The Messiah of the Cylinder* was written with two goals in mind. First, Emanuel disagreed with H. G. Wells' *When the Sleeper Wakes*. Emanuel wanted a proletarian revolt against the bourgeoisie rulers, and true socialism to prevail. Second, fame. Emanuel was dead set that this novel would eliminate past debts and losses to Chapman's IPB and simultaneously launch himself into the literary

limelight. Unfortunately for him, the novel failed to be printed for over three years. But why?

The Messiah of the Cylinder circulated through all the quality magazines: *Popular* in June, to *People's* in July, *Everybody's* in late July literally salivated over the novel but had enough fiction on hand to last them into the next year; 1915 it cycled through *Collier's* in March, *Ainslee's* in late March, and finally in May was returned to *Everybody's*. Finally accepted in June, Gilman Hall expressed an interest to serialize *The Messiah of the Cylinder* in four installments at $500 per, but required that Emanuel cut the novel down, which he did; 44,000 words of the original 75,000 were removed. The novel remained in stasis while Hall was on vacation. Upon returning and examining the massacred manuscript, Hall blanched, and got his staff to work to re-create the masterpiece. Massive editing lasted a month, but to placate an exasperated Chapman over the printing delay, the first of two $1000 checks arrived in late September, the second one following in October. Months passed and with Chapman and Emanuel's frustration mounting, Hall announced Ridgway's intentions for a May 1916 release, but in February retracted the pledge. Frank H. Spearman's *Nan of Music Mountain* was concluding in April and Talbot Mundy's *King, of the Khyber Rifles* was filling the May slot, to run 9 installments. Ridgway had no interest in running two expensively acquired serials simultaneously. That would have left the road clear for a February 1917 release, but before his resignation, Ridgway scheduled Mary Roberts Rinehart's *Long Live the King*. With Howard Wheeler now at the helm, and other changes in the editorial staff, Wheeler firmly promised on the 31st of January that *The Messiah of the Cylinder* would appear in four complete installments beginning with the June number. The June issue was attractively illustrated by Joseph Clement Coll, and Everett Shinn illustrated the cover stunningly with the villain, heroine, and our hero trapped within a cylinder.

Sadly, the novel was too many years too late to effect the fame that Emanuel had initially sought in 1914; it became Emanuel's second bound novel in print, released later that same year by Chicago's A. C. McClurg & Company and appeared in 1918 by Hodder & Stoughton, as *The Apostle of the Cylinder*.

A. C. McClurg & Company paid an advance of $250. Royalties were to be paid 10% on the first 2500 sold, 12.5% on the next 2500, 15% on the next 20,000, and 20% thereafter. They were restricted to US and Canadian rights. Sales figures through the 31st of December 1917 amounted to 845 copies sold; May 1919, the figure had risen to 1270.

In December 1917, Hodder & Stoughton agreed to publish the novel, but required that "*Messiah*" be replaced, to which Emanuel supplied "*Apostle*." They were given the Great Britain and Australian rights, along with Colonial distribution, agreeing to pay £50 advance on account of 15% royalty on the English published price of every copy sold up to 3000, 20% to 6000, and 25% thereafter. Colonial editions would remit a low sum, 3d per copy royalty. Royalties on a future "cheap edition" were to receive an altered royalty, but no such edition came to fruition. Based purely on how well the book sold, H&S had under consideration the option to print *The Sea Demons*, as well as the series *The Devil Chair* and *The Tracer of Egos*. *The Apostle of the Cylinder* was poorly advertised and failed to effect a generous sale with H&S, nullifying their interests in the other titles. Furthermore, Emanuel's constant interference in text corrections, manuscript revisions, and being a general nuisance negated H&S from considering working with Emanuel on any future novels. The first payment arrived in October 1918 to Chapman, a check for $214.43, representing the advance and royalties. Emanuel was given half, and Chapman retained the other $107.21.

The Messiah of the Cylinder subsequently has been reprinted in 1976 by Hyperion, available in hard and softcover editions, making it a readily obtaining novel; *The Apostle of the Cylinder* recently was digitized and published by various print-on-demand presses.

The Great War Years: 1914-1918

Between projects early in 1914, Emanuel reassociated himself with anti-saloon activist William Eugene "Pussyfoot" Johnson. Acquiring "Pussyfoot's" personal scrapbooks, Emanuel drafted five true-temperance short stories in May 1914, written strictly for the IPB syndicate. "Pussyfoot" reviewed the drafts and was ecstatic that the Indians were properly portrayed and not maligned. With his approval, the stories released months later, yet were met with little enthusiasm by newspaper editors. With their acquaintance renewed, Emanuel also supplied "Pussyfoot's" sister magazine, *The American Patriot*, with many rejected short stories originally written for the Sunday syndicates.

He was also writing that summer the *Revelations of an Ambassador-at-Large* series, which landed with *Popular Magazine* in October. Editor Charles Agnew MacLean initially purchased four of the original twelve at $60 per. With hopes of landing the next eight, Chapman set the proofs up on four more, only to have MacLean refuse them. November, the third set of four was sent in, and MacLean accepted only one, making a fifth sale, the last being "Kitchener's Coup." As it turns out, MacLean made a wise move. Running weekly in England was *The Saturday Journal*, published by Cassell & Co. Letters began pouring into MacLean from loyal readers expressing that they had already read these international spy stories in an English publication. MacLean was rightfully outraged, but Chapman could not control the fact that MacLean took so long to run the stories and *The Saturday Journal* ran them immediately.

This effectively ruined their relationship. MacLean, like any American editor, wanted a guarantee that they were running first serial rights. And like its predecessors, this political series was largely syndicated, with first regional rights appearing only a few short months after *Popular* finished the series.

Emanuel wrote another literary failure in the Fall of 1914; *The Genius of Aaron Lapwing*. It circulated amongst every pulp, popular magazine, and the supplements before becoming embarrassingly printed weekly in the *Chicago Ledger*, as *Aaron Lapwing's Genius* (10 April 1915—22 May 1915). The *Chicago Ledger* was a pulp writer's last gasp at obtaining any funds for a written story. If the *Chicago Ledger* wouldn't touch your story, chances were nobody would. To avoid humiliation and identification, a new byline was created: Leonard Britten. The serial was far from genius; it involved fake kingdoms, fake royalty, and a horrible plot. The elaborately created English kingdoms failed to impress even Chapman's English agent at Curtis Brown. Hanshew expressed that they had real castles and kingdoms and personages, that their clients hardly could consider imaginary ones. They were also in the midst of a real war.

With the war developing into becoming a major selling point in fiction, Emanuel turned to churning out a series of war stories told humorously from the viewpoint of a French aviator. Written late 1914, *The Flights of Francois* circulated a year before landing with *Ainslee's*. Initially *Ainslee's* reviewed half the stories in November, however, editor Robert Budd Whiting felt that their German audience might be offended and asked if changes could be effected. Despite the necessary changes, Whiting rejected the series again in late December. The series went out to *Adventure* in February, *Popular* and *Holland's* in March too, before returning to *Ainslee's* as a slightly rewritten series again. The offensive German elements were handled, but Whiting was only interested in four of the stories, and offered $250 for the lot. By combining elements in two other installments, Chapman was able to sell a fifth at $50 in August. The series ran September 1915 to January 1916, and the remaining tales sold to the *Chicago Tribune* (31 October—12 December 1915), concurrently in direct competition with *Ainslee's. Ainslee's* never accepted another Victor Rousseau story again, despite Chapman's repeated attempts into the early 1920s.

Emanuel began his second attempt at fame in mid-1915, creating a novel with New England as the backdrop, titled *The Labyrinth*. Little is known about the novel, save for that it reportedly may never have seen American publication, and was re-written many times over. The novel appears to have only frequented the popular class of magazine, being unsuitable for the pulps. *McClure's, Collier's, Everybody's*, they each saw the novel on more than one occasion from 1915 to 1922. By 1919, the novel had been to 16 magazines, and even bore the new title *A Garden Eastward*. It was still unsold when offered to the *Toronto Star*, in 1942. A novel appearing only in England—*Middle Years,* by V. R. Emanuel—is the same novel, rewritten and sold directly by Emanuel without Chapman's knowledge.

He turned afterward to what has been considered his first published science fiction novel. Written during the summer of 1915, *The Sea Demons* made a lasting splash on the science fiction field for many decades. Originally titled *Brood of Behemoth* when sold to the Frank A. Munsey Company for $600 in December, the 54,000-word novel was immediately pressed into print, appearing in *All-Story Weekly* (1—22 January 1916) in four installments. It syndicated nationally as *The Deep Sea Peril*. Eight years after the initial debut, English publisher John Long issued the serial as a bound novel, as *The Sea Demons*.

Emanuel was able to turn out two 40,000-word novels in the back half of 1915. The first was a peaceful war novel, *Midsummer*

Madness, which made the rounds heavily until the Munsey group acquired it in May 1916 for $250. They released it two months later in *Munsey's Magazine* (July 1916). The second was *The Mask*, Emanuel's third attempt at fame. It hit the magazine market heavily, making the rounds of *Popular* and *Ainslee's* (July), *Adventure* (August), and died with the *Chicago Herald* (September). While the short novel certainly failed amongst the magazines, Chapman had his hands dipped in the photoplay market. The Essanay Film Manufacturing Company released it as *The Truant Soul* (25 December 1916). Harry B. Walthall played dual leads, as the morphine addicted brilliant surgeon Dr. John Lancaster and as his oddly identical half-brother, Dr. John Lawson. The film was heavily advertised and led *The Truant Soul* to be eventually released in print within the *Chicago Tribune* (26 August—28 October 1917) as *His Second Self*. The novel achieved continuous success into the next decade, syndicating in numerous small-press magazines and rurally via the WNU. The story was also reprinted as "A Strange Bargain" in *Brief Stories* (June 1927), debuting as its first pulp appearance. While the film and novel sold well, it did not garner Emanuel the fame he so desperately sought.

Elva gave birth 27 December 1915 to their second child, Audrey, in Quebec.

The next year brought in a new humorous series with the war in the background, concerning a businesswoman's attempts to sell munitions and war supplies to various foreign interests. *Peggy Roche, Saleslady* struggled briefly until late 1916, when *Photoplay Magazine* expressed an interest to print fiction by Victor Rousseau, having received advance news of *The Truant Soul's* screen. They acquired the 12-part series for $900, but backed out at the last minute, accepting only 5 of the tales, printing them monthly starting January 1917. The remainder vanished.

Interested in the tale of Aladdin's lamp, Emanuel churned out in 1916 a 70,000-word

humorous spoof in which the djinn is a gorgeous girl, and follows her bizarre adventures with modern civilization. This fantasy was initially rejected by *Collier's* in July, followed by *McClure's* and *Ainslee's* in August and September, then failed to hit the mark all the way down the line to the Sunday supplements. Chapman turned to the Munsey group, whom ran *Fruit of the Lamp* a year later in *The Argosy* (2—23 February 1918) in four installments. The serial later was bound and re-titled as *Mrs. Aladdin*, in England.

Having spent some years in South Africa, Emanuel's experience played a key role in developing *The Blue Pipe* or *The Big Malopo*, an adventure involving romance and the theft of a large diamond. As in the past, this serial too went the circuit, before landing in *All-Story Weekly* (26 January—23 February 1918) as *The Diamond Demons*. London publishers John Long printed it as *The Big Malopo* in 1924, resuscitating one of Emanuel's original titles for the novel. The novel was simultaneously syndicated in the United States' rural newspapers as *Diamonds of Malopo*.

Realizing Emanuel was better suited to writing the currently popular Canadian timber tales, he turned out *Wooden Spoil* during the summer of 1916. Originally titled *Spoil of the Wildwood* and aimed at *The Saturday Evening Post* and *Collier's* markets, both rejected the novel in August and September. The novel concerns a young American whom comes to inherit his uncle's timberland in Quebec. A lawyer informs him that the land is worthless, but the American visits the property and learns otherwise, and that his uncle has been robbed. The plot is a direct rip from an earlier series, *The Devil Chair*, in which John Haynes, an Englishman, learns that he has inherited lands from a wealthy American uncle, only to receive notice from a lawyer that the lands are worth a tenth their true value. A change in locale and the elimination of any scientific devices along with the insertion of the romantic outdoors and a love interest made

Wooden Spoil an instant sale to *The Argosy* (13 October—17 November 1917). The ultimate irony is that Joseph E. Bray, of A. C. McClurg, on 18 June 1917 passed on the novel, citing numerous reasons:

> We do not want to put forth any book by a comparatively new author which will not sell several thousand, and you, on the other hand, would not, I feel certain, want to attach Mr. Rousseau's name to any volume likely to have a comparatively small sale. Frankly, I do not believe that this would be a good book with which to start Mr. Rousseau's career. I cannot help but think that after all it's an early effort of Mr. Rousseau…the misunderstandings, for instance, which keep the principal characters apart are…such as no person unless he is abnormally stupid could possibly be deluded by. There is a jerkiness, too, about the story. It does not go smoothly. The characters are not sufficiently vitalized. Hilary acts at times just like a mutt.

Poorly written or not, George H. Doran purchased the right to bind the serial, paying 0.15% of sold copies less a $300 advance. By January 1920, Doran had sold 2448 copies, disproving Bray's opinion.

Emanuel's third child, Christine, was now born March 3rd 1917, in Quebec.

While the United States outwardly maintained an act of neutrality, Emanuel was a finishing a seriously "untimely" war novel. At Emanuel's encouragement, Chapman offered *The Minotaur* to A. C. McClurg & Co due to two reasons. First, they were soon printing *The Messiah of the Cylinder* and felt the opportunity was too great to pass. Second, he was confident that the United States would soon openly enter the war. *The Minotaur* met with mixed reviews. While most agreed that Emanuel was a competent writer, and had included medical and dental acts of documented inhumane cruelties, all the novel did was serve to anger many patriotic American editors. Joseph Bray, of A. C. McClurg, may have been the most vocal, writing in a 2 February 1918 letter to Chapman, the following excised piece:

> I think that Mr. Rousseau is a sort of a modern Don Quixote, and, in my opinion, the sooner he quits his tilting with windmills the quicker success will come to him. The trouble with him, he is a reactionary and a sentimentalist. He thinks he is a philosopher called upon to right some of the wrongs in the world. One would think he had a special grudge against this country, which, after all, is at the present time furnishing him with a living. It [*The Minotaur*] is likely to do a great deal of mischief if it should meet with success. This is not the time to create social unrest.
>
> It is not the time to point out defects in our social system. It may not be apparent to Mr. Rousseau, because the United States does not seem to meet with his approval. I think he could write a good story with a purpose. I think that is the trouble with *The Messiah* [*of the Cylinder*]. There is too much preaching in it, and so we lose the interest in the characters.

The novel circulated amongst *McClure's* (late February), *Collier's* (March), *Everybody's* (May), *Pearson's* (June), and was surprisingly offered to *Good Housekeeping*. Two years after the novel debuted, the general consensus was that the novel simply was an unsalable proposition due to war conditions.

This did not stop Emanuel from dabbling in war-related fiction. *The Dark Disk*, a 40,000-word pseudo-scientific dramatic serial originally written for the photoplay field, failed to effect a sale there. *The Thrill Book* purchased the serial in January 1919 for $250, but surprisingly failed to print it. Street & Smith eventually ran it a decade later, in their newly created *Complete Stories* (March 1928). It copped the cover but was horribly illustrated; the cover depicted a man falling out of a building while two goons fire down upon him. *The Thrill Book* had also acquired directly from Emanuel a novelette entitled *The Pink Men*, but whether it ever was printed is unclear. Another lost story entitled "The Mordecai"—according to the Street & Smith archives at Syracuse University—was acquired for $120 in September 1919. It is conceivable that some of the unidentified bylines appearing in *The Thrill Book* may be Emanuel.

Created immediately was another 40,000-word serial novel, *The Fifth Guardian*, which circulated through over 22 magazines and photoplay producers by February 1919, before editor T. C. O'Donnell of *Wayside Tales* (July—September 1921) purchased it for an astonishing $750. O'Donnell would come to also purchase other failures for outrageous figures from Chapman's literary graveyard. More on O'Donnell later.

In the Fall, Emanuel returned to writing a series of six related war stories which should have yielded Chapman both a magazine sale and many placements among the newspapers, however, *Leaves From a Diplomatist's Note-Book* failed at its onset with *Short Stories* in January 1918. By April, it was being offered to every major newspaper market and by September it had trickled down to the rural *Holland's* outfit. The series died without a sale in sight and continued the trend of failures.

Animosity & Resolution With the IPB: January 1918—December 1919

With so many failures and an outstanding debt of $1275 owed to Chapman on past purchases, Emanuel turned over *Captain Mark* for a mere $75. Despite the "gift" price, editors Ray Long

for the *Red Book* and *Blue Book* as well as Hiram Greene for *Woman's World* in January 1918 flat-out refused to read *Captain Mark*, strictly due to the war theme. The story involves a young lieutenant during the Spanish-American War whom rescues an orphaned child, adopts her and over the course of years he is promoted. During the Great War, he is sent to France and the two meet by sheer chance. The girl is of course in love with her savior. You can guess the rest. Newly re-packaged as *Bride of Battle*, it sold in February locally to *Chicago Herald's* syndicated Sunday supplement for $200 and began serial-ization in April and May in at least four major cities. After the monetarily disappointing sale, Chapman offered the story to other individual major city markets at $50 to $100, depending on the size of the populated regions. The *Detroit Free Press*, [Philadelphia] *Evening Bulletin*, *Kansas City Star*, and possibly others purchased first regional serial rights.

Emanuel was drafted into the Canadian Army Medical Corps, serving continuously from the 1st of June 1917 until demobilization on 15 January 1919. He was certainly on guard during the anti-conscription riots in Quebec and may have been present when soldiers fired upon the resistance movement. In any case, re-enlistment left him nights only to write fiction.

> I was working in the hospital when the so-called influenza epidemic of 1918 struck the world…It was a dreadful thing to see a healthy man, stricken in the morning, coughing out his lungs in a bloody spray, and dead by nightfall. After several of us orderlies had been stricken, the doctor in charge ordered us to snuff a solution of permanganate of potash three times a day, and there were no further casualties among the staff.

In May 1918, Emanuel turned over a 33,000-word novella entitled *Broken Men*; it failed to find a home due to a "triangular situation" until *Five-Novels Monthly* printed it in their March 1928 issue. The prior issue announced the plot, proclaiming *Broken Men* to be "an absorbing story of the drama war brought into the quiet lives of a group of people…life is stripped of veneer: it becomes inexorable, greedy, and measures men—and the race—with merciless accuracy."

Sometime in 1918, Emanuel wrote and sold on his own a serial to the Munsey group entitled *The Draught of Eternity*, released as *The Draft of Eternity* in *All-Story Weekly* (1—22 June 1918). The serial was later released in England under its original title. Emanuel had also submitted to Chapman an ancient, dilapidated unsold manuscript entitled *The Man on Wheels* to fulfill the quarterly quota. This Chapman rejected as inadequate; since 1910, Emanuel had been typing about four series or serials for Chapman to place per year. With his now being in the Canadian army, Emanuel claimed it was nearly an impossible feat. And yet, here Emanuel was, selling a successful serial on his own, against their gentleman's agreement.

Chapman was hardly interested afterwards in placing his fiction, especially given that they were heatedly embroiled in a legal dispute. The precise origin of the situation is unknown from Chapman's position, but Emanuel provides his side of events as follow:

> I was making a satisfactory income, but new difficulties arose with Chapman. Naturally, he wanted me to write for the magazines that paid the highest rates, the women's publications, and there was no way of making him understand that I hadn't sufficient experience of American life to be able to depict it realistically. I wrote romances for the popular magazines, about the lumber camps and the Mounted Police, but their rates of pay were considerably lower.

Chapman wrote me a letter threatening to bring our agreement to an end… I took a train for New York immediately, and went to see a great editor and fine person, Bob Davis, the friend of uncounted authors. He had already bought two serials from me at six hundred dollars, which money of course I had had to split with Chapman. As a result of my visit, Davis raised my rate of pay to a thousand dollars a serial, and I could do four a year.

By July, Emanuel had obtained the legal advice of Benjamin Stern, of the widely reputed Stern & Reubens firm, in New York. Numerous arguments ensued over the copyright notice applied to *The Apostle of the Cylinder* (agents at Curtis Brown had accidentally attributed ownership to Chapman) and Emanuel was infuriated that Chapman had forced him to apply "Victor Rousseau" onto what he considered an inferior work of fiction (an odd reversal of opinion given his original stance in 1914). Emanuel also contested Chapman's threat forcing him to hand over all fiction to Chapman to solely agent. Additional scuffles emerged over Chapman's supposed breach of faith, offering serials overseas without Emanuel's consent. Chapman actually had never offered any serials to a single American or English publisher without Emanuel's consent, save for *Wooden Spoil*, in an effort to recoup some of his financial losses against Emanuel's debt.

During the course of the legal crossfire, each continued a business-as-usual attitude. The recently submitted novel *Eric of the Strong Heart* appeared in *Railroad Man's Magazine* (16 November—14 December 1918), a publication that soon merged with *Argosy*. The publication certainly made little sense, given that the story was a lost race fantasy involving Vikings in the Arctic. The precise reason for Davis' positioning of the serial here will likely remain a cause for wonder. The serial was bound in England years later.

February 1919, Chapman was exasperated. The potential novelizations of *The Devil Chair*, *The Tracer of Egos*, and *The Sea Demons* were dropped from consideration by Hodder & Stoughton due to Emanuel's continued interference and drama during the past year, in relation to *The Apostle of the Cylinder*, and poor sales of the novel itself. H&S had been receiving correspondence from Emanuel direct, concerning manuscript corrections, a preface not included in the A. C. McClurg edition, which he ultimately denied their usage thereof, copyright attributions, changing words to meet the English vernacular, etc. Tired of being at cross-purposes, he suggested that they meet with their lawyers in New York. Emanuel refused, stating that he had made a similar expression of intent months ago, and—besides, his lawyer, Benjamin Stern, no longer represented him— that Chapman should come to Quebec to settle the various claims.

Refusing to yield, Chapman in mid-March demanded that he submit a first-class novel, under contract of 20% commission and that one quarter of the sums realized from sales be applied to the $1275 debt. Emanuel agreed to submit a new novel by July 1st, but under specific conditions: Chapman gets a $300 novel, not of the popular *Wooden Spoil* variety, but a serializable novel only to be printed in the US and Canada, and that Chapman surrender English book rights. Chapman accepted the offer on contingency that Emanuel makes any suggested alterations to ensure its publication.

Like a pair of old goats, they locked horns for the next month, hammering out conditions of a contractual agreement. By late March through April 1919, relations were slowly on the mend, and Emanuel demanded a full accounting of his stories. Chapman, lying and claiming poor record-keeping, only provided a list of most of his prior written series and serials, the habitant tales, some short stories, some unsold photoplays, with no notations where or when they were placed. Additionally, due to the outstanding debt, Chapman claimed the right to novelize various past magazine serials in order to recoup his losses, and obtained most of the photoplay rights to all the stories, a fact that would haunt Emanuel in later years. The agreement was signed and witnessed on the 29th of April 1919. Minor corrections ensued over the months, as errors were noted or series titles were found to be missing. The original agreement of providing four titles per year was abolished. Just as well. Emanuel had just then directly placed *The Lion's Jaws* in Davis' hands; it ran in *All-Story Weekly* (29 March—26 April 1919) and was later bound in England.

In May, Emanuel demanded to know what series and serials realized a sale in England. The list was provided, but again, sans publication sources. Chapman claimed his English agents never informed him where the stories were printed, clearly marking him as a liar or an inept literary agent. A quick correspondence with Hanshew at Curtis Brown would have cleared up this inquiry. A second sheet in July denoted where all of his various habitant stories were placed and in what issues. The details largely are inaccurate. During an accounting of his stories, it is discovered that the proof copy to story number ten from *The Surgeon of Souls* had at some point been destroyed.

Chapman in August asked permission to offer the old *World-Famous Police Mysteries* series under the byline "George Munson," to which Emanuel had no objection. The question was more or less out of courtesy; Chapman owned all rights to the series, per the recently constructed contract. They printed under the heading *More Inside Histories of Famous Crimes*, following up a series by George Munson similarly titled, sans the *More*. The original series by George Munson—*Inside History of Famous Crimes*—marked its original print incarnation, and is the first and only time the alias was utilized on anything besides syndicated newspaper vignettes. Both series appeared in *Street & Smith's Detective Story Magazine* during 1919. The Munson series was purchased in England by Hutchinson's *True Story Magazine* in the late 1920s (handled by agents at Curtis Brown) and printed in Canada by Superior Publications during the mid-1940s.

The next few months Emanuel turned over to Chapman two short novellas written for and rejected by *The Thrill Book*. The first, *The Beast Maker*, is approximately an 18,000-word thriller of a man's brain inserted into a gorilla. The story is actually a cleverly disguised plagiarism of Harry Stephen Keeler's *Miracle Agent*. The second is *The Cain Ship*, a 25,000-word blood-n-thunder intially a pleasure to read that degrades into a mock Adam and Eve finale. The daughter of a sea captain goes to the Arctic, takes control of her father's ship, only to be at the mercy of a murderous crew. When the ship looses control and mayhem ensues, it crashes upon the icy shelf in the Arctic, and the crew flees to places unknown. The daughter is rescued by an odd Arctic inhabitant, a manly beast with Tarzan-like qualities. Neither story was saleable outside of *The Thrill Book*. Both were relegated to the last outpost for pulp writers. The *Chicago Ledger*, a newsprint fiction magazine specializing in syndicated short stories and novels, sometimes acquired first rights to unsalable fiction. A third story—*The Valley of Sleeping Slaves*—taking place in South Africa, initially offered to *Short Stories*, next was refused by the newly created *Telling Tales* in November, before landing also in the *Chicago Ledger* a few months later.

Two more stories Emanuel had been hawking himself were eventually handed over to Chapman to try his hand at: "The Mask Dance" and "La Rose en Bois." The former had already been to *Adventure*, *Popular*, and *People's*; the latter to *Blue Book*, *Designer*, *McCall's*, and *Everywoman's World*. Neither appear to have found a home.

The Bride of Dorion's Acres arrived at the IPB in late November 1919, and was printed by *Argosy All-Story Weekly* (27 November—25 December 1920) as *While Dorion Lives*. This Canadian novel, however late, might represent the fulfillment of the July 1st agreement, but it is not a certainty. It was later bound as *The Big Man of Bonne Chance*. A novel appearing serially in *The Argosy* (3—24 January 1920) as *The Big Muskeg* may too be a contender. It too was subsequently bound. A short lost-race novella taking place inside the Earth under Australia, *The Eye of Balamok* appeared simultaneously in *All-Story Weekly* (17—31 January 1920), but is not covered in the IPB files. Emanuel had initiated this sale himself. It is not clear when the latter two tales were written in relation to the former.

England: December 1919—June 1922
Emanuel, wife and his two daughters set sail from Portland, Maine, for Glasgow in December 1919, then proceeded into England. Ahead of them were perhaps the most trying years of his life. England was suffering from post-war conditions, cost-of-living criminally unbearable, people were destitute, homeless, living in railway-cars and Emanuel was constantly on the move, often-times without an address, as he became destitute.

During those years, Emanuel did not turn over to Chapman many serials. *My Lady of the Nile*, appearing in *Argosy All-Story Weekly* (7—28 May 1921) was certainly sold directly by Emanuel, as Chapman never laid a hand on it. The serial was later novelized in England. Chapman did receive a romance novelette entitled *Crossroads*, written for *Breezy Stories*, for which they expressed an interest, offering $100 and all photoplay rights. Chapman rejected the offer outright, acceding to only half the rights; Emanuel a week later expressed that the story stood no chance elsewhere, as it was a formula novelette expressly written for that magazine. Chapman returned to *Breezy* Stories, accepting a lower offer of $80.

Other stories mentioned in passing, are either short stories or series, including "Capitulations of Lucia," "Her Letters," and "Red Lilacs," all geared toward the romance pulps. All appear to have failed; the former went the rounds heavily, hitting *Young's*, *Saucy Stories*, and many others. By 1921, with no prospects in sight, Emanuel requested that the stories be destroyed. An earlier African short—"The Mask Dance"—wound up returned to Emanuel late 1920, to be recast.

Everything he wrote came back. Refused by every English publication, Emanuel sent all rejections overseas to Chapman, hoping for sales. However, he churned out at least two known serials under a newly created alias in the *London Daily Mail*, as John Austin. The first was *Legally Dead* (7 Sep through 1 Nov 1920), in forty-eight daily installments (sans Fridays). The second was *The Greater Claim* (8 Feb through 16 March 1921) in thirty-two installments. Chapman was wholly unaware of the byline.

Emanuel in January 1921 stripped a quarter of the length out of the failed *Labyrinth* manuscript and reworked it into a new novel, as *A Garden Eastward*. It lacked plot but played up more on psychology; Emanuel felt the book stood a fairer chance as an English publication now than in America. The IPB was also forwarded a flimsy detective novel entitled *The White Lily Murder*, which had just been rejected by *Street & Smith's Detective Story Magazine*, *Argosy All-Story Weekly*, and *Black Mask*. Undoubtedly Emanuel's inexperience with detective stories, its horrible construction, and weak characters killed the novel; the *Chicago Ledger* accepted the novel, paying $150.

Arriving to Chapman October 1921 were three short stories collectively titled *The Cloud Pirates*, likely a doomed projected English series of twelve shorts. The tales almost read like adventure fiction as found in English boys' periodicals. It is entirely possible that Emanuel was writing locally for the many boys' papers, as he had expressed an interest in the Amalgamated Press, noting that they ran about 75 weeklies, consuming an inordinate amount of literature. The *Chicago Ledger* was interested in the three tales. Editor Harry Stephen Keeler accepted the stories on one condition: that Emanuel create a fourth to end the series. Emanuel accepted, and finished the story in May 1922; Keeler paid $60 for the selection of zeppelin stories.

Financial conditions worsened to the point that Emanuel's wife—Elva—secretly wrote two letters (the first in March 1921, second in October) to Chapman begging him to assist, to suggest that Emanuel write again for Universal Studios, anything. Emanuel refused to work, firmly believing he could make a living as a writer. Clearly this led to marital friction as Elva was interested in the welfare of her children whereas Emanuel was too stubborn to obtain a job.

"The Four Dumb Men" and the detective short "False Fingers" arrived in May—June; they were immediately offered to and rejected by *S&S Detective Story Magazine*. By mid-June, the former was now at *Cartoons Magazine*, a publication that prior had never printed fiction. The editor of *Cartoons Magazine* was changing their title to *Wayside Tales*, looking for stories of adventure, detective, mystery, outdoor stories, and short serials. "The Four Dumb Men" sold to *Wayside* for $250; they also paid $100 for "Out of Arcady," $150 in July for the short story "Pals," and $200 for "Woman and the Law." *Wayside Tales* had already paid $750 for "The Fifth Guardian." Although H. H. Windsor was the editor, it is the managing editor, T. C. O'Donnell, whom is credited with bankrupting the magazine. By December 1921, he had paid $2500 for Randall Parrish's *Gift of the Desert*.

The short "False Fingers" by December had been to over eleven magazines, before selling to *Midnight Mystery Stories*. The magazine collapsed prior to its publication, languishing a decade before *Great Detective* offered to purchase it. It too collapsed. "False Fingers" was eventually released into the service in 1932, ending up in numerous newspapers.

In July, Emanuel announced that he was writing international detective stories for one of the London magazines, the identity of which is unknown. Come August, he had returned to the Canadian serial novel, deciding to specialize in them, but it was put on hold as his family was soon homeless and without any funds. Desperate for any form of income, Emanuel began offering second serial rights to the various *Argosy* tales that he had placed himself for $40 each, including *The Golden Horde*, which had just appeared as *The Bandit of Batakaland* in *Argosy-All-Story Weekly* (28 January—25 February 1922). It later became novelized in England, under its original title.

Emanuel returned early in 1922 to writing storiettes, six for $20, beginning in February. Chapman had a market again for storiettes, but Emanuel killed it effectively a couple years later when he decided he was ruining too many good plots and time on them. The source(s) of publication is entirely unknown.

Sales on the recently novelized *The Big Muskeg* resulted in about 1000 copies sold, but was considered another novelized failure.

Ellis Island documents detail that Elva and the children had arrived in New York, sans Emanuel, on the 31st of January 1922. His father, after threatening to kick his son and family out, was forced to pay for Emanuel's wife and children's fares back to America. Emanuel remained behind, destitute, a pauper, walking the streets and living as a tramp. According to his memoirs, he fell into company with another tramp, whom informed him of how to survive life on the road.

He explained to me the difference between a "kip" and a "spike." A "kip" was a bed in a cheap lodging-house, costing a few coppers, which he expected to pick up by singing outside a pub. The "spike" was the casual ward of a workhouse, and open to all tramps. I would not have to sleep out in the fields. The "spike" was obviously my destination.

Emanuel had also sent in some sample stories in a projected series of twelve, entitled *The Clients of Burton Hall*. Chapman considered the stories a "well-worn topic," and they perished after even the *Chicago Ledger* refused to touch them.

A Canadian novel was completed in March 1922; Emanuel regarded *The Home Trail* as an outstanding story, equivalent in stature to *Wooden Spoil*, and suggested Chapman try to run it by *Wayside Tales*, then *Argosy*. Both passed on it swiftly. Chapman informed Emanuel that the days of the Mounty or Canadian novels were dead. He was wrong. The novel landed magnificently that same year at *People's Story Magazine* (25 August—25 September), acquired for an astounding $1000. The novel was also bound in England.

Soon after the sale of *The Home Trail* and no longer penniless, Emanuel arrived in America on the 8th of July, five full months after Elva and the kids. Immediately, he set to work on another Northern novel, offering it directly to Davis at *Munsey/Argosy*. Davis rejected it, noting too that the Canadian plot device is dead. It may be among the pulps, but that did not stop the rural *People's Popular Monthly* mail-order magazine from paying $1000 to print *The Free Traders* as *Lee of the Northwest Mounted* (January—August 1923). This novella subsequently was nationally syndicated as *The Free Traders* over the ensuing years and sold to *Brief Stories* for $75, appearing in the May 1926 issue as *On the Range*. *The Free Traders* proved to be a colossal commercial success, but, unlike its predecessors, was not bound in England.

The V. R. Emanuel Novels

In late February 1923, Emanuel proudly announced that he had sold to Constable—an English publisher—the original novel *The Story of John Paul*, and it was to be released under V. R. Emanuel. He intended to begin work on a sequel immediately. Success as a serious English-novelist was now within his grasp! His plans never matured, as his brother suppressed the book as being libelous. The novel was semi-autobiographical and anti-Semitic, hence Montague's interference. In fact, the boy's father's name was given to be Montague. The sequel was quashed.

The February 1924 issue of *Delineator*, a women's fashion magazine, carried a short story entitled "The Wife of Midas" by John Austin. Emanuel had been attempting to crash this high-paying magazine for many years. It appears that in this one instance, he finally succeeded.

In March 1925 he snubbed Chapman, noting that he had sold another item that his agent had failed on. *Middle Years* was bylined as V. R. Emanuel, and appeared by Minton, Balch in England, 1925, and had sold 942 copies. By July 1st, that figure had grown to 1391 copies sold. It is unconfirmed, but this novel may well be *The Labyrinth*, as a triangular situation does indeed exist in this novel. When Chapman inquired just what novel was sold that he had failed to place, Emanuel smartly refrained from replying.

Since his sequel to *The Story of John Paul* had been suppressed, it was rewritten as *The Selmans* by V. R. Emanuel, a novel released that Fall by The Dial Press. It portrayed the hypocrisy of England's Jews through the eyes of a family man. With an advance of $200, an April 1926 statement showed sales totaling 313 copies, 20% royalties, less the advance, resulting in a $137.40 check. Later that year, agents Brandt & Brandt were considering the

novella *The Prince of the Plains*, but rejected it. They had recently been the agents of *The Selmans* to The Dial Press.

Emanuel continued to hand over unsold manuscripts to Chapman, such as "Diamonds of Death," "Quick Action," and "Pedigree." The latter pair was returned, unsold, to be rewritten or destroyed by Emanuel. The former was published as an original novel in England, now titled *Salted Diamonds*, in 1926. The novel concerns a disreputable Chicagoan on the lam from a woman he was reportedly betrothed, whom is the erstwhile widow of his ex-business partner. Arriving in South Africa after reading an article concerning the lucrative diamond trade, the greenhorn finds himself fighting against a controlled interest, in love with two women, and constantly under physical assault from seemingly different parties. The Chicago man is a buffoon—not of the lovable variety—but an idiot whom bulls his way through life.

It was followed in 1927 by *Winding Trails*, a novel concerning the plight of petty criminal Alf Collins. Sentenced to life upon false charges of murder, Alf escapes prison and crosses the border into Canada, in search of his ex-crime boss, with the intention of beating the truth out of him. But, his designs are shattered when he lands a job in a lumbering camp, in which more is at play than simply his thirst for vengeance.

The Romantic Westerns: 1923-1942

In February 1923, despite further assurances that the Canadian field was desolate, he sent in another novel, *Sergeant Forbes, Alias*, and just like *The Home Trail*, it sold for $1000, to *People's* (15 August—1 October 1923). This marked the end of an era, and the start of a new one, as what Emanuel terms "specialized magazines" were rapidly taking center stage.

A contact with an editor whom I had known in the past brought me an invitation to write a western novel of thirty thousand words, dealing with gun-play and cattle-rustlers. Although I had never been west of Chicago, I flung myself into the task with zest. That world of cowboys and bad men became my specialty in the years that followed. The demand was insatiable, and the rate of payment steadily rose. With rejections so rare as to be almost non-existent, I could sit down any Monday morning and earn five hundred dollars by keeping at it till Saturday night. I wrote fast, and never revised.

Chapman received an unsold story entitled "Big Sulphur" in April and by May, Emanuel had sold two novelettes to editor Harold Hersey for $600 each. With a new market available, Emanuel turned his hand to a genre he had no former experience writing: westerns. He also eliminated the need to utilize Chapman to place most of his writings; Emanuel took care of this himself once again. His aim was to hit the Street & Smith and Readers' Publishing markets, for which he succeeded largely with the latter and apparently only once with the former, landing "Three Square Meals A Day" in the 8 March 1924 issue of *Western Story Magazine*, released as "Furs That Fed." *Ace-High Magazine* became a source of income for a few years, but Clayton's editor soon moved Emanuel up into *Ranch Romances* and its companion, *Rangleand Love Story Magazine*. The former gobbled up an inordinate quantity of his romantic westerns from 1925 to 1942.

"The Kid" and "Alkali Springs" was sent to Chapman in July 1923; "Big Sulphur" failed to sell and was returned to Emanuel in October; in November, Emanuel expressed an interest in trying his hand at radio stories. With this view in mind, Chapman supplied Hugo Gernsback's mailing address for the Experimenter Publishing, noting that they printed *Radio News* and *Science and Invention*. Emanuel dropped in December to meet the publishers, but found that the magazines were simply far more technical in nature than he was capable of writing. The idea died there.

Then I made another connection, through another editor whom I had known in the past. Bernarr MacFadden, the health culturist, conceived the idea that the public was avid for stories of real life, and started *True Story* magazine, the first of several of the same type. MacFadden's idea was one of genius. This is the only type of story that has survived the wreck of the magazines after the second world war and the introduction of television.

With the ability to write decent, clean romances, he attempted to write for the *True Confessions*, *True Romances*, *Real Life Stories*, and other related magazines. In January 1924, Emanuel confirmed sale of a story to *True Romances* for $67, and three months later one to *True Confessions* for $100. Unless the locale included Africa or Canada and perhaps the usage of some French words, tracking any of his *True* contributions is impossible; stories carried no byline.

Around mid-June, Chapman suggested that Emanuel aim for the new magazine, *Frontier*. Although he failed with initial attempts, Emanuel became a regular contributor to *Frontier* with seven novelettes between 1927 and 1930. By July, Emanuel had successfully cracked McFadden's non-*True* magazines, selling a serial and short story—to the *Muscle Builder* and *Physical Culture*—that had been unsold for many months. Many more followed over the years. He also won a minor prize in Fawcett's *Triple-X* competition, placing the unsold novelette "Alkali Springs" in the February 1925 issue, as "The Feud of Alkali Springs."

He alternated his western field with colorful attempts writing of the Far East and Europe in *Five-Novels Monthly*, from 1928 to 1938. While nearly all were bylined under Victor Rousseau, one appears as C. Cordier and many others surface under his English-created alias, John Austin. The latter was discovered when Emanuel sent in the long novelette "The Mansion Murder" in 1932. Florence McChesney requested it be cut to 20,000 words with an offer of $250 made August 1933; retitled and condensed, "Murder Down East" appeared in the April 1934 issue, by John Austin.

Without the note from *Five-Novels Monthly* to Chapman indicating use of John Austin, the English use of the byline and the American pulp appearances would remain unknown. As he had recently launched into the western field, it is likely his rejected novelettes appeared as John Austin in Dell Publishing's *Five-Novels* to avoid a conflict of interest with Clayton-owned *Ranch Romances.*

Emanuel sent Chapman a novelette simply titled "Alcazar" during the Spring/Summer of 1937. Chapman felt the anti-communism angle should be removed. Four months later, *Five-Novels* (September 1937) released a novelette by C. Cordier entitled "Walls of the Alcazar," taking place in Spain.

A probable alias is Rider West with "Under Western Skies" (October 1933), along with possibly Audrey Carleton's "Murder at the Chalet" (June 1933). The original title to "Treasure of the Moon" has not been confirmed, either. It ran about 23-pages while "Treasure Ranch" ran 29-pages. The tales are likely one-and-the-same.

A short story entitled "Condition Yellow" by John Austin appeared in *Wings*, (Spring 1948) might be Emanuel's if it was a rewritten reject from the *Spicy* field, however, after a hiatus of fourteen years, it seems improbable that John Austin should suddenly reappear, unless the story had originally been printed a decade earlier.

The Motion Pictures

While *The Truant Soul* (released 25 December 1916) is noted as Emanuel's first foray into the photoplays, it was neither his first nor his last. He had, in fact, earlier written numerous 1- to 3-reel plays, reportedly submitted as Oliver Gordon or Gordon Oliver, courtesy of Chapman. These have never been located. Additionally, he wrote story adaptations for Universal, such as for the movie "Scandal" (1915), but was erroneously credited as Victor Rosseau, sans the first "u" in the surname. More than twenty other story adaptations appeared carrying the H. M. Egbert byline, but it is entirely possible he wrote the original screenplays, such as the science-fiction short "The Mysterious Contragrav," "The Phantom of the Violin," "The Whirling Disk," and many other plays that read like it truly was written by Emanuel. It is known that Emanuel had been writing for Universal Film Mfg. Co. between 1914-1917, but nothing has been positively identified. "The Whirling Disk," for instance, dealt with hypnotism, a sure-fire interest that possessed Emanuel.

Emanuel re-entered the black & white silent films from 1926 through 1929 with at the least nine identified films originally printed in the *Ace-High*, *Ranch Romances*, and *Lariat* magazines. Whether he, Chapman, or the magazines themselves were the agents is unclear. Clayton of *Ace-High* was paying for fiction and film rights. Emanuel claims that he made the sales himself.

> I was well known for my western stories, and had sold some dozen movie rights to a company which wanted my name, and changed the stories to suit itself.

Mrs. Aladdin nearly made a splash when Heath of London offered £200 for film rights in 1926. Chapman acknowledged Emanuel's ecstatic announcement and crushed his enthusiasm, noting that Chapman owned the photoplay rights and greedily wanted more money. A strike in England in May 1926 killed the production altogether. Chapman made attempts to sell the screen rights in America, but met with failure.

In early 1932, Chapman attempted to move *The Surgeon of Souls* into the motion picture market, hoping to secure Bela Lugosi to portray Dr. Ivan Brodsky. Obviously this, too, met with failure.

Weird Tales: 1926—1932
When editor Farnsworth Wright in 1926 came calling for new and second serial right fiction for *Weird Tales*, Chapman was all to happy to rife through his files. Wright received three series during March and April 1926: Fredric Reddale's *The Man Who Remembered*, H. M. Egbert's *The Surgeon of Souls* (11 only, as one was destroyed years ago), and Victor Rousseau's *The Tracer of Egos*. Wright began by issuing *The Surgeon of Souls* under the original fiction section, as they had not been seen since 1910. Payment for each story was made 30-days after publication. It is unclear how much was paid for each story, but a check arriving jointly for Oppenheim's "The Tower Ghost" and Emanuel's "The Case of the Jailer's Daughter" was written for $100. In all likelihood, the stories sold for $50 each.

In discussing Emanuel's *The Surgeon of Souls* as an "original" feature, it should be noted that Wright's practices came under intense scrutiny upon acquiring Richard Marsh's "The Adventure of the Pipe" from Chapman; $85 was paid for a firestorm nightmare that haunted and altered Wright's editorial practices forever. If you love *Weird Tales* for their original content, you owe Chapman immensely. When Wright acquired the tale, it was with the understanding that the story had never seen publication outside of England decades ago. In fact, "The Adventure of the Pipe" had been printed many times in America over the years. *Weird Tales* enthusiasts wrote scathing letters, infuriated over Wright's misleading venture to offer reprint literature as original. If Marsh was a reprint, were others? The story appears anonymously as "The Pipe" in *The Lock and Key Library* edited by Julian Hawthorne, as printed by the Review of Reviews Company in 1909. Chapman claimed ignorance to the story having been reprinted once in America, and lay blame at Hawthorne's feet for having apparently pirated the story. Letters continued to arrive, berating Wright, and also citing that the story appeared in a volume entitled *Eight Unusual Tales*, edited by O'Brien. Wright, fearing irreparable damage to his magazine, began an effort that no matter how obscure a story may have prior been, it would be labeled "reprint."

Despite the friction between the pair, Chapman continued to offer what he deemed to be stories suited to the tastes of *Weird Tales*. October 1927, he sent in a 40,000-word serial entitled *The Pink Men* by Victor Rousseau. The story had originally been written and sold to *The Thrill Book* in 1919, and concerned Manhattan Island's mysterious disappearance into the depths of the bay. Street & Smith had considered printing it in *Complete Stories*, but opted to release it to Chapman. Wright enjoyed the start of the story, but the novella degraded into complete chaos. However, by March 1928, Edmund C. Richards, of *Complete Stories*, requested that the manuscript be returned to him, claiming he had an agent whom could immediately place the serial. If printed, it undoubtedly was under a new title and possibly buried in an obscure publication, as its whereabouts remains a complete mystery.

With the last *The Surgeon of Souls* appearing months ago, Chapman re-offered *The Tracer of Egos* for consideration in January 1928, sending in the first three stories; he asked $50 per story. Chapman commented that *Tales of Magic and Mystery* wanted them, but attempted to pay much less. The series as a whole were not up to *Weird Tales'* standards, and with Wright, it was an all or nothing proposition. The series was clean, smooth, and polished, but simply lacked the weird touch combined with a satisfactory explanation for just how precisely did Dr. Immanuel readily obtain his conclusions.

Much to Wright's chagrin, Chapman in the 1930s began to offer what he felt were weird stories, but were actually detective-mysteries, westerns, etc, and Wright was entirely turned off by his offer of reprint material, especially after his prior experience. He did offer one last gem, a story originally part of *The Surgeon of Souls*, which had been excised due to being of a humorous nature rather than horror. Like prior stories, the weird element was not present to warrant a sale, nor was the story—in Wright's mind—very convincing.

Despite Chapman's inability to effect further sales on Emanuel's past works, this did not bar Emanuel from selling a serial himself to Wright; *The Phantom Hand* (July—November 1932) was his only successful sale to *Weird Tales*, but a far-cry from being his only venture into the weird genre.

Supernatural / Science Fiction: 1926—1933

While Emanuel is certainly remembered for his inclusion in *Weird Tales*, he was a regular with their competition, *Ghost Stories*. Emanuel had already been contributing to MacFadden's *True* and *Muscle Builder* magazines when *Ghost Stories* debuted in July 1926. He launched a series of stories featuring the psychic Dr. Martinus, a Dutchman residing in New York, scoring off his simultaneously printed Dr. Ivan Brodsky tales appearing in *Weird Tales*.

Over the succeeding years, Emanuel placed three serials and various short stories; most notably is *The House of the Living Dead* featuring Dr. Martinus, in six installments (December 1927—May 1928).

Although the pseudo-scientific *The Dark Disk* appeared in 1928, it was written in 1917, and could hardly be honestly considered

Emanuel's last scientific story. He reappeared in 1930, with a novelette in *Astounding Stories of Super-Science*. With a cover illustrating *The Beetle Horde* (January—February 1930) copping the cover of the first issue, he followed it with *The Atom-Smasher* in May, *The Lord of Space* in August, *The Invisible Death* in October, and *The Wall of Death* in November. Inexplicably, the rapid-fire supply of novelettes came to an abrupt end.

In 1931, Emanuel supplied two long novelettes to *Miracle Science and Fantasy Stories*. The magazine was printed by Good Story Magazine Co., founded by Harold Hersey, the former editor to *The Thrill Book*, credited with the creation of *Ranch Romances* for the Clayton outfit, and worked briefly with MacFadden before founding his own imprints. Undoubtedly Hersey was very familiar with Emanuel from any of the three, and was able to request novelettes direct.

With Emanuel no longer writing for *Ghost Stories*, he was offered the opportunity to write for Clayton's *Strange Tales of Mystery and Terror*, landing in the first two issues. He was surrounded by a host of some of the most renowned pulp fiction authors ever, including Ray Cummings, Arthur J. Burks, Gordon MacCreagh, Clark Ashton Smith, and many others. Emanuel supplied one last novelette that spawned multiple publications and translations over the decades involving a mummy, entitled *The Curse of Amen-Ra*. Despite the Who's-Who of authors, the magazine lasted only seven issues.

While both *The Curse of Amen-Ra* (October 1932) and *The Phantom Hand* (*Weird Tales*, July—November 1932) were concluding, Emanuel had returned to writing science fiction. The novella *World's End* serialized in *The Argosy* (8—22 July 1933) was one of the few pulp appearances made by Emanuel that year. It was also the last time *Argosy* accepted anything by Emanuel; 1933 was a year of literary crisis all-around for many aging authors.

Financial Ruin / The *Spicy* Age: 1933—1947

The late 20s through early 30s were magical to the Emanuel family. Emanuel was earning about fifteen grand per year. They now owned an automobile. With the destruction of the financial markets, the literary field appeared initially unscathed, but this soon changed.

Emanuel initially had plans in 1933 toward abandoning the western field, but when Clayton filed bankruptcy, the disruption crippled Emanuel financially. He immediately returned to the westerns and *Five-Novels Monthly*, but funds were diminishing. The situation worsened. He was an aging writer, and the old regime of editors were dying and being replaced with young editors with no interest in the old pulp writers. After 14-years of serials, Munsey refused to look at his manuscripts, Street & Smith had him blacklisted, MacFadden dropped him after about 30 romance shorts and serials. Emanuel was sick of writing formula-plots for Fiction House, Dell published cheaply, Doubleday were okay in his opinion, etc.

To make matters worse, although Chapman was no longer Emanuel's literary agent, Chapman had pretty much eliminated the IPB from the pulp-field, with the exclusion of the recently acquired Rollin Brown, preferring to focus on higher quality publications and the rural magazines. Emanuel was utilizing Lurton Blassingame until 1938, before turning his fiction briefly over to Willis Kingsley Wing. For reasons not apparent, Emanuel was not able to maintain a relationship with Wing; he disliked Blassingame intensely for treating him like a child.

If one looks at the 1933—1935 years, notable is the lack of fiction. In a letter dated 6 August 1937 to Chapman, Emanuel boldly claims to have sold MacFadden a sex-story, one per week, for three years, receiving $125 to $150 per title. Clearly at those prices the market could hardly be ignored. With his marketability dissolving, Emanuel turned to the "spicy" pulps, a move that horrified Chapman. The Trojan outfit paid little and Emanuel was required to churn out gobs of sex stories, between three to six monthly; novelettes occasionally effected sales to his regular pulp markets, but even this soon would shift all to the "spicy" pulps. The lack of quality was very apparent. With funds vanishing, he was writing quantity over quality to maintain a standard of living, get his children through school, and put food on the table. They were forced to sell their automobile. Despite all this, he continued the attempt to break the "spicy" shackles and get back into the pulp field, writing for all genres, but met with failure. August 1937, Emanuel notes that he has sold 94 of 110 shorts to the "sex magazines." By the time he had made this frank statement, over 60 had already been printed, illustrating that the "spicy" pulps bought and printed the stories at a very rapid rate, or, there is at least one or two more undiscovered pseudonyms that ought to be attributed to Emanuel.

The *Spicy* field also became a dumping ground for his unsold manuscripts. One such example is "Dark Dominion," a novelette written for *Five Novels* in the early 1930s; it was cut down to a long short story, appearing in *Spicy-Adventure Stories* (October 1937).

For the Trojan outfit, Emanuel churned out the last two known character-series of his literary career. The popularity of Doc Savage prompted the editors to request Emanuel to offer them something comparable. Jim Anthony debuted in *Super Detective* (October 1940) and was bylined as by John Grange. Anthony's heredity is a mix of Irish and Native American descent; wealthy from an inheritance, he hunted villains free-of-charge and utilized a wide-range of gadgets. It is unclear how many of the novels Emanuel should be properly credited, as Robert Leslie Bellem and W. T. Ballard definitely were writing the series with the 16th novel, *Hell's Ice-Box* (October 1942). Beyond a doubt Emanuel likely wrote the first twelve.

Confirmation of the next three titles are up in the air, though they read somewhat in Emanuel's general style.

The second series featured Dr. Gabriel, debuting in "House of Death" (*Speed Mystery*, May 1943) and bylined under Lew Merrill. The character continued thereafter to appear under Hugh Speer at least six times over the next two years.

The voluminous sales to the "spicy" pulps came to an abrupt end with the arrest of editor Kenneth W. Hutchinson, for defrauding the Trojan publishers out of tens of thousands of dollars. Hutchinson was Emanuel's youngest daughter's ex-husband, and it is clear that by his arrest that either Hutchinson was accepting Emanuel's manuscripts out of consideration or that Emanuel severed the tie out of sheer embarrassment. Additionally, at least eight stories were reprinted under a new byline and re-titled, likely without Emanuel's consent nor knowledge, as court records clearly do not indicate the fraudulent use of Emanuel's name save for in one instance. Either way, after a prolific run through December 1946, his output became a mere trickle, ending in 1950.

A Horizon of Hope: *Golden Fleece* and *Fantastic Adventures*

A flicker of light at the end of an otherwise very dark tunnel briefly flared into life when Sun Publications began printing *Golden Fleece*, a historical fiction magazine.

Sun Publications was home over the years to *10-Story Book*, *Live Stories*, *Lulu*, and other magazines. During a time of instability, Sun Publications had in May 1938 suffered the seizure of three truckloads of magazines and printing equipment by Chicago police, whom served a warrant charging the proprietors of Sun with "possession of obscene literature." Despite these and other losses that ensued, such as an inability to collect past-due funds from distributors, *Golden Fleece* debuted months later in October, featuring a variety of pulp fiction's greatest authors: Robert E.

Howard, H. Bedford-Jones, Ralph Milne Farley, Anthony M. Rud, Seabury Quinn, and many others.

Emanuel had succeeded in selling two novels to *Golden Fleece* (one the past Winter and one that Spring) when the magazine abruptly ceased publication with the June 1939 issue. While *The Queen's Mercy* slid into the April issue, the second novel never was published. Worried that he had lost the novel, Emanuel wrote Chapman, asking for his assistance. What precisely became of the novel is unknown; it may have been reworked into the pages of a Trojan publication.

In October 1939, a new magazine appearing by Ziff-Davis briefly aroused Emanuel's hopes: *Fantastic Adventures*. Immediately he set to work, and sent in "The Lifted Veil" and "Woman of Mercury," reviving his old fantasy alias of H. M. Egbert for the first time in nearly two decades. Rejected, both were reworked and sold to the "spicy" pulps, with the latter's title slightly altered to "Woman From Mercury."

While the above were easily reconstructed, many others seemingly vanished, including the novelettes *Queen of Tall Timber*, *The Magic Maze*, *Owlhoot Marshall*, *The Madness of Jean Barthou*, and short stories "Valley of Strife," "Stranger Guest," "Pioneer Stuff," "Angle with Angels," "Eight Minutes of Darkness," "American Mother," "Salvage," and countless others.

In 1941, while down at Leo Margulies office, a young [unnamed] editor interviewed Emanuel for his college magazine, and Margulies requested a 30,000-word fantasy involving Atlantis. It was rejected without comment. Months later, while attending an authors' banquet, he was applauded for his contributions to the literary field. He took it in the negative, as an old-timer receiving recognition.

During the 1940s—1950s, many of his previously printed works and unsold stories ended up in various national newspapers, such as the *Boston Globe*, the *Kansas City Star*. the *Toronto Star*, and possibly the *Boston Post*. While the *Globe* has certainly been indexed in full (courtesy of Victor Berch), the remaining titles have not. It is unknown whether any other newspapers carried his fiction during these years.

Only one field remained open to Emanuel, the "true" confession/romance pulps. He first wrote for the "true" field in 1923, and appears to have continued clear into the 1950s.

> It seemed to me incredible that, after fifty years of avid magazine reading, the public could have lost interest in that form of entertainment, but magazine after magazine dropped from the bookstands. I don't think the introduction of the radio had much to do with it. It was to a large extent the progressive deterioration in education, which left a large section of what had been the reading public incapable of understanding words, and turning for entertainment to the comics. And above all it was the introduction of television.

> The vogue for specialized magazines had lasted about ten years. I had had a miraculous reincarnation after the fall of the serial, and thought I could adapt myself to any change. But this wasn't change.

> It was annihilation.

Alcoholism and Death

Emanuel turned to a vice he and "Pussyfoot" Johnson once advocated against: alcoholism. His attention to the bottle originated in the early 1930s; by the 1940s, he suffered from acute alcoholism.

> I took the weakling's way out, with alcohol. But it does not liberate, it confines. I wrote without hope, but with an imagination excited by the alcohol, working all night until dawn, then drugging myself to sleep with barbiturates. I lived in a fog, in which only the characters of my stories possessed much reality. And about four times a year, when the longing for human intercourse had become intolerable, I would go into New York and spend a weekend with friends in Greenwich Village, drinking, of course. Although for eight years I was always under the influence of alcohol or barbiturates, I never became what is called an alcoholic. When liquor ceased to be my prop, I discarded it. But I can see how disastrous a prop it was. I had sold my soul to a devil with a gin bottle.

Emanuel was impoverished and lonely. Elva— his wife—died in 1955. He had hit the age in which welfare checks began to appear. Drawing a meager income from the State, he was content.

> Now at last I had the opportunity to be an artist, and for ten years, more or less, I devoted myself to writing the kind of novels I had always wanted to write. I received plenty of appreciative letters [from publishers], but "we are afraid we cannot see any prospects of succeeding with this." Well, I used the backs of the typewritten pages for the rough draft of my next novel, so nothing was wasted.

> One thing did break my heart. I had conceived a series of four novels covering New York life throughout the nineteenth century. I think I succeeded in presenting a novel and accurate picture of life in New York during the

early years of that century in the two volumes that I completed.

With my abilities I should have been a successful novelist, but I never knew how to sell myself.

Two unpublished autobiographies survive; one is semi-factual while the second is a fiction novel incorporating his entire life. Both sport a hitherto unknown, and perhaps, unpublished alias: J. Bouillard Frank. The former is entitled *The Frank Memoirs*, and was never intended for publication. The latter, *Penny Point*, was submitted to Halliday and McCloy. It was returned, unsold. Both were constructed during the remaining five years of his life.

A letter dated in 1958 insinuated that Leo Margulies had maintained an amiable association with Emanuel, and he requested some fresh material. It is unclear whether it was for *Satellite Science Fiction* or *Mike Shayne's Mystery Magazine* or some other side venture. Perhaps it was his lost sequel to *The Messiah of the Cylinder*. And, yes, a sequel

was constructed and went the rounds and like all other attempts, it too met with failure.

On 6 April 1960, in Tarrytown, New York, a forgotten soul died.

As an early pioneer of syndicated newspaper tales whose fiction matured into the pulpwood magazine market, Emanuel possessed a vivid imagination and life experiences enough to construct entertaining stories. Emanuel ought to be remembered for more than just his science-fantasy and weird contributions, but, it is those contributions to the genre that will always keep his namesake at the forefront of a forever-dwindling mass of pulp fiction collectors and readers.

Enclosed in this volume is more than an author's life history and bibliography. There are also numerous examples of his early writings, samples from various series he wrote during his first decade of exploration, and numerous memorable short stories, both lost or forgotten. Read these and then answer for yourself: who was Victor Rousseau Emanuel?

LIST OF ABBREVIATIONS

vi – vignette	(under 4 pages; under 1000 words)	
s – short story	(4 to 20 pages; 1000 to 7,499 words)	
ss – short story in a series	(4 to 20 pages; 1000 to 7,499 words)	
nt – novelette	(21 to 45 pages; 7,500 to 17,499 words)	
na – novella	(46 to 100 pages; 17,500 to 39,999 words)	
n – novel	(101 or more pages; 40,000 or more words)	
mv – movie	Photoplay / moving picture	
sa – story adaptation	A motion picture / photoplay presented in story form	
tc – true crime	[Semi-]Factual depiction of a criminous event	
ts – true story	Actual tale that occurred told in story format	
(hb) – hardback	Bound in hard boards	
(sc) – softcover	Trade Paperback or any form of photo reproduction	
(ab) – abridgement	Condensed from original version (noted after story title)	
(rw) – rewritten	Revised from original version (noted after story title)	

LIST OF PSEUDONYMS

Victor Rousseau	V. R. Emanuel	Victor Emanuel	Victor Emmanuel
Victor Rosseau	H. M. Egbert	Leonard Britten	Victoria Ross
Egbert Prentice	John Austin	C. Cordier	
Lew Merrill	Hugh Speer	Clive Trent	
Harold Carter	Frank Filson	George Munson	

HOUSE NAMES

John Grange	John Wayne	Stan Warner	John Phillips
Ray Coleman	William Decatur	George Freeman Tracy	

STORY INDEX by TITLE (sans syndicated vignettes)

Aaron Lapwing's Genius; or, For the Princess Herodias (as Leonard Britten)   sl
  Chicago Ledger, 1915: Apr 10, 17, 24; May 1, 8, 15, 22

—The Adventures of Anne Ives, Mascot (see: Aviator No. 6)

The Adventure of the Three Georges (as Victor Rousseau)   ss
  Photoplay Magazine, 1917: Mar

The Adventure of the Town Pond Submarine (as Victor Rousseau)   ss
  Photoplay Magazine, 1917: Apr

The Aerial War (as Victor Rousseau)   s
  Short Stories, 1914: Dec

The Affair of the North Sea (as H. M. Egbert)   ss
  The New Magazine (UK) 1910: Aug
  Morrison's Chicago Weekly, 1910: Dec 8 (as: The Fisherman and the Fleet)

Afghan Gold (as Victor Rousseau)   s
  Action Stories, 1930: Jun

Air Maiden (as Clive Trent)   nt
  Spicy Mystery Stories, 1940: Oct

Air-Minded (as Victor Rousseau)   s
  The Boston Daily Globe, 1950: Feb 12

Alf Barton's Princess (as Victor Rousseau)   ss
  Holland's Magazine, 1913: Aug
  The Illustrated Buffalo Express, 1914: Apr 5
  THE TRACER OF EGOS
    US: The Spectre Library (hb), Aug 2007 (as Victor Rousseau)

The Alibi That Failed (as George Munson)   tc
  Detective Story Magazine, 1919: Jul 8

Alice of Chalons (as Victor Rousseau)   ss
  Ainslee's Magazine, 1915: Oct

—All For a Girl (see: Lee of the Northwest Mounted)

An Amazon of Tripoli (as H. M. Egbert)   ss
  Stevens Point Journal, 1913: Nov 15

The Amir's Move (as H. M. Egbert)   ss
  The Globe and Commercial Advertiser, 1910: Sep 24
  Morrison's Chicago Weekly, 1911: Jan 5
  Cassell's Magazine of Fiction (UK) 1913: Oct (as: The King's Courier)

Among Those Present (as Hugh Speer)   s
  Speed Mystery, 1944: Jan

The Amulet of Marduk (as Victor Rousseau)   ss
  Holland's Magazine, 1913: Jun
  The Illustrated Buffalo Express, 1914: Mar 15
  THE TRACER OF EGOS
    US: The Spectre Library (hb), Aug 2007 (as Victor Rousseau)
  HIS SECOND SELF: THE BIO-BIBLIOGRAPHY OF VICTOR ROUSSEAU EMANUEL
    US: The Spectre Library (sc), 2011 (as Victor Rousseau)

Angel of Mercy (as Lew Merrill)   s
  Spicy-Adventure Stories, 1936: Jan
  Spicy-Adventure Stories, 1936: Jan (facsimile)

The Angel of the Marne (as Victor Rousseau)   s
  Ghost Stories, 1929: Jul (credited as Capt. Albert Sewell on Contents Page)
  PHANTOM PERFUMES AND OTHER SHADES
    CND: Ash-Tree Press (hb), 2000

Arc of Death (as Lew Merrill)   s
  Spicy Mystery Stories, 1941: Nov

Arc of Death (as Clive Trent)   s
  Speed Mystery, 1943: Sep

Arctic Treasure (as Victor Rousseau)   s
  North-West Stories, 1926: 1st Sep
  North-West Stories (UK) 1927: Early Mar

The Arm of Justice (as H. M. Egbert)   ss
  St. Louis Post-Dispatch, 1913: Nov 1
  The Houston Post, 1913: Nov 2
  The Boston Daily Globe, 1914: Feb 22
  Buffalo Sunday Times, 1916: Apr 2
  THE DEVIL CHAIR
    US: The Spectre Library (hb), Jun 2008 (as Victor Rousseau)

Army of the Dead (as Lew Merrill)   s
  Spicy-Adventure Stories, 1939: May

Astral Murder (as Lew Merrill)   s
  Spicy Mystery Stories, 1936: Mar
  Spicy Mystery Stories, 1936: Mar (facsimile)

The Atom-Smasher (as Victor Rousseau)   na
  Astounding Stories of Super-Science, 1930: May

Aviator No. 6 (as H. M. Egbert)   sl
  Canada West Monthly (Canada) 1911: Oct, Nov, Dec; 1912: Jan, Feb, Mar, Apr
  People's Popular Monthly, 1912: Mar, Apr, May, Jun, Jul, Aug, Sep, Oct, Nov, Dec
    (as: The Adventures of Anne Ives, Mascot)

The Awakening of Edith (as Victor Rousseau)   sl
  Physical Culture, 1925: Mar, Apr, May, Jun, Jul

The Bacillus Prodigiosus (as H. M. Egbert)   vi
  (see Newspaper Vignettes: Belleville News Democrat, 31 Mar 1909)
  Best Stories of All Time, 1927: Feb

Bamboo Flower (as Clive Trent)   s
   Spicy-Adventure Stories, 1936: Mar
   Spicy-Adventure Stories, 1936: Mar (facsimile)

The Bandit Of Batakaland (as Victor Rousseau)   sl
   Argosy All-Story Weekly, 1922: Jan 28; Feb 4, 11, 18, 25
   THE GOLDEN HORDE
      UK: Hodder and Stoughton, 1926

—**Bank Cashier Caught** (see: A Matter of Mathematics)

Banzai Charge (as Victor Rousseau)   s
   Speed Adventure Stories, 1945: Jul

Barbary Brew (as Lew Merrill)   s
   Spicy-Adventure Stories, 1937: May

Bat Man (as Lew Merrill)   s
   Spicy Mystery Stories, 1936: Feb
   Pulp Review # 5, 1992: Jul
   Pulp Review # 5, 2008 (new ads and perfect bound)
   Spicy Mystery Stories 1936: Feb (facsimile)

The Beast Maker (as H. M. Egbert)   sl
   Chicago Ledger, 1920: Jan 24, 31; Feb 7, 14

Beast of the Kremlin (as Lew Merrill)   s
   Spicy-Adventure Stories, 1938: Dec

Bee Flight (as Clive Trent)   s
   Spicy-Adventure Stories, 1942: May

The Beetle Horde (as Victor Rousseau)   sl
   Astounding Stories of Super-Science, 1930: Jan, Feb

Beggar-Ticks (as Hugh Speer)   s
   Speed Mystery, 1944: May

The Belfry Dawn (as Victor Rousseau)   ss
   Chicago Tribune, 1915: Dec 12

Bell-Bottom Trousers (as Lew Merrill)   s
   Super-Detective, 1946: Mar

Bern's Blunder (as Hugh Speer)   s
   Speed Adventure Stories, 1943: Sep

The Bethune Charter (as Victor Rousseau)   ss
   Chicago Tribune, 1915: Nov 14

Beyond Hell's Barriers (as Hugh Speer)   s
   Spicy Mystery Stories, 1938: Jun

Beyond the Veil (as Lew Merrill)   s
   Spicy Mystery Stories, 1936: Sep
   Spicy Mystery Stories, 1936: Sep (facsimile)

A Bid for a Throne (as H. M. Egbert)										ss
  The Blue Book Magazine, 1911: Nov

The Big Muskeg (as Victor Rousseau)										sl
  The Argosy, 1920: Jan 3, 10, 17, 24
  Philadelphia Inquirer, 1921: Sep 18, 25; Oct 2, 9, 16, 23, 30 (incomplete)
  THE BIG MUSKEG
    US: Stewart Kidd (hb), 1921
  THE BIG MUSKEG
    UK: Hodder and Stoughton (hb), 1923
  THE BIG MUSKEG
    US: Kessinger Publishing (sc), 2007: Jun

Big Pierre's Idol (as Victor Rousseau)									ss
  The Blue Book Magazine, 1915: Apr
  Chicago Tribune, 1917: Dec 23
  The Boston Daily Globe, 1930: Dec 28
  Toronto Star Weekly, 1933: Jul 22

Big Swamp (as Victor Rousseau)										na
  Brief Stories, 1927: Nov

Bill Connolly's Christmas (as Victor Rousseau)								s
  Illustrated Sunday Magazine, 1908: Dec 20

Birchall, the Canadian Murderer (as George Munson)							tc
  Detective Story Magazine, 1919: Jun 24

The Black Avatar (as Victor Rousseau)									s
  Thrilling Adventures, 1931: Dec

Black Dawn (as Victor Rousseau)										sl
  McKean County Democrat, 1942: July 9, 16, 23, 30;
    Aug 6, 13, 20, 27; Sep 3, 10, 17, 24; Oct 1

The Blackest Magic of All (as Victor Rousseau)							s
  Ghost Stories, 1928: Jul
  Startling Mystery Stories, 1967: Spring (as: Medium for Justice)

Black Goddess (as Hugh Speer)										s
  Spicy-Adventure Stories, 1937: Jun

Black Gods (as Lew Merrill)										s
  Spicy-Adventure Stories, 1937: Apr

The Black Gods of Ngami (as Victor Rousseau)							s
  Jungle Stories, 1939: Fall

—**The Black Horror** (see: Death's Dancing Partner)

Blind Luck (as Lew Merrill)										s
  Speed Western Stories, 1945: Jun

Bloated Death (as John Grange)										nt
  Super Detective, 1941: Jan

—Blood of the Children (refer to the section on: Story Adaptations)

Blood on the Snow (as Victor Rousseau)   s
    North-West Romances, 1937: Winter

Blood Racket (as Hugh Speer)   s
    Speed Mystery, 1944: Sep

—Blood Taint (see: The Climbing Buddha)

The Blue Dimity Dress (as Victor Rousseau)   s
    Harper's Monthly Magazine, 1914: Mar

Body Divided (as Hugh Speer)   s
    Spicy Mystery Stories, 1938: Feb

The Body in the Box (as George Munson)   tc
    Detective Story Magazine, 1919: May 27
    Famous Crime Cases (Canada) 1946: May

The Body in the Parcel (as H. M. Egbert)   tc
    Washington Post, 1911: Feb 12 (not bylined)
    Buffalo Sunday Times, 1911: Nov 5
    20th Century Crime Cases (Canada) 1946: Aug

Border Napoleon (as John Grange)   nt
    Super Detective, 1941: Aug

Bows of Fortune (as Lew Merrill)   nt
    Speed Adventure Stories, 1946: Jan

Bows of Muscovy (as Victor Rousseau)   na
    Soldiers of Fortune, 1931: Dec

The Box of Borneos (as Harold Carter)   ss
    Buffalo Sunday Times, 1911: Jun 18
    HIS SECOND SELF: THE BIO-BIBLIOGRAPHY OF VICTOR ROUSSEAU EMANUEL
      US: The Spectre Library (sc), 2011 (as Victor Rousseau)

Brain-Buster (as Lew Merrill)   s
    Private Detective Stories, 1944: Nov

The Branded Man (as Victor Rousseau)   sl
    Argosy All-Story Weekly, 1929: Apr 13, 20, 27; May 4
    Toronto Star Weekly, Magazine Section, 1942: Nov 7, 14, 21 (end not known)
    Zane Grey's Western Magazine, 1947: Aug (Condensed version)

The Brazen Bull (as Clive Trent)   s
    Spicy Mystery Stories, 1937: Jul

Bridal Eve (as Victor Rousseau)   s
    Breezy Stories and Young's Magazine, 1936: Dec

Bride of Battle (as Victor Rousseau)   sl
    Fiction Magazine, 1918: Apr 7, 14, 21, 28; May 5, 12, 19
    Detroit Free Press, 1918: May 12, 19, 26; Jun 2, 9, 16, 23

The Bride of Eagle Pass (as Victor Rousseau)   nt
    Western Romances, 1937: Mar

—**The Bride of Golden Mountain** (see: Jacqueline of Golden River)

Bride of the Pyramid (as Hugh Speer)   s
    Spicy-Adventure Stories, 1936: Mar
    Spicy-Adventure Stories, 1936: Mar (facsimile)

Bride of the Sun (as Lew Merrill)   s
    Spicy-Adventure Stories, 1937: Aug
    Speed Mystery, 1943: Jan (as: Sealed In Death; as George Freeman Tracy)

Bride of the Sword (as Lew Merrill)   s
    Spicy-Adventure Stories, 1936: Apr
    Spicy-Adventure Stories, 1936: Apr (facsimile)

The Brides of Coco Island (as Clive Trent)   s
    Speed Adventure Stories, 1945: Jan

Bright Isle of Enchantment (as Lew Merrill)   s
    Spicy Mystery Stories, 1938: Feb

Broccoli Burlesque (as Lew Merrill)   s
    Super-Detective, 1944: Sep

The Broken Heel (as Harold Carter)   ss
    Buffalo Sunday Times, 1911: Aug 6
    The Saturday Blade, 1912: Feb 10

Broken Men (as Victor Rousseau)   nt
    Five-Novels Monthly, 1928: Mar

The Brother of the Moon (as H. M. Egbert)   ss
    The Blue Book Magazine, 1912: Jan
    Public Ledger, 1913: May 11
    The Boston Daily Globe, 1915: Jan 31

Brothers in Blood (as Lew Merrill)   s
    Spicy Mystery Stories, 1935: Dec
    Spicy Mystery Stories, 1935: Dec (facsimile)

Brushless Cream (as Lew Merrill)   s
    Super-Detective, 1946: Nov

Buffalo Trail (as Victor Rousseau)   s
    Fighting Western, 1946: Oct

Bugle Call (as Clive Trent)   s
    Spicy-Adventure Stories, 1939: Feb

The Bulgarian Papers (as H. M. Egbert)   ss
    The Popular Magazine, 1915: Jan 7
    Fiction Magazine, 1915: Jun 6

The Bullet-Proof Mantle (as H. M. Egbert)   ss
  The Popular Magazine, 1915: Jan 23
  Fiction Magazine, 1915: Jul 4

Bulls Have Jaws (as Lew Merrill)   s
  Speed Adventure Stories, 1943: Nov

Burma Road (as Lew Merrill)   s
  Spicy-Adventure Stories, 1941: May

The Burning of Batoum (as H. M. Egbert)   ss
  The Blue Book Magazine, 1911: Aug
  Public Ledger, 1913: Apr 13

Button, Button (as Lew Merrill)   s
  Private Detective Stories, 1945: Jun

By Name of Brown (as Lew Merrill)   s
  Fighting Western, 1946: Jun

By the Deep Sea Transit (as H. M. Egbert)   ss
  St. Louis Post-Dispatch, 1913: Dec 13
  The Houston Post, 1913: Dec 14
  The Boston Daily Globe, 1914: Apr 5
  Buffalo Sunday Times, 1916: May 14
  THE DEVIL CHAIR
    US: The Spectre Library (hb), Jun 2008 (as Victor Rousseau)

Cactus Trail (as Victor Rousseau)   sl
  Ranch Romances, 1931: 2nd Jun, 1st Jul, 2nd Jul, 3rd Jul, 1st Aug, 2nd Aug

The Cain Ship (as H. M. Egbert)   sl
  Chicago Ledger 1920: May 22, 29; Jun 5

Cakes of Judgment (as Victor Rousseau)   s
  Century, 1909: Jun

Canine Verdict (as Lew Merrill)   s
  Super-Detective, 1945: Mar

Captain Ransome's Twenty Minutes (as Victor Rousseau)   s
  The American Patriot, 1915: Nov

The Captain's Hook (as Hugh Speer)   nt
  Spicy Mystery Stories, 1941: Nov

Capt. Cholmunday's Monkey (as Victor Rousseau)   ss
  Ainslee's Magazine, 1915: Sep

Captive's Castle (as Victor Rousseau)   nt
  Five-Novels Monthly, 1934: Dec

Captives of the Arctic Wasteland (as Victor Rousseau)   nt
  North-West Stories, 1936: Winter
  THE NORTHERNERS
    US: Fawcett (sc), 1990

The Carfax Curse (as Victor Rousseau)   ss
   Holland's Magazine, 1913: Nov
   The Illustrated Buffalo Express, 1914: Apr 19
   THE TRACER OF EGOS
      US: The Spectre Library (hb), Aug 2007 (as Victor Rousseau)

The Case of Madame Lafarge (as H. M. Egbert)   tc
   Washington Post, 1910: Dec 18 (not bylined)
   Buffalo Sunday Times, 1911: Sep 10
   Detective Story Magazine, 1919: Oct 21 (as George Munson)

The Case of Mrs. Wharton (as George Munson)   tc
   Detective Story Magazine, 1919: Jun 17
   Famous Crime Cases (Canada) 1946: Aug

The Case of the Jailer's Daughter (as H. M. Egbert)   ss
   The Globe and Commercial Advertiser, 1910: Feb 5
   Weird Tales, 1926: Sep (as Victor Rousseau)
   THE SURGEON OF SOULS
      US: The Spectre Library (hb), Oct 2006 (as Victor Rousseau)

A Casual Champion (as H. M. Egbert)   ss
   Chicago Daily News, 1911: Oct 14
   HIS SECOND SELF: THE BIO-BIBLIOGRAPHY OF VICTOR ROUSSEAU EMANUEL
      US: The Spectre Library (sc), 2011 (as Victor Rousseau)

Cat Woman (as Lew Merrill)   s
   Spicy Mystery Stories, 1936: Aug
   Spicy Mystery Stories, 1936: Aug (facsimile)

The Cats That Looked at Cohen (as H. M. Egbert)   ss
   Canada West Monthly (Canada) 1911: May
   HIS SECOND SELF: THE BIO-BIBLIOGRAPHY OF VICTOR ROUSSEAU EMANUEL
      US: The Spectre Library (sc), 2011 (as Victor Rousseau)

Cave of Canoes (as Lew Merrill)   s
   Spicy-Adventure Stories, 1940: Nov

Cave of Ghosts (as Victor Rousseau)   s
   Leading Western, 1946: Nov

The Chairs of Stuyvesant Baron (as H. M. Egbert)   ss
   The Globe and Commercial Advertiser, 1910: Apr 2
   Weird Tales, 1927: Apr (as Victor Rousseau)
   THE SURGEON OF SOULS
      US: The Spectre Library (hb), Oct 2006 (as Victor Rousseau)

Challenge of the U-212 (as Victor Rousseau)   nt
   Submarine Stories, 1930: Jul

Challenge to Napoleon (as Victor Rousseau)   nt
   Five-Novels Monthly, 1938: Aug

The Champion of the Fleet (as Harold Carter)   ss
   Buffalo Sunday Times, 1911: Jul 9

—**Changed Lives** (refer to the section on: Story Adaptations)

The Chaparral Trail (as John Austin)   na
   Rangeland Love Story Magazine, 1930: Jul

Chapelle Ardente (as Victor Rousseau)   s
   The Red Book Magazine, 1915: Jan
   Chicago Tribune, 1917: Dec 30
   La Canadienne (Canada, French trans.) 1920: Jul
   The Boston Daily Globe, 1930: Nov 2
   Toronto Star Weekly, 1933: Jul 29 (as: Glowing Chapel)

The Cheap Skate (as Victor Rousseau)   s
   Literary Magazine Section, 1909: Sep 26

Child or Demon - Which? (as Victor Rousseau)   ss
   Ghost Stories, 1926: Oct
   Hutchinson's Adventure-Story Magazine (UK) 1927: Jan (as Eugene Branscombe)
   True Twilight Tales, 1964: Spring
      (as: Child or Demon – Which Was She? as Eugene Branscombe)
   WHEN SPIRITS TALK
      UK: The Ghost Story Society (sc), 1990

Chilled Mutton (as Lew Merrill)   s
   Speed Adventure Stories, 1944: Nov

A Christmas Interpretation (as Victor Rousseau)   s
   Canadian Countryman, 1921: Xmas Issue

— **Church Warden Murderer** (see: Churchwarden Murderer)

Churchwarden Murderer (as H. M. Egbert)   tc
   Washington Post, 1911: Jan 22 (not bylined)
   Buffalo Sunday Times, 1911: Oct 15
   Clues, 1929: 1st Jun (as: Church Warden Murderer)

The Circle of Happiness (as Victor Rousseau)   nt
   Five-Novels Monthly, 1930: Jun

City of Doom (as Hugh Speer)   s
   Speed Adventure Stories, 1943: Jul

City of Light (as Hugh Speer)   s
   Spicy-Adventure Stories, 1940: Aug

Claws of the Statue (as Lew Merrill)   s
   Speed Mystery, 1943: Jul

The Climbing Buddha (as Clive Trent)   s
   Spicy-Adventure Stories, 1939: May
   Speed Mystery Stories, 1943: May (as: Blood Taint; as William Decatur)

The Cloud Pirates (as H. M. Egbert)   ss
   Chicago Ledger, 1922: Jul 8

Coconut Cargo (as Clive Trent)   s
    Speed Adventure Stories, 1944: May

Code of the Hills (as Hugh Speer)   s
    Spicy-Adventure Stories, 1938: Apr

Code of the Northland (as Hugh Speer)   s
    Spicy-Adventure Stories, 1935: Nov

Cold Turkey (as John Grange)   nt
    Super Detective, 1942: Feb

Commando (as Lew Merrill)   s
    Spicy-Adventure Stories, 1942: Dec

—**Comment S'accomplit un Miracle** (see: The Curé's Love Story)

Condemned by Woman (as Victor Rousseau)   s
    Detective Story Magazine, 1919: Feb 11

Congo Spears (as Lew Merrill)   s
    Spicy-Adventure Stories, 1938: Mar

Contraband and Whiskers (as H. M. Egbert)   ss
    Chicago Ledger, 1922: Jul 15

Cord of Death (as Lew Merrill)   s
    Spicy-Adventure Stories, 1941: Jan

The Coronation of Nikolai (as H. M. Egbert)   ss
    The Blue Book Magazine, 1911: Sep
    Public Ledger, 1913: Apr 20
    The Boston Daily Globe, 1915: Mar 7

Corpse in the Car (as Clive Trent)   s
    Super-Detective, 1945: Sep

Count Berchtold's Birthday Party (as H. M. Egbert)   ss
    Fiction Magazine, 1915: Jun 27

Cousin Paul (as Victor Rousseau)   s
    Harper's Monthly Magazine, 1914: Oct

Cowboy Courageous (as Victor Rousseau)   nt
    Ranch Romances, 1928: Dec 2nd

Crawford of the Border (as Victor Rousseau)   nt
    Five-Novels Monthly, 1928: Oct
    Complete Adventure Novelettes 1932: Feb (as: East of Suez)

Crazy House (as Hugh Speer)   s
    Speed Mystery, 1945: Jun

The Crescendo of Prof. Zeldenrust (as Victor Rousseau)   s
    Illustrated Sunday Magazine, 1908: Sep 13

The Crimes of the Marchioness (as H. M. Egbert)   tc
   Washington Post, 1911: Feb 5 (not bylined)
   Buffalo Sunday Times, 1911: Oct 29
   Detective Story Magazine, 1919: Nov 25 (as George Munson)
   20th Century Crime Cases (Canada) 1946: Jul (as H. M. Egbert)

The Cripple of Prospect Park (as H. M. Egbert)   ss
   St. Louis Post-Dispatch, 1913: Sep 27
   The Houston Post, 1913: Sep 28
   The Boston Daily Globe, 1914: Jan 18
   Buffalo Sunday Times, 1916: Feb 27
   THE DEVIL CHAIR
      US: The Spectre Library (hb), Jun 2008 (as Victor Rousseau)
   HIS SECOND SELF: THE BIO-BIBLIOGRAPHY OF VICTOR ROUSSEAU EMANUEL
      US: The Spectre Library (sc), 2011 (as Victor Rousseau)

The Crooked Finger (as Victor Rousseau)   s
   Fiction Magazine, 1917: Aug 12
   The Illustrated Buffalo Express, 1918: Mar 31 (as: The Dead Hand)
   Chicago Ledger, 1918: Aug 3 (as: The Dead Hand; as Victor Rosseau)
   Canadian Countryman (Canada) 1920: Jan 24
      (as: A Just Retribution; as Victor Rosseau)
   Police Magazine, 1925: Jun (as: The Dead Hand)
   Mon Magazine Policier (Canada, French trans.) 1941: Jan (as: La Main du Cadavre)

The Crooked Seam (as Harold Carter)   ss
   Buffalo Sunday Times, 1911: Aug 13
   The Saturday Blade, 1912: Jan 13

Crooked Trails (as Victor Rousseau)   na
   Ranch Romances, 1932: 2nd Jun

Crossed Wires (as Hugh Speer)   s
   Speed Mystery, 1944: Mar

Crossroads (as Victor Rousseau)   nt
   Breezy Stories, 1921: Jun

Cross-Trails to Paradise (as Victor Rousseau)   na
   Ranch Romances, 1934: 2nd Feb

Crusoe on Antarctica (as Victor Rousseau)   s
   Speed Adventure Stories, 1945: Oct

A Cry from Beyond (as Victor Rousseau)   s
   Strange Tales of Mystery and Terror, 1931: Sep
   Magazine of Horror, 1968: Mar
   THE FANTASTIC PULPS
      UK: Gollancz (hb), 1975
   THE FANTASTIC PULPS
      US: St. Martins Press (hb), 1976
   THE FANTASTIC PULPS
      US: Vintage Books (sc), 1976
   Strange Tales of Mystery and Terror 1931: Sep (facsimile)

The Curé Goes Hunting (as Victor Rousseau)   ss
   The Blue Book Magazine, 1915: Jan
   The Boston Daily Globe, 1931: Jan 11

The Curé's Love Story (as Victor Rousseau)   ss
   Everywoman's World (Canada) 1917 (1st publication; not found)
   La Canadienne (Canada, French trans.) 1921: Jan
      (as: *Comment S'accomplit un Miracle*)
   The Boston Daily Globe, 1931: Apr 19

The Curse of Amen-Ra (as Victor Rousseau)   nt
   Strange Tales of Mystery and Terror, 1932: Oct
   A Book of Weird Tales (UK) 1960
   Magazine of Horror, 1967: Fall
   Narraciones Géminis de Terror # 11; Argentina: 1968 (as: La Maldición de la Momia)
   MUMMY STORIES
      US: Ballantine (sc), 1990
   MUMMY STORIES
      UK: Severn House (hb), 1991
   ผีมัมมี่คืนชีพ (The Mummy Returns); Nonthaburi, Thailand, 2535 (year: 1992)
   DR. ACULA'S THRILLING TALES OF THE UNCANNY
      US: Sense of Wonder Press (sc), 2004
   GOTICA # 65: LA MALDICION DE LA MOMIA
      Spain, 2006 (as: La Maldición de la Momia)
   Strange Tales of Mystery and Terror, 1932: Oct (facsimile)

Curse of Killarney (as Lew Merrill)   s
   Spicy Mystery Stories, 1939: Oct

Curse of the Ogilvy's (as Lew Merrill)   s
   Spicy Mystery Stories, 1937: Mar

Curse of the Tremaines (as Hugh Speer)   s
   Private Detective Stories, 1944: May

Cyanide (as Lew Merrill)   s
   Super-Detective, 1945: Jan

Cyclops (as Hugh Speer)   s
   Spicy Mystery Stories, 1936: Aug
   Spicy Mystery Stories, 1936: Aug (facsimile)

The Czar's Drive (as H. M. Egbert)   ss
   The Globe and Commercial Advertiser, 1910: Oct 15
   Morrison's Chicago Weekly, 1911: Jan 19 (as: Why Russia Backed Down)
   Cassell's Magazine of Fiction (UK) 1914: Feb (as: The Tsar's Drive)

Dancing-Girl Orchid (as Clive Trent)   s
   Spicy Mystery Stories, 1941: Sep

Dane Raiders (as Lew Merrill)   s
   Spicy-Adventure Stories, 1938: Oct

Danger's Bloody Banner (as Victor Rousseau)   s
   Thrilling Adventures, 1937: Jun

Daniel Webster Said (as Lew Merrill)   s
Speed Mystery, 1944: Sep

The Dark Disk (as Victor Rousseau)   na
Complete Stories, 1928: Mar

Dark Dominion (as Lew Merrill)   s
Spicy-Adventure Stories, 1937: Oct

A Date with the Goat God (as Hugh Speer)   s
Spicy Mystery Stories, 1938: Oct

Daughter of Death (as Lew Merrill)   s
Spicy Mystery Stories, 1936: Nov
Spicy Mystery Stories, 1936: Nov (facsimile)

The Dawn Tide (as Lew Merrill)   s
Speed Adventure Stories, 1944: May

—**The Dead Hand** (see: The Crooked Finger)

Dead Man Rides (as Clive Trent)   s
Spicy Mystery Stories, 1938: May

Dead Man's Arm (as Hugh Speer)   s
Spicy Mystery Stories, 1938: Aug

A Dead Man's Empire (as H. M. Egbert)   ss
Fiction Magazine, 1915: Jul 18

Dead Man's Shoes (as Lew Merrill)   s
Spicy Mystery Stories, 1936: Jun
Spicy Mystery Stories, 1936: Jun (facsimile)

Dead Man's Trail (as Victor Rousseau)   nt
Action Novels, 1931: Aug

Dead Man's Valley (as Victor Rousseau)   nt
Sky Riders, 1929: Oct

Dead Men's Cave (as Victor Rousseau)   s
Fighting Western, 1948: Oct

Dead or Alive! (as Hugh Speer)   s
Spicy-Adventure Stories, 1938: Jul

A Deal in Elephant (as Victor Rousseau)   s
Harper's Weekly, 1909: Aug 7

Dealer in Death (as John Grange)   nt
   Super-Detective, 1940: Oct
   Behind the Mask # 45, 1998: Summer
   THE ADVENTURERS
     US: Black Dog Books (sc), 2008
   SUPER-DETECTIVE JIM ANTHONY # 1
     US: Altus Press (hb), 2009 (as Victor Rousseau)
   SUPER-DETECTIVE JIM ANTHONY # 1
     US: Altus Press (sc), 2009 (as Victor Rousseau)

The Death God Awakes (as Hugh Speer)   s
   Spicy Mystery Stories, 1937: Sep

Death in the Desert (as Lew Merrill)   s
   Spicy-Adventure Stories, 1936: Jun
   Spicy-Adventure Stories, 1936: Jun (facsimile)

The Death in the Dirigible (as Harold Carter)   ss
   Buffalo Sunday Times, 1911: Jul 30
   The Saturday Blade, 1912: Feb 17

Death in the Tank (as Hugh Speer)   nt
   Speed Detective, 1944: May
   RUE MORGUE NO. 1
     US: Creative Age Press (hb), 1946

The Death March (as H. M. Egbert)   s
   Short Stories, 1911: Feb

Death Patrol (as Lew Merrill)   s
   Speed Adventure Stories, 1945: Apr

Death Ride (as Hugh Speer)   s
   Spicy-Adventure Stories, 1939: Apr

—**Death Rides High** (see: God of the Pit)

Death's Dancing Partner (as Hugh Speer)   s
   Spicy Mystery Stories, 1936: Nov
   Spicy Mystery Stories, 1942: Nov (as: The Black Horror; as Ray Coleman)
   Spicy Mystery Stories, 1936: Nov (facsimile)

Death Stalks Through Walls (as Hugh Speer)   s
   Spicy-Adventure Stories, 1938: Nov

Death Trail (as Clive Trent)   s
   Spicy-Adventure Stories, 1936: Sep
   Spicy-Adventure Stories, 1936: Sep (facsimile)

Death Treasure (as Clive Trent)   s
   Spicy-Adventure Stories, 1937: Feb

—**Demons of the Sea** (see: The Sea Demons)

Derelict of the Arctic Sea (as Victor Rousseau)   s
   North-West Romances, 1939: Fall

Desert Lovers (as Victor Rousseau)   ???
  Ranch Romances, 1931: 1st Sep

Desert Sanctuary (as Hugh Speer)   s
  Spicy-Adventure Stories, 1941: Jan

Desperate Outlaws Put a Price on Head of 'Pussyfoot' Johnson (uncredited)   ts
  The Stevens Point Journal, 1917: May 5

The Desperation of St. Jean (as Victor Rousseau)   ss
  The Blue Book Magazine, 1915: May
  The Boston Daily Globe, 1931: Jun 14

Detective Anchisi and the Fort Wayne Gang (as George Munson)   tc
  Detective Story Magazine, 1919: Sep 23

Devil Doctor (as Lew Merrill)   s
  Spicy Mystery Stories, 1936: Jul
  Spicy Mystery Stories, 1936: Jul (facsimile)

Devil Drums (as Lew Merrill)   s
  Spicy-Adventure Stories, 1935: Dec

The Devil's Tower (as Victor Rousseau)   nt
  Ace-High Magazine, 1923: 2nd Dec
  MOTION PICTURE: as "Devil's Tower," (released: June 1928)
  Detektivmagasinet # 9 (Sweden), 1962 (as: Djävulstornet)

Devil Trail (as Lew Merrill)   s
  Spicy-Adventure Stories, 1937: Mar

The Diamond Demons (as Victor Rousseau)   sl
  All-Story Weekly, 1918: Jan 26; Feb 2, 9, 16, 23
  THE BIG MALOPO
    UK: John Long, 1924 (as H. M. Egbert)

The Diamond Tiara (as H. M. Egbert)   ss
  Chicago Daily News, 1911: Sep 23

Diamonds of Death (as Clive Trent)   s
  Spicy-Adventure Stories, 1937: May

Diamonds of Doom (as Victor Rousseau)   nt
  Frontier Stories, 1929: Feb
  Empire Frontier (UK) 1929: Aug

The Dinner at the White House (as H. M. Egbert)   ss
  The Globe and Commercial Advertiser, 1910: Sep 10
  Morrison's Chicago Weekly, 1910: Dec 15 (as: An Episode at the Whitehouse)
  Cassell's Magazine of Fiction (UK) 1913: Nov (as: title unknown)

Doctor and the Wealthy Patient (as George Munson)   tc
  Detective Story Magazine, 1919: Jun 3
  Famous Crime Cases, 1946: Jun

The Doctor's Supreme Test (as Victor Rousseau)   s
    Illustrated Sunday Magazine, 1910: Oct 23
    Literary Magazine Section, 1912: Nov (as: Victor Rosseau)

The Doll That Came to Life (as Victor Rousseau)   ss
    Ghost Stories, 1927: Jan
    Hutchinson's Mystery Story Magazine (UK) 1927: Jul

Doom Prisoners (as Victor Rousseau)   nt
    Action Stories, 1929: Dec

Doubling for Death (as Clive Trent)   s
    Super-Detective, 1945: Mar

Doughnuts for Discord (as Victor Rousseau)   nt
    Ranch Romances, 1936: 1st Mar

Draft of Eternity (as Victor Rousseau)   sl
    All-Story Weekly, 1918: June 1, 8, 15, 22
    DRAUGHT OF ETERNITY
      UK: John Long (hb), 1924 (as H. M. Egbert)
    DRAFT OF ETERNITY
      US: Beb Books (sc OCR), 2008 (as Victor Rousseau)

The Dream That Came True (as H. M. Egbert)   ss
    The Globe and Commercial Advertiser, 1910: Apr 30
    Weird Tales, 1927: Jun (as Victor Rousseau)
    THE SURGEON OF SOULS
      US: The Spectre Library (hb), Oct 2006 (as Victor Rousseau)

Dry Death (as Clive Trent)   s
    Speed Mystery, 1944: Mar

—**The Duchess** (refer to the section on: Story Adaptations)

A Dutch Music Lesson (as H. M. Egbert)   ss
    Stevens Point Journal, 1913: Dec 6

Dwindling Death (as Lew Merrill)   nt
    Spicy Mystery Stories, 1942: Oct
    Spicy Mystery Stories, 1942: Oct (facsimile)
    High Adventure # 80, 2005

Eagle Flight (as Clive Trent)   s
    Spicy-Adventure Stories, 1937: Sep

Eagle of Tibet (as Victor Rousseau)   nt
    Action Stories, 1942: Dec

The Earth Tides (as Victor Rousseau)   s
    The Dearborn Independent, 1919: Mar 22

—**East of Suez** (see: Crawford of the Border)

The Education of Edward (as H. M. Egbert)   ss
    Stevens Point Journal, 1913: Dec 20

Elephant Girl (as Hugh Speer)   s
  Spicy-Adventure Stories, 1939: Dec
  Spicy-Adventure Stories, 1939: Dec (facsimile)

Elephant God (as Lew Merrill)   s
  Speed Adventure Stories, 1943: May

Emerald of Death (as Clive Trent)   s
  Spicy Mystery Stories, 1938: Jun

The Emperor's Double (as H. M. Egbert)   ss
  The Globe and Commercial Advertiser, 1910: Aug 27
  The New Magazine (UK) 1910: Sep
  Morrison's Chicago Weekly, 1910: Dec 1 (as: His Majesty's Counterpart)

Empire of the Skies (as Victor Rousseau)   na
  Ranch Romances, 1942: 3rd Oct

Enter—the Mounted (as Victor Rousseau)   nt
  North West Stories, 1927: 2nd Aug

—An Episode at the Whitehouse (see: The Dinner at the White House)

Eric of the Strong Heart (as Victor Rousseau)   sl
  Railroad Man's Magazine, 1918: Nov 16, 23, 30; Dec 7, 14
  ERIC OF THE STRONG HEART
    UK: John Long (hb), 1925 (as H. M. Egbert)
  ERIC OF THE STRONG HEART
    US: Pulpdom (sc), 2000

An Error of Longitude (as H. M. Egbert)   ss
  Cassell's Magazine of Fiction (UK) 1912: Dec

The Essayan Statue (as H. M. Egbert)   ss
  The Blue Book Magazine, 1911: Jul
  Public Ledger, 1913: Apr 6
  The Boston Daily Globe, 1915: Feb 21

The Eve of the Hospital (as Victor Rousseau)   ss
  Ainslee's Magazine, 1916: Jan

Even Scores (as Lew Merrill)   s
  Spicy Western Stories, 1938: Dec

Evened Scores (as Victor Rousseau)   nt
  North-West Stories, 1927: 1st Aug

The Evil Shore (as Victor Rousseau)   ss
  The Blue Book Magazine, 1914: Oct
  Chicago Tribune, 1918: Mar 31
  The Boston Daily Globe, 1930: Nov 16

The Evil Three (as Victor Rousseau)   sl
  Ghost Stories, 1930: Dec; 1931: Jan, Feb, Mar, Apr

Exploits of 'Pussyfoot' Johnson in Cleaning Up Indian Territory (uncredited)   ts
   The Stevens Point Journal, 1917: Apr 21

The Eye of Balamok (as Victor Rousseau)   sl
   All-Story Weekly, 1920: Jan 17, 24, 31
   Fantastic Novels, 1949: May (Condensed Edition)
   Fantastic Novels (UK Edition) 1950: Dec (Condensed Edition)
   L'ŒIL DE BALAMOK
      France: La Valette-du-Var: Antares, L'Or du Temps 1, Apr 1991
   PULP EDICIONES # 6
      Guadalajara, Spain: 2004 (as: El Ojo de Balamok)
   THE EYE OF BALAMOK
      US: Beb Books (sc), 2006

The Eyes of Pere Sebastian (as Victor Rousseau)   ss
   Extension Magazine, 1919: Aug
   Toronto Star Weekly, 1933: Aug 12

Eyes of the East (as Victor Rousseau)   nt
   Five-Novels Monthly, 1929: May
   Complete Adventure Novelettes, 1933: Feb

Face in the Crystal (as Lew Merrill)   s
   Spicy Mystery Stories, 1939: Jun

The Face of the Clock (as Harold Carter)   ss
   The Saturday Blade, 1912: Feb 3

The Fair American (as Victor Rousseau)   ss
   Chicago Tribune, 1915: Oct 31

The Faith of Paul Duchaine (as Victor Rousseau)   s
   The Red Book Magazine, 1914: Oct
   Chicago Tribune, 1918: Jan 6
   The Boston Daily Globe, 1931: Feb 22

False Fingers (as Victor Rousseau)   sl
   Los Angeles Times, 1932: Apr 17, 24; May 1, 8
   Western Home Monthly (of Canada) 1932: Aug, Sep
   The Boston Daily Globe, 1932: Sep 25

A Family Reunion (as H. M. Egbert)   ss
   Chicago Daily News, 1911: Nov 18

The Fangs of the Mill (as Victor Rousseau)   s
   Harper's Weekly, 1912: Jul 8
   The Novel Magazine (UK) 1912: Aug

Farrell's Double (as Lew Merrill)   nt
   Spicy Mystery Stories, 1941: Oct
   Spicy Mystery Stories, 1941: Oct (facsimile)

Feathers (as Clive Trent)   s
   Private Detective Stories, 1945: Apr

The Fetish of the Waxworks (as H. M. Egbert)   ss
  The Globe and Commercial Advertiser, 1910: Mar 19
  Weird Tales, 1927: Feb (as Victor Rousseau)
  THE SURGEON OF SOULS
    US: The Spectre Library (hb), Oct 2006 (as Victor Rousseau)

The Feud of Alkali Springs (as Victor Rousseau)   nt
  Fawcett's Triple-X Magazine, 1925: Feb

Feud of the Forest (as Victor Rousseau)   na
  Ranch Romances, 1941: May 2nd

The Fifth Guardian (as Victor Rousseau)   sl
  Cartoons Magazine and Wayside Tales, 1921: Jul, (continued then in…)
  Wayside Tales and Cartoons Magazine, 1921: Aug, Sep

Final Curtain (as Victor Rousseau)   s
  Zane Grey's Western Magazine, 1948: Apr

Fire-Escapes (as Victor Rousseau)   s
  Breezy Stories and Young's Magazine, 1937: May

Fire-Land Queen (as Clive Trent)   s
  Spicy-Adventure Stories, 1939: Sep

Fire—Water—and What? (as Victor Rousseau)   ss
  Ghost Stories, 1927: Jun

The First Victim (as H. M. Egbert)   ss
  St. Louis Post-Dispatch, 1913: Oct 11
  The Houston Post, 1913: Oct 12
  The Boston Daily Globe, 1914: Feb 1
  Buffalo Sunday Times, 1916: Mar 12
  THE DEVIL CHAIR
    US: The Spectre Library (hb), Jun 2008 (as Victor Rousseau)

A Fisher for Souls (as Victor Rousseau)   ss
  The Illustrated Buffalo Express, 1914: May 10
  THE TRACER OF EGOS
    US: The Spectre Library (hb), Aug 2007 (as Victor Rousseau)

—The Fisherman and the Fleet (see: The Affair of the North Sea)

Five Aces (as Victor Rousseau)   s
  Associated Sunday Magazine, 1911: Apr 30
  The Story-Teller (UK) 1911: Jul
  HIS SECOND SELF: THE BIO-BIBLIOGRAPHY OF VICTOR ROUSSEAU EMANUEL
    US: The Spectre Library (sc), 2011 (as Victor Rousseau)

The Five Army Corps (as Victor Rousseau)   ss
  Chicago Tribune, 1915: Nov 28

Fix Bayonets! (as Lew Merrill)   s
  Speed Adventure Stories, 1943: Jul

Flat-Boat (as Lew Merrill)   s
Spicy-Adventure Stories, 1940: Jan

The Flight Magnificent (as Clive Trent)   nt
Speed Mystery, 1944: May

The Flight of Abdul Hamid (as H. M. Egbert)   ss
Canada West Monthly (Canada) 1913: Aug

The Flight of the Princess (as H. M. Egbert)   ss
The Blue Book Magazine, 1911: Oct
Public Ledger, 1913: Apr 27
The Boston Daily Globe, 1915: Mar 14

Flower Boat (as Lew Merrill)   s
Spicy-Adventure Stories, 1937: Jan
Spicy-Adventure Stories, 1937: Jan (facsimile)

Fog Over Kiska (as Lew Merrill)   s
Speed Mystery, 1943: Sep

Follow the Fish (as Clive Trent)   s
Speed Adventure Stories, 1944: Sep

The Forbidden Shrine (as Victor Rousseau)   nt
Five-Novels Monthly, 1934: May

Forest Fury (as Lew Merrill)   s
Spicy-Adventure Stories, 1936: Jul
Spicy-Adventure Stories, 1936: Jul (facsimile)

For Love of Scotland's Queen (as Clive Trent)   s
Spicy-Adventure Stories, 1937: Jun

For Scotland's Queen (as Victor Rousseau)   s
Speed Adventure Stories, 1945: Apr

For the Honor of the Crown (as H. M. Egbert)   ss
Cassell's Magazine of Fiction (UK) 1912: Oct

For the Honor of the Duchess (as Lew Merrill)   s
Spicy-Adventure Stories, 1936: Dec

For the Honor of the Union (as Victor Rousseau)   s
Illustrated Sunday Magazine, 1910: May 29

Four Dumb Men (as H. M. Egbert)   sl
Wayside Tales and Cartoons Magazine, 1921: Oct, Nov

Four-Footed Justice (as Lew Merrill)   s
Speed Adventure Stories, 1943: Mar

Four Who Fled (as Lew Merrill)   s
Speed Adventure Stories, 1943: Jan

Fox Fury (as Lew Merrill)   s
  Spicy-Adventure Stories, 1939: Feb

'Fraid-Cat Hero (as Lew Merrill)   s
  Speed Mystery, 1944: Jan

Framed (as Victor Rousseau)   na
  Ranch Romances, 1935: 3rd Dec

Frame-Up (as Lew Merrill)   s
  Super-Detective, 1945: Jun
  Speed Detective, 1945: Dec

Free, High, and Handsome (as Lew Merrill)   s
  Spicy Western Stories, 1936: Dec
  Spicy Western Stories, 1936: Dec (facsimile)

—**The Free Traders** (see: Lee of the Northwest Mounted)

From Crook to Hero (as Victor Rousseau)   sl
  Muscle Builder, 1925: Dec; 1926: Jan, Feb, Mar, Apr

Frozen Hell (as Victor Rousseau)   nt
  North-West Romances, 1941: Fall
  North-West Romances, 1951: Spring

Fruit Of The Lamp (as Victor Rousseau)   sl
  The Argosy, 1918: Feb 2, 9, 16, 23
  MRS. ALADDIN
    UK: John Long (hb), 1925 (as H. M. Egbert)
  FRUIT OF THE LAMP
    US: Beb Books (sc), 2010 (as Victor Rousseau)

—**Fruits of Betrayal** (see: Return of the Beast)

A Frustrated Alliance (as H. M. Egbert)   ss
  Chicago Daily News, 1911: Oct 28

Fungus and Arsenic (as Victor Rousseau)   s
  Private Detective Stories, 1945: Sep

Furs That Fed (as Victor Rousseau)   s
  Western Story Magazine, 1924: Mar 8

The Further Ranges (as Victor Rousseau)   nt
  Ace-High Magazine, 1923: 1st Aug

Fury of the Jungle (as Victor Rousseau)   sa
  Sure-Fire Screen Stories, 1934: Feb

Future in Reverse (as Lew Merrill)   s
  Spicy Mystery Stories, 1941: Dec

The Gallows-Bird (as Victor Rousseau)   s
  Harper's Weekly, 1910: Jul 2
  The Novel Magazine (UK) 1911: Nov

Gallows Buster (as Lew Merrill)   s
  Spicy Mystery Stories, 1939: Aug

The Garden of Illusion (as Victor Rousseau)   s
  Harper's Weekly, 1912: Feb 17

Gate of Death (as Victor Rousseau)   s
  Speed Mystery, 1945: Jun

The Gates of Rocky River (as Victor Rousseau)   ss
  The American Patriot, 1916: Jan

The General's Decoration (as Victor Rousseau)   s
  All-Story Cavalier Weekly, 1914: May 30

The General's Knave-Trap (as Victor Rousseau)   ss
  Ainslee's Magazine, 1915: Nov

Get Your Man! (as Victor Rousseau)   nt
  North-West Stories, 1926: 2nd Oct
  North-West Stories (UK) 1927: Late Apr

Get Your Man! (as Lew Merrill)   s
  Speed Adventure Stories, 1945: Jan

Ghost Island (as Victor Rousseau)   nt
  All-Fiction, 1930: Nov

Ghost of Empire (as Victor Rousseau)   s
  Speed Adventure Stories, 1944: Jul

The Ghost of the Red Cavalier (as Victor Rousseau)   ss
  Ghost Stories, 1927: Mar
  Hutchinson's Mystery Story Magazine (UK) 1927: May

Ghost Plane (as Hugh Speer)   s
  Speed Adventure Stories, 1946: Jan

Ghosts of Time (as Lew Merrill)   s
  Spicy Mystery Stories, 1941: Apr

Ghost-Wife (as Clive Trent)   s
  Speed Mystery, 1943: Jan

The Ghost Will Walk Tonight (as Hugh Speer)   s
  Super-Detective, 1944: Jun

Giant from Babel (as Lew Merrill)   nt
  Spicy Mystery Stories, 1940: Aug

The Girl at Three Mile Fork (as H. M. Egbert)   s
  MacLean's Magazine (Canada) 1911: Aug
  HIS SECOND SELF: THE BIO-BIBLIOGRAPHY OF VICTOR ROUSSEAU EMANUEL
    US: The Spectre Library (sc), 2011 (as Victor Rousseau)

Girl from Green Gap (as Victor Rousseau)   nt
    Western Romances, 1936: Sep

Girl from Spain (as Lew Merrill)   s
    Saucy Detective, 1937: Mar

Girl from the Nebula (as Lew Merrill)   nt
    Spicy Mystery Stories, 1942: Jan

Girl of the Mounties (as Lew Merrill)   s
    Saucy Movie Tales, 1937: May

Girl of the Night (as Lew Merrill)   s
    Spicy Mystery Stories, 1937: Aug

The Girl Who Stayed at Home (as H. M. Egbert)   s
    The Boston Daily Globe, 1914: Jun 28

Glacier Girl (as Clive Trent)   s
    Spicy-Adventure Stories, 1942: Aug

—Glowing Chapel (see: Chapelle Ardente)

Goat in the Stable (as Lew Merrill)   s
    Speed Detective, 1946: Feb

The God from Beyond (as Lew Merrill)   s
    Spicy Mystery Stories, 1941: Sep

The God From the Pagoda (as H. M. Egbert)   ss
    The Houston Post, 1913: Nov 30
    St. Louis Post-Dispatch, 1913: Dec 6
    The Boston Daily Globe, 1914: Mar 29
    Buffalo Sunday Times, 1916: May 7
    THE DEVIL CHAIR
      US: The Spectre Library (hb), Jun 2008 (as Victor Rousseau)

The God in the Tomb (as Lew Merrill)   s
    Speed Adventure Stories, 1945: Oct

God of the Pit (as Lew Merrill)   s
    Spicy-Adventure Stories, 1938: May
    Speed Mystery, 1943: May (as: Death Rides High; as John Wayne)

The Golden Crocodile (as Lew Merrill)   s
    Spicy-Adventure Stories, 1937: Jun

The Golden Death (as H. M. Egbert)   ss
    Fiction Magazine, 1915: Jul 11
    HIS SECOND SELF: THE BIO-BIBLIOGRAPHY OF VICTOR ROUSSEAU EMANUEL
      US: The Spectre Library (sc), 2011 (as Victor Rousseau)

The Golden Stool (as Hugh Speer)   s
    Spicy-Adventure Stories, 1942: Nov

Good Night, Eve (as Victor Rousseau)   sl
 Physical Culture, 1932: Apr, May, Jun, Jul, Aug

Gorilla Man (as Lew Merrill)   s
 Spicy-Adventure Stories, 1938: Aug

The Great Experiment (as Victor Rousseau)   s
 Harper's Weekly, 1912: Apr 13

The Great God Harris (as Lew Merrill)   s
 Spicy-Adventure Stories, 1940: Dec

The Greater Claim (as John Austin)   sl
 London Daily Mail (UK) 1921: Feb 8, 9, 10, 11, 12, 14, 15, 16, 17, 18, 19,
   21, 22, 23, 24, 25, 26, 28; Mar 1, 2, 3, 4, 5, 7, 8, 9, 10, 11, 12, 14, 15, 16

Gun Round-up (as Victor Rousseau)   s
 Leading Western, 1947: Aug

Gunman's Wages (as Victor Rousseau)   s
 Action Stories, 1927: Jun

Gypsy Tent (as Clive Trent)   s
 Spicy-Adventure Stories, 1940: Oct

Half-Way House (as Hugh Speer)   s
 Spicy Mystery Stories, 1942: Oct
 Spicy Mystery Stories, 1942: Oct (facsimile)

Halsey of the Mounted (as Victor Rousseau)   nt
 Ace-High Magazine, 1924: 2nd Jan

Hammock Land (as Hugh Speer)   s
 Spicy-Adventure Stories, 1941: Oct

Hands Across the Sea (as Victor Rousseau)   s
 War Stories, 1926: Dec
 C'EST LA GUERRE!
   US: Boston: The Stratford Co. (hb), 1927

—**Haunted Hearts** (refer to the section on: Story Adaptations)

Hawk of the Himalayas (as Victor Rousseau)   nt
 Frontier Stories, 1929: Nov

Heads Shall Roll (as Lew Merrill)   s
 Spicy-Adventure Stories, 1942: Apr

—**The Heart of Lincoln** (refer to the section on: Story Adaptations)

Hearts and Diamonds (as Victor Emmanuel)   sl
 Physical Culture, 1926: Nov, Dec; 1927: Jan

Hearts and Sixes (as Victor Rousseau)   nt
 Western Romances, 1929: Nov

Hearts Astray (as Victor Rousseau)   s
   Harper's Monthly Magazine, 1912: Oct

Heaven's Son-in-Law (as Clive Trent)   s
   Speed Mystery, 1945: Jan

A Helen of New York (as George Munson)   tc
   Detective Story Magazine, 1919: Apr 29
   Best Detective Magazine, 1936: Jun

The Hellion Brood (as Victor Rousseau)   nt
   War Stories, 1929: May 23

Hell's Castle (as Lew Merrill)   s
   Speed Mystery, 1944: Jul

Hell's Robots (as Lew Merrill)   s
   Spicy Mystery Stories, 1937: Feb
   Spicy Mystery Stories, 1937: Feb (facsimile)

Hell's Station (as Victor Rousseau)   nt
   Frontier Stories, 1929: Jul

Hell's Tryst (as Hugh Speer)   s
   Spicy Mystery Stories, 1937: Oct
   Spicy Mystery Stories, 1939: Dec (as: Queen of the Witches; as John Phillips)
   Spicy Mystery Stories, 1937: Oct (facsimile)

He Told Me He Married a Ghost! (as Victor Rousseau)   s
   Ghost Stories, 1927: May

Her Home Region (as Victor Rousseau)   sl
   Toronto Star Weekly, 1945: Jan 6, 13, 20, 27; Feb 3, 10, 17, 24

Her Last 'Story' (as H. M. Egbert)   ss
   Cassell's Magazine of Fiction (UK) 1913: Feb

The Hidden Bride (as Victor Rousseau)   s
   Pall Mall Magazine (UK) 1912: Aug

High Andes (as Victor Rousseau)   s
   Short Stories, 1933: Sep 10
   Short Stories (UK) 1934: Mid Jan
   Short Stories, 1952: Mar
   The Boston Daily Globe, 1953: Mar 15

High Andes (as Lew Merrill)   s
   Spicy-Adventure Stories, 1940: May

Hi-Jacking Rustlers (as Victor Rousseau)   nt
   Ace-High Magazine, 1926: 2nd Jan
   MOTION PICTURE: as "Hi-Jacking Rustlers," (released: Nov 1926)
   FREDLOS I TEXAS
     Sweden: Romanförlaget-Göteborg (sc), 1962

His Father's Dishonor (as Victor Rousseau)							s
  Illustrated Sunday Magazine, 1909: Dec 12

—**His Majesty's Barber** (see: The Kaiser's Hairdresser)

—**His Majesty's Counterpart** (see: The Emperor's Double)

His People's Covenant (as Victor Rousseau)							s
  Morrison's Chicago Weekly, 1910: Nov 24

—**His Second Self** (see: The Truant Soul)

Holocaust (as John Austin)									nt
  Five-Novels Monthly, 1932: Jan

Home-Town Soldier (as Lew Merrill)								s
  Private Detective Stories, 1945: Apr

The Home Trail (as Victor Rousseau)							sl
  People's Story Magazine, 1922: Aug 25; Sep 10, 25; Oct 10, 25

Homo Homunculus (as H. M. Egbert)								ss
  The Globe and Commercial Advertiser, 1910: Apr 23
  THE SURGEON OF SOULS
    US: The Spectre Library (hb), Oct 2006 (as Victor Rousseau)

Honor for a Harrigan (as Lew Merrill)							s
  Speed Western Stories, 1947: Oct

Honor of the Sea (as Victor Rousseau)							s
  Red Blooded Stories, 1928: Nov

The Horrible Marionettes (as John Grange)							nt
  Super Detective, 1941: Jun
  Nemesis Incorporated # 17, 18, 19, Frank Lewandowski, 1984—1985

Hostage of Battle (as Hugh Speer)								s
  Spicy-Adventure Stories, 1941: Jul

Hot Stuff (as Lew Merrill)									s
  Speed Mystery, 1945: Jun

House of Death (as Lew Merrill)								s
  Speed Mystery, 1943: May

The House Of Gingras (as Victor Rousseau)							ss
  The Argosy, 1917: Dec 22

House of Hell (as Clive Trent)								s
  Spicy-Adventure Stories, 1938: Dec

The House of Honor (as H. M. Egbert)							vi
  Young's Magazine, 1912: Aug

The House of the Living Dead (as Victor Rousseau)						sl
  Ghost Stories, 1927: Dec; 1928: Jan, Feb, Mar, Apr, May

The House With the Brass Door-Knobs (as Victor Rousseau)   s
 Young's Magazine, 1914: Nov

How 'Pussyfoot' Johnson Made Good Citizens of Indian Charges (uncredited)   ts
 The Stevens Point Journal, 1917: May 19

How 'Pussyfoot' Johnson Wiped Out the Monte Carlo of No Man's Land (uncredited)   ts
 The Stevens Point Journal, 1917: Apr 28

How the Kaiser Went to Paris (as H. M. Egbert)   ss
 Stevens Point Journal, 1913: Nov 1

Human Boomerang (as Clive Trent)   s
 Spicy-Adventure Stories, 1940: Aug

The Human Factor (as Victor Rousseau)   s
 The American Patriot, 1914: Aug

Human Pyramid (as Clive Trent)   s
 Spicy-Adventure Stories, 1941: Apr
 Science Fiction (Canada) 1942: Jun
 Spicy-Adventure Stories, 1941: Apr (facsimile)

I'll Buy Your Appetites (as Lew Merrill)   s
 Spicy Mystery Stories, 1937: Oct
 Spicy Mystery Stories, 1942: Sep (as: More Precious Than Rubies; as Stan Warner)
 Spicy Mystery Stories, 1937: Oct (facsimile)

In the Last Minute (as Victor Rousseau)   s
 War Stories, 1929: Aug 29

Inca Gold (as Lew Merrill)   s
 Spicy-Adventure Stories, 1941: Nov

Indian Dawn (as Victor Rousseau)   nt
 Five-Novels Monthly, 1930: Feb

Indigo Island (as Clive Trent)   s
 Spicy-Adventure Stories, 1941: Feb
 Spicy-Adventure Stories, 1941: Feb (facsimile)

The Ingratitude of Kings (as H. M. Egbert)   ss
 The Globe and Commercial Advertiser, 1910: Nov 12
 Morrison's Chicago Weekly, 1911: Feb 9
 Cassell's Magazine of Fiction (UK) 1914: Mar (as: My Last Case)

Inspector Denovan and Mackoull (as H. M. Egbert)   tc
 Washington Post, 1911: Jan 29 (not bylined)
 Buffalo Sunday Times, 1911: Oct 22
 Detective Story Magazine, 1919: Nov 11 (as George Munson)
   (as: Inspector Denovan and the Paisley Bank Case)

—**Inspector Denovan and the Paisley Bank Case** (see: Inspector Denovan and Mackoull)

The Invisible Death (as Victor Rousseau)   na
   Astounding Stories of Super-Science, 1930: Oct
   LA NOVELA FANTASTICA # 3
      Spain, circa 1932 (as: La Muerte Invisible)
   LA NOVELA FANTASTICA # 4
      Spain, circa 1944-1945 (as: El Rayo Invisible)

An Involuntary Ally (as H. M. Egbert)   ss
   St. Louis Post-Dispatch, 1913: Oct 18
   The Houston Post, 1913: Oct 19
   The Boston Daily Globe, 1914: Feb 8
   Buffalo Sunday Times, 1916: Mar 19
   THE DEVIL CHAIR
      US: The Spectre Library (hb), Jun 2008 (as Victor Rousseau)

I. O. U. Murder (as John Grange)   nt
   Super Detective, 1941: Dec
   Thrilling Novels # 37, Fun Stuff Imaginations/Underground Press, Apr 1996
   Private Detective Stories # 2, Pulp Tales Press, Sept 2007

The Iron Bride (as Clive Trent)   s
   Spicy Mystery Stories, 1938: Aug

The Island of Doom (as Victor Rousseau)   na
   The Danger Trail, 1927: Aug

The Isle of Enchantment (as Victor Rousseau)   s
   Harper's Weekly, 1912: Aug 31

Isle of Refuge (as Hugh Speer)   nt
   Spicy Mystery Stories, 1940: Jun

Isle of the Gods (as Lew Merrill)   s
   Spicy Mystery Stories, 1941: Jan

Isle of the Unborn (as Clive Trent)   s
   Spicy Mystery Stories, 1936: Nov
   Spicy Mystery Stories, 1936: Nov (facsimile)

It Is For France (as Victor Rousseau)   s
   Soldiers of Fortune, 1931: Oct

Jackaroo (as Clive Trent)   s
   Spicy-Adventure Stories, 1939: Oct

Jackson's Wife (as Victor Rousseau)   s
   The Smart Set, 1909: May
   Wendigo # 1 (France, trans.) 2010
   HIS SECOND SELF: THE BIO-BIBLIOGRAPHY OF VICTOR ROUSSEAU EMANUEL
      US: The Spectre Library (sc), 2011 (as Victor Rousseau)

Jacqueline of Golden River (as Victor Rousseau)   sl
   All-Story Cavalier Weekly, 1915: Feb 13, 20, 27; Mar 6
   Chicago Ledger, 1918: Nov 2, 9 (incomplete) (as: The Bride of Golden Mountain)
   JACQUELINE OF GOLDEN RIVER
     US: Doubleday Page (hb), 1920 (as H. M. Egbert)
   JACQUELINE OF GOLDEN RIVER
     UK: Hodder and Stoughton (hb), 1924 (as H. M. Egbert)

Jailbreak (as Hugh Speer)   s
   Speed Mystery, 1944: Jul

The Jam God (as H. M. Egbert)   s
   Short Stories, 1909: May
   GOLDEN STORIES
     US: The Short Stories Company (hb), 1909
   Fiction Magazine, 1917: Apr 22
   HIS SECOND SELF: THE BIO-BIBLIOGRAPHY OF VICTOR ROUSSEAU EMANUEL
     US: The Spectre Library (sc), 2011 (as Victor Rousseau)

Jean of the Silence (as Victor Rousseau)   s
   The Smart Set, 1911: Jun
   HIS SECOND SELF: THE BIO-BIBLIOGRAPHY OF VICTOR ROUSSEAU EMANUEL
     US: The Spectre Library (sc), 2011 (as Victor Rousseau)

Jest of Death (as Hugh Speer)   s
   Spicy-Adventure Stories, 1942: Jan

A Jest That Saved (as Victor Rousseau)   ss
   Chicago Tribune, 1915: Dec 5

The Jeweled Throne (as Victor Rousseau)   nt
   Five-Novels Monthly, 1938: Dec

Jewels of Death (as Victor Rousseau)   nt
   Ace-High Magazine, 1934: Oct

Jewels of Empire (as Victor Rousseau)   nt
   Five-Novels Monthly, 1931: Nov

Jim Blair's Girl (as John Austin)   sl
   Ranch Romances, 1925: Nov, Dec; 1926: Jan, Feb, Mar

Jinx (as Lew Merrill)   nt
   Spicy Mystery Stories, 1942: Mar

The Judas Bottle (as Lew Merrill)   s
   Speed Mystery, 1944: Mar

A Judith of '75 (as Victor Rousseau)   s
   The American Patriot, 1915: Jan

The Jungle Knights (as Victor Rousseau)   ss
   Photoplay Magazine, 1917: Jul

Jungle Loot (as Victor Rousseau)   s
   The Danger Trail, 1928: Jul

Jungle Lords (as Lew Merrill)   s
  Spicy-Adventure Stories, 1940: Feb

Jungle Tin (as Lew Merrill)   s
  Spicy-Adventure Stories, 1942: Aug

Jungle Trap (as Clive Trent)   s
  Speed Adventure Stories, 1944: Jan

Justice and the Moose Call (as Victor Rousseau)   s
  Short Stories, 1914: Mar

—A Just Retribution (see: The Crooked Finger)

The Kaiser's Hairdresser (as H. M. Egbert)   ss
  The New Magazine (UK) 1910: Jul (as: The Toilet That Saved France)
  The Globe and Commercial Advertiser, 1910: Aug 20
  Morrison's Chicago Weekly, 1910: Nov 24 (as: His Majesty's Barber)

Kali's Vine (as Hugh Speer)   s
  Spicy Mystery Stories, 1936: Dec
  Spicy Mystery Stories, 1936: Dec (facsimile)

The Keeper of the Light (as Victor Rousseau)   s
  Harper's Weekly, 1910: Dec 10

Kenney's Stooge (as Hugh Speer)   s
  Speed Mystery, 1943: Sep

The Kidnapped Cabinet Minister (as H. M. Egbert)   ss
  Cassell's Magazine of Fiction (UK) 1912: Sep

The Kidnaped King (as H. M. Egbert)   ss
  The Globe and Commercial Advertiser, 1910: Oct 8
  Morrison's Chicago Weekly, 1911: Jan 12 (as: The Race in Mid-Air)
  Cassell's Magazine of Fiction (UK) 1914: Jan

The Kidnapping of Charley Ross (as H. M. Egbert)   tc
  Washington Post, 1911: Feb 26 (not bylined)
  20th Century Crime Cases (Canada) 1946: Oct

Killer Car (as Lew Merrill)   s
  Speed Mystery, 1945: Jan

Killer in Yellow (as John Grange)   nt
  Super Detective, 1941: Feb

King of the Cocoa Trail (as Victor Rousseau)   nt
  Red Blooded Stories, 1928: Dec

King Silver Rides (as Hugh Speer)   s
  Speed Adventure Stories, 1943: Jan

King Silver's Last Ride (as Hugh Speer)   s
  Speed Adventure Stories, 1943: Mar

The King Spy (as Victor Rousseau)   nt
   Frontier Stories, 1930: May

The Kingdom of the North (as H. M. Egbert)   ss
   St. Louis Post-Dispatch, 1913: Nov 15
   The Houston Post, 1913: Dec 7
   The Boston Daily Globe, 1914: Mar 8
   Buffalo Sunday Times, 1916: May 21
   THE DEVIL CHAIR
      US: The Spectre Library (hb), Jun 2008 (as Victor Rousseau)

The Kings of No Man's Land (as Victor Rousseau)   s
   Harper's Weekly, 1909: Apr 3

The King's Proctor (as Victor Rousseau)   s
   Harper's Weekly, 1912: Nov 23

Kit Carson, Renegade (as Victor Rousseau)   nt
   Leading Western, 1946: Aug

—**Kitachi's Torpedoes** (see: The Peril of Magellan Strait)

Kitchener's Coup (as H. M. Egbert)   ss
   The Popular Magazine, 1915: Mar 7
   Illustrated Buffalo Express, 1915: Jul 4
   Fiction Magazine, 1915: Aug 22

—**La Main du Cadavre** (see: The Crooked Finger)

Lady Luck (as Lew Merrill)   s
   Speed Mystery, 1944: May

Lady of Fortune (as Hugh Speer)   s
   Spicy-Adventure Stories, 1936: Feb
   Spicy-Adventure Stories, 1936: Feb (facsimile)

Lady of the Law (as Lew Merrill)   s
   Spicy-Adventure Stories, 1938: Nov

Lady Sheriff (as Hugh Speer)   s
   Spicy-Adventure Stories, 1938: Jun

Lafe Evens Up (as Victor Rousseau)   ss
   All-Story Weekly, 1915: Sep 11
   Chicago Tribune, 1918: Jan 27
   Philadelphia Inquirer, 1922: Mar 12

Larry of the Yards (as Victor Rousseau)   s
   The Popular Magazine, 1916: 1st Feb
   The Railroad Trainman, 1918: Jun

The Last Adam (as Lew Merrill)   s
   Spicy-Adventure Stories, 1941: Aug

The Last Cartridge (as Victor Rousseau)   vi
  The Munsey, 1907: Sep
  HIS SECOND SELF: THE BIO-BIBLIOGRAPHY OF VICTOR ROUSSEAU EMANUEL
    US: The Spectre Library (sc), 2011 (as Victor Rousseau)

The Last of the Bushrangers (as H. M. Egbert)   tc
  Washington Post, 1911: Jan 15 (not bylined)
  Buffalo Sunday Times, 1911: Oct 8
  Clues, 1927: May
  Complete Mystery Novelettes, 1932: Oct

The Laughing Moor (as Lew Merrill)   s
  Spicy-Adventure Stories, 1939: Nov
  Spicy-Adventure Stories, 1939: Nov (facsimile)

Lee of the Northwest Mounted (as Victor Rousseau)   sl
  People's Popular Monthly, 1923: Jan, Feb, Mar, Apr, May, Jun, Jul, Aug
  —national newspaper syndication, 1924-onward, as "The Free Traders"
  Brief Stories, 1926: May (as: On the Range)
  Boston Sunday Post Magazine, 1931: Mar 29; Apr 5, 12, 19, 26; May 3, 10, 17, 24, 31
    (as: All For a Girl)

The Left-Hand Wife (as H. M. Egbert)   ss
  The Globe and Commercial Advertiser, 1910: Sep 17
  Morrison's Chicago Weekly, 1910: Dec 22
  Cassell's Magazine of Fiction (UK) 1913: Dec

The Legacy of Hate (as H. M. Egbert)
  The Globe and Commercial Advertiser, 1910: Mar 5
  Weird Tales, 1926: Nov (as Victor Rousseau)
  THE SURGEON OF SOULS
    US: The Spectre Library (hb), Oct 2006 (as Victor Rousseau)

Legally Dead (as John Austin)   sl
  London Daily Mail (UK) 1920: Sep 7, 8, 9, 10, 11, 13, 14, 15, 16, 17, 18, 20,
    21, 22, 23, 24, 25, 27, 28, 29, 30; Oct 1, 2, 4, 5, 6, 7, 8, 9, 11, 12, 13,
    14, 15, 16, 18, 19, 20, 21, 22, 23, 25, 26, 27, 28, 29, 30; Nov 1

Legion of Robots (as John Grange)   nt
  Super-Detective, 1940: Nov
  SUPER DETECTIVE FLIP BOOK
    US: Off-Trail Publications (sc), March 2008
  SUPER-DETECTIVE JIM ANTHONY # 1
    US: Altus Press (hb), 2009 (as Victor Rousseau)
  SUPER-DETECTIVE JIM ANTHONY # 1
    US: Altus Press (sc), 2009 (as Victor Rousseau)

Legion of the Dead (as Victor Rousseau)   nt
  Five-Novels Monthly, 1928: Jul
  Complete Adventure Novelettes, 1932: Nov

Letters of Marque (as Clive Trent)   s
  Speed Adventure Stories, 1946: Jan

Liddle Red-Head (as Lew Merrill)   s
  Spicy Detective Stories, 1939: Feb

The Lie of Pere Sebastian (as Victor Rousseau)   ss
   The Blue Book Magazine, 1914: Dec
   The Boston Daily Globe, 1930: Oct 26

Lieutenant Limey Brown (as Victor Rousseau)   s
   War Stories, 1929: Sep 12

Lieutenant Merriman—Missing (as Victor Rousseau)   s
   The American Patriot, 1914: Jun

—Life (refer to the section on: Story Adaptations)

The Lifted Veil (as Lew Merrill)   s
   Spicy Mystery Stories, 1940: Dec

The Lighthouse of the North (as H. M. Egbert)   ss
   The Blue Book Magazine, 1911: Jun
   Public Ledger, 1913: Mar 30
   The Boston Daily Globe, 1915: Feb 14

The Lightnin' Shot (as Victor Rousseau)   nt
   Ace-High Magazine, 1925: 2nd May
   MOTION PICTURE: as "Lightnin' Shot," (released: May 1928)

Like a Tiger (as Lew Merrill)   nt
   Speed Mystery, 1943: Nov

Lilith (as Lew Merrill)   s
   Spicy Mystery Stories, 1937: Jun

Lion Guard (as Lew Merrill)   s
   Spicy-Adventure Stories, 1942: Mar

The Lion's Jaws (as Victor Rousseau)   sl
   All-Story Weekly, 1919: Mar 29; Apr 5, 12, 19, 26
   THE LION'S JAWS
      UK: Hodder and Stoughton (hb), 1923

Living Dead Man (as Hugh Speer)   s
   Speed Mystery, 1945: Mar

Lobster Girl (as Lew Merrill)   s
   Spicy Mystery Stories, 1941: Mar

The Lone Patrol (as Victor Rousseau)   nt
   North West Stories, 1928: Mar 22

Lone Pyramid (as Lew Merrill)   s
   Spicy-Adventure Stories, 1939: Jul

Lone Rider (as Victor Rousseau)   na
   Ranch Romances, 1939: 1st Mar

Long Pig (as Hugh Speer)   s
   Speed Adventure Stories, 1944: Mar

The Long Trail (as Victor Rousseau)   nt
   Ranch Romances, 1927: Sep 2nd

Loot of Lost Lode (as Victor Rousseau)   nt
   Ace-High Magazine, 1934: Mar
   World Stories (UK) 1934: Apr
   The Boston Daily Globe, 1947: Sep 14 (as: Lost Lode)
   Kansas City Times, 1949: Nov 16, 17, 18, 19 [odd installments]
   Kansas City Star, 1949: Nov 16, 17, 18 [even installments]

Loot of the Wolf (as Victor Rousseau)   nt
   North West Stories, 1930: Jan
   La Novela Fantastica # 20; Madrid: circa 1932 (as: Dentelladas de Lobo)

The Lord of Space (as Victor Rousseau)   s
   Astounding Stories of Super-Science, 1930: Aug

The Lord of Space (as Hugh Speer)   nt
   Spicy-Adventure Stories, 1941: May

Lord of Two Worlds (as Hugh Speer)   s
   Spicy-Adventure Stories, 1940: Oct

Lords of Folly (as Lew Merrill)   s
   Spicy-Adventure Stories, 1937: Nov

Lost Fingerprints (as Victor Rousseau)   s
   Speed Mystery, 1944: Jan

—**Lost Lode** (see: Loot of Lost Lode)

Lost Men's Eden (as Victor Rousseau)   nt
   North-West Stories, 1927: 1st Jan
   North-West Stories (UK) 1927: Early Jul

Lost Ranch (as Victor Rousseau)   na
   Ranch Romances, 1931: 2nd Dec

The Lost Shadow (as Clive Trent)   nt
   Spicy Mystery Stories, 1942: Nov

Love Rides the Sage (as Victor Rousseau)   nt
   Rangeland Love Story Magazine, 1931: Jun

Loyalties (as Victor Rousseau)   s
   Breezy Stories and Young's Magazine, 1936: May

Luck of the Cromwells (as Hugh Speer)   s
   Spicy Mystery Stories, 1939: Oct

Madame Murder (as John Grange)   nt
   Super-Detective, 1940: Dec
   High Adventure # 89, 2006: Jul
   SUPER-DETECTIVE JIM ANTHONY # 1
     US: Altus Press (hb), 2009 (as Victor Rousseau)
   SUPER-DETECTIVE JIM ANTHONY # 1
     US: Altus Press (sc), 2009 (as Victor Rousseau)

Mad Charioteers (as Lew Merrill)   nt
  Spicy Mystery Stories, 1938: Aug

The Madness of M'Shane (as Clive Trent)   s
  Speed Adventure Stories, 1945: Apr

Mad Woman Massacre (as Lew Merrill)   s
  Spicy Western Stories, 1937: Jan

Magic Mountain (as Victor Rousseau)   nt
  Rangeland Love Story Magazine, 1932: Jan

The Mahratta's Revenge (as H. M. Egbert)   tc
  Washington Post, 1911: Feb 19 (not bylined)
  Detective Story Magazine, 1919: Dec 2 (as George Munson)

Maid of Osiris (as Lew Merrill)   s
  Spicy Mystery Stories, 1937: Dec

Maid of the Valley (as Victor Rousseau)   nt
  Ranch Romances, 1930: 2nd Jan

The Major's Menagerie (as H. M. Egbert)   ss
  The Globe and Commercial Advertiser, 1910: Mar 12
  Weird Tales, 1927: Jan (as Victor Rousseau)
  THE SURGEON OF SOULS
      US: The Spectre Library (hb), Oct 2006 (as Victor Rousseau)
  Weird Tales, 1927: Jan (facsimile)

The Making of a Man (as Victor Emanuel)   sl
  Muscle Builder, 1924: Oct, Nov, Dec; 1925: Jan, Feb

Manchu Guns (as Victor Rousseau)   nt
  Navy Stories, 1929: May

The Man and the Maelstrom (as H. M. Egbert)   ss
  The Houston Post, 1913: Nov 16
  St. Louis Post-Dispatch, 1913: Nov 22
  The Boston Daily Globe, 1914: Mar 15
  Buffalo Sunday Times, 1916: Apr 23
  THE DEVIL CHAIR
      US: The Spectre Library (hb), Jun 2008 (as Victor Rousseau)

A Man From Montana (as Victor Rousseau)   sl
  Rangeland Love Story Magazine, 1931: Aug, Sep, Oct, Nov, Dec

Man Hunt For the Mounted (as Victor Rousseau)   nt
  North-West Romances, 1938: Spring

The Man in the Balance (as H. M. Egbert)   ss
  The Houston Post, 1913: Nov 23
  St. Louis Post-Dispatch, 1913: Nov 29
  The Boston Daily Globe, 1914: Mar 22
  Buffalo Sunday Times, 1916: Apr 30
  THE DEVIL CHAIR
      US: The Spectre Library (hb), Jun 2008 (as Victor Rousseau)

The Man in the Bottle (as Victor Rousseau)   s
   Harper's Weekly, 1911: Mar 18

The Man-Master (as Victor Rousseau)   nt
   North-West Romances, 1937: Fall

The Man of Pelican Key (as Victor Rousseau)   s
   Ainslee's Magazine, 1912: Jul

The Man on the Heath (as H. M. Egbert)   ss
   Cassell's Magazine of Fiction (UK) 1912: Nov

The Man Who "Killed" a Corpse (as George Munson)   tc
   Detective Story Magazine, 1919: May 20
   Famous Crime Cases (Canada) 1946: Apr

The Man Who Lost His Luck (as H. M. Egbert)   ss
   The Globe and Commercial Advertiser, 1910: Apr 16
   Weird Tales, 1927: May (as Victor Rousseau)
   THE SURGEON OF SOULS
      US: The Spectre Library (hb), Oct 2006 (as Victor Rousseau)

The Man Who Wasn't (as Victor Rousseau)   s
   Illustrated Sunday Magazine, 1909: May 9

The Man Who Went Back (as Victor Rousseau)   s
   Harper's Weekly, 1911: Oct 28

The Man With the Peaked Beard (as Victor Rousseau)   ss
   Ainslee's Magazine, 1915: Dec

—**Månplaneten** (see: Moon Patrol)

A Man's Birthright (as Victor Rousseau)   s
   Literary Magazine Section, 1909: May 9
   HIS SECOND SELF: THE BIO-BIBLIOGRAPHY OF VICTOR ROUSSEAU EMANUEL
      US: The Spectre Library (sc), 2011 (as Victor Rousseau)

Mark of the Spider (as John Grange)   nt
   Super Detective, 1942: Aug
   Pulp Review # 2, Pulp Collector Press, Jan 1992
   Pulp Review # 2, Pulp Collector Press, 2008 (new ads and perfect bound)

Marooned on Eros (as Hugh Speer)   nt
   Spicy Mystery Stories, 1940: Oct

Marsh Murder (as Clive Trent)   s
   Spicy Mystery Stories, 1942: Jul
   Spicy Mystery Stories, 1942: Jul (facsimile)

Mary Rothway's Memory (as Victor Rousseau)   ss
   Holland's Magazine, 1913: Jul
   The Illustrated Buffalo Express, 1914: Mar 22
   THE TRACER OF EGOS
      US: The Spectre Library (hb), Aug 2007 (as Victor Rousseau)

Masai Spears (as Clive Trent)   s
  Spicy-Adventure Stories, 1940: Jan

The Mask of Juno (as Victor Rousscau)   s
  Young's Magazine, 1914: Sep

Master and Man (as H. M. Egbert)   ss
  Chicago Daily News, 1911: Nov 4

Matched Slugs (as Lew Merrill)   s
  Speed Detective, 1944: Dec

A Matrimonial Disentanglement (as H. M. Egbert)   ss
  Chicago Daily News, 1911: Sep 16

A Matter of Mathematics (as Harold Carter)   ss
  The Saturday Blade, 1912: Jan 6 (as: Bank Cashier Caught)

—**Matty's Decision** (refer to the section on: Story Adaptations)

Maverick of Mustang Mesa (as Victor Rousseau)   nt
  Red Seal Western, 1936: Dec

Mayor of No Man's Land (as Lew Merrill)   s
  Spicy-Adventure Stories, 1940: Apr

Medical Officer (as Hugh Speer)   s
  Speed Adventure Stories, 1944: Sep

—**Medium for Justice** (see: The Blackest Magic of All)

Men-at-Arms (as Lew Merrill)   s
  Spicy-Adventure Stories, 1939: Sep

Men of Empire (as Victor Rousseau)   nt
  Five-Novels Monthly, 1938: Nov

The Mesquite Trail (as Victor Rousseau)   nt
  Frontier Stories, 1928: Sep

The Messiah of the Cylinder (as Victor Rousseau)   sl
  Everybody's Magazine, 1917: Jun, Jul, Aug, Sep
  THE MESSIAH OF THE CYLINDER
    US: A. C. McClurg (hb), 1917
  THE APOSTLE OF THE CYLINDER
    UK: Hodder and Stoughton (hb), 1918
  THE MESSIAH OF THE CYLINDER
    US: Hyperion (hb), 1973: Jun
  THE MESSIAH OF THE CYLINDER
    US: Hyperion (sc), 1973: Dec
  APOSTLE OF THE CYLINDER
    US: Kessinger Publishing (sc), 2007: Nov
  THE MESSIAH OF THE CYLINDER AND OTHER STORIES
    CND: Girasol (hb), 2009

A Midnight Elopement (as H. M. Egbert)   ss
  Chicago Daily News, 1911: Sep 30

Midnight Riders (as Victor Rousseau)   nt
  Rangeland Love Story Magazine, 1930: Sep

Midsummer Madness (as Victor Rousseau)   na
  Munsey's Magazine, 1916: Jul

The Misplaced Dream (as H. M. Egbert)   ss
  Stevens Point Journal, 1913: Nov 8

The Misplaced Pigment (as Harold Carter)   ss
  Buffalo Sunday Times, 1911: Aug 20
  The Saturday Blade, 1912: Jan 20

Mississippi Trail (as Hugh Speer)   s
  Spicy-Adventure Stories, 1938: Dec

Monkey Bones (as Clive Trent)   s
  Spicy-Adventure Stories, 1938: Apr

—Monkey-Face and Mrs. Thorpe (see: The Soul that Lost Its Way)

The Montenegrin Ciphers (as H. M. Egbert)   ss
  Fiction Magazine, 1915: Jun 20

Moon Patrol (as Victor Rousseau)   s
  Thrilling Wonder Stories, 1941: Oct
  Jules Verne-Magasinet # 44 (Sweden), 1941 (as: Månplaneten)

—More Precious Than Rubies (see: I'll Buy Your Appetites)

The Moroccan Treaty (as H. M. Egbert)   ss
  Stevens Point Journal, 1913: Oct 25

Mr. Axel's Shady Past (as Victor Rousseau)   ss
  Holland's Magazine, 1913: Dec
  The Illustrated Buffalo Express, 1914: Apr 26
  THE TRACER OF EGOS
    US: The Spectre Library (hb), Aug 2007 (as Victor Rousseau)

Mr. Bill, Come Back (as Lew Merrill)   s
  Speed Western Stories, 1946: Nov

Mrs. Big (as John Grange)   nt
  Super Detective 1942: Apr

Mud In Your Eye! (as Victor Rousseau)   s
  Fighting Western, 1946: Jun

Mulligan and the Pull-Through (as Victor Rousseau)   s
  The American Patriot, 1915: Mar

Murder Down East (as John Austin)   nt
  Five-Novels Monthly, 1934: Apr
  Kansas City Times, 1952: Jul 28, 29, 30, 31; Aug 1, 2 (as Victor Rousseau)
    [odd installments](as: The Mansion Murder)
  Kansas City Star, 1952: Jul 28, 29, 30, 31; Aug 1, 2 (as Victor Rousseau)
    [even installments](as: The Mansion Murder)

Murder House (as Lew Merrill)   s
  Super-Detective, 1946: Sep

Murder in Paradise (as John Grange)   nt
  Super Detective, 1941: Mar
  Super Detective (CND) 1942: Aug

The Murder in the Rue Mazarin (as H. M. Egbert)   tc
  Washington Post, 1911: Jan 1 (not bylined)
  Buffalo Sunday Times, 1911: Sep 24
  Clues, 1927: Mar
  Complete Mystery Novelettes, 1932: Oct
  Keyhole Detective Cases (Canada) 1946: Feb

The Murder of Benjamin Nathan (as H. M. Egbert)   tc
  Washington Post, 1911: Mar 5 (not bylined)
  Detective Story Magazine, 1919: Dec 16 (as George Munson)
  20th Century Crime Cases (Canada) 1946: Nov (as H. M. Egbert)

The Murder of Doctor Burdell (as George Munson)   tc
  Detective Story Magazine, 1919: Jul 1
  Famous Crime Cases (Canada) 1946: Oct

Murder Syndicate (as John Grange)   nt
  Super Detective, 1941: Apr
  Action Adventure Stories # 72, Fading Shadows Inc., Apr 2000

Murderer's Doom (as Clive Trent)   s
  Spicy Mystery Stories, 1941: Feb

My Lady Of The Nile (as H. M. Egbert)   sl
  Argosy All-Story Weekly, 1921: May 7, 14, 21, 28
  MY LADY OF THE NILE
    UK: Hodder and Stoughton (hb), 1923
  MY LADY OF THE NILE
    US: Beb Books (sc OCR), 2011

—**My Last Case** (see: The Ingratitude of Kings)

—**The Mysterious Contragrav** (refer to the section on: Story Adaptations)

Nailed (as Lew Merrill)   s
  Private Detective Stories, 1946: Feb

Neal Effendi - American (as Victor Rousseau)   s
  War Novels, 1929: Sep

Needle's Eye (as John Grange)   nt
  Super Detective, 1942: Jun

Nelly of the Sluice Gate (as H. M. Egbert)   ss
   Chicago Daily News, 1911: Nov 11

Nemesis (as H. M. Egbert)   vi
   (see Newspaper Vignettes: The Day Book, 17 Feb 1914; as: Art For Art's Sake)
   Best Stories of All Time, 1927: Jun

Nero's Ring (as Lew Merrill)   s
   Spicy-Adventure Stories, 1942: Nov

—**New York Takes the Count** (see: The Square Peg)

Night Invasion (as Lew Merrill)   s
   Spicy-Adventure Stories, 1942: Feb

Night of Action (as Hugh Speer)   s
   Spicy-Adventure Stories, 1940: Apr

Night Raid (as Hugh Speer)   s
   Spicy-Adventure Stories, 1937: Oct

Night Raiders (as Victor Rousseau)   nt
   Ranch Romances, 1938: 1st Jul

No Compromise (as Victor Rousseau)   s
   The Boston Daily Globe, 1950: Aug 20

No More Romance (as Lew Merrill)   s
   Spicy-Adventure Stories, 1938: Jul

No Witnesses (as Lew Merrill)   s
   Super-Detective, 1945: Nov

North of Fifty-Three (as Victor Rousseau)   nt
   Three Star Magazine, 1928: Jun 1
   Empire Frontier (UK) 1930: Dec

Nothing North of Nagatok (as Victor Rousseau)   nt
   North-West Stories, 1929: Mar

Noureddin Bey's Sacrifice (as Victor Rousseau)   ss
   Holland's Magazine, 1914: Feb
   The Illustrated Buffalo Express, 1914: May 31
   THE TRACER OF EGOS
      US: The Spectre Library (hb), Aug 2007 (as Victor Rousseau)

Ogre Island (as Hugh Speer)   s
   Spicy Mystery Stories, 1939: Apr

Old-Fashioned Lady (as Lew Merrill)   s
   Super-Detective, 1946: Jul

—**On the Range** (see: Lee of the Northwest Mounted)

On Secret Service (as Hugh Speer)   s
   Spicy-Adventure Stories, 1938: Sep

One-Girl Ranch (as John Austin)   nt
  Five-Novels Monthly, 1928: Aug

Our Astral Honeymoon (as Victor Rousseau)   s
  Ghost Stories, 1928: Jun

Outlaw Guns (as Lew Merrill)   s
  Spicy Western Stories, 1937: Jun

Outlaws of the Sun (as Victor Rousseau)   nt
  Miracle Science and Fantasy Stories, 1931: Apr-May

Out of Aden (as Lew Merrill)   s
  Spicy-Adventure Stories, 1937: Dec
  Spicy-Adventure Stories, 1937: Dec (facsimile)

Out of Arcady (as Victor Rousseau)   s
  Wayside Tales and Cartoons Magazine, 1921: Oct

Out of the Night (as Victor Rousseau)   s
  Red Blooded Stories, 1928: Oct

The Oyster Boom of Avenue B (as Victor Rousseau)   s
  Illustrated Sunday Magazine, 1909: Dec 26

The Pacification of Anne (as Victor Rousseau)   ss
  The Blue Book Magazine, 1915: Mar
  The Boston Daily Globe, 1931: Mar 29

The Palm-Bringer (as Victor Rousseau)   s
  Harper's Weekly, 1910: Feb 5
  Pall Mall Magazine (UK) 1911: Nov

Pals (as Victor Rousseau)   s
  Wayside Tales and Cartoons Magazine, 1921: Nov
  Philadelphia Inquirer, 1922: Jul 16
  The Boston Daily Globe, 1922: Oct 29

Paradise Island (as Hugh Speer)   s
  Spicy-Adventure Stories, 1936: Jan
  Spicy-Adventure Stories, 1936: Jan (facsimile)

Passion's Puppets (as Lew Merrill)   s
  Spicy-Adventure Stories, 1936: Nov
  Spicy-Adventure Stories, 1936: Nov (facsimile)

A Patriot's Dilemma (as H. M. Egbert)   ss
  Illustrated Buffalo Express, 1915: Jun 6
  Fiction Magazine, 1915: Jul 25

Pawns of Empire (as Victor Rousseau)   nt
  The Danger Trail, 1928: Apr

Peace Comes to Bongo (as Hugh Speer)   s
  Speed Adventure Stories, 1944: May

Pearls of Panama (as Lew Merrill)   s
  Spicy-Adventure Stories, 1939: Mar

The Perfect Crime (as Clive Trent)   s
  Speed Mystery, 1944: Jan

The Peril of Magellan Strait (as H. M. Egbert)   ss
  The New Magazine (UK) 1910: Jun
  The Globe and Commercial Advertiser, 1910: Aug 13
  Morrison's Chicago Weekly, 1910: Nov 17 (as: Kitachi's Torpedoes)
  HIS SECOND SELF: THE BIO-BIBLIOGRAPHY OF VICTOR ROUSSEAU EMANUEL
    US: The Spectre Library (sc), 2011 (as Victor Rousseau)

—**The Persecuted Rector** (see: The Persecution of the Rector)

The Persecution of the Rector (as H. M. Egbert)   tc
  Washington Post, 1910: Dec 25 (not bylined)
  Buffalo Sunday Times, 1911: Sep 17
  Flynn's Weekly, 1926: Sep 18 (as: The Persecuted Rector)

The Phantom City (as Victor Rousseau)   ss
  Chicago Tribune, 1915: Nov 21

The Phantom Hand (as Victor Rousseau)   sl
  Weird Tales, 1932: Jul, Aug, Sep, Oct, Nov

The Phantom in the Wooden Well (as Victor Rousseau)   s
  Ghost Stories, 1927: Jul
  Hutchinson's Mystery Story Magazine (UK) 1927: Aug

—**The Phantom of the Violin** (refer to the section on: Story Adaptations)

Phantom Lips (as Victor Rousseau)   s
  Ghost Stories, 1929: Sep

Phantom Throne (as Hugh Speer)   s
  Spicy-Adventure Stories, 1937: Nov

Pharaoh's Princess (as Victor Rousseau)   s
  Illustrated Sunday Magazine, 1909: Jun 13

Philtre of Death (as Hugh Speer)   s
  Spicy Mystery Stories, 1936: Apr
  Spicy Mystery Stories, 1936: Apr (facsimile)

Picked Off (as Victor Rousseau)   s
  Harper's Weekly, 1908: Jan 4
  HIS SECOND SELF: THE BIO-BIBLIOGRAPHY OF VICTOR ROUSSEAU EMANUEL
    US: The Spectre Library (sc), 2011 (as Victor Rousseau)

Pierre and Paul (as Victor Rousseau)   ss
  Extension Magazine, 1918: June
  The Railroad Trainman, 1919: Jan
  Magazine Section [of] The Sunday Star, 1919: Apr 6 (as: The Story of Pierre and Paul)
  Detroit Free Press, 1920: Mar 7
  Los Angeles Times, 1921: Apr 3

The Pilot of the Fleet (as H. M. Egbert)   ss
   Stevens Point Journal, 1913: Nov 29

Pipes of Doom (as Hugh Speer)   s
   Spicy Mystery Stories, 1939: Jun

Planted Fingerprints (as Lew Merrill)   s
   Private Detective Stories, 1945: Jan

Playthings of War (as Hugh Speer)   s
   Spicy-Adventure Stories, 1936: Aug
   Spicy-Adventure Stories, 1936: Aug (facsimile)

Plunder Ranch (as Victor Rousseau)   nt
   Ace-High Magazine, 1924: 1st Aug

Point of Eternity (as Lew Merrill)   s
   Spicy Mystery Stories, 1938: Oct

Poison Gold (as Victor Rousseau)   nt
   Action Novels, 1932/1933: Dec/Jan

Pony Express (as Lew Merrill)   s
   Fighting Western, 1945: Aug

Postponed Verdict (as Lew Merrill)   s
   Private Detective Stories, 1945: Aug

Pride of Place (as Victor Rousseau)   s
   Fiction Magazine, 1916: Oct 22
   The Household Guest, 1917: Oct

Prince of the Plains (as Victor Rousseau)   nt
   Ranch Romances, 1925: May
   MOTION PICTURE: as "Prince of the Plains," (released: Sep 1927)

The Prince's Ring (as H. M. Egbert)   vi
   Home Life, 1910: Oct
   —newspaper syndication
   The Day Book, 1912: Jul 30

The Prisoner of Hofberg (as H. M. Egbert)   ss
   Stevens Point Journal, 1913: Nov 22

The Prisoner of Life (as Victor Rousseau)   sl
   Ghost Stories, 1928: Aug, Sep, Oct, Nov, Dec; 1929: Jan

Prize of Peru (as Lew Merrill)   s
   Spicy-Adventure Stories, 1938: Jun

The Professor's Peach Trees (as Victor Rousseau)   ss
   Holland's Magazine, 1913: Oct
   The Illustrated Buffalo Express, 1914: Mar 29
   THE TRACER OF EGOS
      US: The Spectre Library (hb), Aug 2007 (as Victor Rousseau)

Proving Poe (as H. M. Egbert)   s
  People's Ideal Fiction Magazine, 1911: Jul

Proxy Murder (as Lew Merrill)   s
  Private Detective Stories, 1945: Sep

Puppet Princess (as Lew Merrill)   s
  Spicy-Adventure Stories, 1936: May
  Spicy-Adventure Stories, 1936: May (facsimile)

'Pussyfoot' Performs One of Most Daring Deeds in Frontier History (uncredited)   ts
  The Stevens Point Journal, 1917: May 12

—Queen of the Witches (see: Hell's Tryst)

The Queen's Mercy (as Victor Rousseau)   na
  Golden Fleece, 1939: Apr
  Golden Fleece, 1939: Apr (facsimile)

Quisling's Daughter (as Lew Merrill)   s
  Speed Adventure Stories, 1943: Sep

—The Race in Mid-Air (see: The Kidnaped King)

Rachel (as Victor Rousseau)   s
  The Red Book Magazine, 1914: May
  Chicago Tribune, 1917: Dec 2

Rainbow's End (as Hugh Speer)   s
  Spicy-Adventure Stories, 1936: Nov
  Spicy-Adventure Stories, 1936: Nov (facsimile)

Rangeland Fury (as Victor Rousseau)   na
  Ranch Romances, 1942: 2nd Jan

A Rangeland Renegade (as Victor Rousseau)   na
  Ranch Romances, 1928: Aug 1st

Rangeland Trickery (as Victor Rousseau)   na
  Ranch Romances, 1931: 2nd Mar

Ranger Bait (as Lew Merrill)   s
  Speed Western Stories, 1945: Feb

Ranger Breed (as Victor Rousseau)   s
  All-Fiction, 1930: Dec

The Range Rider (as Victor Rousseau)   sl
  Rangeland Love Story Magazine, 1930: Feb, Mar

Rat-Run (as V. R. Emanuel)   s
  Speed Adventure Stories, 1944: Sep

Rats Never Learn (as Lew Merrill)   s
  Speed Adventure Stories, 1944: Mar

Rat Trap (as Lew Merrill)   s
  Spicy-Adventure Stories, 1941: Jul

Rebel Planet (as Hugh Spccr)   s
  Spicy-Adventure Stories, 1940: Nov

The Record on the Screen (as Harold Carter)   ss
  Buffalo Sunday Times, 1911: Jul 16

Red Coat Patrol (as Victor Rousseau)   nt
  North-West Stories, 1928: 2nd Jul

Red-Coat Patrol (as Victor Rousseau)   nt
  Thrilling Adventures, 1934: Jan

The Red-Coat Rebel (as Victor Rousseau)   nt
  North-West Romances, 1943: Winter

The Red Cross Train (as Victor Rousseau)   s
  Harper's Weekly, 1910: Oct 1

Red Dawn (as Lew Merrill)   s
  Spicy-Adventure Stories, 1939: Aug

Red Diamonds (as Victor Rousseau)   s
  Brief Stories, 1930: Jan

Red Eden (as Hugh Speer)   s
  Spicy-Adventure Stories, 1939: Nov
  Spicy-Adventure Stories, 1939: Nov (facsimile)

The Red Envelope (as H. M. Egbert)   ss
  The Popular Magazine, 1915: Feb 23
  Illustrated Buffalo Express, 1915: Jun 27
  Fiction Magazine, 1915: Aug 15

Red Harvest (as Victor Rousseau)   nt
  Five-Novels Monthly, 1928: Sep

Red Rose and White (as Victor Rousseau)   nt
  Soldiers of Fortune, 1932: May

Red Star of India (as Victor Rousseau)   s
  Speed Adventure Stories, 1944: Nov

The Red Stronghold (as Victor Rousseau)   s
  War Stories, 1929: Oct 10

The Red Trail (as Victor Rousseau)   sl
  The Boston Daily Globe, 1951: Sep 30; Oct 7, 14, 21
  Kansas City Times, 1954: Apr 3, 4, 5, 6, 7, 8, 9 [odd installments]
  Kansas City Star, 1954: Apr 3, 4, 5, 6, 7, 8 [even installments]

Refugee Ship (as Lew Merrill)   s
  Speed Detective, 1944: Jul

Reindeer Rustlers (as Victor Rousseau)   nt
  Action Stories, 1925: Feb

The Resurrection Men (as H. M. Egbert)   tc
  Washington Post, 1911: Jan 8 (not bylined)
  Buffalo Sunday Times, 1911: Oct 1
  Detective Story Magazine, 1919: Oct 28 (as George Munson)
  Keyhole Detective Cases (CND) 1946: Mar (as H. M. Egbert)

The Return of Bill (as H. M. Egbert)   s
  The Novel Magazine (UK) 1913: Apr
  NOTE: Rewritten and condensed version, originally: The Return of Ephraim

The Return of Claudia (as Victor Rousseau)   ss
  The Illustrated Buffalo Express, 1914: May 17
  THE TRACER OF EGOS
    US: The Spectre Library (hb), Aug 2007 (as Victor Rousseau)

The Return of Ephraim (as H. M. Egbert)   s
  Young's Magazine, 1913: Jan
  NOTE: see: The Return of Bill

Return of the Beast (as Lew Merrill)   s
  Spicy Mystery Stories, 1936: Oct
  Spicy Mystery Stories, 1941: Jul (as: Fruits of Betrayal; as John Phillips)

Revolt on Inferno (as Victor Rousseau)   nt
  Miracle Science and Fantasy Stories, 1931: Jun-Jul

Riders of the Border (as Victor Rousseau)   s
  Speed Western Stories, 1946: Dec

Riders of the Buttes (as Victor Rousseau)   sl
  Ranch Romances, 1932: 2nd Jan, 3rd Jan; 1st Feb, 2nd Feb; 1st Mar, 2nd Mar

Riders of the Stars (as Victor Rousseau)   nt
  Ranch Romances, 1928: 1st Oct

A Ridin' Gent (as Victor Rousseau)   nt
  Ace-High Magazine, 1924: 1st May
  MOTION PICTURE: as "A Ridin' Gent," (released: Dec 1926)
  EN VIRVEL AV PISTOLER
    Sweden: Romanförlaget-Göteborg (sc), 1962

The Right to Motherhood (as Victoria Ross)   sl
  Physical Culture, 1926: Jan, Feb, Mar, Apr, May

Rio Riders (as Victor Rousseau)   nt
  Ranch Romances, 1937: 2nd Jan

River of Tears (as Clive Trent)   s
  Speed Adventure Stories, 1943: May

The River Rats (as H. M. Egbert)   ss
    The Globe and Commercial Advertiser, 1910: Oct 29
    The New Magazine (UK) 1910: Nov
    Morrison's Chicago Weekly, 1911: Feb 2

The Road to Biskra (as Victor Rousseau)   ss
    Photoplay Magazine, 1917: Jun

Road to Tolosa (as Hugh Speer)   s
    Spicy-Adventure Stories, 1937: May

The Robbery at the Tower (as Harold Carter)   ss
    Buffalo Sunday Times, 1911: Jun 25

The Robinson Diamonds (as H. M. Egbert)   ss
    The Blue Book Magazine, 1911: Mar
    Public Ledger, 1913: Mar 9 (erroneously as E. M. Egbert)
    The Boston Daily Globe, 1915: Jan 24

The Robot Awakes (as Lew Merrill)   s
    Spicy-Adventure Stories, 1940: Oct
    SENSUOUS SCIENCE FICTION FROM THE WEIRD AND SPICY PULPS
        US: Bowling Green State University Popular Press (hb), 1984
    SENSUOUS SCIENCE FICTION FROM THE WEIRD AND SPICY PULPS
        US: Bowling Green State University Popular Press (sc), 1984

Roles Reversed (as H. M. Egbert)   ss
    St. Louis Post-Dispatch, 1913: Oct 25
    The Houston Post, 1913: Oct 26
    The Boston Daily Globe, 1914: Feb 15
    Buffalo Sunday Times, 1916: Mar 26
    THE DEVIL CHAIR
        US: The Spectre Library (hb), Jun 2008 (as Victor Rousseau)

—**Le Roman de Fanchette** (see: The Wooing of Fanchette)

Romance of the Rio (as Victor Rousseau)   sl
    Ranch Romances, 1929: 2nd Mar [Part 1] 1st Apr [Part 2] 2nd Apr [Part 3]

The Rubber Eagles (as H. M. Egbert)   ss
    Chicago Ledger, 1922: Jul 29

Rubies of Empire (as Lew Merrill)   s
    Spicy-Adventure Stories, 1939: Oct

The Rubies of the Sacrifice (as H. M. Egbert)   ss
    The Blue Book Magazine, 1911: Dec
    Public Ledger, 1913: May 4
    The Boston Daily Globe, 1915: Mar 21

Ruby of Revolt (as Victor Rousseau)   s
    All-Adventure Action Novels, 1939: Spring

Ruckus at Red River (as Lew Merrill)   s
    Fighting Western, 1949: Aug

Rustlers' Trail (as Victor Rousseau)   nt
   Ranch Romances, 1937: 2nd Nov

The Rustlin' Trail (as Victor Rousseau)   nt
   Two Gun Western Stories, 1928: Nov

Ryder's Lights (as Clive Trent)   nt
   Speed Mystery, 1943: Feb

Rye and Die (as Lew Merrill)   s
   Private Detective Stories, 1946: Mar

Sailing — Midnight (as Lew Merrill)   s
   Hollywood Detective, 1944: Dec

Sailor's Luck (as Clive Trent)   s
   Spicy-Adventure Stories, 1942: Dec

Saint Unsealed (as Victor Rousseau)   s
   Six-Gun Western, 1946: Aug

Salvation M'Shane (as Victor Rousseau)   s
   Speed Adventure Stories, 1944: Mar

The Samurai Sword (as Clive Trent)   s
   Speed Mystery 1943: May

Sand and Diamonds (as Victor Rousseau)   s
   Action Stories, 1926: Sep

Sauce for the Gander (as H. M. Egbert)   ss
   Chicago Daily News, 1911: Nov 25

Satan's Music (as Clive Trent)   s
   Spicy Mystery Stories, 1937: Feb
   Spicy Mystery Stories, 1937: Feb (facsimile)

Savage Spears (as Lew Merrill)   s
   Spicy-Adventure Stories, 1936: Mar
   Spicy-Adventure Stories, 1936: Mar (facsimile)

—**Scandal** (refer to the section on: Story Adaptations)

The Scar (as H. M. Egbert)   ss
   Fiction Magazine, 1917: Dec 9
   The Railway Conductor, 1918: Jul

The Scourge of the Mohilla (as Victor Rousseau)   nt
   The Danger Trail, 1927: Feb

Scourge of Women (as Hugh Speer)   s
   Spicy Mystery Stories, 1941: Apr

Scrambled Destiny (as Clive Trent)   s
   Spicy Mystery Stories, 1941: Jul
   Spicy Mystery Stories, 1941: Jul (facsimile)

The Sea Demons (as Victor Rousseau)   sl
  All-Story Weekly, 1916: Jan 1, 8, 15, 22
  Chicago Ledger, 1918: Nov 16 (as: Demons of the Sea; as H. M. Egbert)
  THE SEA DEMONS
    UK: John Long (hb), 1924 (as H. M. Egbert)
  THE SEA DEMONS
    US: Hyperion (hb), 1976 (as Victor Rousseau)
  THE SEA DEMONS
    US: Hyperion (sc), 1976 (as Victor Rousseau)

Sea-Haven (as Lew Merrill)   s
  Spicy-Adventure Stories, 1939: Apr

—Sealed In Death (see: Bride of the Sun)

The Seal Maiden (as Victor Rousseau)   s
  The Cavalier, 1913: Nov 15
  A. Merritt's Fantasy Magazine, 1950: Feb

Sea-Lubber M'Shane (as Clive Trent)   s
  Speed Adventure Stories, 1944: Jul

Sea Raiders (as Lew Merrill)   s
  Spicy-Adventure Stories, 1939: Jan

The Séance of Nishikoff (as H. M. Egbert)   ss
  Stevens Point Journal, 1913: Dec 13

A Seaside Comedy (as H. M. Egbert)   ss
  Chicago Daily News, 1911: Oct 7

The Secret Altar (as Victor Rousseau)   s
  Harper's Weekly, 1911: May 27

The Secret Channel (as Clive Trent)   s
  Speed Adventure Stories, 1943: Nov

The Secret of Old Farm (as Clive Trent)   s
  Spicy Mystery Stories, 1936: Sep
  Spicy Mystery Stories, 1936: Sep (facsimile)

Secret Weapon (as Hugh Speer)   s
  Speed Adventure Stories, 1944: Nov

The Seeing Eye (as Lew Merrill)   s
  Private Detective Stories, 1944: Apr

September Peaches (as Lew Merrill)   s
  Super-Detective, 1946: Jan

Sergeant Forbes, Alias— (as Victor Rousseau)   sl
  People's Magazine, 1923: Aug 15; Sep 1, 15; Oct 1

Sergeant Joe's Return (as Hugh Speer)   nt
  Speed Mystery, 1943: Nov

A Servant of His King (as H. M. Egbert)   ss
   Cassell's Magazine of Fiction (UK) 1913: Jan

The Seven League Boots (as H. M. Egbert)   ss
   St. Louis Post-Dispatch, 1913: Oct 4
   The Houston Post, 1913: Oct 5
   The Boston Daily Globe, 1914: Jan 25
   Buffalo Sunday Times, 1916: Mar 5
   THE DEVIL CHAIR
     US: The Spectre Library (hb), Jun 2008 (as Victor Rousseau)

The Seventeenth Star (as Victor Rousseau)   s
   War Stories, 1929: Jun 20

The Seventh Symphony (as H. M. Egbert)   ss
   —NOTE: this installment was not included with the Globe and Commercial Advertiser
     Other regional sources for the 1910 first publication have not been located
   Weird Tales, 1927: Mar (as Victor Rousseau)
   THE SURGEON OF SOULS
     US: The Spectre Library (hb), Oct 2006 (as Victor Rousseau)

Shadow Man (as Lew Merrill)   s
   Spicy Mystery Stories, 1937: May

Shane of the Fifty-Third (as Victor Rousseau)   s
   War Stories, 1929: Jul 18

—Shattered Memories (refer to the section on: Story Adaptations)

The Shaving of M'Shane (as Clive Trent)   s
   Speed Adventure Stories, 1945: Oct

Shawn of the Stars (as Hugh Speer)   s
   Spicy-Adventure Stories, 1940: Sep
   SENSUOUS SCIENCE FICTION FROM THE WEIRD AND SPICY PULPS
     US: Bowling Green State University Popular Press (hb), 1984
   SENSUOUS SCIENCE FICTION FROM THE WEIRD AND SPICY PULPS
     US: Bowling Green State University Popular Press (sc), 1984

Sheriff Barbara (as Hugh Speer)   s
   Spicy-Adventure Stories, 1939: Aug

Sheriff Nan (as Victor Rousseau)   nt
   Ranch Romances, 1928: Apr 1st

Sheriff-Tooth (as Hugh Speer)   s
   Super-Detective, 1945: Nov

The Sheriff Wanted Peace (as Clive Trent)   s
   Speed Western Stories, 1945: Jul

She-Sheriff Barbara (as Hugh Speer)   s
   Spicy-Adventure Stories, 1939: Oct

She Who Was He! (as Hugh Speer)   s
  Spicy Mystery Stories, 1935: Dec
  Spicy Mystery Stories, 1935: Dec (facsimile)

Shifting Sands (as Victor Rousseau)   sl
  Sunday Magazine, 1935: Jan 13, 20, 27; Feb 3, 10, 17

The Shooting of Colonel Fisk (as George Munson)   tc
  Detective Story Magazine, 1919: Apr 29

The Shunted Man of Europe (as H. M. Egbert)   ss
  St. Louis Post-Dispatch, 1913: Nov 8
  The Houston Post, 1913: Nov 9
  The Boston Daily Globe, 1914: Mar 1
  Buffalo Sunday Times, 1916: Apr 9
  THE DEVIL CHAIR
    US: The Spectre Library (hb), Jun 2008 (as Victor Rousseau)

Sicilian Night (as Lew Merrill)   s
  Speed Adventure Stories, 1944: Jan

The Silent Partner (as Victor Rousseau)   s
  The Railroad Trainman, 1935: Aug
  The Boston Daily Globe, 1947: May 18
  (NOTE: reportedly first printed in the Toronto Star Weekly, circa 1935)

The Sin-Eater (as Lew Merrill)   s
  Spicy Mystery Stories, 1942: Sep

The Singing Utes (as Victor Rousseau)   nt
  Six-Gun Western, 1946: Dec

Skidding (as Lew Merrill)   s
  Spicy Western Stories, 1937: Sep

Skinner (as Lew Merrill)   s
  Spicy-Adventure Stories, 1937: Feb

Sky Goddess (as Clive Trent)   s
  Spicy-Adventure Stories, 1937: Mar

Slave of Alhambra (as Victor Rousseau)   nt
  Thrilling Adventures, 1938: Mar

Slim Uncle Piet (as Victor Rousseau)   s
  Harper's Monthly Magazine, 1913: Jun

Slo Pay (as Lew Merrill)   s
  Fighting Western, 1950: Jul

—Smugglers' Island (refer to the section on: Story Adaptations)

Snake Bride (as Lew Merrill)   s
  Spicy-Adventure Stories, 1937: Sep

The Snow Trail (as Victor Rousseau)   s
North-West Stories, 1926: 2nd Mar

Sons of the Boiling Blanket (as Lew Merrill)   s
Spicy-Adventure Stories, 1942: Oct

Soul Asleep (as Lew Merrill)   s
Spicy Mystery Stories, 1938: Apr

Soul at Strife (as Hugh Speer)   s
Speed Detective, 1946: Dec

The Soul That Lost Its Way (as Victor Rousseau)   ss
Ghost Stories, 1927: Aug
Prize Ghost Stories, 1963: Spring (as: Monkey-Face and Mrs. Thorpe)
Uncredited, abridged and revised

Space Burial (as Lew Merrill)   s
Spicy-Adventure Stories, 1941: Feb
Spicy-Adventure Stories, 1941: Feb (facsimile)

The Spanish Treaty (as H. M. Egbert)   ss
The New Magazine (UK) 1910: Oct
The Globe and Commercial Advertiser, 1910: Oct 22
Morrison's Chicago Weekly, 1911: Jan 26 (as: A Treaty With Spain)

Spawn of Siva (as Clive Trent)   s
Spicy-Adventure Stories, 1937: Jul
Spicy-Adventure Stories, 1937: Jul (facsimile)

Spell of the Serpent (as Lew Merrill)   s
Spicy Mystery Stories, 1941: Jul
Spicy Mystery Stories, 1941: Jul (facsimile)

The Spider's Web (as Victor Rousseau)   nt
Five-Novels Monthly, 1937: Apr

Spies of Destiny (as John Grange)   nt
Super Detective, 1941: Oct

Split Seams (as Lew Merrill)   s
Super-Detective, 1945: Sep

Spoil of the Sea (as Hugh Speer)   s
Speed Adventure Stories, 1944: Jan

The Square Peg (as Victor Rousseau)   s
McClure's Magazine, 1923: May
Everywoman's World, 1923: Oct (as: New York Takes the Count)
The Boston Daily Globe, 1923: Nov 18 (as: New York Takes the Count)
Hearth & Home, 1928: Apr

Stakes on the Black (as Hugh Speer)   s
Spicy-Adventure Stories, 1940: Jul

Stand Up, Ye Dead (as Clive Trent)   s
    Speed Adventure Stories, 1943: Mar

The Starlight Trail (as Victor Rousseau)   na
    Ranch Romances, 1930: 2nd Nov

The Steadfast Heart (as Victor Rousseau)   na
    Ranch Romances, 1930: 3rd Aug

Steel of Death (as Lew Merrill)   nt
    Speed Mystery, 1943: Feb

Steeled by Struggle (as Victor Rousseau)   sl
    Muscle Builder, 1925: Jul, Aug, Sep, Oct, Nov

The Stolen Appendix (as Victor Rousseau)   s
    Illustrated Sunday Magazine, 1911: Jun 25

The Stolen Submarine (as H. M. Egbert)   ss
    The Blue Book Magazine, 1911: May
    Public Ledger, 1913: Mar 23
    The Boston Daily Globe, 1915: Feb 7

The Stone Men of Ignota (as Victor Rousseau)   s
    Future Fiction, 1941: Aug
    Science Fiction (Canada) 1942: Feb (as Victor Rosseau)

Storm Over Athabasca (as Victor Rousseau)   sl
    Farmer's Magazine (CND) 1940: Aug, Sep, Oct, Nov++
    Kansas City Star, 1944: May 1, 2, 3, 4, 5, 6

—**The Story of Pierre and Paul** (see: Pierre and Paul)

Story of the Runaway Bride (as H. M. Egbert)   ss
    Chicago Daily News, 1911: Oct 21

—**A Strange Bargain** (see: The Truant Soul)

The Stuffed Shirt (as Victor Rousseau)   s
    Speed Mystery, 1944: Nov

—**The Sun God** (refer to the section on: Story Adaptations)

Sunburst Valley (as Victor Rousseau)   na
    Ranch Romances, 1928: Jan 1st
    MOTION PICTURE: as "When Dreams Come True," (released: 15 Jan 1929)

The Superfluous Husband (as George Munson)   tc
    Detective Story Magazine, 1919: Jun 10
    Famous Crime Cases (Canada) 1946: Jul

Suzette (as Victor Rousseau)   ss
    Chicago Tribune, 1915: Nov 7

Swamp Soil (as Victor Rousseau)   sl
    Fawcett's Triple-X, 1925: Jul, Aug, Sep

Sweeping Tides (as Victor Rousseau)   nt
  The Boston Daily Globe, 1946: May 5
  NOTE: small-town papers serialized the tale under the H. M. Egbert byline

Sword Play at Dawn! (as Victor Rousseau)   nt
  Five-Novels Monthly, 1938: Jan

Swords for Florence (as Victor Rousseau)   s
  Speed Adventure Stories, 1945: Jan

Swords for Navarre (as Victor Rousseau)   nt
  Five-Novels Monthly, 1934: Feb

Sword-Slasher (as Lew Merrill)   s
  Speed Detective, 1946: May

Swordsman's Choice (as Hugh Speer)   s
  Spicy-Adventure Stories, 1941: Nov

Synthetic Husband (as Lew Merrill)   s
  Spicy Mystery Stories, 1937: Sep
  Speed Mystery, 1943: Mar (as: Too Bad to Kill; as Stan Warner)
  SPICY MYSTERY STORIES
    US: Malibu Graphics (sc), 1990

Tag For A Crown (as Victor Rousseau)   s
  Argosy and Railroad Man's Magazine, 1919: Apr 19
  The Novel Magazine (UK) 1920: Mar

A Tailor Never Pricks His Finger (as Victor Rousseau)   s
  Speed Adventure Stories, 1943: Nov

Taos Trail (as Lew Merrill)   s
  Six-Gun Western, 1946: Mar

The Tell-Tale Arm (as Lew Merrill)   s
  Private Detective Stories, 1944: Dec

The Tell-Tale Glove (as Harold Carter)   ss
  Buffalo Sunday Times, 1911: Jul 2

Temple of Death (as Victor Rousseau)   s
  Triple-X Magazine, 1930: Oct

Temple of Death (as Hugh Speer)   s
  Spicy-Adventure Stories, 1937: Sep

Tennant - of the U. S. A. (as Victor Rousseau)   s
  War Stories, 1930: Dec

The Tenth Commandment (as H. M. Egbert)   ss
  The Globe and Commercial Advertiser, 1910: Feb 26
  Weird Tales, 1926: Dec (as Victor Rousseau)
  THE SURGEON OF SOULS
    US: The Spectre Library (hb), Oct 2006 (as Victor Rousseau)

Terror by Night (as Lew Merrill)   s
    Private Detective Stories, 1946: Nov

Terror Range (as Victor Rousseau)   sl
    Ranch Romances, 1934: 2nd Jun, 3rd Jun, 1st Jul, 2nd Jul, 3rd Jul, 1st Aug

The Test of the Hills (as Victor Rousseau)   s
    Illustrated Sunday Magazine, 1912: Jan 28

Their Honors the Aldermen (as Victor Rousseau)   s
    Harper's Weekly, 1909: Jul 24

—**Their Hour** (refer to the section on: Story Adaptations)

There are Pearls in Dargan (as Victor Rousseau)   s
    Brief Stories, 1929: Dec

There Can't Be Two O'Haras (as Lew Merrill)   s
    Spicy-Adventure Stories, 1939: Dec
    Spicy-Adventure Stories, 1939: Dec (facsimile)

They Shall Not Pass (as Victor Rousseau)   s
    War Birds, 1929: Nov

Things That Were Men (as Clive Trent)   s
    Spicy-Adventure Stories, 1940: Dec

This Was Grandison (as Lew Merrill)   s
    Speed Mystery, 1944: Nov

Thorne, the Throne-Maker (as Victor Rousseau)   na
    The Danger Trail, 1927: Oct

Thorns and Iron (as Victor Rousseau)   nt
    Frontier Stories, 1927: Sep
    Master Thriller Series # 7: Tales of African Adventure (UK) 1934: Dec

The Three Melons (as Victor Rousseau)   s
    The American Patriot, 1914: Apr

Throne of Straw (as Clive Trent)   s
    Spicy-Adventure Stories, 1941: Mar

Thrones of Dust (as Victor Rousseau)   nt
    Five-Novels Monthly, 1932: Apr

Thunderstone (as Lew Merrill)   s
    Spicy Mystery Stories, 1938: Jun

Tidewater (as Lew Merrill)   s
    Spicy Mystery Stories, 1936: Dec
    Spicy Mystery Stories, 1936: Dec (facsimile)

Tides of Conquest (as Victor Rousseau)   sl
    Ranch Romances, 1930: 1st Mar, 2nd Mar, 1st Apr, 2nd Apr, 1st May, 2nd May

The Time Dissolver (as Hugh Speer)   s
  Spicy Mystery Stories, 1937: Feb
  Pulp Review # 22, 1995
  Spicy Mystery Stories, 1937: Feb (facsimile)

Time Lag (as Hugh Speer)   s
  Speed Mystery, 1943: Jul

The Time-Twister (as Lew Merrill)   s
  Spicy Mystery Stories, 1938: May

Titanium Ship (as Clive Trent)   s
  Speed Mystery, 1943: Jul

To Carve a New World (as Victor Rousseau)   nt
  Five-Novels Monthly, 1938: Feb

—**The Toilet That Saved France** (see: The Kaiser's Hairdresser)

—**Too Bad to Kill** (see: Synthetic Husband)

Torpedo Broker (as Victor Rousseau)   ss
  Photoplay Magazine, 1917: May

Trailin' Back (as Victor Rousseau)   nt
  Lariat Story Magazine, 1926: Jul
  Cowboy Story Magazine (UK) 1927: Feb
  MOTION PICTURE: as "Trailin' Back," (released: March 1928)

The Trail of Terror (as Victor Rousseau)   nt
  Rangeland Love Story Magazine, 1932: May

The Trail of the Wolf (as Victor Rousseau)   s
  The American Patriot, 1914: Mar

Trail of the Wolf (as Victor Rousseau)   na
  Ranch Romances, 1935: 1st May

Trail of Wanted Men (as Victor Rousseau)   nt
  Frontier Stories, 1930: Apr

Trails End (as Lew Merrill)   s
  Spicy-Adventure Stories, 1938: Apr

Traitress' Wages (as Lew Merrill)   s
  Spicy-Adventure Stories, 1935: Nov

Treasure Lake (as Victor Rousseau)   nt
  Ace-High Magazine, 1934: Apr

Treasure of Andes (as Hugh Speer)   s
  Spicy-Adventure Stories, 1939: Sep

The Treasure of Cos (as H. M. Egbert)   ss
  Chicago Ledger, 1922: Jul 22

The Treasure of Egypt (as H. M. Egbert)   ss
  The Blue Book Magazine, 1912: Feb
  Public Ledger, 1913: May 18
  The Boston Daily Globe, 1915: Mar 28

The Treasure of Spandau (as H. M. Egbert)   ss
  The Blue Book Magazine, 1911: Apr
  Public Ledger, 1913: Mar 16
  The Boston Daily Globe, 1915: Feb 28

Treasure of the Moon (as John Austin)   s
  Empire Frontier (UK) 1930: Dec
      NOTE: original currently unknown, possibly: Treasure Ranch

Treasure Ranch (as John Austin)   nt
  Five-Novels Monthly, 1928: May

Treasure Trove (as H. M. Egbert)   vi
  The Evening Telegram, 1910: Jun 13

—A Treaty With Spain (see: The Spanish Treaty)

Tree Mother (as Clive Trent)   s
  Spicy-Adventure Stories, 1942: Jul

Tree of Life (as Lew Merrill)   s
  Spicy-Adventure Stories, 1941: Apr
  Spicy-Adventure Stories, 1941: Apr (facsimile)

Trickery Trail (as Victor Rousseau)   nt
  Ranch Romances, 1940: 2nd May

Trigger-Quick (as Lew Merrill)   s
  Speed Western Stories, 1945: Oct

Trigger Trail (as Victor Rousseau)   nt
  All Western Magazine, 1932: Mar

Trouble Wrangler (as Lew Merrill)   s
  Leading Western, 1947: Nov

The Truant Soul (as Victor Rousseau)   mv
  MOTION PICTURE: as "The Truant Soul," (released: 25 Dec 1916)
  Chicago Tribune, 1917: Aug 26; Sep 2, 9, 16, 23, 30; Oct 7, 14, 21, 28 (as: His Second Self)
  —nationally syndicated in the smaller presses (as: The Truant Soul)
  Brief Stories, 1927: Jun (as: A Strange Bargain)
  Western Home Monthly (CND) 1927-1928 (unconfirmed)

Trumps & Tolliver (as Victor Rousseau)   s
  The American Patriot, 1915: Oct

The Turning of the Worm (as Victor Rousseau)   s
  Illustrated Sunday Magazine, 1910: Apr 3

Turnover in Tannersville (as Lew Merrill)   s
  Super-Detective, 1944: Dec

Twisted Time (as Lew Merrill)   nt
   Spicy Mystery Stories, 1942: Nov

The Two Charioteers (as Victor Rousseau)   ss
   Holland's Magazine 1913: Sep
   The Illustrated Buffalo Express, 1914: Apr 12
   THE TRACER OF EGOS
     US: The Spectre Library (hb), Aug 2007 (as Victor Rousseau)

Two on a Trail (as Lew Merrill)   s
   Spicy-Adventure Stories, 1938: Jan

The Two Parricides (as George Munson)   tc
   Detective Story Magazine, 1919: Jul 15

Typed (as Lew Merrill)   s
   Super-Detective, 1945: Apr

Tyrants Die by the Sword (as Victor Rousseau)   nt
   Five-Novels Monthly, 1936: Nov

The Ultimate Problem (as H. M. Egbert)   ss
   The Globe and Commercial Advertiser, 1910: May 7
   Weird Tales, 1927: Jul (as Victor Rousseau)
   THE SURGEON OF SOULS
     US: The Spectre Library (hb), Oct 2006 (as Victor Rousseau)

Unborn Terror (as Hugh Speer)   s
   Speed Mystery, 1944: Nov

Uncle Hendrick's Parlor Organ (as Victor Rousseau)   s
   The American Patriot, 1915: Jul/Aug

—**Under the Black Flag** (see: Under the Striped Man's Flag)

Under the Striped Man's Flag (as H. M. Egbert)   sl
   Chicago Ledger, 1919: Nov 29; Dec 6, 13, 20, 27
   The Corner, 1927: Jan, Feb, Mar, Apr, May (as: Under the Black Flag)

Undertow (as Victor Rousseau)   nt
   Five-Novels Monthly, 1931: Jan

The Unknown Factor (as Hugh Speer)   nt
   Speed Mystery, 1943: Feb

Unwritten Law (as Lew Merrill)   s
   Hollywood Detective, 1945: May

The Upper Window (as Victor Rousseau)   s
   Harper's Weekly, 1909: Apr 24

Valley of Blood (as Lew Merrill)   s
   Spicy-Adventure Stories, 1936: Sep
   Spicy-Adventure Stories, 1936: Sep (facsimile)

Valley of Gold (as Victor Rousseau)   nt
  North-West Romances, 1938: Summer

The Valley of Sleeping Slaves (as Victor Rousseau)   sl
  Chicago Ledger, 1920: Jun 5, 12, 19, 26

Vampire (as Lew Merrill)   s
  Spicy Mystery Stories, 1942: Jul
  Spicy Mystery Stories, 1942: Jul (facsimile)

The Vampire Doll (as Hugh Speer)   s
  Spicy Mystery Stories, 1937: Dec

Van Dam's Heads (as Clive Trent)   s
  Spicy-Adventure Stories, 1937: Oct

Vault of Horror (as Clive Trent)   s
  Spicy Mystery Stories, 1937: Aug

The Vengeance Trail (as Victor Rousseau)   nt
  Argosy, 1931: Mar 21

Venus of Troy (as Clive Trent)   s
  Spicy Mystery Stories, 1936: Aug
  Spicy Mystery Stories, 1936: Aug (facsimile)

Viking's Daughter (as Hugh Speer)   nt
  Spicy Mystery Stories, 1941: Oct
  Spicy Mystery Stories, 1941: Oct (facsimile)

The Virgin of Okiak (as Victor Rousseau)   s
  Harper's Weekly, 1911: Jul 8

Vision of Death (as Lew Merrill)   s
  Spicy Mystery Stories, 1940: Jun

The Voice in the Mist (as Victor Rousseau)   ss
  The Blue Book Magazine, 1914: Sep
  Chicago Tribune, 1918: Mar 10
  The Boston Daily Globe, 1930: Nov 30

The Wall of Death (as Victor Rousseau)   s
  Astounding Stories of Super-Science, 1930: Nov

Walls of the Alcazar (as C. Cordier)   nt
  Five-Novels Monthly, 1937: Sep

A Wanderer of the West (as Victor Rousseau)   nt
  Ace-High Magazine, 1924: 2nd Oct
  MOTION PICTURE: as "Wanderer of the West," (released: Dec 1927)
  EN COWBOY SLAR KNOCKOUT
    Sweden: Romanförlaget-Göteborg (sc), 1961

War Time (as Lew Merrill)   s
  Hollywood Detective, 1945: Aug

The Water Gate (as Lew Merrill)   s
  Spicy-Adventure Stories, 1938: Sep

Water Witch (as Lew Merrill)   s
  Spicy Mystery Stories, 1939: Apr

The Wax Clavette (as H. M. Egbert)   ss
  The Popular Magazine, 1915: Feb 7
  Illustrated Buffalo Express, 1915: Jun 20
  Fiction Magazine, 1915: Aug 8

The Ways of Women (as Victor Rosseau)   s
  Illustrated Sunday Magazine, 1910: Sep 18

Webs of Sand (as Victor Rousseau)   nt
  Five-Novels Monthly, 1931: Jul

West of Rainbow's End (as Victor Rousseau)   nt
  Ranch Romances, 1925: Sep
  MOTION PICTURE: as "West of the Rainbow's End," (released: 13 Aug 1926)

When Dead Gods Wake (as Victor Rousseau)   s
  Strange Tales of Mystery and Terror, 1931: Nov
  Magazine of Horror, 1969: Jan
  13 HISTOIRES DE SORCELLERIE
    Belgium: Verviers, 1975
  Strange Tales of Mystery and Terror, 1931: Nov (facsimile)

—**When Dreams Come True** (see: Sunburst Valley)

When It Grew Cold (as Lew Merrill)   s
  Spicy Mystery Stories, 1942: Feb

When Planets Mate (as Lew Merrill)   s
  Spicy-Adventure Stories, 1941: Sep
  Spicy-Adventure Stories, 1941: Sep (facsimile)

When the Shark Turns (as Victor Rousseau)   s
  Illustrated Sunday Magazine, 1909: Sep 12

While Dorion Lives (as Victor Rousseau)   sl
  Argosy All-Story Weekly, 1920: Nov 27; Dec 4, 11, 18, 25
  THE BIG MAN OF BONNE CHANCE
    UK: Hodder and Stoughton (hb), 1925

The Whirl of Death (as Harold Carter)   ss
  The Saturday Blade, 1912: Jan 27

—**The Whirling Disk** (refer to the section on: Story Adaptations)

White Girl (as Lew Merrill)   s
  Speed Adventure Stories, 1943: Feb

The White Goddess (as Lew Merrill)   s
  Spicy-Adventure Stories, 1936: Aug
  Spicy-Adventure Stories, 1936: Aug (facsimile)

The White Lily Murder (as H. M. Egbert)   sl
    Chicago Ledger, 1921: Oct 22, 29; Nov 5, 12, 19, 26; Dec 3, 10, 17, 24

—Why Russia Backed Down (see: The Czar's Drive)

The Wife and the Other Man (as George Munson)   tc
    Detective Story Magazine, 1919: May 13

The Wife of Ira Hopkins (as Victor Rousseau)   ss
    The Illustrated Buffalo Express, 1914: May 24
    THE TRACER OF EGOS
       US: The Spectre Library (hb), Aug 2007 (as Victor Rousseau)

The Wife of Midas (as John Austin)   s
    Delineator, 1924: Feb

Wildcats Have Wings (as Victor Rousseau)   s
    War Stories, 1930: Oct

Wild Ice (as Victor Rousseau)   nt
    Action Novels, 1932: Oct/Nov

—A Wild Irish Rose (refer to the section on: Story Adaptations)

The Wing Wonder (as Victor Rousseau)   nt
    Air Stories, 1930: May

Witch's Island (as Lew Merrill)   s
    Spicy Mystery Stories, 1940: Feb

Witch's Sabbath (as Lew Merrill)   s
    Spicy Mystery Stories, 1937: Apr

With Swords Unsheathed (as Victor Rousseau)   nt
    Five-Novels Monthly, 1935: Apr

The Wolf Trail (as Victor Rousseau)   na
    Short Stories 1927: Nov 10
    Short Stories (UK) 1928: Early Apr
    Real Northwest Adventures, 1937: Mar
    The Boston Daily Globe, 1947: Jan 26
    Kansas City Times, 1944: Jan 25, 26, 27, 28, 29, 30, 31; Feb 1 [odd installments]
    Kansas City Star, 1944: Jan 25, 26, 27, 28, 29, 30, 31; Feb 1 [even installments]

The Wolf Trail (a Romance in the Southwest) (as Victor Rousseau)   nt
    Ranch Romances, 1933: Oct 1

The Wolf Trap (as H. M. Egbert)   s
    Fiction Magazine, 1916: Aug 27
    The House hold Guest, 1917: Sep
    Washington Post, 1918: Aug 11
    The Illustrated Buffalo Express, 1918: Sep 1
    HIS SECOND SELF: THE BIO-BIBLIOGRAPHY OF VICTOR ROUSSEAU EMANUEL
       US: The Spectre Library (sc), 2011 (as Victor Rousseau)

Wolf Woman (as Clive Trent)   s
 Speed Mystery, 1944: Nov

Woman and the Law (as Victor Rousseau)   nt
 Wayside Tales, 1922: Feb
 Kansas City Star, 1956: Jun 5, 6, 7, 8, 9
  [odd installments](as: The Woman and the Law)
 Kansas City Times, 1956: Jun 6, 7, 8, 9
  [even installments](as: The Woman and the Law)

Woman from Mercury (as Lew Merrill)   s
 Spicy-Adventure Stories, 1940: Jul

The Woman from the Sea (as H. M. Egbert)   ss
 Stevens Point Journal, 1913: Oct 18
 HIS SECOND SELF: THE BIO-BIBLIOGRAPHY OF VICTOR ROUSSEAU EMANUEL
  US: The Spectre Library (sc), 2011 (as Victor Rousseau)

Woman in Yellow (as Lew Merrill)   s
 Romantic Western, 1938: Nov

The Woman of Atlantis (as Victor Rousseau)   ss
 Holland's Magazine, 1914: Jan
 The Illustrated Buffalo Express, 1914: May 3
 THE TRACER OF EGOS
  US: The Spectre Library (hb), Aug 2007 (as Victor Rousseau)

The Woman of Cayenne (as Hugh Speer)   s
 Spicy-Adventure Stories, 1936: Jun
 Spicy-Adventure Stories, 1936: Jun (facsimile)

The Woman With the Crooked Nose (as H. M. Egbert)   ss
 The Globe and Commercial Advertiser, 1910: Feb 12
 Weird Tales, 1926: Oct (as Victor Rousseau)
 THE SURGEON OF SOULS
  US: The Spectre Library (hb), Oct 2006 (as Victor Rousseau)

—**A Woman's Debt** (refer to the section on: Story Adaptations)

Wooden Spoil (as Victor Rousseau)   sl
 The Argosy, 1917: Oct 13, 20, 27; Nov 3, 10, 17
 WOODEN SPOIL
  US: George H. Doran (hb), 1919
 WOODEN SPOIL
  US: Grosset and Dunlap (hb), 1919
 WOODEN SPOIL
  UK: Hodder and Stoughton (hb), 1919
 Detroit Free Press, 1920: Jun 13, 20, 27; Jul 4, 11, 18, 25; Aug 1, 8, 15
 Boston Daily Globe, 1921: Jan 9, 16, 23, 30; Feb 6, 13, 20 (as Victor Rousseau)
 Philadelphia Inquirer, 1922: Apr 23, 30; May 7, 14, 21, 28; Jun 4, 11, 18, 25;
  Jul 2, 9, 16 (as Victor Rousseau)
 Chicago Ledger, 1922: Aug 5, 12, 19, 26; Sept 2, 9, 16, 23, 30;
  Oct 7, 14, 21 (as H. M. Egbert)
 Grit, 1933: Aug 13, 20, 27; Sep 3, 10, 17++ (as Victor Rousseau)
 WOODEN SPOIL
  US: Kessinger (hb), 2010: Jan

The Wooing of Fanchette (as Victor Rousseau)   ss
  The Blue Book Magazine, 1915: Feb
  Chicago Tribune, 1918: Mar 24
  Everywoman's World (Canada) 1920: Apr
  La Canadienne (Canada, French trans.) 1920: Aug (as: Le Roman de Fanchette)
  The Boston Daily Globe, 1931: Jan 18

World's End (as Victor Rousseau)   sl
  Argosy, 1933: Jul 8, 15, 22
  RED TWILIGHT/WORLD'S END: TWO NOVELS FROM ARGOSY
    US: Starmont House (hb), 1991

The Wrath of Paul Dupuy (as Victor Rousseau)   ss
  The Blue Book Magazine, 1914: Nov
  Chicago Tribune, 1918: Mar 17
  The Boston Daily Globe, 1931: Feb 8
  Toronto Star Weekly, 1933: Sep 30

The "X" Bacillus (as H. M. Egbert)   ss
  Illustrated Buffalo Express, 1915: Jun 13
  Fiction Magazine, 1915: Aug 1

Yellow Gold Trails (as Victor Rousseau)   nt
  Novelets, 1925: Apr

Youth the Conqueror (as H. M. Egbert)   s
  Young's Magazine, 1909: Mar
  HIS SECOND SELF: THE BIO-BIBLIOGRAPHY OF VICTOR ROUSSEAU EMANUEL
    US: The Spectre Library (sc), 2011 (as Victor Rousseau)

Zang the Creator (as Lew Merrill)   s
  Spicy Mystery Stories, 1936: Apr
  Spicy Mystery Stories, 1936: Apr (facsimile)

MAGAZINE INDEX
Pulp, Slick & Newspaper Tabloid Format

Year Month, Day Story Title   **Byline**

ACE-HIGH MAGAZINE (US: Clayton Magazines)

1923	Aug	1st	nt	The Further Ranges	Victor Rousseau
1923	Dec	2nd	nt	The Devil's Tower	Victor Rousseau
1924	Jan	2nd	nt	Halsey of the Mounted	Victor Rousseau
1924	May	1st	nt	A Ridin' Gent	Victor Rousseau
1924	Aug	1st	nt	Plunder Ranch	Victor Rousseau
1924	Oct	2nd	nt	A Wanderer of the West	Victor Rousseau
1925	May	2nd	nt	The Lightnin' Shot	Victor Rousseau
1926	Jan	2nd	nt	Hi-Jacking Rustlers	Victor Rousseau

ACE-HIGH MAGAZINE (US: Dell Publishing)

1934	Mar	nt	Loot of Lost Lode	Victor Rousseau
1934	Apr	nt	Treasure Lake	Victor Rousseau
1934	Oct	nt	Jewels of Death	Victor Rousseau

ACTION ADVENTURE STORIES (US: Fading Shadows Inc.)

2000	Apr	# 72 nt	Murder Syndicate	John Grange

ACTION NOVELS (US: Fiction House)

1931	Aug	nt	Dead Man's Trail	Victor Rousseau
1932	Oct/Nov	nt	Wild Ice	Victor Rousseau
32/33	Dec/Jan	nt	Poison Gold	Victor Rousseau

ACTION STORIES (US: Fiction House)

1925	Feb	nt	Reindeer Rustlers	Victor Rousseau
1926	Sep	s	Sand and Diamonds	Victor Rousseau
1927	Jun	s	Gunman's Wages	Victor Rousseau
1929	Dec	nt	Doom Prisoners	Victor Rousseau
1930	Jun	s	Afghan Gold	Victor Rousseau
1942	Dec	nt	Eagle of Tibet	Victor Rousseau

AINSLEE'S MAGAZINE (US: Ainslee Magazine Co.)

1912	Jul	s	The Man of Pelican Key	Victor Rousseau

The Flights of Francois (Series: Sep 1915 through Jan 1916)

1915	Sep	ss	Capt. Cholmunday's Monkey	Victor Rousseau
1915	Oct	ss	Alice of Chalons	Victor Rousseau
1915	Nov	ss	The General's Knave-Trap	Victor Rousseau
1915	Dec	ss	The Man With the Peaked Beard	Victor Rousseau
1916	Jan	ss	The Eve of the Hospital	Victor Rousseau

AIR STORIES (US: Fiction House)

1930	May	nt	The Wing Wonder	Victor Rousseau

ALL-ADVENTURE ACTION NOVELS (US: Fiction House)

1939	Spring	s	Ruby of Revolt	Victor Rousseau

ALL-FICTION (US: Dell Publishing Co.)

1930	Nov	nt	Ghost Island	Victor Rousseau
1930	Dec	s	Ranger Breed	Victor Rousseau

ALL-STORY CAVALIER WEEKLY (US: Frank A. Munsey Co.)

1914	May	30	s	The General's Decoration	Victor Rousseau
1915	Feb	13	sl	Jacqueline of Golden River	Victor Rousseau
1915	Feb	20	sl	Jacqueline of Golden River	Victor Rousseau
1915	Feb	27	sl	Jacqueline of Golden River	Victor Rousseau
1915	Mar	6	sl	Jacqueline of Golden River	Victor Rousseau

ALL-STORY WEEKLY (US: Frank A. Munsey Co.)

1915	Sep	11	s	Lafe Evens Up	Victor Rousseau
1916	Jan	1	sl	The Sea Demons	Victor Rousseau
1916	Jan	8	sl	The Sea Demons	Victor Rousseau
1916	Jan	15	sl	The Sea Demons	Victor Rousseau
1916	Jan	22	sl	The Sea Demons	Victor Rousseau
1918	Jan	26	sl	The Diamond Demons	Victor Rousseau
1918	Feb	2	sl	The Diamond Demons	Victor Rousseau
1918	Feb	9	sl	The Diamond Demons	Victor Rousseau
1918	Feb	16	sl	The Diamond Demons	Victor Rousseau
1918	Feb	23	sl	The Diamond Demons	Victor Rousseau
1918	Jun	1	sl	Draft of Eternity	Victor Rousseau
1918	Jun	8	sl	Draft of Eternity	Victor Rousseau
1918	Jun	15	sl	Draft of Eternity	Victor Rousseau
1918	Jun	22	sl	Draft of Eternity	Victor Rousseau
1919	Mar	29	sl	The Lion's Jaws	Victor Rousseau
1919	Apr	5	sl	The Lion's Jaws	Victor Rousseau
1919	Apr	12	sl	The Lion's Jaws	Victor Rousseau
1919	Apr	19	sl	The Lion's Jaws	Victor Rousseau
1919	Apr	26	sl	The Lion's Jaws	Victor Rousseau
1920	Jan	17	sl	The Eye of Balamok	Victor Rousseau
1920	Jan	24	sl	The Eye of Balamok	Victor Rousseau
1920	Jan	31	sl	The Eye of Balamok	Victor Rousseau

ALL WESTERN MAGAZINE (US: Dell Publishing Co.)

1932	Mar		nt	Trigger Trail	Victor Rousseau

AMERICAN PATRIOT, THE (US: American Issue Publishing Co.)

1914	Mar		s	The Trail of the Wolf	Victor Rousseau
1914	Apr		s	The Three Melons	Victor Rousseau
1914	Jun		s	Lieutenant Merriman—Missing	Victor Rousseau
1914	Aug		s	The Human Factor	Victor Rousseau
1915	Jan		s	A Judith of '75	Victor Rousseau
1915	Mar		s	Mulligan and the Pull-Through	Victor Rousseau
1915	Jul/Aug		s	Uncle Hendrick's Parlor Organ	Victor Rousseau
1915	Oct		s	Trumps & Tolliver	Victor Rousseau
1915	Nov		s	Captain Ransome's Twenty Minutes	Victor Rousseau
1916	Jan		ss	The Gates of Rocky River	Victor Rousseau

A. MERRITT'S FANTASY MAGAZINE (US: Recreational Reading)

1950	Feb		s	The Seal Maiden	Victor Rousseau

ARGOSY, THE (US: Frank A. Munsey Co.)

1917	Oct	13	sl	Wooden Spoil	Victor Rousseau
1917	Oct	20	sl	Wooden Spoil	Victor Rousseau
1917	Oct	27	sl	Wooden Spoil	Victor Rousseau
1917	Nov	3	sl	Wooden Spoil	Victor Rousseau
1917	Nov	10	sl	Wooden Spoil	Victor Rousseau
1917	Nov	17	sl	Wooden Spoil	Victor Rousseau

1917	Dec	22	ss	The House of Gingras	Victor Rousseau
1918	Feb	2	sl	Fruit of the Lamp	Victor Rousseau
1918	Feb	9	sl	Fruit of the Lamp	Victor Rousseau
1918	Feb	16	sl	Fruit of the Lamp	Victor Rousseau
1918	Feb	23	sl	Fruit of the Lamp	Victor Rousseau
1920	Jan	3	sl	The Big Muskeg	Victor Rousseau
1920	Jan	10	sl	The Big Muskeg	Victor Rousseau
1920	Jan	17	sl	The Big Muskeg	Victor Rousseau
1920	Jan	24	sl	The Big Muskeg	Victor Rousseau
1931	Mar	21	nt	The Vengeance Trail	Victor Rousseau
1933	Jul	8	sl	World's End	Victor Rousseau
1933	Jul	15	sl	World's End	Victor Rousseau
1933	Jul	22	sl	World's End	Victor Rousseau

ARGOSY ALL-STORY WEEKLY (US: Frank A. Munsey Co.)

1920	Nov	27	sl	While Dorion Lives	Victor Rousseau
1920	Dec	4	sl	While Dorion Lives	Victor Rousseau
1920	Dec	11	sl	While Dorion Lives	Victor Rousseau
1920	Dec	18	sl	While Dorion Lives	Victor Rousseau
1920	Dec	25	sl	While Dorion Lives	Victor Rousseau
1921	May	7	sl	My Lady of the Nile	H. M. Egbert
1921	May	14	sl	My Lady of the Nile	H. M. Egbert
1921	May	21	sl	My Lady of the Nile	H. M. Egbert
1921	May	28	sl	My Lady of the Nile	H. M. Egbert
1922	Jan	28	sl	The Bandit of Batakaland	Victor Rousseau
1922	Feb	4	sl	The Bandit of Batakaland	Victor Rousseau
1922	Feb	11	sl	The Bandit of Batakaland	Victor Rousseau
1922	Feb	18	sl	The Bandit of Batakaland	Victor Rousseau
1922	Feb	25	sl	The Bandit of Batakaland	Victor Rousseau
1929	Apr	13	sl	The Branded Man	Victor Rousseau
1929	Apr	20	sl	The Branded Man	Victor Rousseau
1929	Apr	27	sl	The Branded Man	Victor Rousseau
1929	May	4	sl	The Branded Man	Victor Rousseau

ARGOSY AND RAILROAD MAN'S MAGAZINE (US: Frank A. Munsey Co.)

1919	Apr	19	s	Tag For a Crown	Victor Rousseau

ASTOUNDING STORIES OF SUPER-SCIENCE (US: Publishers' Fiscal Corp.)

1930	Jan		sl	The Beetle Horde	Victor Rousseau
1930	Feb		sl	The Beetle Horde	Victor Rousseau
1930	May		na	The Atom-Smasher	Victor Rousseau
1930	Aug		s	The Lord of Space	Victor Rousseau
1930	Oct		na	The Invisible Death	Victor Rousseau
1930	Nov		s	The Wall of Death	Victor Rousseau

BEHIND THE MASK (US: Fading Shadows)

1998	Summer		nt	Dealer in Death	John Grange

BEST DETECTIVE MAGAZINE (US: Street & Smith Corp.)

Inside History of Famous Crimes (Series: Jun 1936 through Jul 1936)

1936	Jun		tc	A Helen of New York	George Munson
1936	Jul		tc	The Body in the Box	George Munson

BEST STORIES OF ALL TIME (US: Clever Truths Publishing Company)

1927	Feb		vi	The Bacillus Prodigiosus	H. M. Egbert
1927	Jun		vi	Nemesis	H. M. Egbert

BLUE BOOK MAGAZINE, THE (US: The Story Press Corp.)
The King of Knaves (Series: Mar 1911 through Feb 1912)

1911	Mar	ss	The Robinson Diamonds	H. M. Egbert
1911	Apr	ss	The Treasure of Spandau	H. M. Egbert
1911	May	ss	The Stolen Submarine	H. M. Egbert
1911	Jun	ss	The Lighthouse of the North	H. M. Egbert
1911	Jul	ss	The Essayan Statue	H. M. Egbert
1911	Aug	ss	The Burning of Batoum	H. M. Egbert
1911	Sep	ss	The Coronation of Nikolai	H. M. Egbert
1911	Oct	ss	The Flight of the Princess	H. M. Egbert
1911	Nov	ss	A Bid for a Throne	H. M. Egbert
1911	Dec	ss	The Rubies of the Sacrifice	H. M. Egbert
1912	Jan	ss	The Brother of the Moon	H. M. Egbert
1912	Feb	ss	The Treasure of Egypt	H. M. Egbert

Tales of the St. Lawrence Riverway (Series: Sep 1914 through May 1915)

1914	Sep	ss	The Voice in the Mist	Victor Rousseau
1914	Oct	ss	The Evil Shore	Victor Rousseau
1914	Nov	ss	The Wrath of Paul Dupuy	Victor Rousseau
1914	Dec	ss	The Lie of Pere Sebastian	Victor Rousseau
1915	Jan	ss	The Curé Goes Hunting	Victor Rousseau
1915	Feb	ss	The Wooing of Fanchette	Victor Rousseau
1915	Mar	ss	The Pacification of Anne	Victor Rousseau
1915	Apr	ss	Big Pierre's Idol	Victor Rousseau
1915	May	ss	The Desperation of St. Jean	Victor Rousseau

BOOK OF WEIRD TALES, A (UK: Veevers and Hensman Ltd.)

1960		nt	The Curse of Amen-Ra	Victor Rousseau

BREEZY STORIES (US: C. H. Young Publishing Co.)

1921	Jun	nt	Crossroads	Victor Rousseau

BREEZY STORIES AND YOUNG'S MAGAZINE (US: C. H. Young Publishing Co.)

1936	May	s	Loyalties	Victor Rousseau
1936	Dec	s	Bridal Eve	Victor Rousseau
1937	May	s	Fire-Escapes	Victor Rousseau

BRIEF STORIES (US: Personal Arts Co., then Novel Magazine Corp.)

1926	May	na	On the Range	Victor Rousseau
1927	Jun	nt	A Strange Bargain	Victor Rousseau
1927	Nov	na	Big Swamp	Victor Rousseau
1929	Dec	s	There Are Pearls in Dargan	Victor Rousseau
1930	Jan	s	Red Diamonds	Victor Rousseau

CANADA WEST MONTHLY (CND: W. E. Gunn Co.)

1911	May	ss	The Cats That Looked at Cohen	H. M. Egbert
1911	Oct	sl	Aviator No. 6	H. M. Egbert
1911	Nov	sl	Aviator No. 6	H. M. Egbert
1911	Dec	sl	Aviator No. 6	H. M. Egbert
1912	Jan	sl	Aviator No. 6	H. M. Egbert
1912	Feb	sl	Aviator No. 6	H. M. Egbert
1912	Mar	sl	Aviator No. 6	H. M. Egbert
1912	Apr	sl	Aviator No. 6	H. M. Egbert
1913	Aug	ss	The Flight of Abdul Hamid	H. M. Egbert

CANADIAN COUNTRYMAN (CND: Canadian Countryman Publishing Co.)

1920	Jan	24	s	A Just Retribution	Victor Rosseau
1921	Xmas		s	A Christmas Interpretation	Victor Rousseau

LA CANADIENNE (CND: Continental Publishing Co; printed in French)

1920	Jul	ss	Chapelle Ardente	Victor Rousseau
1920	Aug	ss	Le Roman de Fanchette	Victor Rousseau
1921	Jan	ss	Comment S'accomplit un Miracle	Victor Rousseau

CARTOONS MAGAZINE AND WAYSIDE TALES (US: H. H. Windsor)

1921	Jul	sl	The Fifth Guardian	Victor Rousseau

—continues in *Wayside Tales and Cartoons Magazine*

CASSELL'S MAGAZINE OF FICTION (UK: Cassell & Co.)

Isabel Marston, Star Reporter (Series: Sep 1912 through Feb 1913; never in the USA)

1912	Sep	ss	The Kidnapped Cabinet Minister	H. M. Egbert
1912	Oct	ss	For the Honor of the Crown	H. M. Egbert
1912	Nov	ss	The Man on the Heath	H. M. Egbert
1912	Dec	ss	An Error of Longitude	H. M. Egbert
1913	Jan	ss	A Servant of His King	H. M. Egbert
1913	Feb	ss	Her Last 'Story'	H. M. Egbert

A King's Courier (Series: Oct 1913 through March 1914)

(for the first six in the UK, see *The New Magazine*)

NOTE: The Oct issue should be "The Amir's Move;" the missing Nov title should be "The Dinner at the White House," but it remains unconfirmed

1913	Oct	ss	A King's Courier	H. M. Egbert
1913	Nov	ss		H. M. Egbert
1913	Dec	ss	The Left-Hand Wife	H. M. Egbert
1914	Jan	ss	The Kidnaped King	H. M. Egbert
1914	Feb	ss	The Tsar's Drive	H. M. Egbert
1914	Mar	ss	My Last Case	H. M. Egbert

CAVALIER, THE (US: Frank A. Munsey Co.)

1913	Nov	15	s	The Seal Maiden	Victor Rousseau

CENTURY MAGAZINE (US: The Century Company)

1909	Jun	s	Cakes of Judgment	Victor Rousseau

CHICAGO LEDGER (US: W. D. Boyce Co.)

1915	Apr	10	sl	Aaron Lapwing's Genius	Leonard Britten
1915	Apr	17	sl	Aaron Lapwing's Genius	Leonard Britten
1915	Apr	24	sl	Aaron Lapwing's Genius	Leonard Britten
1915	May	1	sl	Aaron Lapwing's Genius	Leonard Britten
1915	May	8	sl	Aaron Lapwing's Genius	Leonard Britten
1915	May	15	sl	Aaron Lapwing's Genius	Leonard Britten
1915	May	22	sl	Aaron Lapwing's Genius	Leonard Britten
1918	Aug	3	s	The Dead Hand	Victor Rosseau

Note: The Bride of Golden Mountain (length of serial unknown)

1918	Nov	2	sl	The Bride of Golden Mountain	Victor Rousseau
1918	Nov	9	sl	The Bride of Golden Mountain	Victor Rousseau
1918	Nov	16	sl	The Bride of Golden Mountain	Victor Rousseau

Note: Demons of the Sea (length of serial unknown)

1918	Nov	16	sl	Demons of the Sea	H. M. Egbert
1918	Nov	23	sl	Demons of the Sea	H. M. Egbert
1918	Nov	30	sl	Demons of the Sea	H. M. Egbert
1919	Nov	29	sl	Under the Striped Man's Flag	H. M. Egbert

1919	Dec	6	sl	Under the Striped Man's Flag	H. M. Egbert
1919	Dec	13	sl	Under the Striped Man's Flag	H. M. Egbert
1919	Dec	20	sl	Under the Striped Man's Flag	H. M. Egbert
1919	Dec	27	sl	Under the Striped Man's Flag	H. M. Egbert
1920	Jan	24	sl	The Beast Maker	H. M. Egbert
1920	Jan	31	sl	The Beast Maker	H. M. Egbert
1920	Feb	7	sl	The Beast Maker	H. M. Egbert
1920	Feb	14	sl	The Beast Maker	H. M. Egbert
1920	May	22	sl	The Cain Ship	H. M. Egbert
1920	May	29	sl	The Cain Ship	H. M. Egbert
1920	Jun	5	sl	The Cain Ship	H. M. Egbert
1920	Jun	5	sl	The Valley of Sleeping Slaves	Victor Rousseau
1920	Jun	12	sl	The Valley of Sleeping Slaves	Victor Rousseau
1920	Jun	19	sl	The Valley of Sleeping Slaves	Victor Rousseau
1920	Jun	26	sl	The Valley of Sleeping Slaves	Victor Rousseau
1921	Oct	22	sl	The White Lily Murder	H. M. Egbert
1921	Oct	29	sl	The White Lily Murder	H. M. Egbert
1921	Nov	5	sl	The White Lily Murder	H. M. Egbert
1921	Nov	12	sl	The White Lily Murder	H. M. Egbert
1921	Nov	19	sl	The White Lily Murder	H. M. Egbert
1921	Nov	26	sl	The White Lily Murder	H. M. Egbert
1921	Dec	3	sl	The White Lily Murder	H. M. Egbert
1921	Dec	10	sl	The White Lily Murder	H. M. Egbert
1921	Dec	17	sl	The White Lily Murder	H. M. Egbert
1921	Dec	24	sl	The White Lily Murder	H. M. Egbert

The Cloud Pirates (Series: 8 Jul through 29 Jul 1922)

1922	Jul	8	ss	The Cloud Pirates	H. M. Egbert
1922	Jul	15	ss	Contraband and Whiskers	H. M. Egbert
1922	Jul	22	ss	Treasure of Cos	H. M. Egbert
1922	Jul	29	ss	The Rubber Eagles	H. M. Egbert
1922	Aug	5	sl	Wooden Spoil	H. M. Egbert
1922	Aug	12	sl	Wooden Spoil	H. M. Egbert
1922	Aug	19	sl	Wooden Spoil	H. M. Egbert
1922	Aug	26	sl	Wooden Spoil	H. M. Egbert
1922	Sep	2	sl	Wooden Spoil	H. M. Egbert
1922	Sep	9	sl	Wooden Spoil	H. M. Egbert
1922	Sep	16	sl	Wooden Spoil	H. M. Egbert
1922	Sep	23	sl	Wooden Spoil	H. M. Egbert
1922	Sep	30	sl	Wooden Spoil	H. M. Egbert
1922	Oct	7	sl	Wooden Spoil	H. M. Egbert
1922	Oct	14	sl	Wooden Spoil	H. M. Egbert
1922	Oct	21	sl	Wooden Spoil	H. M. Egbert

CLUES (US: Clayton Magazines)

1927	Mar		tc	The Murder in the Rue Mazarin	H. M. Egbert
1927	May		tc	The Last of the Bushrangers	H. M. Egbert
1929	Jun	1st	tc	Church Warden Murderer	H. M. Egbert

COMPLETE ADVENTURE NOVELETTES (US: Clayton Magazines)

1932	Feb		nt	East of Suez	Victor Rousseau
1932	Nov		nt	Legion of the Dead	Victor Rousseau
1933	Feb		nt	Eyes of the East	Victor Rousseau

COMPLETE MYSTERY NOVELETTES (US: Clayton Magazines)

1932	Oct		tc	The Last of the Bushrangers	H. M. Egbert
1932	Oct		tc	The Murder in the Rue Mazarin	H. M. Egbert

COMPLETE STORIES (US: Street & Smith Corp.)
1928	Mar		na	The Dark Disk	Victor Rousseau

THE CORNER (UK: Cassell & Co.)
Note: Under the Black Flag (serial length unconfirmed, but likely in five parts)
1927	Jan		sl	Under the Black Flag: Hoisting the Black Flag	H. M. Egbert
1927	Feb		sl		
1927	Mar		sl	Under the Black Flag: The Vengeance of Nicolai	H. M. Egbert
1927	Apr		sl		
1927	May		sl		

COWBOY STORY MAGAZINE (UK: Anchor Press)
1927	Feb		nt	Trailin' Back	Victor Rousseau

DANGER TRAIL, THE (US: Clayton Magazines)
1927	Feb		nt	The Scourge of the Mohilla	Victor Rousseau
1927	Aug		na	The Island of Doom	Victor Rousseau
1927	Oct		na	Thorne, the Throne-Maker	Victor Rousseau
1928	Apr		nt	Pawns of Empire	Victor Rousseau
1928	Jul		s	Jungle Loot	Victor Rousseau

DEARBORN INDEPENDENT, THE (US: Dearborn Publishing Company)
1919	Mar	22	s	The Earth-Tides	Victor Rousseau

DELINEATOR, THE (US: Butterick Publishing)
1924	Feb		s	The Wife of Midas	John Austin

DETECTIVE STORY MAGAZINE (US: Street & Smith Corp.)
1919	Feb	11	s	Condemned by Woman	Victor Rousseau

Inside History of Famous Crimes (Series: 29 April through 15 July 1919)
1919	Apr	29	tc	The Shooting of Colonel Fisk [I]	George Munson
1919	May	6	tc	A Helen of New York [II]	George Munson
1919	May	13	tc	The Wife and the Other Man [III]	George Munson
1919	May	20	tc	The Man Who "Killed" a Corpse [IV]	George Munson
1919	May	27	tc	The Body in the Box [V]	George Munson
1919	Jun	3	tc	The Doctor and the Wealthy Patient [VI]	George Munson
1919	Jun	10	tc	The Superfluous Husband [VII]	George Munson
1919	Jun	17	tc	The Case of Mrs. Wharton [VIII]	George Munson
1919	Jun	24	tc	Birchall, the Canadian Murderer [IX]	George Munson
1919	Jul	1	tc	The Murder of Doctor Burdell [X]	George Munson
1919	Jul	8	tc	The Alibi That Failed [XI]	George Munson
1919	Jul	15	tc	The Two Parricides [XII]	George Munson
1919	Sep	23	tc	Detective Anchisi and the Fort Wayne Gang	George Munson

More Inside Histories of Famous Crimes (Series: 21 Oct through 16 Dec 1919)
1919	Oct	21	tc	The Case of Madame Lafarge	George Munson
1919	Oct	28	tc	The Resurrection Men	George Munson
1919	Nov	11	tc	Inspector Denovan and the Paisley Bank Case	George Munson
1919	Nov	25	tc	The Crimes of the Marchioness	George Munson
1919	Dec	2	tc	The Mahratta's Revenge	George Munson
1919	Dec	16	tc	The Murder of Benjamin Nathan	George Munson

EMPIRE FRONTIER (UK: World's Work)
1929	Aug		nt	Diamonds of Doom	Victor Rousseau
1930	Dec		nt	North of Fifty-Three	Victor Rousseau
1930	Dec		ss	Treasure of the Moon	John Austin

EVERYBODY'S MAGAZINE (US: Ridgway Co.)

1917	Jun	sl	The Messiah of the Cylinder	Victor Rousseau
1917	Jul	sl	The Messiah of the Cylinder	Victor Rousseau
1917	Aug	sl	The Messiah of the Cylinder	Victor Rousseau
1917	Sep	sl	The Messiah of the Cylinder	Victor Rousseau

EVERYWOMAN'S WORLD (CND: Continental Publishing Co.)

| 1920 | Apr | ss | The Wooing of Fanchette | Victor Rousseau |
| 1923 | Oct | s | New York Takes the Count | Victor Rousseau |

EXTENSION MAGAZINE (US: Catholic Church Extension Society)

| 1918 | Jun | ss | Pierre and Paul | Victor Rousseau |
| 1919 | Aug | ss | The Eyes of Pere Sebastian | Victor Rousseau |

FAMOUS CRIME CASES (CND: Duchess Printing and Publishing)

Inside History of Famous Crimes (Series: Titles unconfirmed, should parallel *S&S's DSM*)

1946	Feb	tc		
1946	Mar	tc		
1946	Apr	tc	The Man Who Killed a Corpse	George Munson
1946	May	tc	The Body in the Box	George Munson
1946	Jun	tc	Doctor and the Wealthy Patient	George Munson
1946	Jul	tc	The Superfluous Husband	George Munson
1946	Aug	tc	Case of Mrs. Wharton	George Munson
1946	Sep	tc		
1946	Oct	tc	The Murder of Doctor Burdell	George Munson
1946	Nov	tc		
1946	Dec	tc		
1947	Jan	tc		

FANTASTIC NOVELS (US: New Publications [Popular Publications])

| 1949 | May | nt | The Eye of Balamok (condensed edition) | Victor Rousseau |

FANTASTIC NOVELS (UK: Pemberton's)

| 1950 | Dec | nt | The Eye of Balamok (condensed edition) | Victor Rousseau |

FARMER'S MAGAZINE (CND: Consolidated)

Note: Storm Over Athabasca (conclusion of serial not established)

1940	Aug	sl	Storm Over Athabasca	Victor Rousseau
1940	Sep	sl	Storm Over Athabasca	Victor Rousseau
1940	Oct	sl	Storm Over Athabasca	Victor Rousseau
1940	Nov	sl	Storm Over Athabasca	Victor Rousseau

FIGHTING WESTERN (US: Trojan Publishing)

1945	Aug	s	Pony Express	Lew Merrill
1946	Jun	s	By Name of Brown	Lew Merrill
		s	Mud In Your Eye!	Victor Rousseau
1946	Oct	s	Buffalo Trail	Victor Rousseau
1948	Oct	s	Dead Men's Cave	Victor Rousseau
1949	Aug	s	Ruckus at Red River	Lew Merrill
1950	Jul	s	Slo Pay	Lew Merrill

FIVE-NOVELS MONTHLY (US: Eff-Enn Publishing Corp. [Clayton Magazines])

1928	Mar	nt	Broken Men	Victor Rousseau
1928	May	nt	Treasure Ranch	John Austin
1928	Jul	nt	Legion of the Dead	Victor Rousseau
1928	Aug	nt	One-Girl Ranch	John Austin

1928	Sep		nt	Red Harvest	Victor Rousseau
1928	Oct		nt	Crawford of the Border	Victor Rousseau
1929	May		nt	Eyes of the East	Victor Rousseau
1930	Feb		nt	Indian Dawn	Victor Rousseau
1930	Jun		nt	The Circle of Happiness	Victor Rousseau
1931	Jan		nt	Undertow	Victor Rousseau
1931	Jul		nt	Webs of Sand	Victor Rousseau
1931	Nov		nt	Jewels of Empire	Victor Rousseau
1932	Jan		nt	Holocaust	John Austin
1932	Apr		nt	Thrones of Dust	Victor Rousseau
1934	Feb		nt	Swords for Navarre	Victor Rousseau
1934	Apr		nt	Murder Down East	John Austin
1934	May		nt	The Forbidden Shrine	Victor Rousseau
1934	Dec		nt	Captive's Castle	Victor Rousseau
1935	Apr		nt	With Swords Unsheathed	Victor Rousseau
1936	Nov		nt	Tyrants Die By the Sword	Victor Rousseau
1937	Apr		nt	The Spider's Web	Victor Rousseau
1937	Sep		nt	[The] Walls of the Alcazar	C. Cordier
1938	Jan		nt	Sword Play at Dawn!	Victor Rousseau
1938	Feb		nt	To Carve a New World	Victor Rousseau
1938	Aug		nt	Challenge to Napoleon	Victor Rousseau
1938	Nov		nt	Men of Empire	Victor Rousseau
1938	Dec		nt	The Jeweled Throne	Victor Rousseau

FLYNN'S WEEKLY (US: The Red Star News Co. [Frank A. Munsey Co.])

| 1926 | Sep | 18 | tc | The Persecuted Rector | H. M. Egbert |

FRONTIER STORIES (US: Doubleday, Page & Co. to July 1928; Doubleday, Doran & Co.)

1927	Sep		nt	Thorns and Iron	Victor Rousseau
1928	Sep		nt	The Mesquite Trail	Victor Rousseau
1929	Feb		nt	Diamonds of Doom	Victor Rousseau
1929	Jul		nt	Hell's Station	Victor Rousseau
1929	Nov		nt	Hawk of the Himalayas	Victor Rousseau
1930	Apr		nt	Trail of Wanted Men	Victor Rousseau
1930	May		nt	The King Spy	Victor Rousseau

FUTURE FICTION (US: Columbia Publications)

| 1941 | Aug | | s | The Stone Men of Ignota | Victor Rousseau |

GHOST STORIES (US: Constructive [Jun 26—Mar 30]; Good Story Magazine [Apr 30—Dec 31])
  NOTE: Oct '26, Jan '27, Mar '27, Jun '27, and Dec '27—May '28 all have Dr. Martinus

1926	Oct		ss	Child or Demon—Which?	Victor Rousseau
1927	Jan		ss	The Doll That Came to Life	Victor Rousseau
1927	Mar		ss	The Ghost of the Red Cavalier	Victor Rousseau
1927	May		s	He Told Me He Married a Ghost!	Victor Rousseau
1927	Jun		ss	Fire—Water—and What?	Victor Rousseau
1927	Jul		s	The Phantom in the Wooden Well	Victor Rousseau
1927	Aug		ss	The Soul That Lost Its Way	Victor Rousseau
1927	Dec		sl	The House of the Living Dead	Victor Rousseau
1928	Jan		sl	The House of the Living Dead	Victor Rousseau
1928	Feb		sl	The House of the Living Dead	Victor Rousseau
1928	Mar		sl	The House of the Living Dead	Victor Rousseau
1928	Apr		sl	The House of the Living Dead	Victor Rousseau
1928	May		sl	The House of the Living Dead	Victor Rousseau
1928	Jun		s	Our Astral Honeymoon	Victor Rousseau
1928	Jul		s	The Blackest Magic of All	Victor Rousseau

1928	Aug		sl	The Prisoner of Life	Victor Rousseau
1928	Sep		sl	The Prisoner of Life	Victor Rousseau
1928	Oct		sl	The Prisoner of Life	Victor Rousseau
1928	Nov		sl	The Prisoner of Life	Victor Rousseau
1928	Dec		sl	The Prisoner of Life	Victor Rousseau
1929	Jan		sl	The Prisoner of Life	Victor Rousseau
1929	Jul		s	The Angel of the Marne	Victor Rousseau
1929	Sep		s	Phantom Lips	Victor Rousseau
1930	Dec		sl	The Evil Three	Victor Rousseau
1931	Jan		sl	The Evil Three	Victor Rousseau
1931	Feb		sl	The Evil Three	Victor Rousseau
1931	Mar		sl	The Evil Three	Victor Rousseau
1931	Apr		sl	The Evil Three	Victor Rousseau

GOLDEN FLEECE (US: Sun Publications)

1939	Apr		na	The Queen's Mercy	Victor Rousseau

HARPER'S MONTHLY MAGAZINE (US: Harper & Bros.)

1912	Oct		s	Hearts Astray	Victor Rousseau
1913	Jun		s	Slim Uncle Piet	Victor Rousseau
1914	Mar		s	The Blue Dimity Dress	Victor Rousseau
1914	Oct		s	Cousin Paul	Victor Rousseau

HARPER'S WEEKLY (US: Harper & Bros.)

1908	Jan	4	s	Picked Off	Victor Rousseau
1909	Apr	3	s	The Kings of No Man's Land	Victor Rousseau
1909	Apr	24	s	The Upper Window	Victor Rousseau
1909	Jul	24	s	Their Honors the Aldermen	Victor Rousseau
1909	Aug	7	s	A Deal in Elephant	Victor Rousseau
1910	Feb	5	s	The Palm-Bringer	Victor Rousseau
1910	Jul	2	s	The Gallows-Bird	Victor Rousseau
1910	Oct	1	s	The Red Cross Train	Victor Rousseau
1910	Dec	10	s	The Keeper of the Light	Victor Rousseau
1911	Mar	18	s	The Man in the Bottle	Victor Rousseau
1911	May	27	s	The Secret Altar	Victor Rousseau
1911	Jul	8	s	The Virgin of Okiak	Victor Rousseau
1911	Oct	28	s	The Man Who Went Back	Victor Rousseau
1912	Feb	17	s	The Garden of Illusion	Victor Rousseau
1912	Apr	13	s	The Great Experiment	Victor Rousseau
1912	Jul	8	s	The Fangs of the Mill	Victor Rousseau
1912	Aug	31	s	The Isle of Enchantment	Victor Rousseau
1912	Nov	23	s	The King's Proctor	Victor Rousseau

HEARTH & HOME (US: P. O. Vickery)

1928	Apr		s	The Square Peg	Victor Rousseau

HIGH ADVENTURE (US: Adventure House)

2005	Jan	# 80	nt	Dwindling Death	Lew Merrill
2006	Jul	# 89	nt	Madame Murder	John Grange

HOLLAND'S MAGAZINE (US: Texas Farm and Ranch Pub. Co.)
   The Tracer of Egos (Series: Jun 1913 through Feb 1914; ran 9 of 12 out of sequence)

1913	Jun		ss	The Amulet of Marduk	Victor Rousseau
1913	Jul		ss	Mary Rothway's Memory	Victor Rousseau
1913	Aug		ss	Alf Barton's Princess	Victor Rousseau
1913	Sep		ss	The Two Charioteers	Victor Rousseau

1913	Oct	ss	The Professor's Peach Trees	Victor Rousseau
1913	Nov	ss	The Carfax Curse	Victor Rousseau
1913	Dec	ss	Mr. Axel's Shady Past	Victor Rousseau
1914	Jan	ss	The Woman of Atlantis	Victor Rousseau
1914	Feb	ss	Noureddin Bey's Sacrifice	Victor Rousseau

HOLLYWOOD DETECTIVE (US: Trojan Publishing)

1944	Dec	s	Sailing—Midnight	Lew Merrill
1945	May	s	Unwritten Law	Lew Merrill
1945	Aug	s	War Time	Lew Merrill

HOME LIFE (US: Balch Publishing Co.)

| 1910 | Oct | vi | The Prince's Ring | H. M. Egbert |

HOUSEHOLD GUEST, THE (US: Household Guest)

| 1917 | Sep | s | The Wolf Trap | H. M. Egbert |
| 1917 | Oct | s | Pride of Place | Victor Rousseau |

HUTCHINSON'S ADVENTURE-STORY MAGAZINE (UK: Hutchinson's)

| 1927 | Jan | ss | Child or Demon—Which? | Eugene Branscombe |

HUTCHINSON'S MYSTERY-STORY MAGAZINE (UK: Hutchinson's)

1927	May	ss	The Ghost of the Red Cavalier	Eugene Branscombe
1927	Jul	ss	The Doll That Came to Life	Victor Rousseau
1927	Aug	ss	The Phantom in the Wooden Well	Victor Rousseau

JUNGLE STORIES (US: Glen-Kel Pub.)

| 1939 | Fall | s | The Black Gods of Ngami | Victor Rousseau |

KEYHOLE DETECTIVE CASES (CND: Duchess Printing and Publishing)
—becomes *20th Century Crime Cases*
   (Series: World-Famous Police Mysteries, 11 parts)

| 1946 | Feb | tc | The Murder in the Rue Mazarin | H. M. Egbert |
| 1946 | Mar | tc | The Resurrection Men | H. M. Egbert |

LARIAT STORY MAGAZINE (US: Real Adventures Pub. Co.)

| 1926 | Jul | nt | Trailin' Back | Victor Rousseau |

LEADING WESTERN (US: Trojan Publishing)

1946	Aug	nt	Kit Carson, Renegade	Victor Rousseau
1946	Nov	s	Cave of Ghosts	Victor Rousseau
1947	Aug	s	Gun Round-up	Victor Rousseau
1947	Nov	s	Trouble Wrangler	Lew Merrill

MacLEAN'S MAGAZINE (CND: MacLean Publishing Co.)

| 1911 | Aug | s | The Girl at Three Mile Fork | H. M. Egbert |

MAGAZINE OF HORROR (US: Health Knowledge)

1967	Fall	nt	The Curse of Amen-Ra	Victor Rousseau
1968	Mar	nt	A Cry from Beyond	Victor Rousseau
1969	Jan	nt	When Dead Gods Wake	Victor Rousseau

MASTER THRILLER SERIES (UK: World's Work)

| 1934 | # 7 | s | Thorns and Iron | Victor Rousseau |

MIRACLE SCIENCE AND FANTASY STORIES (US: Good Story Publishing Co.)

1931	Apr-May	nt	Outlaws of the Sun	Victor Rousseau
1931	Jun-Jul	nt	Revolt on Inferno	Victor Rousseau

McCLURE'S MAGAZINE (US: McClure Co.)

1923	May	s	The Square Peg	Victor Rousseau

MON MAGAZINE POLICIER (CND: Montreal)

1941	Jan	V1#1 s	La Main du Cadavre	Victor Rousseau

MORRISON'S CHICAGO WEEKLY (US: Morrison Publishing Co.)

1910	Nov	24	s	His People's Covenant	Victor Rousseau

A King's Courier (Series: 17 Nov 1910 through 9 Feb 1911) (First regional syndication)

1910	Nov	17	ss	Kitachi's Torpedoes	H. M. Egbert
1910	Nov	24	ss	His Majesty's Barber	H. M. Egbert
1910	Dec	1	ss	His Majesty's Counterpart	H. M. Egbert
1910	Dec	8	ss	The Fisherman and the Fleet	H. M. Egbert
1910	Dec	15	ss	An Episode at the Whitehouse	H. M. Egbert
1910	Dec	22	ss	The Left-Hand Wife	H. M. Egbert
1911	Jan	5	ss	The Amir's Move	H. M. Egbert
1911	Jan	12	ss	The Race in Mid-Air	H. M. Egbert
1911	Jan	19	ss	Why Russia Backed Down	H. M. Egbert
1911	Jan	26	ss	A Treaty With Spain	H. M. Egbert
1911	Feb	2	ss	The River Rats	H. M. Egbert
1911	Feb	9	ss	The Ingratitude of Kings	H. M. Egbert

MUNSEY, THE (US: Frank A. Munsey Co.)

1907	Sep	vi	The Last Cartridge	Victor Rousseau

MUNSEY'S MAGAZINE (US: Frank A. Munsey Co.)

1916	Jul	na	Midsummer Madness	Victor Rousseau

MUSCLE BUILDER (US: Physical Culture Pub. Co.)

1924	Oct	sl	The Making of a Man	Victor Emanuel
1924	Nov	sl	The Making of a Man	Victor Emanuel
1924	Dec	sl	The Making of a Man	Victor Emanuel
1925	Jan	sl	The Making of a Man	Victor Emanuel
1925	Feb	sl	The Making of a Man	Victor Emanuel
1925	Jul	sl	Steeled by Struggle	Victor Rousseau
1925	Aug	sl	Steeled by Struggle	Victor Rousseau
1925	Sep	sl	Steeled by Struggle	Victor Rousseau
1925	Oct	sl	Steeled by Struggle	Victor Rousseau
1925	Nov	sl	Steeled by Struggle	Victor Rousseau
1925	Dec	sl	From Crook to Hero	Victor Rousseau
1926	Jan	sl	From Crook to Hero	Victor Rousseau
1926	Feb	sl	From Crook to Hero	Victor Rousseau
1926	Mar	sl	From Crook to Hero	Victor Rousseau
1926	Apr	sl	From Crook to Hero	Victor Rousseau

NAVY STORIES (US: Dell Publishing Co.)

1929	May	nt	Manchu Guns	Victor Rousseau

NEMESIS INCORPORATED (US: Frank Lewandowski)

1984	# 17	nt	The Horrible Marionettes	John Grange
1984	# 18	nt	The Horrible Marionettes	John Grange
1985	# 19	nt	The Horrible Marionettes	John Grange

NEW MAGAZINE, THE (UK: Cassell & Co.)
　　A King's Courier (Series: Jun 1910 through Nov 1910)
　　(continues in *Cassell's Magazine of Fiction*)

1910	Jun	ss	The Peril of Magellan Strait	H. M. Egbert
1910	Jul	ss	The Toilet That Saved France	H. M. Egbert
1910	Aug	ss	The Affair of the North Sea	H. M. Egbert
1910	Sep	ss	The Emperor's Double	H. M. Egbert
1910	Oct	ss	The Spanish Treaty	H. M. Egbert
1910	Nov	ss	The River Rats	H. M. Egbert

NORTH-WEST ROMANCES (US: Fiction House)
—formerly *North-West Stories*

1937	Fall	nt	The Man-Master	Victor Rousseau
1937	Winter	s	Blood on the Snow	Victor Rousseau
1938	Spring	nt	Man Hunt for the Mounted	Victor Rousseau
1938	Summer	nt	Valley of Gold	Victor Rousseau
1938	Fall	s	Derelict of the Arctic Sea	Victor Rousseau
1941	Fall	nt	Frozen Hell	Victor Rousseau
1943	Winter	nt	The Red-Coat Rebel	Victor Rousseau
1951	Spring	nt	Frozen Hell	Victor Rousseau

NORTH-WEST STORIES (US: Fiction House)
—formerly *Novelets*; becomes *North-West Romances*

1926	Mar	2nd	s	The Snow Trail	Victor Rousseau
1926	Sep	1st	s	Arctic Treasure	Victor Rousseau
1926	Oct	2nd	nt	Get Your Man!	Victor Rousseau
1927	Jan	1st	nt	Lost Men's Eden	Victor Rousseau
1927	Aug	1st	nt	Evened Scores	Victor Rousseau
1927	Aug	2nd	nt	Enter—the Mounted!	Victor Rousseau
1928	Jul	2nd	nt	Red Coat Patrol	Victor Rousseau
1929	Mar		nt	Nothing North of Nagatok	Victor Rousseau
1930	Jan		nt	Loot of the Wolf	Victor Rousseau
1936	Winter		nt	Captives of the Arctic Wasteland	Victor Rousseau

NORTH-WEST STORIES (UK: Atlas Publishing)

1927	Mar	Early	s	Arctic Treasure	Victor Rousseau
1927	Apr	Late	nt	Get Your Man!	Victor Rousseau
1927	Jul	Early	nt	Lost Men's Eden	Victor Rousseau

NOVELETS (US: Fiction House)
—formerly *Illustrated Novelets*; becomes *North-West Stories*

1925	Apr	nt	Yellow Gold Trails	Victor Rousseau

NOVEL MAGAZINE, THE (UK: C. A. Pearson)

1911	Nov	s	The Gallows-Bird	Victor Rousseau
1912	Aug	s	Fangs of the Mill	Victor Rousseau
1913	Apr	s	The Return of Bill (rw)	H. M. Egbert
1920	Mar	s	Tag For a Crown	Victor Rousseau

PALL MALL MAGAZINE (UK: George Rutledge & Sons)

1911	Nov	s	The Palm-Bringer	Victor Rousseau
1912	Aug	s	The Hidden Bride	Victor Rousseau

PEOPLE'S (US: Street & Smith Corp.)
1923	Aug	15	sl	Sergeant Forbes, Alias—	Victor Rousseau
1923	Sep	1	sl	Sergeant Forbes, Alias—	Victor Rousseau
1923	Sep	15	sl	Sergeant Forbes, Alias	Victor Rousseau
1923	Oct	1	sl	Sergeant Forbes, Alias—	Victor Rousseau

PEOPLE'S (IDEAL FICTION) MAGAZINE (US: Street & Smith Corp.)
| 1911 | Jul | | s | Proving Poe | H. M. Egbert |

PEOPLE'S POPULAR MONTHLY (US: The People's Monthly Co.)
1912	Mar		sl	The Adventures of Anne Ives, Mascot	H. M. Egbert
1912	Apr		sl	The Adventures of Anne Ives, Mascot	H. M. Egbert
1912	May		sl	The Adventures of Anne Ives, Mascot	H. M. Egbert
1912	Jun		sl	The Adventures of Anne Ives, Mascot	H. M. Egbert
1912	Jul		sl	The Adventures of Anne Ives, Mascot	H. M. Egbert
1912	Aug		sl	The Adventures of Anne Ives, Mascot	H. M. Egbert
1912	Sep		sl	The Adventures of Anne Ives, Mascot	H. M. Egbert
1912	Oct		sl	The Adventures of Anne Ives, Mascot	H. M. Egbert
1912	Nov		sl	The Adventures of Anne Ives, Mascot	H. M. Egbert
1912	Dec		sl	The Adventures of Anne Ives, Mascot	H. M. Egbert
1923	Jan		sl	Lee of the Northwest Mounted	Victor Rousseau
1923	Feb		sl	Lee of the Northwest Mounted	Victor Rousseau
1923	Mar		sl	Lee of the Northwest Mounted	Victor Rousseau
1923	Apr		sl	Lee of the Northwest Mounted	Victor Rousseau
1923	May		sl	Lee of the Northwest Mounted	Victor Rousseau
1923	Jun		sl	Lee of the Northwest Mounted	Victor Rousseau
1923	Jul		sl	Lee of the Northwest Mounted	Victor Rousseau
1923	Aug		sl	Lee of the Northwest Mounted	Victor Rousseau

PEOPLE'S STORY MAGAZINE (US: Street & Smith Corp.)
1922	Aug	25	sl	The Home Trail	Victor Rousseau
1922	Sep	10	sl	The Home Trail	Victor Rousseau
1922	Sep	25	sl	The Home Trail	Victor Rousseau
1922	Oct	10	sl	The Home Trail	Victor Rousseau
1922	Oct	25	sl	The Home Trail	Victor Rousseau

PHOTOPLAY MAGAZINE (US: Photoplay Pub. Co.)
   Peggy Roche, Saleslady (Series: Mar 1917 through Jul 1917)
1917	Mar		ss	The Adventure of the Three Georges	Victor Rousseau
1917	Apr		ss	The Adventure of the Town Pond Submarine	Victor Rousseau
1917	May		ss	Torpedo Broker	Victor Rousseau
1917	Jun		ss	The Road to Biskra	Victor Rousseau
1917	Jul		ss	The Jungle Knights	Victor Rousseau

PHYSICAL CULTURE (US: Physical Culture Pub. Co.)
1925	Mar		sl	The Awakening of Edith	Victor Rousseau
1925	Apr		sl	The Awakening of Edith	Victor Rousseau
1925	May		sl	The Awakening of Edith	Victor Rousseau
1925	Jun		sl	The Awakening of Edith	Victor Rousseau
1925	Jul		sl	The Awakening of Edith	Victor Rousseau
1926	Jan		sl	The Right to Motherhood	Victoria Ross
1926	Feb		sl	The Right to Motherhood	Victoria Ross
1926	Mar		sl	The Right to Motherhood	Victoria Ross
1926	Apr		sl	The Right to Motherhood	Victoria Ross
1926	May		sl	The Right to Motherhood	Victoria Ross
1926	Nov		sl	Hearts and Diamonds	Victor Emmanuel

1926	Dec		sl	Hearts and Diamonds	Victor Emmanuel
1927	Jan		sl	Hearts and Diamonds	Victor Emmanuel
1932	Apr		sl	Good Night, Eve	Victor Rousseau
1932	May		sl	Good Night, Eve	Victor Rousseau
1932	Jun		sl	Good Night, Eve	Victor Rousseau
1932	Jul		sl	Good Night, Eve	Victor Rousseau
1932	Aug		sl	Good Night, Eve	Victor Rousseau

POLICE MAGAZINE (US: Police Publishing Co.)

| 1925 | Jun | | s | The Dead Hand | Victor Rousseau |

POPULAR MAGAZINE, THE (US: Street & Smith Corp.)

Revelations of an Ambassador at Large (Series: 7 Jan 1915 through 7 Mar 1915)

1915	Jan	7	ss	The Bulgarian Papers	H. M. Egbert
1915	Jan	23	ss	The Bullet-Proof Mantle	H. M. Egbert
1915	Feb	7	ss	The Wax Clavette	H. M. Egbert
1915	Feb	23	ss	The Red Envelope	H. M. Egbert
1915	Mar	7	ss	Kitchener's Coup	H. M. Egbert
1916	Feb		ss	Larry of the Yards	Victor Rousseau

PRIVATE DETECTIVE STORIES (US: Trojan Publishing)

1944	Apr		s	The Seeing Eye	Lew Merrill
1944	May		s	Curse of the Tremaines	Hugh Speer
1944	Nov		s	Brain-Buster	Lew Merrill
1944	Dec		s	The Tell-Tale Arm	Lew Merrill
1945	Jan		s	Planted Fingerprints	Lew Merrill
1945	Apr		s	Feathers	Clive Trent
			s	Home-Town Soldier	Lew Merrill
1945	Jun		s	Button, Button	Lew Merrill
1945	Aug		s	Postponed Verdict	Lew Merrill
1945	Sep		s	Fungus and Arsenic	Victor Rousseau
			s	Proxy Murder	Lew Merrill
1946	Feb		s	Nailed	Lew Merrill
1946	Mar		s	Rye and Die	Lew Merrill
1946	Nov		s	Terror By Night	Lew Merrill

PRIVATE DETECTIVE STORIES (US: Pulp Tales Press)

| 2007 | Sep | # 2 | nt | I. O. U. Murder | John Grange |

PRIZE GHOST STORIES (US: League Publications)

| 1963 | Spring | | ss | Monkey-Face and Mrs. Thorpe (abridged and revised) | Uncredited |

PULP REVIEW (US: The Pulp Collector Press)

1992	Jan	# 2	nt	The Mark of the Spider	John Grange
1992	July	# 5	s	Bat Man	Lew Merrill
1995	July	# 22	s	The Time Dissolver	Hugh Speer
2008		# 2	nt	The Mark of the Spider	John Grange
2008		# 5	s	Bat Man	Lew Merrill

RAILROAD MAN'S MAGAZINE (US: Frank A. Munsey Co.)

1918	Nov	16	sl	Eric of the Strong Heart	Victor Rousseau
1918	Nov	23	sl	Eric of the Strong Heart	Victor Rousseau
1918	Nov	30	sl	Eric of the Strong Heart	Victor Rousseau
1918	Dec	7	sl	Eric of the Strong Heart	Victor Rousseau
1918	Dec	14	sl	Eric of the Strong Heart	Victor Rousseau

RAILROAD TRAINMAN, THE (US: The Brotherhood of Railroad Trainmen)

1918	Jun	s	Larry of the Yards	Victor Rousseau
1919	Jan	ss	Pierre and Paul	Victor Rousseau
1935	Aug	s	The Silent Partner	Victor Rousseau

RAILWAY CONDUCTOR, THE (US: Order of Railway Conductors)

1918	Jul	ss	The Scar	H. M. Egbert

RANCH ROMANCES (US: Western Stories Pub. Co. [Clayton] to 1933; Warner Pub. 1933 onward)

1925	May		nt	Prince of the Plains	Victor Rousseau
1925	Sep		nt	West of Rainbow's End	Victor Rousseau
1925	Nov		sl	Jim Blair's Girl	John Austin
1925	Dec		sl	Jim Blair's Girl	John Austin
1926	Jan		sl	Jim Blair's Girl	John Austin
1926	Feb		sl	Jim Blair's Girl	John Austin
1926	Mar		sl	Jim Blair's Girl	John Austin
1927	Sep	2nd	nt	The Long Trail	Victor Rousseau
1928	Jan	1st	na	Sunburst Valley	Victor Rousseau
1928	Apr	1st	nt	Sheriff Nan	Victor Rousseau
1928	Aug	1st	na	A Rangeland Renegade	Victor Rousseau
1928	Oct	1st	nt	Riders of the Stars	Victor Rousseau
1928	Dec	2nd	nt	Cowboy Courageous	Victor Rousseau

Note: Romance of the Rio (serial length unconfirmed, likely in 2 or 3 more parts)

1929	Mar	2nd	sl	Romance of the Rio	Victor Rousseau
1929	Apr	1st	sl	Romance of the Rio	Victor Rousseau
1929	Apr	2nd	sl	Romance of the Rio	Victor Rousseau
1930	Jan	2nd	nt	Maid of the Valley	Victor Rousseau
1930	Mar	1st	sl	Tides of Conquest	Victor Rousseau
1930	Mar	2nd	sl	Tides of Conquest	Victor Rousseau
1930	Apr	1st	sl	Tides of Conquest	Victor Rousseau
1930	Apr	2nd	sl	Tides of Conquest	Victor Rousseau
1930	May	1st	sl	Tides of Conquest	Victor Rousseau
1930	May	2nd	sl	Tides of Conquest	Victor Rousseau
1930	Aug	3rd	na	The Steadfast Heart	Victor Rousseau
1930	Nov	2nd	na	The Starlight Trail	Victor Rousseau
1931	Mar	2nd	na	Rangeland Trickery	Victor Rousseau
1931	Jun	2nd	sl	Cactus Trail	Victor Rousseau
1931	Jul	1st	sl	Cactus Trail	Victor Rousseau
1931	Jul	2nd	sl	Cactus Trail	Victor Rousseau
1931	Jul	3rd	sl	Cactus Trail	Victor Rousseau
1931	Aug	1st	sl	Cactus Trail	Victor Rousseau
1931	Aug	2nd	sl	Cactus Trail	Victor Rousseau

Note: Desert Lover (unconfirmed length as a serial, novelette, or novella)

1931	Sep	1st	??	Desert Lover	Victor Rousseau
1931	Dec	2nd	na	Lost Ranch	Victor Rousseau
1932	Jan	2nd	sl	Riders of the Buttes	Victor Rousseau
1932	Jan	3rd	sl	Riders of the Buttes	Victor Rousseau
1932	Feb	1st	sl	Riders of the Buttes	Victor Rousseau
1932	Feb	2nd	sl	Riders of the Buttes	Victor Rousseau
1932	Mar	1st	sl	Riders of the Buttes	Victor Rousseau
1932	Mar	2nd	sl	Riders of the Buttes	Victor Rousseau
1932	Jun	2nd	na	Crooked Trails	Victor Rousseau
1933	Oct	1st	nt	The Wolf Trail (Romance in the Southwest)	Victor Rousseau
1934	Feb	2nd	na	Cross-Trails to Paradise	Victor Rousseau
1934	Jun	2nd	sl	Terror Range	Victor Rousseau
1934	Jun	3rd	sl	Terror Range	Victor Rousseau

1934	Jul	1st	sl	Terror Range	Victor Rousseau
1934	Jul	2nd	sl	Terror Range	Victor Rousseau
1934	Jul	3rd	sl	Terror Range	Victor Rousseau
1934	Aug	1st	sl	Terror Range	Victor Rousseau
1935	May	1st	na	Trail of the Wolf	Victor Rousseau
1935	Dec	3rd	na	Framed	Victor Rousseau
1936	Mar	1st	nt	Doughnuts for Discord	Victor Rousseau
1937	Jan	2nd	nt	Rio Riders	Victor Rousseau
1937	Nov	2nd	nt	Rustlers' Trail	Victor Rousseau
1938	Jul	1st	nt	Night Raiders	Victor Rousseau
1939	Mar	1st	na	Lone Rider	Victor Rousseau
1940	May	2nd	nt	Trickery Trail	Victor Rousseau
1941	May	2nd	na	Feud of the Forest	Victor Rousseau
1942	Jan	2nd	na	Rangeland Fury	Victor Rousseau
1942	Oct	3rd	na	Empire of the Skies	Victor Rousseau

RANGELAND LOVE STORY MAGAZINE (US: Climax, then Clayton Magazines)

1930	Feb	sl	The Range Rider	Victor Rousseau
1930	Mar	sl	The Range Rider	Victor Rousseau
1930	Jul	na	The Chaparral Trail	John Austin
1930	Sep	nt	Midnight Riders	Victor Rousseau
1931	Jun	nt	Love Rides the Sage	Victor Rousseau
1931	Aug	sl	A Man from Montana	Victor Rousseau
1931	Sep	sl	A Man from Montana	Victor Rousseau
1931	Oct	sl	A Man from Montana	Victor Rousseau
1931	Nov	sl	A Man from Montana	Victor Rousseau
1931	Dec	sl	A Man from Montana	Victor Rousseau
1932	Jan	nt	Magic Mountain	Victor Rousseau
1932	May	nt	The Trail of Terror	Victor Rousseau

REAL NORTHWEST ADVENTURES (US: Northwest Pub. Co.)

1937	Mar	nt	The Wolf Trail	Victor Rousseau

RED BLOODED STORIES (US: New Metropolitan Fiction)

1928	Oct	s	Out of the Night	Victor Rousseau
1928	Nov	s	Honor of the Sea	Victor Rousseau
1928	Dec	nt	King of the Cocoa Trail	Victor Rousseau

RED BOOK MAGAZINE, THE (US: The Red Book Corporation)

1914	May	s	Rachel	Victor Rousseau
1914	Oct	s	The Faith of Paul Duchaine	Victor Rousseau
1915	Jan	s	Chapelle Ardente	Victor Rousseau

RED SEAL WESTERN (US: Periodical House)

1936	Dec	nt	Maverick of Mustang Mesa	Victor Rousseau

ROMANTIC WESTERN (US: Trojan Publishing)

1938	Nov	s	Woman in Yellow	Lew Merrill

SAUCY DETECTIVE (US: Movie Digest)

1937	Mar	s	Girl From Spain	Lew Merrill

SAUCY MOVIE TALES (US: Movie Digest)

1937	May	s	Girl of the Mounties	Lew Merrill

SCIENCE FICTION (CND: Duchess Printing and Publishing)
1942	Feb		s	The Stone Men of Ignota	Victor Rousseau
1942	Jun		s	Human Pyramid	Clive Trent

SHORT STORIES (US: Short Stories Co.)
1909	May		s	The Jam God	H. M. Egbert
1911	Feb		s	The Death March	H. M. Egbert
1914	Mar		s	Justice and the Moose Call	Victor Rousseau
1914	Dec		s	The Aerial War	Victor Rousseau
1927	Nov	10	na	The Wolf Trail	Victor Rousseau
1933	Sep	10	s	High Andes	Victor Rousseau
1952	Mar		s	High Andes	Victor Rousseau

SHORT STORIES (UK: World's Work)
1928	Apr	early	na	The Wolf Trail	Victor Rousseau
1934	Jan	mid	s	High Andes	Victor Rousseau

SIX-GUN WESTERN (US: Trojan Publishing)
1946	Mar	s	Taos Trail	Lew Merrill
1946	Aug	s	Saint Unsealed	Victor Rousseau
1946	Dec	nt	The Singing Utes	Victor Rousseau

SKY RIDERS (US: Dell Publishing Co.)
1929	Oct	nt	Dead Man's Valley	Victor Rousseau

SMART SET, THE (US: Ess Ess Publishing Co.)
1909	May	s	Jackson's Wife	Victor Rousseau
1911	June	s	Jean of the Silence	Victor Rousseau

SOLDIERS OF FORTUNE (US: Clayton Magazines)
1931	Oct	s	It Is For France	Victor Rousseau
1931	Dec	na	Bows of Muscovy	Victor Rousseau
1932	May	nt	Red Rose and White	Victor Rousseau

SPEED ADVENTURE STORIES (US: Trojan Publishing / Arrow Publications)
—formerly *Spicy-Adventure Stories*
1943	Jan	s	Four Who Fled	Lew Merrill
		s	King Silver Rides	Hugh Speer
1943	Feb	s	White Girl	Lew Merrill
1943	Mar	s	Four-Footed Justice	Lew Merrill
		s	King Silver's Last Ride	Hugh Speer
		s	Stand Up, Ye Dead	Clive Trent
1943	May	s	Elephant God	Lew Merrill
		s	River of Tears	Clive Trent
1943	Jul	s	City of Doom	Hugh Speer
		s	Fix Bayonets!	Lew Merrill
1943	Sep	s	Bern's Blunder	Hugh Speer
		s	Quisling's Daughter	Lew Merrill
1943	Nov	s	Bulls Have Jaws	Lew Merrill
		s	The Secret Channel	Clive Trent
		s	A Tailor Never Pricks His Finger	Victor Rousseau
1944	Jan	s	Jungle Trap	Clive Trent
		s	Sicilian Night	Lew Merrill
		s	Spoil of the Sea	Hugh Speer

1944	Mar	s	Long Pig	Hugh Speer
		s	Rats Never Learn	Lew Merrill
		s	Salvation M'Shane	Victor Rousseau
1944	May	s	Coconut Cargo	Clive Trent
		s	The Dawn Tide	Lew Merrill
		s	Peace Comes to Bongo	Hugh Speer
1944	Jul	s	Ghost of Empire	Victor Rousseau
		s	Sea-Lubber M'Shane	Clive Trent
1944	Sep	s	Follow the Fish	Clive Trent
		s	Medical Officer	Hugh Speer
		s	Rat-Run	V. R. Emanuel
1944	Nov	s	Chilled Mutton	Lew Merrill
		s	Red Star of India	Victor Rousseau
		s	Secret Weapon	Hugh Speer
1945	Jan	s	The Brides of Coco Island	Clive Trent
		s	Get Your Man!	Lew Merrill
		s	Swords for Florence	Victor Rousseau
1945	Apr	s	Death Patrol	Lew Merrill
		s	For Scotland's Queen	Victor Rousseau
		s	The Madness of M'Shane	Clive Trent
1945	Jul	s	Banzai Charge	Victor Rousseau
1945	Oct	s	Crusoe on Antarctica	Victor Rousseau
		s	The God in the Tomb	Lew Merrill
		s	The Shaving of M'Shane	Clive Trent
1946	Jan	s	Ghost Plane	Hugh Speer
		s	Letters of Marque	Clive Trent
		nt	Bows of Fortune	Lew Merrill

SPEED DETECTIVE (US: Trojan Publishing)
—formerly *Spicy Detective Stories*

1944	May	nt	Death in the Tank	Hugh Speer
1944	Jul	s	Refugee Ship	Lew Merrill
1944	Dec	s	Matched Slugs	Lew Merrill
1945	Dec	s	Frame-Up	Lew Merrill
1946	Feb	s	Goat in the Stable	Lew Merrill
1946	May	s	Sword-Slasher	Lew Merrill
1946	Dec	s	Soul at Strife	Hugh Speer

SPEED MYSTERY (US: Trojan Publishing)
—formerly *Spicy Mystery Stories*

1943	Jan	s	Ghost-Wife	Clive Trent
		s	Sealed In Death	George Freeman Tracy
1943	Feb	nt	Ryder's Lights	Clive Trent
		nt	Steel of Death	Lew Merrill
		nt	The Unknown Factor	Hugh Speer
1943	Mar	s	Too Bad to Kill	Stan Warner
1943	May	s	House of Death	Lew Merrill
		s	The Samurai Sword	Clive Trent
		s	Death Rides High	John Wayne
		s	Blood Taint	William Decatur
1943	Jul	s	Claws of the Statue	Lew Merrill
		s	Time Lag	Hugh Speer
		s	Titanium Ship	Clive Trent
1943	Sep	s	Arc of Death	Clive Trent
		s	Fog Over Kiska	Lew Merrill
		s	Kenney's Stooge	Hugh Speer

1943	Nov	nt	Like a Tiger	Lew Merrill
		nt	Sergeant Joe's Return	Hugh Speer
1944	Jan	s	Among Those Present	Hugh Speer
		s	'Fraid-Cat Hero	Lew Merrill
		s	Lost Fingerprints	Victor Rousseau
		s	The Perfect Crime	Clive Trent
1944	Mar	s	Crossed Wires	Hugh Speer
		s	Dry Death	Clive Trent
		s	The Judas Bottle	Lew Merrill
1944	May	s	Beggar-Ticks	Hugh Speer
		nt	The Flight Magnificent	Clive Trent
		s	Lady Luck	Lew Merrill
1944	Jul	s	Hell's Castle	Lew Merrill
		s	Jailbreak	Hugh Speer
1944	Sep	s	Blood Racket	Hugh Speer
		s	Daniel Webster Said	Lew Merrill
1944	Nov	s	The Stuffed Shirt	Victor Rousseau
		s	This Was Grandison	Lew Merrill
		s	Unborn Terror	Hugh Speer
		s	Wolf Woman	Clive Trent
1945	Jan	s	Heaven's Son-in-Law	Clive Trent
		s	Killer Car	Lew Merrill
1945	Mar	s	Living Dead Man	Hugh Speer
1945	Jun	s	Crazy House	Hugh Speer
		s	Gate of Death	Hugh Speer
		s	Hot Stuff	Lew Merrill

SPEED WESTERN STORIES (US: Trojan Publishing)
—formerly *Spicy Western Stories*

1945	Feb	s	Ranger Bait	Lew Merrill
1945	Jun	s	Blind Luck	Lew Merrill
1945	Jul	s	The Sheriff Wanted Peace	Clive Trent
1945	Oct	s	Trigger-Quick	Lew Merrill
1946	Nov	s	Mr. Bill, Come Back	Lew Merrill
1946	Dec	s	Riders of the Border	Victor Rousseau
1947	Oct	s	Honor for a Harrigan	Lew Merrill

SPICY-ADVENTURE STORIES (US: Trojan Publishing)
—becomes *Speed Adventure Stories*

1935	Nov	s	Code of the Northland	Hugh Speer
		s	Traitress' Wages	Lew Merrill
1935	Dec	s	Devil Drums	Lew Merrill
1936	Jan	s	Angel of Mercy	Lew Merrill
		s	Paradise Island	Hugh Speer
1936	Feb	s	Lady of Fortune	Hugh Speer
1936	Mar	s	Bamboo Flower	Clive Trent
		s	Bride of the Pyramid	Hugh Speer
		s	Savage Spears	Lew Merrill
1936	Apr	s	Bride of the Sword	Lew Merrill
1936	May	s	Puppet Princess	Lew Merrill
1936	Jun	s	The Woman of Cayenne	Hugh Speer
1936	Jul	s	Forest Fury	Lew Merrill
1936	Aug	s	Playthings of War	Hugh Speer
		s	The White Goddess	Lew Merrill

1936	Sep	s	Death in the Desert	Lew Merrill
		s	Death Trail	Clive Trent
		s	Valley of Blood	Lew Merrill
1936	Nov	s	Passion's Puppets	Lew Merrill
		s	Rainbow's End	Hugh Speer
1936	Dec	s	For the Honor of the Duchess	Lew Merrill
1937	Jan	s	Flower Boat	Lew Merrill
1937	Feb	s	Death Treasure	Clive Trent
		s	Skinner	Lew Merrill
1937	Mar	s	Devil Trail	Lew Merrill
		s	Sky Goddess	Clive Trent
1937	Apr	s	Black Gods	Lew Merrill
1937	May	s	Barbary Brew	Lew Merrill
		s	Diamonds of Death	Clive Trent
		s	Road to Tolosa	Hugh Speer
1937	Jun	s	Black Goddess	Hugh Speer
		s	For Love of Scotland's Queen	Clive Trent
		s	The Golden Crocodile	Lew Merrill
1937	Jul	s	Spawn of Siva	Clive Trent
1937	Aug	s	Bride of the Sun	Lew Merrill
1937	Sep	s	Eagle Flight	Clive Trent
		s	Snake Bride	Lew Merrill
		s	Temple of Death	Hugh Speer
1937	Oct	s	Dark Dominion	Lew Merrill
		s	Night Raid	Hugh Speer
		s	Van Dam's Heads	Clive Trent
1937	Nov	s	Lords of Folly	Lew Merrill
		s	Phantom Throne	Hugh Speer
1937	Dec	s	Out of Aden	Lew Merrill
1938	Jan	s	Two on a Trail	Lew Merrill
1938	Mar	s	Congo Spears	Lew Merrill
1938	Apr	s	Code of the Hills	Hugh Speer
		s	Monkey Bones	Clive Trent
		s	Trails End	Lew Merrill
1938	May	s	God of the Pit	Lew Merrill
1938	Jun	s	Lady Sheriff	Hugh Speer
		s	Prize of Peru	Lew Merrill
1938	Jul	s	Dead or Alive!	Hugh Speer
		s	No More Romance	Lew Merrill
1938	Aug	s	Gorilla Man	Lew Merrill
1938	Sep	s	On Secret Service	Hugh Speer
		s	The Water Gate	Lew Merrill
1938	Oct	s	Dane Raiders	Lew Merrill
1938	Nov	s	Death Stalks Through Walls	Hugh Speer
		s	Lady of the Law	Lew Merrill
1938	Dec	s	Beast of the Kremlin	Lew Merrill
		s	House of Hell	Clive Trent
		s	Mississippi Trail	Hugh Speer
1939	Jan	s	Sea Raiders	Lew Merrill
1939	Feb	s	Bugle Call	Clive Trent
		s	Fox Fury	Lew Merrill
1939	Mar	s	Pearls of Panama	Lew Merrill
1939	Apr	s	Death Ride	Hugh Speer
		s	Sea-Haven	Lew Merrill
1939	May	s	Army of the Dead	Lew Merrill
		s	The Climbing Buddha	Clive Trent

1939	Jul	s	Lone Pyramid	Lew Merrill
1939	Aug	s	Red Dawn	Lew Merrill
		s	Sheriff Barbara	Hugh Speer
1939	Sep	s	Fire-Land Queen	Clive Trent
		s	Men-At-Arms	Lew Merrill
		s	Treasure of Andes	Hugh Speer
1939	Oct	s	Jackaroo	Clive Trent
		s	Rubies of Empire	Lew Merrill
		s	She-Sheriff Barbara	Hugh Speer
1939	Nov	s	The Laughing Moor	Lew Merrill
		s	Red Eden	Hugh Speer
1939	Dec	s	Elephant Girl	Hugh Speer
		s	There Can't Be Two O'Haras	Lew Merrill
1940	Jan	s	Flat-Boat	Lew Merrill
		s	Masai Spears	Clive Trent
1940	Feb	s	Jungle Lords	Lew Merrill
1940	Apr	s	Mayor of No Man's Land	Lew Merrill
		s	Night of Action	Hugh Speer
1940	May	s	High Andes	Lew Merrill
1940	Jul	s	Stakes on the Black	Hugh Speer
		s	Woman from Mercury	Lew Merrill
1940	Aug	s	City of Light	Hugh Speer
		s	Human Boomerang	Clive Trent
1940	Sep	s	Shawn of the Stars	Hugh Speer
1940	Oct	s	Gypsy Tent	Clive Trent
		s	Lord of Two Worlds	Hugh Speer
		s	The Robot Awakes	Lew Merrill
1940	Nov	s	Cave of Canoes	Lew Merrill
		s	Rebel Planet	Hugh Speer
1940	Dec	s	The Great God Harris	Lew Merrill
		s	Things That Were Men	Clive Trent
1941	Jan	s	Cord of Death	Lew Merrill
		s	Death Sanctuary	Hugh Speer
1941	Feb	s	Indigo Island	Clive Trent
		s	Space Burial	Lew Merrill
1941	Mar	s	Throne of Straw	Clive Trent
1941	Apr	s	Human Pyramid	Clive Trent
		s	Tree of Life	Lew Merrill
1941	May	s	Burma Road	Lew Merrill
		s	The Lord of Space	Hugh Speer
1941	Jul	s	Hostage of Battle	Hugh Speer
		s	Rat Trap	Lew Merrill
1941	Aug	s	The Last Adam	Lew Merrill
1941	Sep	s	When Planets Mate	Lew Merrill
1941	Oct	s	Hammock Land	Hugh Speer
1941	Nov	s	Inca Gold	Lew Merrill
		s	Swordsman's Choice	Hugh Speer
1942	Jan	s	Jest of Death	Hugh Speer
1942	Feb	s	Night Invasion	Lew Merrill
1942	Apr	s	Heads Shall Roll	Lew Merrill
1942	May	s	Bee Flight	Clive Trent
1942	Jun	s	Lion Guard	Lew Merrill
1942	Jul	s	Tree Mother	Clive Trent
1942	Aug	s	Glacier Girl	Clive Trent
		s	Jungle Tin	Lew Merrill
1942	Oct	s	Sons of the Boiling Blanket	Lew Merrill

1942	Nov	s	The Golden Stool	Hugh Speer
		s	Nero's Ring	Lew Merrill
1942	Dec	s	Commando	Lew Merrill
		s	Sailor's Luck	Clive Trent

SPICY DETECTIVE STORIES (US: Trojan Publishing)
—becomes *Speed Detective*

1939	Feb	s	Liddle Red-Head	Lew Merrill

SPICY MYSTERY STORIES (US: Trojan Publishing)
—becomes *Speed Mystery*

1935	Dec	s	Brothers in Blood	Lew Merrill
		s	She Who Was He!	Hugh Speer
1936	Feb	s	Bat Man	Lew Merrill
1936	Mar	s	Astral Murder	Lew Merrill
1936	Apr	s	Philtre of Death	Hugh Speer
		s	Zang the Creator	Lew Merrill
1936	Jun	s	Dead Man's Shoes	Lew Merrill
1936	Jul	s	Devil Doctor	Lew Merrill
1936	Aug	s	Cat Woman	Lew Merrill
		s	Cyclops	Hugh Speer
		s	Venus of Troy	Clive Trent
1936	Sep	s	Beyond the Veil	Lew Merrill
		s	The Secret of Old Farm	Clive Trent
1936	Oct	s	Return of the Beast	Lew Merrill
1936	Nov	s	Daughter of Death	Lew Merrill
		s	Death's Dancing Partner	Hugh Speer
		s	Isle of the Unborn	Clive Trent
1936	Dec	s	Kali's Vine	Hugh Speer
		s	Tidewater	Lew Merrill
1937	Feb	s	Hell's Robots	Lew Merrill
		s	Satan's Music	Clive Trent
		s	The Time Dissolver	Hugh Speer
1937	Mar	s	Curse of the Ogilvy's	Lew Merrill
1937	Apr	s	Witch's Sabbath	Lew Merrill
1937	May	s	Shadow Man	Lew Merrill
1937	Jun	s	Lilith	Lew Merrill
1937	Jul	s	The Brazen Bull	Clive Trent
1937	Aug	s	Girl of the Night	Lew Merrill
		s	Vault of Horror	Clive Trent
1937	Sep	s	The Death God Awakes	Hugh Speer
		s	Synthetic Husband	Lew Merrill
1937	Oct	s	Hell's Tryst	Hugh Speer
		s	I'll Buy Your Appetites	Lew Merrill
1937	Dec	s	Maid of Osiris	Lew Merrill
		s	The Vampire Doll	Hugh Speer
1938	Feb	s	Body Divided	Hugh Speer
		s	Bright Isle of Enchantment	Lew Merrill
1938	Apr	s	Soul Asleep	Lew Merrill
1938	May	s	Dead Man Rides	Clive Trent
		s	The Time-Twister	Lew Merrill
1938	Jun	s	Beyond Hell's Barriers	Hugh Speer
		s	Emerald of Death	Clive Trent
		s	Thunderstone	Lew Merrill

1938	Aug	s	Dead Man's Arm	Hugh Speer
		s	The Iron Bride	Clive Trent
		nt	Mad Charioteers	Lew Merrill
1938	Oct	s	A Date With the Goat God	Hugh Speer
		s	Point of Eternity	Lew Merrill
1939	Apr	s	Ogre Island	Hugh Speer
		s	Water Witch	Lew Merrill
1939	Jun	s	Face in the Crystal	Lew Merrill
		s	Pipes of Doom	Hugh Speer
1939	Aug	s	Gallows Buster	Lew Merrill
1939	Oct	s	Curse of Killarney	Lew Merrill
		s	Luck of the Cromwells	Hugh Speer
1939	Dec	s	Queen of the Witches	John Phillips
1940	Feb	s	Witches' Island	Lew Merrill
1940	Jun	nt	Isle of Refuge	Hugh Speer
		s	Vision of Death	Lew Merrill
1940	Aug	nt	Giant from Babel	Lew Merrill
1940	Oct	nt	Air Maiden	Clive Trent
		nt	Marooned on Eros	Hugh Speer
1940	Dec	s	The Lifted Veil	Lew Merrill
1941	Jan	s	Isle of the Gods	Lew Merrill
1941	Feb	s	Murderer's Doom	Clive Trent
1941	Mar	s	Lobster Girl	Lew Merrill
1941	Apr	s	Ghosts of Time	Lew Merrill
		s	Scourge of Women	Hugh Speer
1941	Jul	s	Scrambled Destiny	Clive Trent
		s	Spell of the Serpent	Lew Merrill
		s	Fruits of Betrayal	John Phillips
1941	Sep	s	Dancing-Girl Orchid	Clive Trent
		s	The God From Beyond	Lew Merrill
1941	Oct	nt	Farrell's Double	Lew Merrill
		nt	Viking's Daughter	Hugh Speer
1941	Nov	s	Arc of Death	Lew Merrill
		nt	The Captain's Hook	Hugh Speer
1941	Dec	s	Future in Reverse	Lew Merrill
1942	Jan	nt	Girl From the Nebula	Lew Merrill
1942	Feb	s	When It Grew Cold	Lew Merrill
1942	Mar	nt	Jinx	Lew Merrill
1942	Jul	s	Marsh Murder	Clive Trent
		s	Vampire	Lew Merrill
1942	Sep	s	The Sin-Eater	Lew Merrill
		s	More Precious Than Rubies	Stan Warner
1942	Oct	nt	Dwindling Death	Lew Merrill
		s	Half-Way House	Hugh Speer
1942	Nov	nt	The Lost Shadow	Clive Trent
		nt	Twisted Time	Lew Merrill
		s	The Black Horror	Ray Coleman

SPICY WESTERN STORIES (US: Trojan Publishing)
—becomes *Speed Western Stories*

1936	Dec	s	Free, High, and Handsome	Lew Merrill
1937	Jan	s	Man Woman Massacre	Lew Merrill
1937	Jun	s	Outlaw Guns	Lew Merrill
1937	Sep	s	Skidding	Lew Merrill
1938	Dec	s	Even Scores	Lew Merrill

STARTLING MYSTERY STORIES (US: Health Knowledge)
1967	Spring	s	Medium for Justice	Victor Rousseau

STORY-TELLER, THE (UK: Cassell & Co.)
1911	Jul	s	Five Aces	Victor Rousseau

STRANGE TALES OF MYSTERY AND TERROR (US: Clayton Magazines)
1931	Sep	s	A Cry From Beyond	Victor Rousseau
1931	Nov	s	When Dead Gods Wake	Victor Rousseau
1932	Oct	nt	The Curse of Amen-Ra	Victor Rousseau

SUBMARINE STORIES (US: Dell Publishing Co.)
1930	Jul	nt	Challenge of the U-212	Victor Rousseau

SUPER-DETECTIVE (US: Trojan Publishing)
NOTE: The John Grange bylined tales are confirmed up through "Cold Turkey" only; the remaining three have yet to be firmly determined
1940	Oct	nt	Dealer in Death	John Grange
1940	Nov	nt	Legion of Robots	John Grange
1940	Dec	nt	Madame Murder	John Grange
1941	Jan	nt	Bloated Death	John Grange
1941	Feb	nt	Killer in Yellow	John Grange
1941	Mar	nt	Murder in Paradise	John Grange
1941	Apr	nt	Murder Syndicate	John Grange
1941	Jun	nt	The Horrible Marionettes	John Grange
1941	Aug	nt	Border Napoleon	John Grange
1941	Oct	nt	Spies of Destiny	John Grange
1941	Dec	nt	I. O. U. Murder	John Grange
1942	Feb	nt	Cold Turkey	John Grange
1942	Apr	nt	Mrs. Big	John Grange
1942	Jun	nt	Needle's Eye	John Grange
1942	Aug	nt	Mark of the Spider	John Grange
1944	Jun	s	The Ghost Will Walk Tonight	Hugh Speer
1944	Sep	s	Broccoli Burlesque	Lew Merrill
1944	Dec	s	Turnover in Tannersville	Lew Merrill
1945	Jan	s	Cyanide	Lew Merrill
1945	Mar	s	Canine Verdict	Lew Merrill
		s	Doubling for Death	Clive Trent
1945	Apr	s	Typed	Lew Merrill
1945	Jun	s	Frame-Up	Lew Merrill
1945	Sep	s	Corpse in the Car	Clive Trent
		s	Split Seams	Lew Merrill
1945	Nov	s	No Witnesses	Lew Merrill
		s	Sheriff-Tooth	Hugh Speer
1946	Jan	s	September Peaches	Lew Merrill
1946	Mar	s	Bell-Bottom Trousers	Lew Merrill
1946	Jul	s	Old-Fashioned Lady	Lew Merrill
1946	Sep	s	Murder House	Lew Merrill
1946	Nov	s	Brushless Cream	Lew Merrill

SUPER-DETECTIVE (CND: Superior Publishing)
Reprint Edition is Volume 1 # 3. Prior editions have not been found. Later editions might exist.
1942	Aug	nt	Murder in Paradise	John Grange

SURE-FIRE SCREEN STORIES (US: Dell Publishing)
1934	Feb	sa	Fury of the Jungle	Victor Rousseau

THREE STAR MAGAZINE (US: Three Star Publishing [Clayton])
| 1928 | Jun | 1 | nt | North of Fifty-Three | Victor Rousseau |

THRILLING ADVENTURES (US: Metropolitan Magazines / Standard Magazines)
1931	Dec		s	The Black Avatar	Victor Rousseau
1934	Jan		nt	Red-Coat Patrol	Victor Rousseau
1937	Jun		s	Danger's Bloody Banner	Victor Rousseau
1938	Mar		nt	Slave of Alhambra	Victor Rousseau

THRILLING NOVELS (US: Fun Stuff Imaginations/Underground Reprints)
| 1996 | Apr # 37 | nt | I. O. U. Murder | John Grange |

THRILLING WONDER STORIES (US: Better Publications)
| 1941 | Oct | s | Moon Patrol | Victor Rousseau |

TRIPLE-X MAGAZINE (US: Fawcett Publications)
1925	Feb	nt	The Feud of Alkali Springs	Victor Rousseau
1925	Jul	sl	Swamp Soil	Victor Rousseau
1925	Aug	sl	Swamp Soil	Victor Rousseau
1925	Sep	sl	Swamp Soil	Victor Rousseau
1930	Oct	s	Temple of Death	Victor Rousseau

TRUE TWILIGHT TALES (US: League Publications)
| 1964 | Spring | ss | Child or Demon—Which? | Eugene Branscombe |

20ᵗʰ CENTURY CRIME CASES (CND: Duchess Printing and Publishing)
—formerly *Keyhole Detective Cases*
  Series: World-Famous Police Mysteries, continued from prior magazine title
1946	Jul	tc	Crimes of the Marchioness	H. M. Egbert
1946	Aug	tc	The Body in the Parcel	H. M. Egbert
1946	Sep	tc		
1946	Oct	tc	The Kidnapping of Charley Ross	H. M. Egbert
1946	Nov	tc	The Murder of Benjamin Nathan	H. M. Egbert

TWO GUN WESTERN STORIES (US: Metropolitan Publishers)
| 1928 | Nov | nt | The Rustlin' Trail | Victor Rousseau |

WAR BIRDS (US: Dell Publishing)
| 1929 | Nov | s | They Shall Not Pass | Victor Rousseau |

WAR NOVELS (US: Dell Publishing)
| 1929 | Sep | s | Neal Effendi—American | Victor Rousseau |

WAR STORIES (US: Dell Publishing)
1926	Dec		s	Hands Across the Sea	Victor Rousseau
1929	May	23	nt	The Hellion Brood	Victor Rousseau
1929	Jun	20	s	The Seventeenth Star	Victor Rousseau
1929	Jul	18	s	Shane of the Fifty-Third	Victor Rousseau
1929	Aug	29	s	In the Last Minute	Victor Rousseau
1929	Sep	12	s	Lieutenant Limey Brown	Victor Rousseau
1929	Oct	10	s	The Red Stronghold	Victor Rousseau
1930	Oct		s	Wildcats Have Wings	Victor Rousseau
1930	Dec		s	Tennant—of the U.S.A.	Victor Rousseau

WAYSIDE TALES (US: H. H. Windsor)
—formerly *Wayside Tales and Cartoons Magazine*
| 1922 | Feb | nt | Woman and the Law | Victor Rousseau |

WAYSIDE TALES AND CARTOONS MAGAZINE (US: H. H. Windsor)
—formerly *Cartoons Magazine and Wayside Tales*

1921	Aug	sl	The Fifth Guardian	Victor Rousseau
1921	Sep	sl	The Fifth Guardian	Victor Rousseau
1921	Oct	sl	Four Dumb Men	H. M. Egbert
1921	Oct	s	Out of Arcady	Victor Rousseau
1921	Nov	sl	Four Dumb Men	H. M. Egbert
1921	Nov	s	Pals	Victor Rousseau

WEIRD TALES (US: Popular Fiction Publishing Co.)
   The Surgeon of Souls (Series: Sep 1926 through Jul 1927)

1926	Sep	ss	The Case of the Jailer's Daughter	Victor Rousseau
1926	Oct	ss	The Woman With the Crooked Nose	Victor Rousseau
1926	Nov	ss	The Legacy of Hate	Victor Rousseau
1926	Dec	ss	The Tenth Commandment	Victor Rousseau
1927	Jan	ss	The Major's Menagerie	Victor Rousseau
1927	Feb	ss	The Fetish of the Waxworks	Victor Rousseau
1927	Mar	ss	The Seventh Symphony	Victor Rousseau
1927	Apr	ss	The Chairs of Stuyvesant Baron	Victor Rousseau
1927	May	ss	The Man Who Lost His Luck	Victor Rousseau
1927	Jun	ss	The Dream That Came True	Victor Rousseau
1927	Jul	ss	The Ultimate Problem	Victor Rousseau
1932	Jul	sl	The Phantom Hand	Victor Rousseau
1932	Aug	sl	The Phantom Hand	Victor Rousseau
1932	Sep	sl	The Phantom Hand	Victor Rousseau
1932	Oct	sl	The Phantom Hand	Victor Rousseau
1932	Nov	sl	The Phantom Hand	Victor Rousseau

WESTERN HOME MONTHLY (CND: Stovel)
   Note: Reportedly serialized "The Truant Soul" late 1927 to early 1928; unconfirmed

1932	Aug	sl	False Fingers	Victor Rousseau
1932	Sep	sl	False Fingers	Victor Rousseau

WESTERN ROMANCES (US: Dell Publishing)

1929	Nov	nt	Hearts and Sixes	Victor Rousseau
1936	Sep	nt	Girl from Green Gap	Victor Rousseau
1937	Mar	nt	The Bride of Eagle Pass	Victor Rousseau

WESTERN STORY MAGAZINE (US: Street & Smith Corp.)

1924	Mar	8	s	Furs That Fed	Victor Rousseau

WORLD STORIES (UK: Atlas Publishing and Distributing)

1934	Apr	nt	Loot of Lost Lode	Victor Rousseau

YOUNG'S MAGAZINE (US: C. H. Young Publishing Co.)

1909	Mar	s	Youth the Conqueror	H. M. Egbert
1912	Aug	vi	The House of Honor	H. M. Egbert
1913	Jan	s	The Return of Ephraim	H. M. Egbert
1914	Sep	s	The Mask of Juno	Victor Rousseau
1914	Nov	s	The House with the Brass Door-Knobs	Victor Rousseau

ZANE GREY'S WESTERN MAGAZINE (US: Dell Publishing)

1947	Aug	nt	The Branded Man (ab)	Victor Rousseau
1948	Apr	s	Final Curtain	Victor Rousseau

NEWSPAPERS & SUPPLEMENTS
Short Stories and Regional First Serial Rights

Year	Month/Day		Story Title	Byline

(ASSOCIATED) SUNDAY MAGAZINE (Syndicated Newspaper Supplement)

Year	Month/Day		Story Title	Byline
1911	Apr	30	s	Five Aces	Victor Rousseau

BOSTON DAILY GLOBE, THE (Boston, Massachusetts)

The Devil Chair (Series: 18 Jan through 5 Apr 1914)

Year	Month/Day		Story Title	Byline
1914	Jan	18	ss	The Cripple of Prospect Park	H. M. Egbert
1914	Jan	25	ss	The Seven League Boots	H. M. Egbert
1914	Feb	1	ss	The First Victim	H. M. Egbert
1914	Feb	8	ss	An Involuntary Ally	H. M. Egbert
1914	Feb	15	ss	Roles Reversed	H. M. Egbert
1914	Feb	22	ss	The Arm of Justice	H. M. Egbert
1914	Mar	1	ss	The Shunted Man of Europe	H. M. Egbert
1914	Mar	8	ss	The Kingdom of the North	H. M. Egbert
1914	Mar	15	ss	The Man and the Maelstrom	H. M. Egbert
1914	Mar	22	ss	The Man in the Balance	H. M. Egbert
1914	Mar	29	ss	The God From the Pagoda	H. M. Egbert
1914	Apr	5	ss	By the Deep Sea Transit	H. M. Egbert
1914	Jun	28	s	The Girl Who Stayed at Home	H. M. Egbert

The King of Knaves (Series: 24 Jan through 28 Mar 1915; out of sequence)
('The Burning of Batoum' and 'A Bid for a Throne' were not accepted by The Globe)

Year	Month/Day		Story Title	Byline
1915	Jan	24	ss	The Robinson Diamonds	H. M. Egbert
1915	Jan	31	ss	The Brother of the Moon	H. M. Egbert
1915	Feb	7	ss	The Stolen Submarine	H. M. Egbert
1915	Feb	14	ss	The Lighthouse of the North	H. M. Egbert
1915	Feb	21	ss	The Essayan Statue	H. M. Egbert
1915	Feb	28	ss	The Treasure of Spandau	H. M. Egbert
1915	Mar	7	ss	The Coronation of Nikolai	H. M. Egbert
1915	Mar	14	ss	The Flight of the Princess	H. M. Egbert
1915	Mar	21	ss	The Rubies of the Sacrifice	H. M. Egbert
1915	Mar	28	ss	The Treasure of Egypt	H. M. Egbert
1921	Jan	9	sl	Wooden Spoil	Victor Rousseau
1921	Jan	16	sl	Wooden Spoil	Victor Rousseau
1921	Jan	23	sl	Wooden Spoil	Victor Rousseau
1921	Jan	30	sl	Wooden Spoil	Victor Rousseau
1921	Feb	6	sl	Wooden Spoil	Victor Rousseau
1921	Feb	13	sl	Wooden Spoil	Victor Rousseau
1921	Feb	20	sl	Wooden Spoil	Victor Rousseau
1922	Oct	29	s	Pals	Victor Rousseau
1923	Nov	18	s	New York Takes the Count	Victor Rousseau
1930	Oct	26	ss	The Lie of Pere Sebastian	Victor Rousseau
1930	Nov	2	ss	Chapelle Ardente	Victor Rousseau
1930	Nov	16	ss	The Evil Shore	Victor Rousseau
1930	Nov	30	ss	The Voice in the Mist	Victor Rousseau
1930	Dec	28	ss	Big Pierre's Idol	Victor Rousseau
1931	Jan	11	ss	The Curé Goes Hunting	Victor Rousseau
1931	Jan	18	ss	The Wooing of Fanchette	Victor Rousseau
1931	Feb	8	ss	The Wrath of Paul Dupuy	Victor Rousseau
1931	Feb	22	ss	The Faith of Paul Duchaine	Victor Rousseau
1931	Mar	29	ss	The Pacification of Anne	Victor Rousseau
1931	Apr	19	ss	The Curé's Love Story	Victor Rousseau

1931	Jun	14	ss	The Desperation of St. Jean	Victor Rousseau
1932	Sep	25	nt	False Fingers	Victor Rousseau
1946	May	5	nt	Sweeping Tides	Victor Rousseau
1947	Jan	26	nt	The Wolf Trail	Victor Rousseau
1947	May	18	s	The Silent Partner	Victor Rousseau
1947	Sep	14	nt	Lost Lode	Victor Rousseau
1950	Feb	12	s	Air-Minded	Victor Rousseau
1950	Aug	20	s	No Compromise	Victor Rousseau
1951	Sep	30	sl	The Red Trail	Victor Rousseau
1951	Oct	7	sl	The Red Trail	Victor Rousseau
1951	Oct	14	sl	The Red Trail	Victor Rousseau
1951	Oct	21	sl	The Red Trail	Victor Rousseau
1953	Mar	15	nt	High Andes	Victor Rousseau

BOSTON POST (Boston, Massachusetts)— in the *Boston Sunday Post Magazine*

1931	Mar	29	sl	All For a Girl	Victor Rousseau
1931	Apr	5	sl	All For a Girl	Victor Rousseau
1931	Apr	12	sl	All For a Girl	Victor Rousseau
1931	Apr	19	sl	All For a Girl	Victor Rousseau
1931	Apr	26	sl	All For a Girl	Victor Rousseau
1931	May	3	sl	All For a Girl	Victor Rousseau
1931	May	10	sl	All For a Girl	Victor Rousseau
1931	May	17	sl	All For a Girl	Victor Rousseau
1931	May	24	sl	All For a Girl	Victor Rousseau
1931	May	31	sl	All For a Girl	Victor Rousseau

BUFFALO SUNDAY TIMES (Buffalo, New York)
The Man With the Camera Eyes (Series: 18 Jun through 20 Aug 1911; only 9 of 12 found)

1911	Jun	18	ss	The Box of Borneos	Harold Carter
1911	Jun	25	ss	The Robbery of the Tower	Harold Carter
1911	Jul	2	ss	The Tell-Tale Glove	Harold Carter
1911	Jul	9	ss	The Champion of the Fleet	Harold Carter
1911	Jul	16	ss	The Record on the Screen	Harold Carter
1911	Jul	30	ss	The Death in the Dirigible	Harold Carter
1911	Aug	6	ss	The Broken Heel	Harold Carter
1911	Aug	13	ss	The Crooked Seam	Harold Carter
1911	Aug	20	ss	The Misplaced Pigment	Harold Carter

World Famous Police Mysteries (Series: 10 Sep through 5 Nov 1911; only 9 of 12 found)

1911	Sep	10	tc	The Case of Madame Lafarge	H. M. Egbert
1911	Sep	17	tc	The Persecution of the Rector	H. M. Egbert
1911	Sep	24	tc	The Murder in the Rue Mazarin	H. M. Egbert
1911	Oct	1	tc	The Resurrection Men	H. M. Egbert
1911	Oct	8	tc	The Last of the Bushrangers	H. M. Egbert
1911	Oct	15	tc	The Churchwarden Murderer	H. M. Egbert
1911	Oct	22	tc	Inspector Denovan and Mackoull	H. M. Egbert
1911	Oct	29	tc	The Crimes of the Marchioness	H. M. Egbert
1911	Nov	5	tc	The Body in the Parcel	H. M. Egbert

CHICAGO DAILY NEWS, THE (Chicago, Illinois)
The Quest of Gentle Hazard (Series: 16 Sep through 25 Nov 1911; only 11 of 12 found,
and they are printed out of sequential order)

1911	Sep	16	ss	A Matrimonial Disentanglement	H. M. Egbert
1911	Sep	23	ss	The Diamond Tiara	H. M. Egbert
1911	Sep	30	ss	A Midnight Elopement	H. M. Egbert
1911	Oct	7	ss	A Seaside Comedy	H. M. Egbert
1911	Oct	14	ss	A Casual Champion	H. M. Egbert

1911	Oct	21	ss	Story of the Runaway Bride	H. M. Egbert
1911	Oct	28	ss	A Frustrated Alliance	H. M. Egbert
1911	Nov	4	ss	Master and Man	H. M. Egbert
1911	Nov	11	ss	Nelly of the Sluice Gate	H. M. Egbert
1911	Nov	18	ss	A Family Reunion	H. M. Egbert
1911	Nov	25	ss	Sauce for the Gander	H. M. Egbert

CHICAGO TRIBUNE, THE (Chicago, Illinois)
The Flights of Francois (Series: 31 Oct through 12 Dec 1915)

1915	Oct	31	ss	The Fair American	Victor Rousseau
1915	Nov	7	ss	Suzette	Victor Rousseau
1915	Nov	14	ss	The Bethune Charter	Victor Rousseau
1915	Nov	21	ss	The Phantom City	Victor Rousseau
1915	Nov	28	ss	The Five Army Corps	Victor Rousseau
1915	Dec	5	ss	A Jest That Saved	Victor Rousseau
1915	Dec	12	ss	The Belfry Dawn	Victor Rousseau

His Second Self (Novelisation of 'The Truant Soul' photoplay)

1917	Aug	26	sl	His Second Self	Victor Rousseau
1917	Sep	2	sl	His Second Self	Victor Rousseau
1917	Sep	9	sl	His Second Self	Victor Rousseau
1917	Sep	16	sl	His Second Self	Victor Rousseau
1917	Sep	23	sl	His Second Self	Victor Rousseau
1917	Sep	30	sl	His Second Self	Victor Rousseau
1917	Oct	7	sl	His Second Self	Victor Rousseau
1917	Oct	14	sl	His Second Self	Victor Rousseau
1917	Oct	21	sl	His Second Self	Victor Rousseau
1917	Oct	28	sl	His Second Self	Victor Rousseau
1917	Dec	2	ss	Rachel	Victor Rousseau
1917	Dec	23	ss	Big Pierre's Idol	Victor Rousseau
1917	Dec	30	ss	Chapelle Ardente	Victor Rousseau
1918	Jan	6	ss	The Faith of Paul Duchaine	Victor Rousseau
1918	Jan	27	ss	Lafe Evens Up	Victor Rousseau
1918	Mar	10	ss	The Voice in the Mist	Victor Rousseau
1918	Mar	17	ss	The Wrath of Paul Dupuy	Victor Rousseau
1918	Mar	24	ss	The Wooing of Fanchette	Victor Rousseau
1918	Mar	31	ss	The Evil Shore	Victor Rousseau

DETROIT FREE PRESS (Detroit, Michigan)

1918	May	12	sl	Bride of Battle	Victor Rousseau
1918	May	19	sl	Bride of Battle	Victor Rousseau
1918	May	26	sl	Bride of Battle	Victor Rousseau
1918	Jun	2	sl	Bride of Battle	Victor Rousseau
1918	Jun	9	sl	Bride of Battle	Victor Rousseau
1918	Jun	16	sl	Bride of Battle	Victor Rousseau
1918	Jun	23	sl	Bride of Battle	Victor Rousseau
1920	Mar	7	ss	Pierre and Paul	Victor Rousseau
1920	Jun	13	sl	Wooden Spoil	Victor Rousseau
1920	Jun	20	sl	Wooden Spoil	Victor Rousseau
1920	Jun	27	sl	Wooden Spoil	Victor Rousseau
1920	Jul	4	sl	Wooden Spoil	Victor Rousseau
1920	Jul	11	sl	Wooden Spoil	Victor Rousseau
1920	Jul	18	sl	Wooden Spoil	Victor Rousseau
1920	Jul	25	sl	Wooden Spoil	Victor Rousseau
1920	Aug	1	sl	Wooden Spoil	Victor Rousseau
1920	Aug	8	sl	Wooden Spoil	Victor Rousseau
1920	Aug	15	sl	Wooden Spoil	Victor Rousseau

EVENING TELEGRAM, THE (New York, New York)
| 1910 | Jun | 13 | vi | Treasure Trove | H. M. Egbert |

FICTION MAGAZINE (Newspaper Supplement, owned by the *Chicago Record-Herald*)
The Revelations of an Ambassador-at-Large (Series: 6 June through 22 August 1915)
1915	Jun	6	ss	The Bulgarian Papers	H. M. Egbert
1915	Jun	13	ss	The Bookworm of Potsdam	H. M. Egbert
1915	Jun	20	ss	The Montenegrin Ciphers	H. M. Egbert
1915	Jun	27	ss	Count Berchtold's Birthday Party	H. M. Egbert
1915	Jul	4	ss	The Bullet-Proof Mantle	H. M. Egbert
1915	Jul	11	ss	The Golden Death	H. M. Egbert
1915	Jul	18	ss	A Dead Man's Empire	H. M. Egbert
1915	Jul	25	ss	A Patriot's Dilemma	H. M. Egbert
1915	Aug	1	ss	The "X" Bacillus	H. M. Egbert
1915	Aug	8	ss	The Wax Clavette	H. M. Egbert
1915	Aug	15	ss	The Red Envelope	H. M. Egbert
1915	Aug	22	ss	Kitchener's Coup	H. M. Egbert
1916	Aug	27	s	The Wolf Trap	H. M. Egbert
1916	Oct	22	s	Pride of Place	Victor Rousseau
1917	Apr	22	s	The Jam God	H. M. Egbert
1917	Aug	12	s	The Crooked Finger	Victor Rousseau
1917	Dec	9	ss	The Scar	H. M. Egbert
1918	Apr	7	sl	Bride of Battle	Victor Rousseau
1918	Apr	14	sl	Bride of Battle	Victor Rousseau
1918	Apr	21	sl	Bride of Battle	Victor Rousseau
1918	Apr	28	sl	Bride of Battle	Victor Rousseau
1918	May	5	sl	Bride of Battle	Victor Rousseau
1918	May	12	sl	Bride of Battle	Victor Rousseau
1918	May	19	sl	Bride of Battle	Victor Rousseau

GLOBE AND COMMERCIAL ADVERTISER, THE (New York, New York)
The Surgeon of Souls (Series: 5 Feb through 7 May 1910; lacks 'The Seventh Symphony')
1910	Feb	5	ss	The Case of the Jailer's Daughter	H. M. Egbert
1910	Feb	12	ss	The Woman With the Crooked Nose	H. M. Egbert
1910	Feb	26	ss	The Tenth Commandment	H. M. Egbert
1910	Mar	5	ss	The Legacy of Hate	H. M. Egbert
1910	Mar	12	ss	The Major's Menagerie	H. M. Egbert
1910	Mar	19	ss	The Fetish of the Waxworks	H. M. Egbert
1910	Apr	2	ss	The Chairs of Stuyvesant Baron	H. M. Egbert
1910	Apr	16	ss	The Man Who Lost His Luck	H. M. Egbert
1910	Apr	23	ss	Homo Homunculus	H. M. Egbert
1910	Apr	30	ss	The Dream That Came True	H. M. Egbert
1910	May	7	ss	The Ultimate Problem	H. M. Egbert

A King's Courier (Series: 13 Aug through 12 Nov 1910; lacks 'The Affair of the North Sea')
1910	Aug	13	ss	The Peril of Magellan Strait	H. M. Egbert
1910	Aug	20	ss	The Kaiser's Hairdresser	H. M. Egbert
1910	Aug	27	ss	The Emperor's Double	H. M. Egbert
1910	Sep	10	ss	The Dinner at the White House	H. M. Egbert
1910	Sep	17	ss	The Left-Hand Wife	H. M. Egbert
1910	Sep	24	ss	The Amir's Move	H. M. Egbert
1910	Oct	8	ss	The Kidnaped King	H. M. Egbert
1910	Oct	15	ss	The Czar's Drive	H. M. Egbert
1910	Oct	22	ss	The Spanish Treaty	H. M. Egbert
1910	Oct	29	ss	The River Rats	H. M. Egbert
1910	Nov	12	ss	The Ingratitude of Kings	H. M. Egbert

GRIT (Williamsport, Pennsylvania)
> Note: Wooden Spoil (serial incomplete; begins 13 Aug in the *Grit Story Section*)

1933	Aug	13	sl	Wooden Spoil	Victor Rousseau
1933	Aug	20	sl	Woodcn Spoil	Victor Rousseau
1933	Aug	27	sl	Wooden Spoil	Victor Rousseau
1933	Sep	3	sl	Wooden Spoil	Victor Rousseau
1933	Sep	10	sl	Wooden Spoil	Victor Rousseau
1933	Sep	17	sl	Wooden Spoil	Victor Rousseau

HOUSTON POST, THE (Houston, Texas)
> The Devil Chair (Series: 28 Sep through 14 Dec 1913; out of sequence)

1913	Sep	28	ss	The Cripple of Prospect Park	H. M. Egbert
1913	Oct	5	ss	The Seven League Boots	H. M. Egbert
1913	Oct	12	ss	The First Victim	H. M. Egbert
1913	Oct	19	ss	An Involuntary Ally	H. M. Egbert
1913	Oct	26	ss	Roles Reversed	H. M. Egbert
1913	Nov	2	ss	The Arm of Justice	H. M. Egbert
1913	Nov	9	ss	The Shunted Man of Europe	H. M. Egbert
1913	Nov	16	ss	The Man and the Maelstrom	H. M. Egbert
1913	Nov	23	ss	The Man in the Balance	H. M. Egbert
1913	Nov	30	ss	The God From the Pagoda	H. M. Egbert
1913	Dec	7	ss	The Kingdom of the North	H. M. Egbert
1913	Dec	14	ss	By the Deep Sea Transit	H. M. Egbert

ILLUSTRATED BUFFALO EXPRESS, THE (Buffalo, New York)
> The Tracer of Egos (Series: 15 Mar through 31 May 1914; byline oft misspelled)

1914	Mar	15	ss	The Amulet of Marduk	Victor Rousseau
1914	Mar	22	ss	Mary Rothway's Memory	Victor Rosseau
1914	Mar	29	ss	The Professor's Peach Trees	Victor Rousseau
1914	Apr	5	ss	Alf Barton's Princess	Victor Rosseau
1914	Apr	12	ss	The Two Charioteers	Victor Rousseau
1914	Apr	19	ss	The Carfax Curse	Victor Rosseau
1914	Apr	26	ss	Mr. Axel's Shady Past	Victor Rosseau
1914	May	3	ss	The Woman of Atlantis	Victor Rousseau
1914	May	10	ss	A Fisher for Souls	Victor Rousseau
1914	May	17	ss	The Return of Claudia	Victor Rousseau
1914	May	24	ss	The Wife of Ira Hopkins	Victor Rousseau
1914	May	31	ss	Noureddin Bey's Sacrifice	Victor Rousseau

> Revelations of an Ambassador at Large (Series: incomplete data, ends 4 Jul 1915)

1915	Jun	6	ss	A Patriot's Dilemma	H. M. Egbert
1915	Jun	13	ss	The "X" Bacillus	H. M. Egbert
1915	Jun	20	ss	The Wax Clavette	H. M. Egbert
1915	Jun	27	ss	The Red Envelope	H. M. Egbert
1915	Jul	4	ss	Kitchener's Coup	H. M. Egbert
1918	Mar	31	s	The Dead Hand	Victor Rousseau
1918	Sep	1	s	The Wolf Trap	H. M. Egbert

ILLUSTRATED SUNDAY MAGAZINE (Syndicated Newspaper Supplement)

1908	Sep	13	s	The Crescendo of Prof. Zeldenrust	Victor Rousseau
1908	Dec	20	s	Bill Connolly's Christmas	Victor Rousseau
1909	May	9	s	The Man Who Wasn't	Victor Rousseau
1909	Jun	13	s	Pharaoh's Princess	Victor Rousseau
1909	Sep	12	s	When the Shark Turns	Victor Rousseau
1909	Dec	12	s	His Father's Dishonor	Victor Rousseau
1909	Dec	26	s	The Oyster Boom of Avenue B	Victor Rousseau
1910	Apr	3	s	The Turning of the Worm	Victor Rousseau

1910	May	29	s	For the Honor of The Union	Victor Rousseau
1910	Sep	18	s	The Ways of Women	Victor Rosseau
1910	Oct	23	s	The Doctor's Supreme Test	Victor Rousseau
1911	Jun	25	s	The Stolen Appendix	Victor Rousseau
1912	Jan	12	s	The Test of the Hills	Victor Rousseau

KANSAS CITY STAR (Kansas City, Missouri)
   NOTE: Missing installments appear in the Kansas City Times
   The exception is "Storm Over Athabasca," which ran entirely in this paper.

1944	Jan	25	sl	The Wolf Trail (2 of 16)	Victor Rousseau
1944	Jan	26	sl	The Wolf Trail (4 of 16)	Victor Rousseau
1944	Jan	27	sl	The Wolf Trail (6 of 16)	Victor Rousseau
1944	Jan	28	sl	The Wolf Trail (8 of 16)	Victor Rousseau
1944	Jan	29	sl	The Wolf Trail (10 of 16)	Victor Rousseau
1944	Jan	30	sl	The Wolf Trail (12 of 16)	Victor Rousseau
1944	Jan	31	sl	The Wolf Trail (14 of 16)	Victor Rousseau
1944	Feb	1	sl	The Wolf Trail (16 of 16)	Victor Rousseau
1944	May	1	sl	Storm Over Athabasca (1 of 6)	Victor Rousseau
1944	May	2	sl	Storm Over Athabasca (2 of 6)	Victor Rousseau
1944	May	3	sl	Storm Over Athabasca (3 of 6)	Victor Rousseau
1944	May	4	sl	Storm Over Athabasca (4 of 6)	Victor Rousseau
1944	May	5	sl	Storm Over Athabasca (5 of 6)	Victor Rousseau
1944	May	6	sl	Storm Over Athabasca (6 of 6)	Victor Rousseau
1949	Nov	16	sl	The Lost Lode (2 of 7)	Victor Rousseau
1949	Nov	17	sl	The Lost Lode (4 of 7)	Victor Rousseau
1949	Nov	18	sl	The Lost Lode (6 of 7)	Victor Rousseau
1952	Jul	28	sl	The Mansion Murder (2 of 11)	Victor Rousseau
1952	Jul	29	sl	The Mansion Murder (4 of 11)	Victor Rousseau
1952	Jul	30	sl	The Mansion Murder (6 of 11)	Victor Rousseau
1952	Jul	31	sl	The Mansion Murder (8 of 11)	Victor Rousseau
1952	Aug	1	sl	The Mansion Murder (10 of 11)	Victor Rousseau
1954	Apr	3	sl	The Red Trail (2 of 13)	Victor Rousseau
1954	Apr	4	sl	The Red Trail (4 of 13)	Victor Rousseau
1954	Apr	5	sl	The Red Trail (6 of 13)	Victor Rousseau
1954	Apr	6	sl	The Red Trail (8 of 13)	Victor Rousseau
1954	Apr	7	sl	The Red Trail (10 of 13)	Victor Rousseau
1954	Apr	8	sl	The Red Trail (12 of 13)	Victor Rousseau
1956	Jun	5	sl	The Woman and the Law (1 of 9)	Victor Rousseau
1956	Jun	6	sl	The Woman and the Law (3 of 9)	Victor Rousseau
1956	Jun	7	sl	The Woman and the Law (5 of 9)	Victor Rousseau
1956	Jun	8	sl	The Woman and the Law (7 of 9)	Victor Rousseau
1956	Jun	9	sl	The Woman and the Law (9 of 9)	Victor Rousseau

KANSAS CITY TIMES (Kansas City, Missouri)
   NOTE: Missing installments appear in the Kansas City Star

1944	Jan	25	sl	The Wolf Trail (1 of 16)	Victor Rousseau
1944	Jan	26	sl	The Wolf Trail (3 of 16)	Victor Rousseau
1944	Jan	27	sl	The Wolf Trail (5 of 16)	Victor Rousseau
1944	Jan	28	sl	The Wolf Trail (7 of 16)	Victor Rousseau
1944	Jan	29	sl	The Wolf Trail (9 of 16)	Victor Rousseau
1944	Jan	30	sl	The Wolf Trail (11 of 16)	Victor Rousseau
1944	Jan	31	sl	The Wolf Trail (13 of 16)	Victor Rousseau
1944	Feb	1	sl	The Wolf Trail (15 of 16)	Victor Rousseau
1949	Nov	16	sl	The Lost Lode (1 of 7)	Victor Rousseau
1949	Nov	17	sl	The Lost Lode (3 of 7)	Victor Rousseau
1949	Nov	18	sl	The Lost Lode (5 of 7)	Victor Rousseau

1949	Nov	19	sl	The Lost Lode (7 of 7)	Victor Rousseau
1952	Jul	28	sl	The Mansion Murder (1 of 11)	Victor Rousseau
1952	Jul	29	sl	The Mansion Murder (3 of 11)	Victor Rousseau
1952	Jul	30	sl	The Mansion Murder (5 of 11)	Victor Rousseau
1952	Jul	31	sl	The Mansion Murder (7 of 11)	Victor Rousseau
1952	Aug	1	sl	The Mansion Murder (9 of 11)	Victor Rousseau
1952	Aug	2	sl	The Mansion Murder (11 of 11)	Victor Rousseau
1954	Apr	3	sl	The Red Trail (1 of 13)	Victor Rousseau
1954	Apr	4	sl	The Red Trail (3 of 13)	Victor Rousseau
1954	Apr	5	sl	The Red Trail (5 of 13)	Victor Rousseau
1954	Apr	6	sl	The Red Trail (7 of 13)	Victor Rousseau
1954	Apr	7	sl	The Red Trail (9 of 13)	Victor Rousseau
1954	Apr	8	sl	The Red Trail (11 of 13)	Victor Rousseau
1954	Apr	9	sl	The Red Trail (13 of 13)	Victor Rousseau
1956	Jun	6	sl	The Woman and the Law (2 of 9)	Victor Rousseau
1956	Jun	7	sl	The Woman and the Law (4 of 9)	Victor Rousseau
1956	Jun	8	sl	The Woman and the Law (6 of 9)	Victor Rousseau
1956	Jun	9	sl	The Woman and the Law (8 of 9)	Victor Rousseau

LITERARY MAGAZINE SECTION (Syndicated Newspaper Supplement)

1909	May	9	s	A Man's Birthright	Victor Rousseau
1909	Sep	26	s	The Cheap Skate	Victor Rousseau

LITERARY MAGAZINE SECTION (Small-town Syndicated Supplement)
NOTE: Acquired after the prior owner's went bankrupt in early 1910, the new owners—the *Illustrated Sunday Magazine*—reprinted their fiction in its pages.

1912	Nov		s	The Doctor's Supreme Test	Victor Rosseau

LOS ANGELES TIMES (Los Angeles, California)

1921	Apr	3	ss	Pierre and Paul	Victor Rousseau
1932	Apr	17	sl	False Fingers	Victor Rousseau
1932	Apr	24	sl	False Fingers	Victor Rousseau
1932	May	1	sl	False Fingers	Victor Rousseau
1932	May	8	sl	False Fingers	Victor Rousseau

LONDON DAILY MAIL (London, England)

1920	Sep	7	sl	Legally Dead	John Austin
1920	Sep	8	sl	Legally Dead	John Austin
1920	Sep	9	sl	Legally Dead	John Austin
1920	Sep	10	sl	Legally Dead	John Austin
1920	Sep	11	sl	Legally Dead	John Austin
1920	Sep	13	sl	Legally Dead	John Austin
1920	Sep	14	sl	Legally Dead	John Austin
1920	Sep	15	sl	Legally Dead	John Austin
1920	Sep	16	sl	Legally Dead	John Austin
1920	Sep	17	sl	Legally Dead	John Austin
1920	Sep	18	sl	Legally Dead	John Austin
1920	Sep	20	sl	Legally Dead	John Austin
1920	Sep	21	sl	Legally Dead	John Austin
1920	Sep	22	sl	Legally Dead	John Austin
1920	Sep	23	sl	Legally Dead	John Austin
1920	Sep	24	sl	Legally Dead	John Austin
1920	Sep	25	sl	Legally Dead	John Austin
1920	Sep	27	sl	Legally Dead	John Austin
1920	Sep	28	sl	Legally Dead	John Austin
1920	Sep	29	sl	Legally Dead	John Austin

1920	Sep	30	sl	Legally Dead	John Austin
1920	Oct	1	sl	Legally Dead	John Austin
1920	Oct	2	sl	Legally Dead	John Austin
1920	Oct	4	sl	Legally Dead	John Austin
1920	Oct	5	sl	Legally Dead	John Austin
1920	Oct	6	sl	Legally Dead	John Austin
1920	Oct	7	sl	Legally Dead	John Austin
1920	Oct	8	sl	Legally Dead	John Austin
1920	Oct	9	sl	Legally Dead	John Austin
1920	Oct	11	sl	Legally Dead	John Austin
1920	Oct	12	sl	Legally Dead	John Austin
1920	Oct	13	sl	Legally Dead	John Austin
1920	Oct	14	sl	Legally Dead	John Austin
1920	Oct	15	sl	Legally Dead	John Austin
1920	Oct	16	sl	Legally Dead	John Austin
1920	Oct	18	sl	Legally Dead	John Austin
1920	Oct	19	sl	Legally Dead	John Austin
1920	Oct	20	sl	Legally Dead	John Austin
1920	Oct	21	sl	Legally Dead	John Austin
1920	Oct	22	sl	Legally Dead	John Austin
1920	Oct	23	sl	Legally Dead	John Austin
1920	Oct	25	sl	Legally Dead	John Austin
1920	Oct	26	sl	Legally Dead	John Austin
1920	Oct	27	sl	Legally Dead	John Austin
1920	Oct	28	sl	Legally Dead	John Austin
1920	Oct	29	sl	Legally Dead	John Austin
1920	Oct	30	sl	Legally Dead	John Austin
1920	Nov	1	sl	Legally Dead	John Austin
1921	Feb	8	sl	The Greater Claim	John Austin
1921	Feb	9	sl	The Greater Claim	John Austin
1921	Feb	10	sl	The Greater Claim	John Austin
1921	Feb	1	sl	The Greater Claim	John Austin
1921	Feb	12	sl	The Greater Claim	John Austin
1921	Feb	14	sl	The Greater Claim	John Austin
1921	Feb	15	sl	The Greater Claim	John Austin
1921	Feb	16	sl	The Greater Claim	John Austin
1921	Feb	17	sl	The Greater Claim	John Austin
1921	Feb	18	sl	The Greater Claim	John Austin
1921	Feb	19	sl	The Greater Claim	John Austin
1921	Feb	21	sl	The Greater Claim	John Austin
1921	Feb	22	sl	The Greater Claim	John Austin
1921	Feb	23	sl	The Greater Claim	John Austin
1921	Feb	24	sl	The Greater Claim	John Austin
1921	Feb	25	sl	The Greater Claim	John Austin
1921	Feb	26	sl	The Greater Claim	John Austin
1921	Feb	28	sl	The Greater Claim	John Austin
1921	Mar	1	sl	The Greater Claim	John Austin
1921	Mar	2	sl	The Greater Claim	John Austin
1921	Mar	3	sl	The Greater Claim	John Austin
1921	Mar	4	sl	The Greater Claim	John Austin
1921	Mar	5	sl	The Greater Claim	John Austin
1921	Mar	7	sl	The Greater Claim	John Austin
1921	Mar	8	sl	The Greater Claim	John Austin
1921	Mar	9	sl	The Greater Claim	John Austin
1921	Mar	10	sl	The Greater Claim	John Austin
1921	Mar	11	sl	The Greater Claim	John Austin

1921	Mar	12	sl	The Greater Claim	John Austin
1921	Mar	14	sl	The Greater Claim	John Austin
1921	Mar	15	sl	The Greater Claim	John Austin
1921	Mar	16	sl	The Greater Claim	John Austin

MAGAZINE SECTION [OF] THE SUNDAY STAR (Washington, D.C.)

| 1919 | Apr | 6 | ss | The Story of Pierre and Paul | Victor Rousseau |

McKEAN COUNTY DEMOCRAT (Smethport, Pennsylvania)

NOTE: First Regional publication not located. This is a small-town serialization.

1942	Jul	9	sl	Black Dawn	Victor Rousseau
1942	Jul	16	sl	Black Dawn	Victor Rousseau
1942	Jul	23	sl	Black Dawn	Victor Rousseau
1942	Jul	30	sl	Black Dawn	Victor Rousseau
1942	Aug	6	sl	Black Dawn	Victor Rousseau
1942	Aug	13	sl	Black Dawn	Victor Rousseau
1942	Aug	20	sl	Black Dawn	Victor Rousseau
1942	Aug	27	sl	Black Dawn	Victor Rousseau
1942	Sep	3	sl	Black Dawn	Victor Rousseau
1942	Sep	10	sl	Black Dawn	Victor Rousseau
1942	Sep	17	sl	Black Dawn	Victor Rousseau
1942	Sep	24	sl	Black Dawn	Victor Rousseau
1942	Oct	1	sl	Black Dawn	Victor Rousseau

PHILADELPHIA INQUIRER (Philadelphia, Pennsylvania)

NOTE: Serialization data on "The Big Muskeg" is incomplete

1921	Sep	18	sl	The Big Muskeg	Victor Rousseau
1921	Sep	25	sl	The Big Muskeg	Victor Rousseau
1921	Oct	2	sl	The Big Muskeg	Victor Rousseau
1921	Oct	9	sl	The Big Muskeg	Victor Rousseau
1921	Oct	16	sl	The Big Muskeg	Victor Rousseau
1921	Oct	23	sl	The Big Muskeg	Victor Rousseau
1921	Oct	30	sl	The Big Muskeg	Victor Rousseau
1922	Mar	12	ss	Lafe Evens Up	Victor Rousseau
1922	Apr	23	sl	Wooden Spoil	Victor Rousseau
1922	Apr	30	sl	Wooden Spoil	Victor Rousseau
1922	May	7	sl	Wooden Spoil	Victor Rousseau
1922	May	14	sl	Wooden Spoil	Victor Rousseau
1922	May	21	sl	Wooden Spoil	Victor Rousseau
1922	May	28	sl	Wooden Spoil	Victor Rousseau
1922	Jun	4	sl	Wooden Spoil	Victor Rousseau
1922	Jun	11	sl	Wooden Spoil	Victor Rousseau
1922	Jun	18	sl	Wooden Spoil	Victor Rousseau
1922	Jun	25	sl	Wooden Spoil	Victor Rousseau
1922	Jul	2	sl	Wooden Spoil	Victor Rousseau
1922	Jul	9	sl	Wooden Spoil	Victor Rousseau
1922	Jul	16	sl	Wooden Spoil	Victor Rousseau
1922	Jul	16	s	Pals	Victor Rousseau

PUBLIC LEDGER (Philadelphia, Pennsylvania) in the 'Magazine Section'

Audacious Hazard aka The King of Knaves (Series: 9 Mar through 18 May 1913)

("A Bid For A Throne" was not printed)

1913	Mar	9	ss	The Robinson Diamonds	E. M. Egbert (sic)
1913	Mar	16	ss	The Treasure of Spandau	H. M. Egbert
1913	Mar	23	ss	The Stolen Submarine	H. M. Egbert
1913	Mar	30	ss	The Lighthouse of the North	H. M. Egbert

1913	Apr	6	ss	The Essayan Statue	H. M. Egbert
1913	Apr	13	ss	The Burning of Batoum	H. M. Egbert
1913	Apr	20	ss	The Coronation of Nikolai	H. M. Egbert
1913	Apr	27	ss	The Flight of the Princess	H. M. Egbert
1913	May	4	ss	The Rubies of the Sacrifice	H. M. Egbert
1913	May	11	ss	The Brother of the Moon	H. M. Egbert
1913	May	18	ss	The Treasure of Egypt	H. M. Egbert

ST. LOUIS POST-DISPATCH (St. Louis, Missouri)
The Devil Chair (Series: title printed as 'The Wheel' 27 Sep through 13 Dec 1913)

1913	Sep	27	ss	The Cripple of Prospect Park	H. M. Egbert
1913	Oct	4	ss	The Seven League Boots	H. M. Egbert
1913	Oct	11	ss	The First Victim	H. M. Egbert
1913	Oct	18	ss	An Involuntary Ally	H. M. Egbert
1913	Oct	25	ss	Roles Reversed	H. M. Egbert
1913	Nov	1	ss	The Arm of Justice	H. M. Egbert
1913	Nov	8	ss	The Shunted Man of Europe	H. M. Egbert
1913	Nov	15	ss	The Kingdom of the North	H. M. Egbert
1913	Nov	22	ss	The Man and the Maelstrom	H. M. Egbert
1913	Nov	29	ss	The Man in the Balance	H. M. Egbert
1913	Dec	6	ss	The God From the Pagoda	H. M. Egbert
1913	Dec	13	ss	By the Deep Sea Transit	H. M. Egbert

ST. LOUIS REPUBLIC (St. Louis, Missouri)
World-Famous Police Mysteries by H M Egbert (Series: 18 Dec 1910 through 26 Feb 1911)

SATURDAY BLADE, THE (Chicago, Illinois)
The Man With the Camera Eyes (Series: title printed as 'Peter Crewe, Detective'
appears 6 Jan through 17 Feb 1912; the first five tales not located)

1912	Jan	6	ss	Bank Cashier Caught	Harold Carter
1912	Jan	13	ss	The Crooked Seam	Harold Carter
1912	Jan	20	ss	The Misplaced Pigment	Harold Carter
1912	Jan	27	ss	The Whirl of Death	Harold Carter
1912	Feb	3	ss	The Face of the Clock	Harold Carter
1912	Feb	10	ss	The Broken Heel	Harold Carter
1912	Feb	17	ss	The Death in the Dirigible	Harold Carter

STEVENS POINT JOURNAL, THE (Stevens Point, Wisconsin)
League of Lost Causes (Series: 18 Oct – 20 Dec 1913, no first Regional Rights found)
NOTE: Only 10 titles known to exist in the series.
First World Rights sold to Cassell in England, late 1912; only 7 sold. Printing: Unknown

1913	Oct	18	ss	The Woman From the Sea	H. M. Egbert
1913	Oct	25	ss	The Moroccan Treaty	H. M. Egbert
1913	Nov	1	ss	How the Kaiser Went to Paris	H. M. Egbert
1913	Nov	8	ss	The Misplaced Dream	H. M. Egbert
1913	Nov	15	ss	An Amazon of Tripoli	H. M. Egbert
1913	Nov	22	ss	The Prisoner of Hofberg	H. M. Egbert
1913	Nov	29	ss	The Pilot of the Fleet	H. M. Egbert
1913	Dec	6	ss	A Dutch Music Lesson	H. M. Egbert
1913	Dec	13	ss	The Séance of Nishikoff	H. M. Egbert
1913	Dec	20	ss	The Education of Edward	H. M. Egbert

NOTE: No first-syndication locations have yet been found; none were bylined.

1917	Apr	21	ts	Exploits of 'Pussyfoot' Johnson in Cleaning up Indian Territory.	Uncredited
1917	Apr	28	ts	How 'Pussyfoot' Johnson Wiped Out the Monte Carlo of No Man's Land	Uncredited

1917	May	5	ts	Desperate Outlaws Put a Price on Head of 'Pussyfoot' Johnson	Uncredited
1917	May	12	ts	'Pussyfoot' Performs One of Most Daring Deeds in Frontier History	Uncredited
1917	May	19	ts	How 'Pussyfoot' Johnson Made Good Citizens of Indian Charges	Uncredited

SUNDAY MAGAZINE (see under 'Associated Sunday Magazine')

SUNDAY MAGAZINE, THE (of *The Milwaukee Journal*, Milwaukee, Wisconsin)

1935	Jan	13	sl	Shifting Sands	Victor Rousseau
1935	Jan	20	sl	Shifting Sands	Victor Rousseau
1935	Jan	27	sl	Shifting Sands	Victor Rousseau
1935	Feb	3	sl	Shifting Sands	Victor Rousseau
1935	Feb	10	sl	Shifting Sands	Victor Rousseau
1935	Feb	17	sl	Shifting Sands	Victor Rousseau

TIMES-PICAYUNE (New Orleans, Louisiana)
NOTE: originally was sold circa 1944 to an unknown publication and subsequently since

| 1948 | Mar | 14 | vi | The Vital Clue | Victor Rousseau |

TORONTO STAR WEEKLY (Toronto, Canada)
Unconfirmed: the short story "Silent Partner" reportedly printed circa 1935-1936

1933	Jul	22	ss	Big Pierre's Idol	Victor Rousseau
1933	Jul	29	ss	Glowing Chapel	Victor Rousseau
1933	Aug	12	ss	Eyes of Pere Sebastien (sic)	Victor Rousseau
1933	Sep	30	ss	Wrath of Paul Dupuy	Victor Rousseau
1942	Nov	7	sl	The Branded Man	Victor Rousseau
1942	Nov	14	sl	The Branded Man	Victor Rousseau
1942	Nov	21	sl	The Branded Man	Victor Rousseau

Unconfirmed: unclear duration of the above reprinted serial "The Branded Man"

1945	Jan	6	sl	Her Home Region	Victor Rousseau
1945	Jan	13	sl	Her Home Region	Victor Rousseau
1945	Jan	20	sl	Her Home Region	Victor Rousseau
1945	Jan	27	sl	Her Home Region	Victor Rousseau
1945	Feb	3	sl	Her Home Region	Victor Rousseau
1945	Feb	10	sl	Her Home Region	Victor Rousseau
1945	Feb	17	sl	Her Home Region	Victor Rousseau
1945	Feb	24	sl	Her Home Region	Victor Rousseau

WASHINGTON POST (Washington D. C.)
World Famous Police Mysteries (Series: 18 Dec 1910 through 5 Mar 1911; none were bylined)

1910	Dec	18	tc	The Case of Madame Lafarge	
1910	Dec	25	tc	The Persecution of the Rector	
1911	Jan	1	tc	The Murder in the Rue Mazarin	
1911	Jan	8	tc	The Resurrection Men	
1911	Jan	15	tc	The Last of the Bushrangers	
1911	Jan	22	tc	The Churchwarden Murderer	
1911	Jan	29	tc	Inspector Denovan and Mackoull	
1911	Feb	5	tc	The Crimes of the Marchioness	
1911	Feb	12	tc	The Body in the Parcel	
1911	Feb	19	tc	The Mahratta's Revenge	
1911	Feb	26	tc	The Kidnapping of Charley Ross	
1911	Mar	5	tc	The Murder of Benjamin Nathan	
1918	Aug	11	ss	The Wolf Trap	H. M. Egbert

MAGAZINE AND NEWSPAPER
Journalistic Articles or Essays (All Print Mediums)

Year	Month, Day	Article Title	Byline

THE ANACONDA STANDARD (Newspaper: Anaconda, Montana)

Year	Month	Day	Article Title	Byline
1906	Jan	21	Scenes in a Turpentine Camp	Victor Rousseau
1906	Jun	10	Harvesters of the Seas	Victor Rousseau

BALTIMORE AMERICAN (Newspaper: Baltimore, Maryland)

1907	Feb	3	A Ramble in Dickens' Land	Victor Rousseau
1907	May	5	The Romance of the Thames	Victor Rousseau
1907	Jun	16	The Season in London	Victor Rousseau
1907	Jul	21	The City of Gold	Victor Rousseau

EVERY WHERE (Magazine edited by Will Carleton)

| 1907 | Sep | | The Call of September | Egbert Prentice |
| 1907 | Oct | | The Trail of October | Egbert Prentice |

HARPER'S WEEKLY (Tabloid Magazine)

1908	Jan	25	Low Rent or No Rent: The Tenement Dwellers Rebellion in New York	Victor Rousseau
1908	Mar	14	The Lengthening Bread Line	Victor Rousseau
1908	Mar	21	Wanted: Soldiers	Victor Rousseau
1908	Mar	28	Rex Beach and the Barrier	Victor Rousseau
1908	Apr	4	Hoop-la! The Circus	Victor Rousseau
1908	Apr	11	Unlocking $47,000,000	Victor Rousseau
1908	Apr	18	When Women Ruled	Victor Rousseau
1908	May	30	Court of Sorrows	Victor Rousseau
1908	Aug	23	Cupid and the Law	Victor Rousseau
1908	Oct	3	The Poor of London	Victor Rousseau
1908	Oct	3	The Puppet Play Which Lasts Two Months	Victor Rousseau
1908	Oct	10	The Doom of English Liberalism	Victor Rousseau
1908	Dec	19	Lawless New York – Part One	Victor Rousseau
1908	Dec	26	Helping the Filipinos to Fight Disease	H. M. Egbert
1909	Jan	9	Lawless New York – Part Two	Victor Rousseau
1909	Jan	23	Laura Jean Libbey	Victor Rousseau
1909	Feb	13	Bargaining With Criminals	Victor Rousseau
1909	Feb	20	Discovery of the Soul	Victor Rousseau
1909	Oct	2	Uncle Sam, Pickpocket	Victor Rousseau
1909	Oct	9	School for Souls	Victor Rousseau
1910	Feb	26	Pussyfoot	Victor Rousseau
1910	May	14	Britain's World-mourned King	Victor Rousseau
1913	Jun	7	Japan and the Philippines	Victor Rousseau

IRISH WEEKLY TIMES (Dublin, Ireland)

1907	Feb	16	A Ramble in Dickens' Land	Victor Rousseau
1907	May	18	The Romance of the Thames	Victor Rousseau
1907	Jun	22	The Season in London	Victor Rousseau
1907	Jul	27	The City of Gold	Victor Rousseau

NEW YORK TIMES (Newspaper: New York City, New York)

| 1911 | Nov | 19 | The Man Roosevelt | Harold Carter |
| 1914 | Apr | 19 | New Writers: Mr. Harrison's View of Their Opportunities | Victor Rousseau |

1923	Jun	10	Evolution	V. R. Emanuel
1926	Dec	17	The Rights of Foreigners	V. R. Emanuel
1935	Jul	21	The Dies Bill	V. R. Emanuel
1935	Sep	10	A Writer Defends the Pulps	Victor Rousseau Emanuel
1936	Aug	21	Concerning Rabies	V. R. Emanuel
1938	May	31	The Problem of the Alien	V. R. Emanuel
1939	Jul	2	An Impenitent Alien	V. R. Emanuel
1942	Jul	16	Old-Time Razors Preferred	V. R. Emanuel
1942	Aug	26	Fashion Note for Men	V. R. Emanuel
1942	Sep	17	Trials of a Shirt Owner	V. R. Emanuel
1945	Mar	25	Japanese and Aztec	V. R. Emanuel

SAN ANTONIO LIGHT (Newspaper: San Antonio, Texas)

1906	Feb	25	The Orange Industry in Florida	Victor Rousseau

NOVELS AND STORY COLLECTIONS

Book Title
Location, Publisher, Date, Format, Pages   **Byline**
  Original Title or, Additional Notes

THE APOSTLE OF THE CYLINDER
UK: Hodder and Stoughton, 1918, hb, 319pp   Victor Rousseau
  Originally: The Messiah of the Cylinder
US: Kessinger Publishing, Nov 2007, sc, 320pp   Victor Rousseau
  Print-on-Demand

THE BIG MALOPO
UK: John Long, 1924, hb, 254pp   H. M. Egbert
  Originally: The Diamond Demons

THE BIG MAN OF BONNE CHANCE
UK: Hodder and Stoughton, 1925, hb, 320pp   Victor Rousseau
  Originally: While Dorion Lives

THE BIG MUSKEG
US: Stewart Kidd, 1921, hb, 302pp   Victor Rousseau
UK: Hodder and Stoughton, 1923, hb, 318pp   Victor Rousseau
US: Kessinger Publishing, Jun 2007, sc, 304pp   Victor Rousseau
  Print-on-Demand

DERWENT'S HORSE
UK: Methuen, 1901, hb, 275pp   Victor Rousseau
  First Publication, author's first novel

THE DEVIL CHAIR
US: The Spectre Library, Jun 2008, hb, 180pp   Victor Rousseau
  Limit: 200, 1st collection of all 12 stories

DRAFT OF ETERNITY
US: Beb Books, 2008, sc, 70pp   Victor Rousseau
  OCR ink-jet octavo photocopy

DRAUGHT OF ETERNITY
UK: John Long, 1924, hb, 254pp   H. M. Egbert
  Originally: Draft of Eternity

ERIC OF THE STRONG HEART
UK: John Long, 1925, hb, 254   H. M. Egbert
US: Pulpdom, 2000, sc, 105pp   H. M. Egbert

THE EYE OF BALAMOK
US: Beb Books, 2006, sc, 57pp   Victor Rousseau

THE FRUIT OF THE LAMP
US: Beb Books, 2010, sc, 80pp   Victor Rousseau
  OCR ink-jet octavo photocopy

GOLDEN HORDE
UK: Hodder and Stoughton, 1926, hb, 317pp   Victor Rousseau
  Originally: The Bandit of Batakaland

THE HOME TRAIL
UK: Hodder and Stoughton, 1924, hb, 287pp   Victor Rousseau

JACQUELINE OF GOLDEN RIVER
US: Doubleday Page, 1920, hb, 248pp   H. M. Egbert
UK: Hodder and Stoughton, 1924, hb, 320pp   H. M. Egbert

THE LION'S JAWS
UK: Hodder and Stoughton, 1923, hb, 319pp   Victor Rousseau

THE MESSIAH OF THE CYLINDER
US: A. C. McClurg, 1917, hb, 319pp   Victor Rousseau
US: Hyperion, Jun 1973, hb, 319pp   Victor Rousseau
  Introduction by Lester del Rey
US: Hyperion, Dec 1973, sc: 319pp   Victor Rousseau
  Introduction by Lester del Rey

MIDDLE YEARS
US: Minton, Balch, 1925, hb, 332pp   V. R. Emanuel
  First Publication

MRS. ALADDIN
UK: John Long, 1925, hb, 254pp   H. M. Egbert
  Originally: Fruit of the Lamp

MY LADY OF THE NILE
UK: Hodder and Stoughton, 1923, hb, 286pp   H. M. Egbert
US: Beb Books, 2011, sc
  OCR ink-jet octavo photocopy

SALTED DIAMONDS
UK: John Long, 1926, hb, 254pp   H. M. Egbert
  First Publication
UK: John Long, 1927-28, hb, 286pp   H. M. Egbert
  Second imprint

THE SEA DEMONS
UK: John Long, 1924, hb, 254pp   H. M. Egbert
US: Hyperion, 1976, hb, 254pp   Victor Rousseau
US: Hyperion, 1976, sc, 254pp   Victor Rousseau

THE SELMANS
US: The Dial Press, 1925, hb, 372pp   V. R. Emanuel
  First Publication

THE STORY OF JOHN PAUL
UK: Constable, 1923, hb, 348pp   V. R. Emanuel
  First Publication

THE SURGEON OF SOULS
US: The Spectre Library, Oct 2006, hb, 172pp   Victor Rousseau
  Limit: 200; 1st collection of all 12 stories

THE TRACER OF EGOS
US: The Spectre Library, Aug 2007, hb, 174pp   Victor Rousseau
  Limit: 200, 1st collection of all 12 stories

WINDING TRAILS
UK: John Long, 1927, hb, 254pp   H. M. Egbert

WOODEN SPOIL
US: George H. Doran, 1919, hb, 312pp   Victor Rousseau
   Unauthorized edition
US: Grosset and Dunlap, 1919, hb, 312pp   Victor Rousseau
UK: Hodder and Stoughton, 1919, hb, 320pp   Victor Rousseau
US: Kessinger Publishing, Jan 2010, hb, 314pp   Victor Rousseau
   Print-on-Demand

ANTHOLOGIES

Title
Story Title and Byline
Country, Publisher, Year, Format, Pages, Editor

THE ADVENTURERS
Dealer in Death, by John Grange
  US: Black Dog Books, 2008, sc, 263pp, edited by Tom Roberts

C'EST LA GUERRE! The Best Stories of the World War
Hands Across the Sea, by Victor Rousseau
  US: The Straford Co., 1927, hb, 338pp, edited by James G. Dunton

DR. ACULA'S THRILLING TALES OF THE UNCANNY
The Curse of Amen-Ra, by Victor Rousseau
  US: Sense of Wonder Press, 2004, sc, 284pp, edited by Rock Lynne

THE FANTASTIC PULPS
A Cry From Beyond, by Victor Rousseau
  UK: Gollancz, 1975, hb, 418pp, edited by Peter Haining
  US: St. Martins Press, 1976, hb, 418pp, edited by Peter Haining
  US: Vintage Books, 1976, sc, 418pp, edited by Peter Haining

GOLDEN STORIES
The Jam God, by H. M. Egbert
  US: The Short Stories Company, 1909, hb, 226pp

HIS SECOND SELF: THE BIO-BIBLIOGRAPHY OF VICTOR ROUSSEAU EMANUEL
The Last Cartridge, by Victor Rousseau
Picked Off, by Victor Rousseau
Youth the Conqueror, by Victor Rousseau
Jackson's Wife, by Victor Rousseau
The Jam God, by Victor Rousseau
A Man's Birthright, by Victor Rousseau
The Peril of Magellan Strait, by Victor Rousseau
Five Aces, by Victor Rousseau
The Cats That Looked at Cohen, by Victor Rousseau
Jean of the Silence, by Victor Rousseau
The Box of Borneos, by Victor Rousseau
The Girl at Three Mile Fork, by Victor Rousseau
A Casual Champion, by Victor Rousseau
The Cripple from Prospect Park, by Victor Rousseau
The Woman from the Sea, by Victor Rousseau
The Amulet of Marduk, by Victor Rousseau
The Golden Death, by Victor Rousseau
The Wolf Trap, by Victor Rousseau
  US: The Spectre Library (sc), 2011 (as Victor Rousseau)

THE MESSIAH OF THE CYLINDER AND OTHER STORIES
The Messiah of the Cylinder, by Victor Rousseau
  CND: Girasol, 2009, hb, 120pp

MUMMY STORIES
The Curse of Amen-Ra by Victor Rousseau
   US: Ballantine, 1990, sc, 225pp, edited by Martine H. Greenberg
   UK: Severn House, 1991, hb, 225pp, edited by Martine H. Greenberg

THE NORTHERNERS
Captives of the Arctic Wasteland by Victor Rousseau
   US: Fawcett, 1990, sc, 256pp, edited by Bill Pronzini

PHANTOM PERFUMES AND OTHER SHADES
The Angel of the Marne, by Victor Rousseau
   CND: Ash-Tree Press, 2000, hb, 244pp, edited by Michael Ashley

RED TWILIGHT / WORLD'S END: Two Novels From Argosy
World's End, by Victor Rousseau
   US: Starmont House, 1991, hb, 123pp

RUE MORGUE NO. 1
Death in the Tank, by Hugh Speer
   US: Creative Age Press, 1946, hb, 403pp, edited by Rex Stout & Louis Greenfield

SENSUOUS SCIENCE FICTION FROM THE WEIRD AND SPICY PULPS
The Robot Awakes, by Lew Merrill
Shawn of the Stars, by Hugh Speer
   US: Bowling Green State University Popular Press, 1984, hb, 164pp, edited by Sheldon Jaffery
   US: Bowling Green State University Popular Press, 1984, sc, 164pp, edited by Sheldon Jaffery

SPICY MYSTERY STORIES
Synthetic Husband by Lew Merrill
   US: Malibu Graphics, 1990, sc, 112pp, edited by Tom Mason

SUPER DETECTIVE FLIP BOOK
Legion of Robots, by John Grange
   US: Off-Trail Publications, March 2008, sc, 176pp

SUPER-DETECTIVE JIM ANTHONY: The Complete Stories, Vol. One
Dealer In Death, by Victor Rousseau
Legion of Robots, by Victor Rousseau
Madame Murder, by Victor Rousseau
   US: Altus Press, 2009, hb, 389pp, edited by Will Murray (limited to 100 copies)
   US: Altus Press, 2009, sc, 389pp, edited by Will Murray

WHEN SPIRITS TALK
Child or Demon—Which?, by Victor Rousseau
   UK: Ghost Story Society, 1990, sc, 32pp, edited by Michael Ashley

CHRONOLOGICAL INDEX

Part One: Chronological Index of all Fiction-Story Titles
1st Publication or Earliest Known Only (excludes syndicated vignettes)

1901

	DERWENT'S HORSE	Methuen (UK)	N

1907

Sep	The Last Cartridge	The Munsey	vi

1908

Jan 4	Picked Off	Harper's Weekly	s
Sep 13	The Crescendo of Prof. Zeldenrust	Illustrated Sunday Magazine	s
Dec 20	Bill Connolly's Christmas	Illustrated Sunday Magazine	s

1909

Mar	Youth the Conqueror	Young's Magazine	s
Apr 3	The Kings of No Man's Land	Harper's Weekly	s
Apr 24	The Upper Window	Harper's Weekly	s
May	Jackson's Wife	The Smart Set	s
May	The Jam God	Short Stories	s
May 9	The Man Who Wasn't	Illustrated Sunday Magazine	s
May 9	A Man's Birthright	Literary Magazine Section	s
Jun	Cakes of Judgment	Century Magazine	s
Jun 13	Pharaoh's Princess	Illustrated Sunday Magazine	s
Jul 24	Their Honors the Aldermen	Harper's Weekly	s
Aug 7	A Deal in Elephant	Harper's Weekly	s
Sep 12	When the Shark Turns	Illustrated Sunday Magazine	s
Sep 26	The Cheap Skate	Literary Magazine Section	s
Dec 12	His Father's Dishonor	Illustrated Sunday Magazine	s

1910

Feb 5	The Palm-Bringer	Harper's Weekly	s

The Surgeon of Souls (syndicated series)
    First regional rights noted below in the *Globe and Commercial Advertiser*
    Note: "The Seventh Symphony" (# 7) not found

Feb 5	The Case of the Jailer's Daughter	Globe and Commercial Advertiser	ss
Feb 12	The Woman With the Crooked Nose	Globe and Commercial Advertiser	ss
Feb 26	The Tenth Commandment	Globe and Commercial Advertiser	ss
Mar 5	The Legacy of Hate	Globe and Commercial Advertiser	ss
Mar 12	The Major's Menagerie	Globe and Commercial Advertiser	ss
Mar 19	The Fetish of the Waxworks	Globe and Commercial Advertiser	ss
Apr 2	The Chairs of Stuyvesant Baron	Globe and Commercial Advertiser	ss
Apr 3	The Turning of the Worm	Illustrated Sunday Magazine	s
Apr 16	The Man Who Lost His Luck	Globe and Commercial Advertiser	ss
Apr 23	Homo Homunculus	Globe and Commercial Advertiser	ss
Apr 30	The Dream That Came True	Globe and Commercial Advertiser	ss
May 7	The Ultimate Problem	Globe and Commercial Advertiser	ss
May 29	For the Honor of the Union	Illustrated Sunday Magazine	s

A King's Courier (syndicated series)
    World first printings overlap between England's *The New Magazine*
    and the United States' *Morrison's Chicago Weekly*, as noted below

Jun	The Peril of Magellan Strait	The New Magazine	ss
Jul	The Toilet that Saved France	The New Magazine	ss

Aug	The Affair of the North Sea	The New Magazine	ss
Aug 27	The Emperor's Double	Globe and Commercial Advertiser	ss
Sep 10	The Dinner at the White House	Globe and Commercial Advertiser	ss
Sep 17	The Left-Hand Wife	Globe and Commercial Advertiser	ss
Sep 24	The Amir's Move	Globe and Commercial Advertiser	ss
Oct	The Spanish Treaty	The New Magazine	ss
Oct 8	The Kidnaped King	Globe and Commercial Advertiser	ss
Oct 15	The Czar's Drive	Globe and Commercial Advertiser	ss
Oct 29	The River Rats	Globe and Commercial Advertiser	ss
Nov 12	The Ingratitude of Kings	Globe and Commercial Advertiser	ss
Jun 13	Treasure Trove	The Evening Telegram	vi
Jul 2	The Gallows-Bird	Harper's Weekly	s
Sep 18	The Ways of Women	Illustrated Sunday Magazine	s
Oct	The Prince's Ring	Home Life	vi
Oct 1	The Red Cross Train	Harper's Weekly	s
Oct 23	The Doctor's Supreme Test	Illustrated Sunday Magazine	s
Nov 24	His People's Covenant	Morrison's Chicago Weekly	s
Dec 10	The Keeper of the Light	Harper's Weekly	s
Dec 18	The Case of Madame LaFarge	Washington Post	tc
Dec 25	The Persecution of the Rector	Washington Post	tc

1911

Jan 1	The Murder in the Rue Mazarin	Washington Post	tc
Jan 8	The Resurrection Men	Washington Post	tc
Jan 15	The Churchwarden Murderer	Washington Post	tc
Jan 22	The Last of the Bushrangers	Washington Post	tc
Jan 29	Inspector Denovan and Mackoull	Washington Post	tc
Feb	The Death March	Short Stories	s
Feb 5	The Crimes of the Marchioness	Washington Post	tc
Feb 12	The Body in the Parcel	Washington Post	tc
Feb 19	The Mahratta's Revenge	Washington Post	tc
Feb 26	The Kidnapping of Charley Ross	Washington Post	tc

The King of Knaves (*Blue Book Magazine*: Mar 1911—Feb 1912)

Mar	The Robinson Diamonds	The Blue Book Magazine	ss
Mar 5	The Murder of Benjamin Nathan	Washington Post	tc
Mar 18	The Man in the Bottle	Harper's Weekly	s
Apr	The Treasure of Spandau	The Blue Book Magazine	ss
Apr 30	Five Aces	Associated Sunday Magazine	s
May	The Stolen Submarine	The Blue Book Magazine	ss
May	The Cats That Looked at Cohen	Canada West Monthly	ss
May 27	The Secret Altar	Harper's Weekly	s
Jun	The Lighthouse of the North	The Blue Book Magazine	ss
Jun	Jean of the Silence	The Smart Set	s

The Man With the Camera Eyes (syndicated series)
First regional rights only found partially in the *Buffalo Sunday Times*.
They were printed out of order. Proper sequence noted after the titles.
See *The Saturday Blade* for Chicago rights to the three titles noted below:

	A Matter of Mathematics (# 6)	(First rights not located)	
	The Whirl of Death (# 7)	(First rights not located)	
	The Face on the Clock (# 10)	(First rights not located)	
Jun 18	The Box of Borneos (# 1)	Buffalo Sunday Times	ss
Jun 25	The Robbery at the Tower (# 2)	Buffalo Sunday Times	ss
Jun 25	The Stolen Appendix	Illustrated Sunday Magazine	s
Jul	The Essayan Statue	The Blue Book Magazine	ss
Jul	Proving Poe	People's Magazine	s
Jul 2	The Tell-Tale Glove (# 3)	Buffalo Sunday Times	ss

Jul 8	The Virgin of Okiak	Harper's Weekly	s
Jul 9	The Champion of the Fleet (# 4)	Buffalo Sunday Times	ss
Jul 16	The Record on the Screen (# 5)	Buffalo Sunday Times	ss
Jul 30	The Death in the Dirigible (# 12)	Buffalo Sunday Times	ss
Aug	The Burning of Batoum	The Blue Book Magazine	ss
Aug	The Girl at Three Mile Fork	MacLean's Magazine	s
Aug 6	The Broken Heel (# 11)	Buffalo Sunday Times	ss
Aug 13	The Crooked Seam (# 8)	Buffalo Sunday Times	ss
Aug 20	The Misplaced Pigment (# 9)	Buffalo Sunday Times	ss
Sep	The Coronation of Nikolai	The Blue Book Magazine	ss

The Quest of Gentle Hazard (syndicated series)
First regional rights in the *Chicago Daily News,* printed out of
sequential order. Proper sequence noted after each title below.
"A Wedding De Luxe" (# 12) is missing

Sep 16	A Matrimonial Disentanglement (# 9)	The Chicago Daily News	ss
Sep 23	The Diamond Tiara (# 6)	The Chicago Daily News	ss
Sep 30	A Midnight Elopement (# 8)	The Chicago Daily News	ss
Oct	The Flight of the Princess	The Blue Book Magazine	ss
Oct	Aviator No. 6 (1 of 7)	Canada West Monthly	sl
Oct 7	A Seaside Comedy (# 2)	The Chicago Daily News	ss
Oct 14	A Casual Champion (# 1)	The Chicago Daily News	ss
Oct 21	Story of the Runaway Bride (# 5)	The Chicago Daily News	ss
Oct 28	A Frustrated Alliance (# 4)	The Chicago Daily News	ss
Oct 28	The Man Who Went Back	Harper's Weekly	s
Nov	A Bid for a Throne	The Blue Book Magazine	ss
Nov	Aviator No. 6 (2 of 7)	Canada West Monthly	sl
Nov 4	Master and Man (# 3)	The Chicago Daily News	ss
Nov 11	Nelly of the Sluice Gate (# 11)	The Chicago Daily News	ss
Nov 18	A Family Reunion (# 7)	The Chicago Daily News	ss
Nov 25	Sauce for the Gander (# 10)	The Chicago Daily News	ss
Dec	The Rubies of the Sacrifice	The Blue Book Magazine	ss
Dec	Aviator No. 6 (3 of 7)	Canada West Monthly	sl

1912

Jan	The Brother of the Moon	The Blue Book Magazine	ss
Jan	Aviator No. 6 (4 of 7)	Canada West Monthly	sl
Jan 28	The Test of the Hills	Illustrated Sunday Magazine	s
Feb	The Treasure of Egypt	The Blue Book Magazine	ss
Feb	Aviator No. 6 (5 of 7)	Canada West Monthly	sl
Feb 17	The Garden of Illusion	Harper's Weekly	s
Mar	Aviator No. 6 (6 of 7)	Canada West Monthly	sl
Apr	Aviator No. 6 (7 of 7)	Canada West Monthly	sl
Apr 13	The Great Experiment	Harper's Weekly	s
Jul	The Man of Pelican Key	Ainslee's Magazine	s
Jul 8	The Fangs of the Mill	Harper's Weekly	s
Aug	The House of Honor	Young's Magazine	vi
Aug	The Hidden Bride	Pall Mall Magazine (UK)	s
Aug 31	The Isle of Enchantment	Harper's Weekly	s

League of Lost Causes (syndicated series)
Seven of ten first sold to a Cassell & Co publication in England
Payment from Cassell received Sep, Oct, and Nov in full.
First U.S.A. rights never found; likely in the *Chicago Ledger*

	The Woman from the Sea	(First Rights Not Located)	ss
	The Moroccan Treaty	(First Rights Not Located)	ss
	How the Kaiser Went to Paris	(First Rights Not Located)	ss
	The Misplaced Dream	(First Rights Not Located)	ss

	An Amazon of Tripoli	(First Rights Not Located)	ss
	The Prisoner of Hofberg	(First Rights Not Located)	ss
	The Pilot of the Fleet	(First Rights Not Located)	ss
	A Dutch Music Lesson	(First Rights Not Located)	ss
	The Séance of Nishikoff	(First Rights Not Located)	ss
	The Education of Edward	(First Rights Not Located)	ss

Isabel Marston, Star Reporter (Sep 1912—Feb 1913)

Sep	The Kidnapped Cabinet Minister	Cassell's Magazine of Fiction (UK)	ss
Oct	For the Honor of the Crown	Cassell's Magazine of Fiction (UK)	ss
Oct	Hearts Astray	Harper's Monthly Magazine	s
Nov	The Man on the Heath	Cassell's Magazine of Fiction (UK)	ss
Nov 23	The King's Proctor	Harper's Weekly	s
Dec	An Error of Longitude	Cassell's Magazine of Fiction (UK)	ss

1913

Jan	A Servant of His King	Cassell's Magazine of Fiction (UK)	ss
Jan	The Return of Ephraim	Young's Magazine	s
Feb	Her Last 'Story'	Cassell's Magazine of Fiction (UK)	ss
Jun	Slim Uncle Piet	Harper's Monthly	s

The Tracer of Egos (syndicated series)
World first rights to *Holland's Magazine*; remaining installments
syndicated in the newspaper field, all noted below and numbered
The *Illustrated Buffalo Express* carried their regions rights; numbered
installments (9, 10, 11) are noted as thus in that publication, in May 1914

Jun	The Amulet of Marduk (# 1)	Holland's Magazine	ss
Jul	Mary Rothway's Memory (# 2)	Holland's Magazine	ss
Aug	The Flight of Abdul Hamid	Canada West Monthly	ss
Aug	Alf Barton's Princess (# 6)	Holland's Magazine	ss
Sep	The Two Charioteers (# 3)	Holland's Magazine	ss

The Devil Chair (syndicated series)
The *St. Louis Post-Dispatch* launched the series in sequential order

Sep 27	The Cripple of Prospect Park (# 1)	St. Louis Post-Dispatch	ss
Oct	The Professor's Peach Trees (# 5)	Holland's Magazine	ss
Oct 4	The Seven League Boots (# 2)	St. Louis Post-Dispatch	ss
Oct 11	The First Victim (# 3)	St. Louis Post-Dispatch	ss
Oct 18	An Involuntary Ally (# 4)	St. Louis Post-Dispatch	ss
Oct 25	Roles Reversed (# 5)	St. Louis Post-Dispatch	ss
Nov	The Carfax Curse (# 4)	Holland's Magazine	ss
Nov 1	The Arm of Justice (# 6)	St. Louis Post-Dispatch	ss
Nov 8	The Shunted Man of Europe (# 7)	St. Louis Post-Dispatch	ss
Nov 15	The Kingdom of the North (# 8)	St. Louis Post-Dispatch	ss
Nov 15	The Seal Maiden	The Cavalier	s
Nov 22	The Man and the Maelstrom (# 9)	St. Louis Post-Dispatch	ss
Nov 29	The Man in the Balance (# 10)	St. Louis Post-Dispatch	ss
Dec	Mr. Axel's Shady Past (# 7)	Holland's Magazine	ss
Dec 6	The God from the Pagoda (# 11)	St. Louis Post-Dispatch	ss
Dec 13	By the Deep Sea Transit (# 12)	St. Louis Post-Dispatch	ss

1914

Jan	The Woman of Atlantis (# 8)	Holland's Magazine	ss
Feb	Noureddin Bey's Sacrifice (# 12)	Holland's Magazine	ss
Mar	The Trail of the Wolf	The American Patriot	s
Mar	The Blue Dimity Dress	Harper's Monthly Magazine	s
Mar	Justice and the Moose Call	Short Stories	s
Apr	The Three Melons	The American Patriot	s
May	Rachael	The Red Book Magazine	s

May 10	A Fisher for Souls (# 9)	Illustrated Buffalo Express	ss
May 17	The Return of Claudia (# 10)	Illustrated Buffalo Express	ss
May 24	The Wife of Ira Hopkins (# 11)	Illustrated Buffalo Express	ss
May 30	The General's Decoration	All-Story Cavalier Weekly	s
Jun	Lieutenant Merriman—Missing	The American Patriot	s
Jun 28	The Girl Who Stayed at Home	The Boston Daily Globe	s
Aug	The Human Factor	The American Patriot	s

Tales of the St. Lawrence Riverway
First rights sold to *The Blue Book Magazine* (Sep 1914—May 1915).
Refer to the Recurring Characters index for solo tales in the series

Sep	The Voice in the Mist	The Blue Book Magazine	ss
Sep	The Mask of Juno	Young's Magazine	s
Oct	Cousin Paul	Harper's Monthly Magazine	s
Oct	The Evil Shore	The Blue Book Magazine	ss
Oct	The Faith of Paul Duchaine	The Red Book Magazine	s
Nov	The Wrath of Paul Dupuy	The Blue Book Magazine	ss
Nov	The House With the Brass Door-Knobs	Young's Magazine	s
Dec	The Aerial War	Short Stories	s
Dec	The Lie of Pere Sebastian	The Blue Book Magazine	ss

1915

Jan	A Judith of '75	The American Patriot	s
Jan	The Curé Goes Hunting	The Blue Book Magazine	ss
Jan	Chapelle Ardente	The Red Book Magazine	s

The Revelations of an Ambassador-at-Large
Five were printed in *The Popular Magazine*, as noted. The whole series
was syndicated in the supplement, the Fiction Magazine. Proper sequence
is noted after each title

Jan 7	The Bulgarian Papers (# 1)	The Popular Magazine	ss
Jan 23	The Bullet-Proof Mantle (# 5)	The Popular Magazine	ss
Feb	The Wooing of Fanchette	The Blue Book Magazine	ss
Feb 7	The Wax Clavette (# 10)	The Popular Magazine	ss
Feb 13	Jacqueline of Golden River (1 of 4)	All-Story Cavalier Weekly	sl
Feb 20	Jacqueline of Golden River (2 of 4)	All-Story Cavalier Weekly	sl
Feb 23	The Red Envelope (# 11)	The Popular Magazine	ss
Feb 27	Jacqueline of Golden River (3 of 4)	All-Story Cavalier Weekly	sl
Mar	Mulligan and the Pull-Through	The American Patriot	s
Mar	The Pacification of Anne	The Blue Book Magazine	ss
Mar 6	Jacqueline of Golden River (4 of 4)	All-Story Cavalier Weekly	sl
Mar 7	Kitchener's Coup (# 12)	The Popular Magazine	ss
Apr	Big Pierre's Idol	The Blue Book Magazine	ss
Apr 10	Aaron Lapwing's Genius (1 of 7)	Chicago Ledger	sl
Apr 17	Aaron Lapwing's Genius (2 of 7)	Chicago Ledger	sl
Apr 24	Aaron Lapwing's Genius (3 of 7)	Chicago Ledger	sl
May	The Desperation of St. Jean	The Blue Book Magazine	ss
May 1	Aaron Lapwing's Genius (4 of 7)	Chicago Ledger	sl
May 8	Aaron Lapwing's Genius (5 of 7)	Chicago Ledger	sl
May 15	Aaron Lapwing's Genius (6 of 7)	Chicago Ledger	sl
May 22	Aaron Lapwing's Genius (7 of 7)	Chicago Ledger	sl
Jun 13	The Bookworm of Potsdam (# 2)	Fiction Magazine	ss
Jun 20	The Montenegrin Ciphers (# 3)	Fiction Magazine	ss
Jun 27	Count Berchtold's Birthday Party (# 4)	Fiction Magazine	ss
Jul 11	The Golden Death (# 6)	Fiction Magazine	ss
Jul 18	A Dead Man's Empire (# 7)	Fiction Magazine	ss
Jul 25	A Patriot's Dilemma (# 8)	Fiction Magazine	ss
Jul/Aug	Uncle Hendrick's Parlor Organ	The American Patriot	s

Aug 1	The "X" Bacillus (# 9)	Fiction Magazine	ss

The Flights of Francois
Partial first rights printed in *Ainslee's Magazine* (Sep 1915—Jan 1916)
Remaining installments printed in the *Chicago Tribune* (Oct 31—Dec 12)

Sep	Capt. Cholmunday's Monkey (# 5)	Ainslee's Magazine	ss
Sep 11	Lafe Evens Up	All-Story Weekly	ss
Oct	Alice of Chalons (# 7)	Ainslee's Magazine	ss
Oct	Trumps & Tolliver	The American Patriot	s
Oct 31	The Fair American (# 1)	The Chicago Tribune	ss
Nov	The General's Knave-Trap (# 8)	Ainslee's Magazine	ss
Nov	Captain Ransome's Twenty Minutes	The American Patriot	s
Nov 7	Suzette (# 2)	The Chicago Tribune	ss
Nov 14	The Bethune Charter (# 3)	The Chicago Tribune	ss
Nov 21	The Phantom City (# 4)	The Chicago Tribune	ss
Nov 28	The Five Army Corps (# 6)	The Chicago Tribune	ss
Dec	The Man With the Peaked Beard (# 10)	Ainslee's Magazine	ss
Dec 5	A Jest that Saved (# 9)	The Chicago Tribune	ss
Dec 12	The Belfry Dawn (# 11)	The Chicago Tribune	ss

1916

Jan	The Eve of the Hospital (# 12)	Ainslee's Magazine	ss
Jan	The Gates of Rocky River	The American Patriot	ss
Jan 1	The Sea Demons (1 of 4)	All-Story Weekly	sl
Jan 8	The Sea Demons (2 of 4)	All-Story Weekly	sl
Jan 15	The Sea Demons (3 of 4)	All-Story Weekly	sl
Jan 22	The Sea Demons (4 of 4)	All-Story Weekly	sl
Feb	Larry of the Yards	The Popular Magazine	s
Jul	Midsummer Madness	Munsey's Magazine	na
Aug 27	The Wolf Trap	Fiction Magazine	s
Oct 22	Pride of Place	Fiction Magazine	s

1917

Peggy Roche, Saleslady
Partially printed in the *Photoplay Magazine* (Mar—Jul 1917)

Mar	The Adventure of the Three Georges	Photoplay Magazine	ss
Apr	The Adventure of the Town Pond Submarine	Photoplay Magazine	ss
May	Torpedo Broker	Photoplay Magazine	ss
Jun	The Road to Biskra	Photoplay Magazine	ss
Jun	The Messiah of the Cylinder (1 of 4)	Everybody's Magazine	sl
Jul	The Jungle Knights	Photoplay Magazine	ss
Jul	The Messiah of the Cylinder (2 of 4)	Everybody's Magazine	sl
Aug	The Messiah of the Cylinder (3 of 4)	Everybody's Magazine	sl
Aug 12	The Crooked Finger	Fiction Magazine	s
Aug 26	His Second Self (1 of 10)	The Chicago Tribune	sl
Sep	The Messiah of the Cylinder (4 of 4)	Everybody's Magazine	sl
Sep 2	His Second Self (2 of 10)	The Chicago Tribune	sl
Sep 9	His Second Self (3 of 10)	The Chicago Tribune	sl
Sep 16	His Second Self (4 of 10)	The Chicago Tribune	sl
Sep 23	His Second Self (5 of 10)	The Chicago Tribune	sl
Sep 30	His Second Self (6 of 10)	The Chicago Tribune	sl
Oct 7	His Second Self (7 of 10)	The Chicago Tribune	sl
Oct 13	Wooden Spoil (1 of 6)	The Argosy	sl
Oct 14	His Second Self (8 of 10)	The Chicago Tribune	sl
Oct 20	Wooden Spoil (2 of 6)	The Argosy	sl
Oct 21	His Second Self (9 of 10)	The Chicago Tribune	sl
Oct 27	Wooden Spoil (3 of 6)	The Argosy	sl

Oct 28	His Second Self (10 of 10)	The Chicago Tribune	sl
Nov 3	Wooden Spoil (4 of 6)	The Argosy	sl
Nov 10	Wooden Spoil (5 of 6)	The Argosy	sl
Nov 17	Wooden Spoil (6 of 6)	The Argosy	sl
Dec 9	The Scar	Fiction Magazine	ss
Dec 22	The House of Gingras	The Argosy	ss

1918

Jan 26	The Diamond Demons (1 of 5)	All-Story Weekly	sl
Feb 2	The Diamond Demons (2 of 5)	All-Story Weekly	sl
Feb 2	Fruit of the Lamp (1 of 4)	The Argosy	sl
Feb 9	The Diamond Demons (3 of 5)	All-Story Weekly	sl
Feb 9	Fruit of the Lamp (2 of 4)	The Argosy	sl
Feb 16	The Diamond Demons (4 of 5)	All-Story Weekly	sl
Feb 16	Fruit of the Lamp (3 of 4)	The Argosy	sl
Feb 23	The Diamond Demons (5 of 5)	All-Story Weekly	sl
Feb 23	Fruit of the Lamp (4 of 4)	The Argosy	sl
Apr 7	Bride of Battle (1 of 7)	Fiction Magazine	sl
Apr 14	Bride of Battle (2 of 7)	Fiction Magazine	sl
Apr 21	Bride of Battle (3 of 7)	Fiction Magazine	sl
Apr 28	Bride of Battle (4 of 7)	Fiction Magazine	sl
May 5	Bride of Battle (5 of 7)	Fiction Magazine	sl
May 12	Bride of Battle (6 of 7)	Fiction Magazine	sl
May 19	Bride of Battle (7 of 7)	Fiction Magazine	sl
Jun	Pierre and Paul	Extension Magazine	ss
Jun 1	Draft of Eternity (1 of 4)	All-Story Weekly	sl
Jun 8	Draft of Eternity (2 of 4)	All-Story Weekly	sl
Jun 15	Draft of Eternity (3 of 4)	All-Story Weekly	sl
Jun 22	Draft of Eternity (4 of 4)	All-Story Weekly	sl
Nov 16	Eric of the Strong Heart (1 of 5)	Railroad Man's Magazine	sl
Nov 23	Eric of the Strong Heart (2 of 5)	Railroad Man's Magazine	sl
Nov 30	Eric of the Strong Heart (3 of 5)	Railroad Man's Magazine	sl
Dec 7	Eric of the Strong Heart (4 of 5)	Railroad Man's Magazine	sl
Dec 14	Eric of the Strong Heart (5 of 5)	Railroad Man's Magazine	sl

1919

Feb 11	Condemned by Woman	Detective Story Magazine	s
Mar 22	The Earth Tides	The Dearborn Independent	s
Mar 29	The Lion's Jaws (1 of 5)	All-Story Weekly	sl
Apr 5	The Lion's Jaws (2 of 5)	All-Story Weekly	sl
Apr 12	The Lion's Jaws (3 of 5)	All-Story Weekly	sl
Apr 19	The Lion's Jaws (4 of 5)	All-Story Weekly	sl
Apr 19	Tag For a Crown	Argosy and Railroad Man's Magazine	s
Apr 26	The Lion's Jaws (5 of 5)	All-Story Weekly	sl
Apr 29	The Shooting of Colonel Fisk	Detective Story Magazine	tc
May 6	A Helen of New York	Detective Story Magazine	tc
May 13	The Wife and the Other Man	Detective Story Magazine	tc
May 20	The Man Who "Killed" a Corpse	Detective Story Magazine	tc
May 27	The Body in the Box	Detective Story Magazine	tc
Jun 3	The Doctor and the Wealthy Patient	Detective Story Magazine	tc
Jun 10	The Superfluous Husband	Detective Story Magazine	tc
Jun 17	The Case of Mrs. Wharton	Detective Story Magazine	tc
Jun 24	Birchall, the Canadian Murderer	Detective Story Magazine	tc
Jul 1	The Murder of Doctor Burdell	Detective Story Magazine	tc
Jul 8	The Alibi That Failed	Detective Story Magazine	tc

Jul 15	The Two Parricides	Detective Story Magazine	tc
Aug	The Eyes of Pere Sebastian	Extension Magazine	ss
Sep 23	Detective Anchisi and the Fort Wayne Gang	Detective Story Magazine	tc
Nov 29	Under the Striped Man's Flag (1 of 5)	Chicago Ledger	sl
Dec 6	Under the Striped Man's Flag (2 of 5)	Chicago Ledger	sl
Dec 13	Under the Striped Man's Flag (3 of 5)	Chicago Ledger	sl
Dec 20	Under the Striped Man's Flag (4 of 5)	Chicago Ledger	sl
Dec 27	Under the Striped Man's Flag (5 of 5)	Chicago Ledger	sl

1920

Jan 3	The Big Muskeg (1 of 4)	The Argosy	sl
Jan 10	The Big Muskeg (2 of 4)	The Argosy	sl
Jan 17	The Big Muskeg (3 of 4)	The Argosy	sl
Jan 17	The Eye of Balamok (1 of 3)	All-Story Weekly	sl
Jan 24	The Big Muskeg (4 of 4)	The Argosy	sl
Jan 24	The Eye of Balamok (2 of 3)	All-Story Weekly	sl
Jan 24	The Beast Maker (1 of 4)	Chicago Ledger	sl
Jan 31	The Eye of Balamok (3 of 3)	All-Story Weekly	sl
Jan 31	The Beast Maker (2 of 4)	Chicago Ledger	sl
Feb 7	The Beast Maker (3 of 4)	Chicago Ledger	sl
Feb 14	The Beast Maker (4 of 4)	Chicago Ledger	sl
May 22	The Cain Ship (1 of 3)	Chicago Ledger	sl
May 29	The Cain Ship (2 of 3)	Chicago Ledger	sl
Jun 5	The Cain Ship (3 of 3)	Chicago Ledger	sl
Jun 5	The Valley of Sleeping Slaves (1 of 4)	Chicago Ledger	sl
Jun 12	The Valley of Sleeping Slaves (2 of 4)	Chicago Ledger	sl
Jun 19	The Valley of Sleeping Slaves (3 of 4)	Chicago Ledger	sl
Jun 26	The Valley of Sleeping Slaves (4 of 4)	Chicago Ledger	sl
Sep 7	Legally Dead (1 of 48)	London Daily Mail	sl
Sep 8	Legally Dead (2 of 48)	London Daily Mail	sl
Sep 9	Legally Dead (3 of 48)	London Daily Mail	sl
Sep 10	Legally Dead (4 of 48)	London Daily Mail	sl
Sep 11	Legally Dead (5 of 48)	London Daily Mail	sl
Sep 13	Legally Dead (6 of 48)	London Daily Mail	sl
Sep 14	Legally Dead (7 of 48)	London Daily Mail	sl
Sep 15	Legally Dead (8 of 48)	London Daily Mail	sl
Sep 16	Legally Dead (9 of 48)	London Daily Mail	sl
Sep 17	Legally Dead (10 of 48)	London Daily Mail	sl
Sep 18	Legally Dead (11 of 48)	London Daily Mail	sl
Sep 20	Legally Dead (12 of 48)	London Daily Mail	sl
Sep 21	Legally Dead (13 of 48)	London Daily Mail	sl
Sep 22	Legally Dead (14 of 48)	London Daily Mail	sl
Sep 23	Legally Dead (15 of 48)	London Daily Mail	sl
Sep 24	Legally Dead (16 of 48)	London Daily Mail	sl
Sep 25	Legally Dead (17 of 48)	London Daily Mail	sl
Sep 27	Legally Dead (18 of 48)	London Daily Mail	sl
Sep 28	Legally Dead (19 of 48)	London Daily Mail	sl
Sep 29	Legally Dead (20 of 48)	London Daily Mail	sl
Sep 30	Legally Dead (21 of 48)	London Daily Mail	sl
Oct 1	Legally Dead (22 of 48)	London Daily Mail	sl
Oct 2	Legally Dead (23 of 48)	London Daily Mail	sl
Oct 4	Legally Dead (24 of 48)	London Daily Mail	sl
Oct 5	Legally Dead (25 of 48)	London Daily Mail	sl
Oct 6	Legally Dead (26 of 48)	London Daily Mail	sl
Oct 7	Legally Dead (27 of 48)	London Daily Mail	sl
Oct 8	Legally Dead (28 of 48)	London Daily Mail	sl

Oct 9	Legally Dead (29 of 48)	London Daily Mail	sl
Oct 11	Legally Dead (30 of 48)	London Daily Mail	sl
Oct 12	Legally Dead (31 of 48)	London Daily Mail	sl
Oct 13	Legally Dead (32 of 48)	London Daily Mail	sl
Oct 14	Legally Dead (33 of 48)	London Daily Mail	sl
Oct 15	Legally Dead (34 of 48)	London Daily Mail	sl
Oct 16	Legally Dead (35 of 48)	London Daily Mail	sl
Oct 18	Legally Dead (36 of 48)	London Daily Mail	sl
Oct 19	Legally Dead (37 of 48)	London Daily Mail	sl
Oct 20	Legally Dead (38 of 48)	London Daily Mail	sl
Oct 21	Legally Dead (39 of 48)	London Daily Mail	sl
Oct 22	Legally Dead (40 of 48)	London Daily Mail	sl
Oct 23	Legally Dead (41 of 48)	London Daily Mail	sl
Oct 25	Legally Dead (42 of 48)	London Daily Mail	sl
Oct 26	Legally Dead (43 of 48)	London Daily Mail	sl
Oct 27	Legally Dead (44 of 48)	London Daily Mail	sl
Oct 28	Legally Dead (45 of 48)	London Daily Mail	sl
Oct 29	Legally Dead (46 of 48)	London Daily Mail	sl
Oct 30	Legally Dead (47 of 48)	London Daily Mail	sl
Nov 1	Legally Dead (48 of 48)	London Daily Mail	sl
Nov 27	While Dorion Lives (1 of 5)	Argosy All-Story Weekly	sl
Dec 4	While Dorion Lives (2 of 5)	Argosy All-Story Weekly	sl
Dec 11	While Dorion Lives (3 of 5)	Argosy All-Story Weekly	sl
Dec 18	While Dorion Lives (4 of 5)	Argosy All-Story Weekly	sl
Dec 25	While Dorion Lives (5 of 5)	Argosy All-Story Weekly	sl

1921

Feb 8	The Greater Claim (1 of 32)	London Daily Mail	sl
Feb 9	The Greater Claim (2 of 32)	London Daily Mail	sl
Feb 10	The Greater Claim (3 of 32)	London Daily Mail	sl
Feb 11	The Greater Claim (4 of 32)	London Daily Mail	sl
Feb 12	The Greater Claim (5 of 32)	London Daily Mail	sl
Feb 14	The Greater Claim (6 of 32)	London Daily Mail	sl
Feb 15	The Greater Claim (7 of 32)	London Daily Mail	sl
Feb 16	The Greater Claim (8 of 32)	London Daily Mail	sl
Feb 17	The Greater Claim (9 of 32)	London Daily Mail	sl
Feb 18	The Greater Claim (10 of 32)	London Daily Mail	sl
Feb 19	The Greater Claim (11 of 32)	London Daily Mail	sl
Feb 21	The Greater Claim (12 of 32)	London Daily Mail	sl
Feb 22	The Greater Claim (13 of 32)	London Daily Mail	sl
Feb 23	The Greater Claim (14 of 32)	London Daily Mail	sl
Feb 24	The Greater Claim (15 of 32)	London Daily Mail	sl
Feb 25	The Greater Claim (16 of 32)	London Daily Mail	sl
Feb 26	The Greater Claim (17 of 32)	London Daily Mail	sl
Feb 28	The Greater Claim (18 of 32)	London Daily Mail	sl
Mar 1	The Greater Claim (19 of 32)	London Daily Mail	sl
Mar 2	The Greater Claim (20 of 32)	London Daily Mail	sl
Mar 3	The Greater Claim (21 of 32)	London Daily Mail	sl
Mar 4	The Greater Claim (22 of 32)	London Daily Mail	sl
Mar 5	The Greater Claim (23 of 32)	London Daily Mail	sl
Mar 7	The Greater Claim (24 of 32)	London Daily Mail	sl
Mar 8	The Greater Claim (25 of 32)	London Daily Mail	sl
Mar 9	The Greater Claim (26 of 32)	London Daily Mail	sl
Mar 10	The Greater Claim (27 of 32)	London Daily Mail	sl
Mar 11	The Greater Claim (28 of 32)	London Daily Mail	sl
Mar 12	The Greater Claim (29 of 32)	London Daily Mail	sl

Mar 14	The Greater Claim (30 of 32)	London Daily Mail	sl
Mar 15	The Greater Claim (31 of 32)	London Daily Mail	sl
Mar 16	The Greater Claim (32 of 32)	London Daily Mail	sl
May 7	My Lady of the Nile (1 of 4)	Argosy All-Story Weekly	sl
May 14	My Lady of the Nile (2 of 4)	Argosy All-Story Weekly	sl
May 21	My Lady of the Nile (3 of 4)	Argosy All-Story Weekly	sl
May 28	My Lady of the Nile (4 of 4)	Argosy All-Story Weekly	sl
Jun	Crossroads	Breezy Stories	nt
Jul	The Fifth Guardian (1 of 3)	Cartoons Magazine and Wayside Tales	sl
Aug	The Fifth Guardian (2 of 3)	Wayside Tales and Cartoons Magazine	sl
Sep	The Fifth Guardian (3 of 3)	Wayside Tales and Cartoons Magazine	sl
Oct	Out of Arcady	Wayside Tales and Cartoons Magazine	s
Oct	Four Dumb Men (1 of 2)	Wayside Tales and Cartoons Magazine	nt
Oct 22	The White Lily Murder (1 of 10)	Chicago Ledger	sl
Oct 29	The White Lily Murder (2 of 10)	Chicago Ledger	sl
Nov	Four Dumb Men (2 of 2)	Wayside Tales and Cartoons Magazine	nt
Nov	Pals	Wayside Tales and Cartoons	s
Nov 5	The White Lily Murder (3 of 10)	Chicago Ledger	sl
Nov 12	The White Lily Murder (4 of 10)	Chicago Ledger	sl
Nov 19	The White Lily Murder (5 of 10)	Chicago Ledger	sl
Nov 26	The White Lily Murder (6 of 10)	Chicago Ledger	sl
Dec 3	The White Lily Murder (7 of 10)	Chicago Ledger	sl
Dec 10	The White Lily Murder (8 of 10)	Chicago Ledger	sl
Dec 17	The White Lily Murder (9 of 10)	Chicago Ledger	sl
Dec 24	The White Lily Murder (10 of 10)	Chicago Ledger	sl

1922

Jan 28	The Bandit of Batakaland (1 of 5)	Argosy All-Story Weekly	sl
Feb	Woman and the Law	Wayside Tales	nt
Feb 4	The Bandit of Batakaland (2 of 5)	Argosy All-Story Weekly	sl
Feb 11	The Bandit of Batakaland (3 of 5)	Argosy All-Story Weekly	sl
Feb 18	The Bandit of Batakaland (4 of 5)	Argosy All-Story Weekly	sl
Feb 25	The Bandit of Batakaland (5 of 5)	Argosy All-Story Weekly	sl

The Cloud Pirates
Printed only in the *Chicago Ledger* (1922: July 2—30)

Jul 8	The Cloud Pirates	Chicago Ledger	ss
Jul 15	Contraband and Whiskers	Chicago Ledger	ss
Jul 22	Treasure of Cos	Chicago Ledger	ss
Jul 29	The Rubber of Eagles	Chicago Ledger	ss
Aug 25	The Home Trail (1 of 5)	People's Story Magazine	sl
Sep 4	The Home Trail (2 of 5)	People's Story Magazine	sl
Sep 11	The Home Trail (3 of 5)	People's Story Magazine	sl
Sep 18	The Home Trail (4 of 5)	People's Story Magazine	sl
Sep 25	The Home Trail (5 of 5)	People's Story Magazine	sl

1923

Jan	Lee of the Northwest Mounted (1 of 8)	People's Popular Monthly	sl
Feb	Lee of the Northwest Mounted (2 of 8)	People's Popular Monthly	sl
Mar	THE STORY OF JOHN PAUL	Constable (UK)	N
Mar	Lee of the Northwest Mounted (3 of 8)	People's Popular Monthly	sl
Apr	Lee of the Northwest Mounted (4 of 8)	People's Popular Monthly	sl
May	Lee of the Northwest Mounted (5 of 8)	People's Popular Monthly	sl
May	The Square Peg	McClure's Magazine	s
Jun	Lee of the Northwest Mounted (6 of 8)	People's Popular Monthly	sl
Jul	Lee of the Northwest Mounted (7 of 8)	People's Popular Monthly	sl
Aug	Lee of the Northwest Mounted (8 of 8)	People's Popular Monthly	sl

Aug 1st	The Further Ranges	Ace-High Magazine	nt
Aug 15	Sergeant Forbes, Alias— (1 of 4)	People's	sl
Sep 1	Sergeant Forbes, Alias— (2 of 4)	People's	sl
Sep 15	Scrgeant Forbes, Alias— (3 of 4)	People's	sl
Oct 1	Sergeant Forbes, Alias— (4 of 4)	People's	sl
2nd Dec	The Devil's Tower	Ace-High Magazine	nt

1924

2nd Jan	Halsey of the Mounted	Ace-High Magazine	nt
Feb	The Wife of Midas	Delineator	s
Mar 8	Furs That Fed	Western Story Magazine	s
1st May	A Ridin' Gent	Ace-High Magazine	nt
1st Aug	Plunder Ranch	Ace-High Magazine	nt
Oct	The Making of a Man (1 of 5)	Muscle Builder	sl
2nd Oct	A Wanderer of the West	Ace-High Magazine	nt
Nov	The Making of a Man (2 of 5)	Muscle Builder	sl
Dec	The Making of a Man (3 of 5)	Muscle Builder	sl

1925

Jan	The Making of a Man (4 of 5)	Muscle Builder	sl
Feb	The Making of a Man (5 of 5)	Muscle Builder	sl
Feb	Reindeer Rustlers	Action Stories	nt
Feb	The Feud of Alkali Springs	Triple-X Magazine	nt
Mar	MIDDLE YEARS	Minton, Balch	N
Mar	The Awakening of Edith (1 of 5)	Physical Culture	sl
Apr	The Awakening of Edith (2 of 5)	Physical Culture	sl
Apr	Yellow Gold Trails	Novelets	nt
May	The Awakening of Edith (3 of 5)	Physical Culture	sl
May	Prince of the Plains	Ranch Romances	nt
2nd May	The Lightnin' Shot	Ace-High Magazine	nt
June	The Awakening of Edith (4 of 5)	Physical Culture	sl
Jul	The Awakening of Edith (5 of 5)	Physical Culture	sl
Jul	Steeled by Struggle (1 of 5)	Muscle Builder	sl
Jul	Swamp Soil (1 of 3)	Triple-X Magazine	sl
Aug	Steeled by Struggle (2 of 5)	Muscle Builder	sl
Aug	Swamp Soil (2 of 3)	Triple-X Magazine	sl
Sep	Steeled by Struggle (3 of 5)	Muscle Builder	sl
Sep	THE SELMANS	The Dial Press	N
Sep	Swamp Soil (3 of 3)	Triple-X Magazine	sl
Sep	West of Rainbow's End	Ranch Romances	nt
Oct	Steeled by Struggle (4 of 5)	Muscle Builder	sl
Nov	Steeled by Struggle (5 of 5)	Muscle Builder	sl
Nov	Jim Blair's Girl (1 of 5)	Ranch Romances	sl
Dec	From Crook to Hero (1 of 5)	Muscle Builder	sl
Dec	Jim Blair's Girl (2 of 5)	Ranch Romances	sl

1926

Jan	From Crook to Hero (2 of 5)	Muscle Builder	sl
Jan	Jim Blair's Girl (3 of 5)	Ranch Romances	sl
Jan	The Right to Motherhood (1 of 5)	Physical Culture	sl
2nd Jan	Hi-Jacking Rustlers	Ace-High Magazine	nt
Feb	From Crook to Hero (3 of 5)	Muscle Builder	sl
Feb	Jim Blair's Girl (4 of 5)	Ranch Romances	sl
Feb	The Right to Motherhood (2 of 5)	Physical Culture	sl
Mar	From Crook to Hero (4 of 5)	Muscle Builder	sl
Mar	Jim Blair's Girl (5 of 5)	Ranch Romances	sl

Mar	The Right to Motherhood (3 of 5)	Physical Culture	sl
2nd Mar	The Snow Trail	North-West Stories	s
Apr	From Crook to Hero (5 of 5)	Muscle Builder	sl
Apr	The Right to Motherhood (4 of 5)	Physical Culture	sl
May	The Right to Motherhood (5 of 5)	Physical Culture	sl
Jul	Trailin' Back	Lariat Story Magazine	nt
Sep	Sand and Diamonds	Action Stories	s
1st Sep	Arctic Treasure	North-West Stories	s
Oct	Child or Demon—Which?	Ghost Stories	ss
2nd Oct	Get Your Man!	North-West Stories	nt
Nov	Hearts and Diamonds (1 of 3)	Physical Culture	sl
Dec	Hands Across the Sea	War Stories	s
Dec 26	Hearts and Diamonds (2 of 3)	Physical Culture	sl
—	SALTED DIAMONDS	John Long (UK)	N

1927

Jan	Hearts and Diamonds (3 of 3)	Physical Culture	sl
Jan	The Doll That Came to Life	Ghost Stories	ss
1st Jan	Lost Men's Eden	North-West Stories	nt
Feb	The Scourge of the Mohilla	The Danger Trail	nt
Mar	The Ghost of the Red Cavalier	Ghost Stories	ss
May	He Told Me He Married a Ghost!	Ghost Stories	s
Jun	Fire—Water—and What?	Ghost Stories	ss
Jun	Gunman's Wages	Action Stories	s
Jul	The Phantom in the Wooden Well	Ghost Stories	s
Aug	The Island of Doom	The Danger Trail	na
Aug	The Soul That Lost Its Way	Ghost Stories	ss
1st Aug	Evened Scores	North-West Stories	nt
2nd Aug	Enter—The Mounted!	North-West Stories	nt
Sep	Thorns and Iron	Frontier Stories	nt
2nd Sep	The Long Trail	Ranch Romances	nt
Oct	Thorne, the Throne-Maker	The Danger Trail	na
Nov	Big Swamp	Brief Stories	na
Nov 10	The Wolf Trail	Short Stories	na
Dec	The House of the Living Dead (1 of 6)	Ghost Stories	sl
—	WINDING TRAILS	John Long (UK)	N

1928

Jan	The House of the Living Dead (2 of 6)	Ghost Stories	sl
1st Jan	Sunburst Valley	Ranch Romances	na
Feb	The House of the Living Dead (3 of 6)	Ghost Stories	sl
Mar	The House of the Living Dead (4 of 6)	Ghost Stories	sl
Mar	Broken Men	Five-Novels Monthly	nt
Mar	The Dark Disk	Complete Stories	na
Apr	The House of the Living Dead (5 of 6)	Ghost Stories	sl
Apr	Pawns of Empire	The Danger Trail	nt
1st Apr	Sheriff Nan	Ranch Romances	nt
May	The House of the Living Dead (6 of 6)	Ghost Stories	sl
May	Treasure Ranch	Five-Novels	nt
Jun	Our Astral Honeymoon	Ghost Stories	s
Jun 1	North of Fifty-Three	Three Star Magazine	nt
Jul	Jungle Loot	The Danger Trail	s
Jul	Legion of the Dead	Five-Novels Monthly	nt
Jul	The Blackest Magic of All	Ghost Stories	s
2nd Jul	Red Coat Patrol	North-West Stories	nt
Aug	One-Girl Ranch	Five-Novels Monthly	nt

Aug	The Prisoner of Life (1 of 6)	Ghost Stories	sl
1st Aug	A Rangeland Renegade	Ranch Romances	na
Sep	The Prisoner of Life (2 of 6)	Ghost Stories	sl
Sep	Red Harvest	Five-Novels Monthly	nt
Sep	The Mesquite Trail	Frontier Stories	nt
Oct	The Prisoner of Life (3 of 6)	Ghost Stories	sl
Oct	Crawford of the Border	Five-Novels Monthly	nt
Oct	Out of the Night	Red Blooded Stories	s
1st Oct	Riders of the Stars	Ranch Romances	nt
Nov	The Prisoner of Life (4 of 6)	Ghost Stories	sl
Nov	The Rustlin' Trail	Two Gun Western Stories	nt
Nov	Honor of the Sea	Red Blooded Stories	s
Dec	The Prisoner of Life (5 of 6)	Ghost Stories	sl
Dec	King of the Cocoa Trail	Red Blooded Stories	nt
2nd Dec	Cowboy Courageous	Ranch Romances	nt

1929

Jan	The Prisoner of Life (6 of 6)	Ghost Stories	sl
Feb	Diamonds of Doom	Frontier Stories	nt
Mar	Nothing North of Nagatok	North-West Stories	nt
2nd Mar	Romance of the Rio (1 of ?)	Ranch Romances	sl
1st Apr	Romance of the Rio (2 of ?)	Ranch Romances	sl
2nd Apr	Romance of the Rio (3 of ?)	Ranch Romances	sl
Apr 13	The Branded Man (1 of 4)	Argosy All-Story Weekly	sl
Apr 20	The Branded Man (2 of 4)	Argosy All-Story Weekly	sl
Apr 27	The Branded Man (3 of 4)	Argosy All-Story Weekly	sl
May	Eyes of the East	Five-Novels Monthly	nt
May	Manchu Guns	Navy Stories	nt
May 4	The Branded Man (4 of 4)	Argosy All-Story Weekly	sl
May 23	The Hellion Brood	War Stories	nt
Jun 20	The Seventeenth Star	War Stories	s
Jul	The Angel of the Marne	Ghost Stories	s
Jul	Hell's Station	Frontier Stories	nt
Jul 18	Shane of the Fifty-Third	War Stories	s
Aug 29	In the Last Minute	War Stories	s
Sep	Phantom Lips	Ghost Stories	s
Sep	Neal Effendi—American	War Novels	s
Sep 12	Lieutenant Limey Brown	War Stories	s
Oct	Dead Man's Valley	Sky Riders	nt
Oct 10	The Red Stronghold	War Stories	s
Nov	Hawk of the Himalayas	Frontier Stories	nt
Nov	Hearts and Sixes	Western Romances	nt
Nov	They Shall Not Pass	War Birds	s
Dec	Doom Prisoners	Action Stories	nt
Dec	There are Pearls in Dargan	Brief Stories	s

1930

Jan	Loot of the Wolf	North-West Stories	nt
Jan	Red Diamonds	Brief Stories	s
Jan	The Beetle Horde (1 of 2)	Astounding	sl
2nd Jan	Maid of the Valley	Ranch Romances	nt
Feb	The Beetle Horde (2 of 2)	Astounding	sl
Feb	Indian Dawn	Five-Novels Monthly	nt
Feb	The Range Rider (1 of 2)	Rangeland Love Story Magazine	sl
Mar	The Range Rider (2 of 2)	Rangeland Love Story Magazine	sl
1st Mar	Tides of Conquest (1 of 6)	Ranch Romances	sl

2nd Mar	Tides of Conquest (2 of 6)	Ranch Romances	sl
Apr	Trail of Wanted Men	Frontier Stories	nt
1st Apr	Tides of Conquest (3 of 6)	Ranch Romances	sl
2nd Apr	Tides of Conquest (4 of 6)	Ranch Romances	sl
May	The Atom-Smasher	Astounding Stories of Super-Science	na
May	The King Spy	Frontier Stories	nt
May	The Wing Wonder	Air Stories	nt
1st May	Tides of Conquest (5 of 6)	Ranch Romances	sl
2nd May	Tides of Conquest (6 of 6)	Ranch Romances	sl
Jun	The Circle of Happiness	Five-Novels Monthly	nt
Jun	Afghan Gold	Action Stories	s
Jul	The Chaparral Trail	Rangeland Love Story Magazine	na
Jul	Challenge of the U-212	Submarine Stories	nt
Aug	The Lord of Space	Astounding Stories of Super-Science	s
3rd Aug	The Steadfast Heart	Ranch Romances	na
Sep	Midnight Riders	Rangeland Love Story Magazine	nt
Oct	Wildcats Have Wings	War Stories	s
Oct	The Invisible Death	Astounding Stories of Super-Science	na
Oct	Temple of Death	Triple-X Magazine	s
Nov	The Wall of Death	Astounding Stories of Super-Science	s
Nov	Ghost Island	All-Fiction	nt
2nd Nov	The Starlight Trail	Ranch Romances	na
Dec	Ranger Breed	All-Fiction	s
Dec	Tennant—of the U.S.A.	War Stories	s
Dec	Treasure of the Moon	Empire Frontier	s
Dec	The Evil Three (1 of 5)	Ghost Stories	sl

1931

Jan	The Evil Three (2 of 5)	Ghost Stories	sl
Jan	Undertow	Five-Novels Monthly	nt
Feb	The Evil Three (3 of 5)	Ghost Stories	sl
Mar	The Evil Three (4 of 5)	Ghost Stories	sl
Mar 21	The Vengeance Trail	The Argosy	nt
2nd Mar	Rangeland Trickery	Ranch Romances	na
Apr	The Evil Three (5 of 5)	Ghost Stories	sl
Apr-May	Outlaws of the Sun	Miracle Science and Fantasy Stories	nt
Jun-Jul	Revolt on Inferno	Miracle Science and Fantasy Stories	nt
Jun	Love Rides the Sage	Rangeland Love Story Magazine	nt
Jul	Webs of Sand	Five-Novels Monthly	nt
2nd Jun	Cactus Trail (1 of 6)	Ranch Romances	sl
1st Jul	Cactus Trail (2 of 6)	Ranch Romances	sl
2nd Jul	Cactus Trail (3 of 6)	Ranch Romances	sl
3rd Jul	Cactus Trail (4 of 6)	Ranch Romances	sl
Aug	Dead Man's Trail	Action Novels	nt
Aug	A Man from Montana (1 of 5)	Rangeland Love Story Magazine	sl
1st Aug	Cactus Trail (5 of 6)	Ranch Romances	sl
2nd Aug	Cactus Trail (6 of 6)	Ranch Romances	sl
Sep	A Man from Montana (2 of 5)	Rangeland Love Story Magazine	sl
Sep	A Cry From Beyond	Strange Tales of Mystery and Terror	s
1st Sep	Desert Lover	Ranch Romances	
Oct	It Is For France	Soldiers of Fortune	s
Oct	A Man from Montana (3 of 5)	Rangeland Love Story Magazine	sl
Nov	A Man from Montana (4 of 5)	Rangeland Love Story Magazine	sl
Nov	Jewels of Empire	Five-Novels Monthly	nt
Nov	When Dead Gods Wake	Strange Tales of Mystery and Terror	s
Dec	The Black Avatar	Thrilling Adventures	s

Dec	A Man from Montana (5 of 5)	Rangeland Love Story Magazine	sl
Dec	Bows of Muscovy	Soldiers of Fortune	na
2nd Dec	Lost Ranch	Ranch Romances	na

1932

Jan	Holocaust	Five-Novels Monthly	nt
Jan	Magic Mountain	Rangeland Love Story Magazine	nt
2nd Jan	Riders of the Buttes (1 of 6)	Ranch Romances	sl
3rd Jan	Riders of the Buttes (2 of 6)	Ranch Romances	sl
1st Feb	Riders of the Buttes (3 of 6)	Ranch Romances	sl
2nd Feb	Riders of the Buttes (4 of 6)	Ranch Romances	sl
Mar	Trigger Trail	All Western Magazine	nt
1st Mar	Riders of the Buttes (5 of 6)	Ranch Romances	sl
2nd Mar	Riders of the Buttes (6 of 6)	Ranch Romances	sl
Apr	Thrones of Dust	Five-Novels Monthly	nt
Apr	Good Night, Eve (1 of 5)	Physical Culture	sl
May	The Trail of Terror	Rangeland Love Story Magazine	nt
May	Red Rose and White	Soldiers of Fortune	nt
May	Good Night, Eve (2 of 5)	Physical Culture	sl
June	Good Night, Eve (3 of 5)	Physical Culture	sl
2nd Jun	Crooked Trails	Ranch Romances	na
Jul	Good Night, Eve (4 of 5)	Physical Culture	sl
Jul	The Phantom Hand (1 of 5)	Weird Tales	sl
Aug	Good Night, Eve (5 of 5)	Physical Culture	sl
Aug	The Phantom Hand (2 of 5)	Weird Tales	sl
Sep	The Phantom Hand (3 of 5)	Weird Tales	sl
Oct	The Curse of Amen-Ra	Strange Tales of Mystery and Terror	nt
Oct	The Phantom Hand (4 of 5)	Weird Tales	sl
Oct/Nov	Wild Ice	Action Novels	nt
Nov	The Phantom Hand (5 of 5)	Weird Tales	sl
Dec/Jan	Poison Gold	Action Novels	nt

1933

Jul 8	World's End (1 of 3)	The Argosy	sl
Jul 15	World's End (2 of 3)	The Argosy	sl
Jul 22	World's End (3 of 3)	The Argosy	sl
Sep 10	High Andes	Short Stories	s
1st Oct	The Wolf Trail	Ranch Romances	nt

1934

Jan	Red-Coat Patrol	Thrilling Adventures	nt
2nd Feb	Cross-Trails to Paradise	Ranch Romances	na
Feb	Swords for Navarre	Five-Novels Monthly	nt
Feb	Fury of the Jungle	Sure-Fire Screen Stories	sa
Mar	Loot of Lost Lode	Ace-High Magazine	nt
Apr	Murder Down East	Five Novels Monthly	nt
Apr	Treasure Lake	Ace-High Magazine	nt
May	The Forbidden Shrine	Five-Novels Monthly	nt
2nd Jun	Terror Range (1 of 6)		
3rd Jun	Terror Range (2 of 6)	Ranch Romances	sl
1st Jul	Terror Range (3 of 6)	Ranch Romances	sl
2nd Jul	Terror Range (4 of 6)	Ranch Romances	sl
3rd Jul	Terror Range (5 of 6)	Ranch Romances	sl
1st Aug	Terror Range (6 of 6)	Ranch Romances	sl
Oct	Jewels of Death	Ace-High Magazine	nt
Dec	Captive's Castle	Five-Novels Monthly	nt

1935

Jan 13	Shifting Sands (1 of 6)	Sunday Magazine	sl
Jan 20	Shifting Sands (2 of 6)	Sunday Magazine	sl
Jan 27	Shifting Sands (3 of 6)	Sunday Magazine	sl
Feb 3	Shifting Sands (4 of 6)	Sunday Magazine	sl
Feb 10	Shifting Sands (5 of 6)	Sunday Magazine	sl
Feb 17	Shifting Sands (6 of 6)	Sunday Magazine	sl
Apr	With Swords Unsheathed	Five-Novels Monthly	nt
1st May	Trail of the Wolf	Ranch Romances	na
Nov	Code of the Northland	Spicy-Adventure Stories	s
Nov	Traitress' Wages	Spicy-Adventure Stories	s
Dec	Devil Drums	Spicy-Adventure Stories	s
Dec	Brothers in Blood	Spicy Mystery Stories	s
Dec	She Who Was He!	Spicy Mystery Stories	s
3rd Dec	Framed	Ranch Romances	na

1936

Jan	Angel of Mercy	Spicy-Adventure Stories	s
Jan	Paradise Island	Spicy-Adventure Stories	s
Feb	Lady of Fortune	Spicy-Adventure Stories	s
Feb	Bat Man	Spicy Mystery Stories	s
1st Mar	Doughnuts for Discord	Ranch Romances	nt
Mar	Bamboo Flower	Spicy-Adventure Stories	s
Mar	Bride of the Pyramid	Spicy-Adventure Stories	s
Mar	Savage Spears	Spicy-Adventure Stories	s
Mar	Astral Murder	Spicy Mystery Stories	s
Apr	Bride of the Sword	Spicy-Adventure Stories	s
Apr	Philtre of Death	Spicy Mystery Stories	s
Apr	Zang the Creator	Spicy Mystery Stories	s
May	Puppet Princess	Spicy-Adventure Stories	s
May	Loyalties	Breezy Stories and Young's Magazine	s
Jun	The Woman of Cayenne	Spicy-Adventure Stories	s
Jun	Dead Man's Shoes	Spicy Mystery Stories	s
Jul	Forest Fury	Spicy-Adventure Stories	s
Jul	Devil Doctor	Spicy Mystery Stories	s
Aug	Playthings of War	Spicy-Adventure Stories	s
Aug	The White Goddess	Spicy-Adventure Stories	s
Aug	Cat Woman	Spicy Mystery Stories	s
Aug	Cyclops	Spicy Mystery Stories	s
Aug	Venus of Troy	Spicy Mystery Stories	s
Sep	Girl from Green Gap	Western Romances	nt
Sep	Death in the Desert	Spicy-Adventure Stories	s
Sep	Death Trail	Spicy-Adventure Stories	s
Sep	Valley of Blood	Spicy-Adventure Stories	s
Sep	Beyond the Veil	Spicy Mystery Stories	s
Sep	The Secret of Old Farm	Spicy Mystery Stories	s
Oct	Return of the Beast	Spicy Mystery Stories	s
Nov	Tyrants Die By the Sword	Five-Novels Monthly	nt
Nov	Passion's Puppets	Spicy-Adventure Stories	s
Nov	Rainbow's End	Spicy-Adventure Stories	s
Nov	Daughter of Death	Spicy Mystery Stories	s
Nov	Death's Dancing Partner	Spicy Mystery Stories	s
Nov	Isle of the Unborn	Spicy Mystery Stories	s
Dec	Maverick of Mustang Mesa	Red Seal Western	nt
Dec	For the Honor of the Duchess	Spicy-Adventure Stories	s

Dec	Kali's Vine	Spicy Mystery Stories	s
Dec	Tidewater	Spicy Mystery Stories	s
Dec	Free, High, and Handsome	Spicy Western Stories	s
Dec	Bridal Eve	Breezy Stories and Young's Magazine	s
Winter	Captives of the Arctic Wasteland	North-West Stories	nt

1937

Jan	Flower Boat	Spicy-Adventure Stories	s
2nd Jan	Rio Riders	Ranch Romances	nt
Jan	Man Woman Massacre	Spicy Western Stories	s
Feb	Death Treasure	Spicy-Adventure Stories	s
Feb	Skinner	Spicy-Adventure Stories	s
Feb	Hell's Robots	Spicy Mystery Stories	s
Feb	Satan's Music	Spicy Mystery Stories	s
Feb	The Time Dissolver	Spicy Mystery Stories	s
Mar	Girl From Spain	Saucy Detective	s
Mar	Devil Trail	Spicy-Adventure Stories	s
Mar	Sky Goddess	Spicy-Adventure Stories	s
Mar	Curse of the Ogilvy's	Spicy Mystery Stories	s
Apr	The Spider's Web	Five-Novels Monthly	nt
Apr	Black Gods	Spicy-Adventure Stories	s
Apr	Witch's Sabbath	Spicy Mystery Stories	s
May	Fire-Escapes	Breezy Stories and Young's Magazine	s
May	Girl of the Mounties	Saucy Movie Tales	s
May	Barbary Brew	Spicy-Adventure Stories	s
May	Diamonds of Death	Spicy-Adventure Stories	s
May	Road to Tolosa	Spicy-Adventure Stories	s
May	Shadow Man	Spicy Mystery Stories	s
Jun	Black Goddess	Spicy-Adventure Stories	s
Jun	For Love of Scotland's Queen	Spicy-Adventure Stories	s
Jun	The Golden Crocodile	Spicy-Adventure Stories	s
Jun	Lilith	Spicy Mystery Stories	s
Jun	Outlaw Guns	Spicy Western Stories	s
Jun	Danger's Bloody Banner	Thrilling Adventures	s
Jul	Spawn of Siva	Spicy-Adventure Stories	s
Jul	The Brazen Bull	Spicy Mystery Stories	s
Aug	Bride of the Sun	Spicy-Adventure Stories	s
Aug	Girl of the Night	Spicy Mystery Stories	s
Aug	Vault of Horror	Spicy Mystery Stories	s
Sep	[The] Walls of the Alcazar	Five-Novels Monthly	nt
Sep	The Bride of Eagle Pass	Western Romances	nt
Sep	Eagle Flight	Spicy-Adventure Stories	s
Sep	Snake Bride	Spicy-Adventure Stories	s
Sep	Temple of Death	Spicy-Adventure Stories	s
Sep	The Death God Awakes	Spicy Mystery Stories	s
Sep	Synthetic Husband	Spicy Mystery Stories	s
Sep	Skidding	Spicy Western Stories	s
Fall	The Man-Master	North-West Romances	nt
Oct	Dark Dominion	Spicy-Adventure Stories	s
Oct	Night Raid	Spicy-Adventure Stories	s
Oct	Van Dam's Heads	Spicy-Adventure Stories	s
Oct	Hell's Tryst	Spicy Mystery Stories	s
Oct	I'll Buy Your Appetites	Spicy Mystery Stories	s
Nov	Lords of Folly	Spicy-Adventure Stories	s
Nov	Phantom Throne	Spicy-Adventure Stories	s
2nd Nov	Rustler's Trail	Ranch Romances	nt

Dec	Out of Aden	Spicy-Adventure Stories	s
Dec	Maid of Osiris	Spicy Mystery Stories	s
Dec	The Vampire Doll	Spicy Mystery Stories	s
Winter	Blood on the Snow	North-West Romances	s

1938

Jan	Sword Play at Dawn!	Five-Novels Monthly	nt
Jan	Two on a Trail	Spicy-Adventure Stories	s
Feb	To Carve a New World	Five-Novels Monthly	nt
Feb	Body Divided	Spicy Mystery Stories	s
Feb	Bright Isle of Enchantment	Spicy Mystery Stories	s
Mar	Congo Spears	Spicy-Adventure Stories	s
Mar	Slave of Alhambra	Thrilling Adventure	nt
Spring	Man Hunt for the Mounted	North-West Romances	nt
Apr	Code of the Hills	Spicy-Adventure Stories	s
Apr	Monkey Bones	Spicy-Adventure Stories	s
Apr	Trails End	Spicy-Adventure Stories	s
Apr	Soul Asleep	Spicy Mystery Stories	s
May	God of the Pit	Spicy-Adventure Stories	s
May	Dead Man Rides	Spicy Mystery Stories	s
May	The Time-Twister	Spicy Mystery Stories	s
Jun	Lady Sheriff	Spicy-Adventure Stories	s
Jun	Prize of Peru	Spicy-Adventure Stories	s
Jun	Beyond Hell's Barriers	Spicy Mystery Stories	s
Jun	Emerald of Death	Spicy Mystery Stories	s
Jun	Thunderstone	Spicy Mystery Stories	s
Summer	Valley of Gold	North-West Romances	nt
Jul	Dead or Alive!	Spicy-Adventure Stories	s
Jul	No More Romance	Spicy-Adventure Stories	s
1st Jul	Night Raiders	Ranch Romances	nt
Aug	Gorilla Man	Spicy-Adventure Stories	s
Aug	Challenge to Napoleon	Five-Novels Monthly	nt
Aug	Dead Man's Arm	Spicy Mystery Stories	s
Aug	The Iron Bride	Spicy Mystery Stories	s
Aug	Mad Charioteers	Spicy Mystery Stories	nt
Sep	On Secret Service	Spicy-Adventure Stories	s
Sep	The Water Gate	Spicy-Adventure Stories	s
Fall	Derelict of the Arctic Sea	North-West Romances	s
Oct	Dane Raiders	Spicy-Adventure Stories	s
Oct	A Date With the Goat God	Spicy Mystery Stories	s
Oct	Point of Eternity	Spicy Mystery Stories	s
Nov	Men of Empire	Five-Novels Monthly	nt
Nov	Woman in Yellow	Romantic Western	s
Nov	Death Stalks Through Walls	Spicy-Adventure Stories	s
Nov	Lady of the Law	Spicy-Adventure Stories	s
Dec	The Jeweled Throne	Five-Novels Monthly	nt
Dec	Beast of the Kremlin	Spicy-Adventure Stories	s
Dec	House of Hell	Spicy-Adventure Stories	s
Dec	Mississippi Trail	Spicy-Adventure Stories	s
Dec	Even Scores	Spicy Western Stories	s

1939

Jan	Sea Raiders	Spicy-Adventure Stories	s
Feb	Bugle Call	Spicy-Adventure Stories	s
Feb	Fox Fury	Spicy-Adventure Stories	s
Feb	Liddle Red-Head	Spicy Detective Stories	s

Mar	Pearls of Panama	Spicy-Adventure Stories	s
1st Mar	Lone Rider	Ranch Romances	na
Spring	Ruby of Revolt	All-Adventure Action Novels	s
Apr	The Queen's Mercy	Golden Fleece	na
Apr	Death Ride	Spicy-Adventure Stories	s
Apr	Sea-Haven	Spicy-Adventure Stories	s
Apr	Ogre Island	Spicy Mystery Stories	s
Apr	Water Witch	Spicy Mystery Stories	s
May	Army of the Dead	Spicy-Adventure Stories	s
May	The Climbing Buddha	Spicy-Adventure Stories	s
Jun	Face in the Crystal	Spicy Mystery Stories	s
Jun	Pipes of Doom	Spicy Mystery Stories	s
Jul	Lone Pyramid	Spicy-Adventure Stories	s
Aug	Red Dawn	Spicy-Adventure Stories	s
Aug	Sheriff Barbara	Spicy-Adventure Stories	s
Aug	Gallows Buster	Spicy Mystery Stories	s
Sep	Fire-Land Queen	Spicy-Adventure Stories	s
Sep	Men-At-Arms	Spicy-Adventure Stories	s
Sep	Treasure of Andes	Spicy-Adventure Stories	s
Fall	The Black Gods of Ngami	Jungle Stories	s
Oct	Jackaroo	Spicy-Adventure Stories	s
Oct	Rubies of Empire	Spicy-Adventure Stories	s
Oct	She-Sheriff Barbara	Spicy-Adventure Stories	s
Oct	Curse of Killarney	Spicy Mystery Stories	s
Oct	Luck of the Cromwells	Spicy Mystery Stories	s
Nov	The Laughing Moor	Spicy-Adventure Stories	s
Nov	Red Eden	Spicy-Adventure Stories	s
Dec	Elephant Girl	Spicy-Adventure Stories	s
Dec	There Can't Be Two O'Haras	Spicy-Adventure Stories	s

1940

Jan	Flat-Boat	Spicy-Adventure Stories	s
Jan	Masai Spears	Spicy-Adventure Stories	s
Feb	Jungle Lords	Spicy-Adventure Stories	s
Feb	Witches' Island	Spicy Mystery Stories	s
Apr	Mayor of No Man's Land	Spicy-Adventure Stories	s
Apr	Night of Action	Spicy-Adventure Stories	s
May	High Andes	Spicy-Adventure Stories	s
2nd May	Trickery Trail	Ranch Romances	nt
Jun	Isle of Refuge	Spicy Mystery Stories	nt
Jun	Vision of Death	Spicy Mystery Stories	s
Jul	Stakes on the Black	Spicy-Adventure Stories	s
Jul	Woman from Mercury	Spicy-Adventure Stories	s
Aug	City of Light	Spicy-Adventure Stories	s
Aug	Human Boomerang	Spicy-Adventure Stories	s
Aug	Giant from Babel	Spicy Mystery Stories	nt
Aug	Storm Over Athabasca (1 of ?)	Farmer's Magazine (CND)	sl
Sep	Shawn of the Stars	Spicy-Adventure Stories	s
Sep	Storm Over Athabasca (2 of ?)	Farmer's Magazine (CND)	sl
Oct	Gypsy Tent	Spicy-Adventure Stories	s
Oct	Lord of Two Worlds	Spicy-Adventure Stories	s
Oct	The Robot Awakes	Spicy-Adventure Stories	s
Oct	Air Maiden	Spicy Mystery Stories	nt
Oct	Marooned on Eros	Spicy Mystery Stories	nt
Oct	Dealer in Death	Super-Detective	nt
Oct	Storm Over Athabasca (3 of ?)	Farmer's Magazine (CND)	sl

Nov	Cave of Canoes	Spicy-Adventure Stories	s
Nov	Rebel Planet	Spicy-Adventure Stories	s
Nov	Legion of Robots	Super-Detective	nt
Nov	Storm Over Athabasca (4 of ?)	Farmer's Magazine (CND)	sl
Dec	The Great God Harris	Spicy-Adventure Stories	s
Dec	Things That Were Men	Spicy-Adventure Stories	s
Dec	The Lifted Veil	Spicy Mystery Stories	s
Dec	Madame Murder	Super-Detective	nt

1941

Jan	Bloated Death	Super Detective	nt
Jan	Cord of Death	Spicy-Adventure Stories	s
Jan	Death Sanctuary	Spicy-Adventure Stories	s
Jan	Isle of the Gods	Spicy Mystery Stories	s
Feb	Killer In Yellow	Super Detective	nt
Feb	Indigo Island	Spicy-Adventure Stories	s
Feb	Space Burial	Spicy-Adventure Stories	s
Feb	Murderer's Doom	Spicy Mystery Stories	s
Mar	Murder in Paradise	Super Detective	nt
Mar	Throne of Straw	Spicy-Adventure Stories	s
Mar	Lobster Girl	Spicy Mystery Stories	s
Apr	Murder Syndicate	Super Detective	nt
Apr	Human Pyramid	Spicy-Adventure Stories	s
Apr	Tree of Life	Spicy-Adventure Stories	s
Apr	Ghosts of Time	Spicy Mystery Stories	s
Apr	Scourge of Women	Spicy Mystery Stories	s
May	Burma Road	Spicy-Adventure Stories	s
May	The Lord of Space	Spicy-Adventure Stories	s
2nd May	Feud of the Forest	Ranch Romances	na
Jun	The Horrible Marionettes	Super Detective	nt
Jul	Hostage of Battle	Spicy-Adventure Stories	s
Jul	Rat Trap	Spicy-Adventure Stories	s
Jul	Scrambled Destiny	Spicy Mystery Stories	s
Jul	Spell of the Serpent	Spicy Mystery Stories	s
Aug	Border Napoleon	Super Detective	nt
Aug	The Stone Men of Ignota	Future Fiction	s
Aug	The Last Adam	Spicy-Adventure Stories	s
Sep	When Planets Mate	Spicy-Adventure Stories	s
Sep	Dancing-Girl Orchid	Spicy Mystery Stories	s
Sep	The God From Beyond	Spicy Mystery Stories	s
Fall	Frozen Hell	North-West Romances	nt
Oct	Spies of Destiny	Super Detective	nt
Oct	Hammock Land	Spicy-Adventure Stories	s
Oct	Farrell's Double	Spicy Mystery Stories	nt
Oct	Viking's Daughter	Spicy Mystery Stories	nt
Oct	Moon Patrol	Thrilling Wonder Stories	s
Nov	Inca Gold	Spicy-Adventure Stories	s
Nov	Swordsman's Choice	Spicy-Adventure Stories	s
Nov	Arc of Death	Spicy Mystery Stories	s
Nov	The Captain's Hook	Spicy Mystery Stories	nt
Dec	I. O. U. Murder	Super Detective	nt
Dec	Future in Reverse	Spicy Mystery Stories	s

1942

Jan	Jest of Death	Spicy-Adventure Stories	s
Jan	Girl From the Nebula	Spicy Mystery Stories	nt

2nd Jan	Rangeland Fury	Ranch Romances	na
Feb	Cold Turkey	Super Detective	nt
Feb	Night Invasion	Spicy-Adventure Stories	s
Feb	Whcn It Grew Cold	Spicy Mystery Stories	s
Mar	Jinx	Spicy Mystery Stories	nt
Apr	Mrs. Big	Super Detective	nt
Apr	Heads Shall Roll	Spicy-Adventure Stories	s
May	Bee Flight	Spicy-Adventure Stories	s
Jun	Needle's Eye	Super Detective	nt
Jun	Lion Guard	Spicy-Adventure Stories	s
Jul	Tree Mother	Spicy-Adventure Stories	s
Jul	Marsh Murder	Spicy Mystery Stories	s
Jul	Vampire	Spicy Mystery Stories	s
Aug	Mark of the Spider	Super Detective	nt
Aug	Glacier Girl	Spicy-Adventure Stories	s
Aug	Jungle Tin	Spicy-Adventure Stories	s
Sep	The Sin-Eater	Spicy Mystery Stories	s
Oct	Sons of the Boiling Blanket	Spicy-Adventure Stories	s
Oct	Dwindling Death	Spicy Mystery Stories	nt
Oct	Half-Way House	Spicy Mystery Stories	s
3rd Oct	Empire of the Skies	Ranch Romances	na
Nov	The Golden Stool	Spicy-Adventure Stories	s
Nov	Nero's Ring	Spicy-Adventure Stories	s
Nov	The Lost Shadow	Spicy Mystery Stories	nt
Nov	Twisted Time	Spicy Mystery Stories	nt
Dec	Eagle of Tibet	Action Stories	nt
Dec	Commando	Spicy-Adventure Stories	s
Dec	Sailor's Luck	Spicy-Adventure Stories	s

1943

Jan	Four Who Fled	Speed Adventure Stories	s
Jan	King Silver Rides	Speed Adventure Stories	s
Jan	Ghost-Wife	Speed Mystery	s
Feb	White Girl	Speed Adventure Stories	s
Feb	Ryder's Lights	Speed Mystery	nt
Feb	Steel of Death	Speed Mystery	nt
Feb	The Unknown Factor	Speed Mystery	nt
Mar	Four-Footed Justice	Speed Adventure Stories	s
Mar	King Silver's Last Ride	Speed Adventure Stories	s
Mar	Stand Up, Ye Dead	Speed Adventure Stories	s
May	Elephant God	Speed Adventure Stories	s
May	River of Tears	Speed Adventure Stories	s
May	House of Death	Speed Mystery	s
May	The Samurai Sword	Speed Mystery	s
Jul	City of Doom	Speed Adventure Stories	s
Jul	Fix Bayonets!	Speed Adventure Stories	s
Jul	Claws of the Statue	Speed Mystery	s
Jul	Time Lag	Speed Mystery	s
Jul	Titanium Ship	Speed Mystery	s
Sep	Bern's Blunder	Speed Adventure Stories	s
Sep	Quisling's Daughter	Speed Adventure Stories	s
Sep	Arc of Death	Speed Mystery	s
Sep	Fog Over Kiska	Speed Mystery	s
Sep	Kenney's Stooge	Speed Mystery	s
Nov	Bulls Have Jaws	Speed Adventure Stories	s
Nov	The Secret Channel	Speed Adventure Stories	s

Nov	A Tailor Never Pricks His Finger	Speed Adventure Stories	s
Nov	Like a Tiger	Speed Mystery	nt
Nov	Sergeant Joe's Return	Speed Mystery	nt
Winter	The Red-Coat Rebel	North-West Romances	nt

1944

Jan	Jungle Trap	Speed Adventure Stories	s
Jan	Sicilian Night	Speed Adventure Stories	s
Jan	Spoil of the Sea	Speed Adventure Stories	s
Jan	Among Those Present	Speed Mystery	s
Jan	'Fraid-Cat Hero	Speed Mystery	s
Jan	Lost Fingerprints	Speed Mystery	s
Jan	The Perfect Crime	Speed Mystery	s
Mar	Long Pig	Speed Adventure Stories	s
Mar	Rats Never Learn	Speed Adventure Stories	s
Mar	Salvation M'Shane	Speed Adventure Stories	s
Mar	Crossed Wires	Speed Mystery	s
Mar	Dry Death	Speed Mystery	s
Mar	The Judas Bottle	Speed Mystery	s
Apr	The Seeing Eye	Private Detective Stories	s
May	Curse of the Tremaines	Private Detective Stories	s
May	Coconut Cargo	Speed Adventure Stories	s
May	The Dawn Tide	Speed Adventure Stories	s
May	Peace Comes to Bongo	Speed Adventure Stories	s
May	Death in the Tank	Speed Detective	nt
May	Beggar-Ticks	Speed Mystery	s
May	The Flight Magnificent	Speed Mystery	nt
May	Lady Luck	Speed Mystery	s
Jun	The Ghost Will Walk Tonight	Super-Detective	s
Jul	Ghost of Empire	Speed Adventure Stories	s
Jul	Sea-Lubber M'Shane	Speed Adventure Stories	s
Jul	Refugee Ship	Speed Detective	s
Jul	Hell's Castle	Speed Mystery	s
Jul	Jailbreak	Speed Mystery	s
Sep	Follow the Fish	Speed Adventure Stories	s
Sep	Medical Officer	Speed Adventure Stories	s
Sep	Rat-Run	Speed Adventure Stories	s
Sep	Blood Racket	Speed Mystery	s
Sep	Daniel Webster Said	Speed Mystery	s
Sep	Broccoli Burlesque	Super-Detective	s
Nov	Brain-Buster	Private Detective Stories	s
Nov	Chilled Mutton	Speed Adventure Stories	s
Nov	Red Star of India	Speed Adventure Stories	s
Nov	Secret Weapon	Speed Adventure Stories	s
Nov	The Stuffed Shirt	Speed Mystery	s
Nov	This Was Grandison	Speed Mystery	s
Nov	Unborn Terror	Speed Mystery	s
Nov	Wolf Woman	Speed Mystery	s
Dec	The Tell-Tale Arm	Private Detective Stories	s
Dec	Sailing—Midnight	Hollywood Detective	s
Dec	Matched Slugs	Speed Detective	s
Dec	Turnover in Tannersville	Super-Detective	s

1945

Jan	Planted Fingerprints	Private Detective Stories	s
Jan	The Brides of Coco Island	Speed Adventure Stories	s

Jan	Get Your Man!	Speed Adventure Stories	s
Jan	Swords for Florence	Speed Adventure Stories	s
Jan	Heaven's Son-in-Law	Speed Mystery	s
Jan	Killer Car	Speed Mystery	s
Jan	Cyanide	Super-Detective	s
Jan 6	Her Home Region (1 of 8)	Toronto Star Weekly	sl
Jan 13	Her Home Region (2 of 8)	Toronto Star Weekly	sl
Jan 20	Her Home Region (3 of 8)	Toronto Star Weekly	sl
Jan 27	Her Home Region (4 of 8)	Toronto Star Weekly	sl
Feb	Ranger Bait	Speed Western Stories	s
Feb 3	Her Home Region (5 of 8)	Toronto Star Weekly	sl
Feb 10	Her Home Region (6 of 8)	Toronto Star Weekly	sl
Feb 17	Her Home Region (7 of 8)	Toronto Star Weekly	sl
Feb 24	Her Home Region (8 of 8)	Toronto Star Weekly	sl
Mar	Living Dead Man	Speed Mystery	s
Mar	Canine Verdict	Super-Detective	s
Mar	Doubling for Death	Super-Detective	s
Apr	Feathers	Private Detective Stories	s
Apr	Home-Town Soldier	Private Detective Stories	s
Apr	Death Patrol	Speed Adventure Stories	s
Apr	For Scotland's Queen	Speed Adventure Stories	s
Apr	The Madness of M'Shane	Speed Adventure Stories	s
Apr	Typed	Super-Detective	s
May	Unwritten Law	Hollywood Detective	s
Jun	Button, Button	Private Detective Stories	s
Jun	Crazy House	Speed Mystery	s
Jun	Gate of Death	Speed Mystery	s
Jun	Hot Stuff	Speed Mystery	s
Jun	Blind Luck	Speed Western Stories	s
Jun	Frame-Up	Super-Detective	s
Jul	Banzai Charge	Speed Adventure Stories	s
Jul	The Sheriff Wanted Peace	Speed Western Stories	s
Aug	War Time	Hollywood Detective	s
Aug	Pony Express	Fighting Western	s
Aug	Postponed Verdict	Private Detective Stories	s
Sep	Fungus and Arsenic	Private Detective Stories	s
Sep	Proxy Murder	Private Detective Stories	s
Sep	Corpse in the Car	Super-Detective	s
Sep	Split Seams	Super-Detective	s
Oct	Crusoe on Antarctica	Speed Adventure Stories	s
Oct	The God in the Tomb	Speed Adventure Stories	s
Oct	The Shaving of M'Shane	Speed Adventure Stories	s
Oct	Trigger-Quick	Speed Western Stories	s
Nov	No Witnesses	Super-Detective	s
Nov	Sheriff-Tooth	Super-Detective	s
Dec	Frame-Up	Speed Detective	s

1946

Jan	Bows of Fortune	Speed Adventure Stories	nt
Jan	Ghost Plane	Speed Adventure Stories	s
Jan	Letters of Marque	Speed Adventure Stories	s
Jan	September Peaches	Super-Detective	s
Feb	Goat in the Stable	Speed Detective	s
Feb	Nailed	Private Detective Stories	s
Mar	Rye and Die	Private Detective Stories	s
Mar	Taos Trail	Six-Gun Western	s

Mar	Bell-Bottom Trousers	Super-Detective	s
May	Sword-Slasher	Speed Detective	s
May 5	Sweeping Tides	The Boston Daily Globe	nt
Jun	By Name of Brown	Fighting Western	s
Jun	Mud In Your Eye!	Fighting Western	s
Jul	Old-Fashioned Lady	Super-Detective	s
Aug	Kit Carson, Renegade	Leading Western	nt
Aug	Saint Unsealed	Six-Gun Western	s
Sep	Murder House	Super-Detective	s
Oct	Buffalo Trail	Fighting Western	s
Nov	Cave of Ghosts	Leading Western	s
Nov	Terror By Night	Private Detective Stories	s
Nov	Mr. Bill, Come Back	Speed Western Stories	s
Nov	Brushless Cream	Super-Detective	s
Dec	The Singing Utes	Six-Gun Western	nt
Dec	Soul at Strife	Speed Detective	s
Dec	Riders of the Border	Speed Western Stories	s

1947

Aug	Gun Round-up	Leading Western	s
Oct	Honor for a Harrigan	Speed Western Stories	s
Nov	Trouble Wrangler	Leading Western	s

1948

Mar 14	The Vital Clue	New Orleans Times-Picayune	vi
Apr	Final Curtain	Zane Grey's Western Magazine	s
Oct	Dead Men's Cave	Fighting Western	s

1949

Aug	Ruckus at Red River	Fighting Western	s

1950

Feb 12	Air-Minded	The Boston Daily Globe	s
Jul	Slo Pay	Fighting Western	s
Aug 20	No Compromise	The Boston Daily Globe	s

1951

Sep 30	The Red Trail (1 of 4)	The Boston Daily Globe	sl
Oct 7	The Red Trail (2 of 4)	The Boston Daily Globe	sl
Oct 14	The Red Trail (3 of 4)	The Boston Daily Globe	sl
Oct 21	The Red Trail (4 of 4)	The Boston Daily Globe	sl

Part Two: Chronological Index of Syndicated Newspaper Vignettes

NOTE: Precise dating of syndicated vignettes is nearly impossible. As thus, the earliest known appearance of each vignette is recorded. Vignettes appearing from 1905 to 1906 are for children, and the service provider is unknown.

The Newspaper Enterprise Association from 1907-1910 and William Gerard Chapman's bureau 1908-1917 and the mid-1920s, handled Emanuel's vignettes. The mid-1920s original vignettes have never been located. They were sold to only one market. The identity of that market is unknown.

Chapman's Daily Short Story service officially launched in the Fall of 1912. To establish a standard form, *The Day Book* will be utilized to represent all of Emanuel's vignette output for the period 1912 through 1917. *The Day Book* represents First Regional Rights in the Chicago area. As a daily paper, it ran the service on a regular schedule, oft-times slightly ahead of other regions or simultaneously. The *Dallas Morning News,* the *St. Louis-Post Dispatch,* and the *Detroit Free Press* also carried the service but not continuously. Sadly, mid-January, February, March, April, May, June and July 1917 issues of *The Day Book* are missing from the Library of Congress. Due to the World War, most national papers had already discontinued the service. *The Day Book* may have been one of the last, leaving those last several months of vignettes currently a mystery.

"Picked Off," in *Harper's Weekly*, was syndicated as "Corporal Herring's First Fight;" these are not noted. "The Cakes of Judgment" from *Century* magazine, likewise was syndicated, worldwide, as far away as in New Zealand's *Hawera & Normanby Star.*

Additionally, many national and rural papers altered the titles of the stories. For example, "The Buddha's Eyes" in *The Day Book* also appears as "The Idol's Eyes" in the *Detroit Free Press.*

A. Children's Vignettes (1905-1906)—syndicate service unidentified

Year	Month/Day		Vignette Title	Byline

Dallas Morning News (Dallas, Texas)

Year	Month/Day		Vignette Title	Byline
1905	Nov	5	Stephanus Paulus Joubert: A Story About a Boer Boy Hero	V. R. Emanuel
1905	Dec	17	The Adventure of a Penny: A Christmas Story	V. Emanuel
1905	Dec	24	The Bad Boy and Santa Claus	V. R. Emanuel
1905	Dec	31	Ling Lee's New Year	V. R. Emanuel
1906	Jan	21	Little Maudie's Party	V. R. Emanuel
1906	Feb	18	Elizabeth's Lesson	V. R. Emanuel

B. Vignettes (1907-1910) via the Newspaper Enterprise Association

Binghamton Press (Binghamton, New York)

Year	Month/Day		Vignette Title	Byline
1907	Sep	18	Swallow	Victor Rousseau

Marshall Expounder (Marshall, Michigan)

Year	Month/Day		Vignette Title	Byline
1908	Mar	20	On Crusoe's Island	Victor Rousseau

The Des Moines Daily News (Des Moines, Iowa)

Year	Month/Day		Vignette Title	Byline
1908	Apr	29	The Voice at the Door	Harold Carter
1908	Aug	3	The Governor's Daughter	Harold Carter

1908	Aug	17	The Tobacco Taster	Harold Carter
1908	Oct	9	The Eyes of the Statue	Harold Carter
1908	Oct	11	Where None Pursueth	Harold Carter
1908	Oct	25	By The Aid of Delilah	Victor Rousseau
1908	Dec	28	The Convict	Harold Carter
1909	Mar	21	How Zucchi Broke Jail	Harold Carter
1909	Jun	28	The Coup That Failed	Harold Carter
1909	Aug	2	The Decoy Peanut	Harold Carter

San Antonio Gazette (San Antonio, Texas)

1908	Jun	18	The Duel	Harold Carter
1908	Jul	6	A Question of Identity	Harold Carter
1908	Jul	7	Under the River	Harold Carter
1908	Jul	21	The Madman	Harold Carter
1908	Sep	2	The Frost King's Conquest	Harold Carter
1908	Dec	14	The Lost Rubens	Harold Carter

San Antonio Light (San Antonio, Texas)

| 1909 | Feb | 10 | Avery's Exploit | Harold Carter |
| 1909 | Feb | 23 | Sol Blumberg's Strategy | Harold Carter |

San Antonio Light and Gazette (San Antonio, Texas)

1909	Jun	15	Artists at Odds	Harold Carter
1909	Jun	29	In the Chair	Harold Carter
1909	Aug	22	Pride of Profession	Harold Carter
1909	Oct	14	Food for Wolves	Harold Carter

Wilkes-Barre Times (Wilkes-Barre, Pennsylvania)

1908	Jan	8	The Wonderful Hour	Victor Rousseau
1908	Jan	9	Only Father	Victor Rousseau
1908	Mar	25	"Noblesse Oblige"	Victor Rousseau
1908	Apr	1	Under the Knife	Harold Carter
1908	Sep	26	Mrs. Briggs—Heroine	Harold Carter
1908	Sep	29	The Trait of the Tiger	Harold Carter
1908	Nov	2	King of the Gamblers	Harold Carter
1909	Feb	5	A Sower of Stony Soil	Harold Carter
1909	May	19	Diamond Cut Diamond	Harold Carter
1909	Jun	7	The Tower of Silence	Harold Carter
1909	Jul	17	When the King Jests	—Uncredited
1909	Aug	3	The Ruling Passion	Harold Carter
1909	Aug	24	Shah's Mate	Harold Carter
1909	Sep	24	—Untitled	Harold Carter
1909	Oct	1	Follow My Leader	Harold Carter
1909	Oct	2	A Woman's Strategy	Harold Carter
1909	Oct	15	The Test of the Preacher	Harold Carter
1909	Oct	20	The Hall of Mirrors	Harold Carter
1909	Nov	1	The Sheik's Granary	Harold Carter
1909	Nov	5	The Peddler's Cross	Harold Carter
1909	Nov	8	Nathanson's Wedding Gift	Harold Carter
1909	Nov	16	Death in the Greenhouse	Harold Carter
1909	Dec	17	The Chinese Reel	Harold Carter
1909	Dec	28	The Teakwood Cane	Harold Carter
1910	Jan	5	The Blind Confederate	Harold Carter
1910	Jan	17	Blue Blade	Harold Carter
1910	Jan	24	The Goddess of Murder	Harold Carter
1910	Jan	27	The Thirteenth Nerve	Harold Carter

1910	Mar	7	The Diamonds and the Dentist	Harold Carter
1910	Apr	1	Clubs and Diamonds	Harold Carter
1910	Apr	15	The Double Transfer	Harold Carter
1910	Jun	14	The Interloper	Harold Carter
1910	Jun	14	The Moose Call	Harold Carter
1910	Jun	20	The Tailor's Temptation	Harold Carter
1910	Aug	5	The Drummer-Major	Harold Carter
1910	Oct	10	The Spy in the Submarine	Harold Carter
1910	Nov	10	The Missing Link	Harold Carter
1910	Nov	11	The Rajah's Trap	Harold Carter
1910	Nov	11	The Hour of Grace	Harold Carter

Pittsburg Press **(Pittsburgh, Pennsylvania)**

1908	Oct	23	The Ashes in the Urn	Harold Carter
1908	Oct	29	The Survival of the Fittest	Harold Carter
1908	Nov	12	The Pearl of El-Safi	Harold Carter
1908	Nov	17	Measure for Measure	Harold Carter
1909	Mar	8	"Wolf"	Harold Carter
1909	Mar	26	Sponge Island	Harold Carter
1909	May	25	Star of the South	Harold Carter
1909	Jun	2	The Red Wolf	Harold Carter
1909	Jun	10	Time's Revenge	Harold Carter
1909	Jun	15	A Jest of Fortune	Harold Carter
1909	Sep	15	Professor's Discovery	Harold Carter
1909	Sep	25	Follow the Leader	Harold Carter
1910	Jan	3	The Fatal Paper	Harold Carter
1910	Jan	20	The Premium Brides	Harold Carter
1910	Feb	8	The Lobster Pots	Harold Carter
1910	Feb	15	The God of Luck	Harold Carter
1910	Feb	22	JOB VII:10	Harold Carter
1910	Mar	10	The Secret Passage	Harold Carter
1910	Mar	17	The Battle of the Aquarium	Harold Carter
1909	Mar	18	The Treasure of the Stream	Harold Carter
1910	Mar	29	The Death Lure	Harold Carter
1910	May	10	The Missing Link	Victor Rousseau
1910	May	16	Nathanson's Natural Foe	Harold Carter
1910	Jun	7	The Mummy of Thoth	Harold Carter
1910	June	7	The Salt Shaker	Harold Carter
1910	Jul	11	The Chain	Harold Carter
1910	Jul	19	The June Bug	Harold Carter
1910	Aug	9	The Green Cockade	Harold Carter
1910	Aug	16	Fool's Luck	Harold Carter
1910	Aug	26	The Spy in the Submarine	Harold Carter
1910	Aug	26	The Duel in the Gorge	Harold Carter

C. Vignettes (1909-1917) via the International Press Bureau

Belleville News Democrat **(Belleville, Illinois)**

1909	Feb	25	Brandy and Soda	H. M. Egbert
1909	Mar	31	Bacillus Prodigiosus	H. M. Egbert

Pine Bluffs Post **(Pine Bluffs, Wyoming)**

1909	Mar	3	The Tailor's Dilemma	H. M. Egbert
1909	Apr	4	The Chameleon's Bite	H. M. Egbert

***The Hamburg Reporter* (Hamburg, Iowa)**
1909 Jun 4   Lodger's Union   H. M. Egbert

***Yampa Leader* (Yampa, Colorado)**
1909 Jun 11   The Third Ingredient   H. M. Egbert

***Oelwein Daily Register* (Oelwein, Iowa)**
1909 Jul 16   The Blue Rose   H. M. Egbert

***The Daily Press* (Sheboygan, Wisconsin)**
1909 Aug 9   A Ghost Misplaced   H. M. Egbert

***The Longmont Ledger* (Marion, Colorado)**
1909 Oct 10   The Professor's Mission   H. M. Egbert

***The Sheboygan Press* (Sheboygan, Wisconsin)**
1909 Oct 12   A Genuine Raphael   H. M. Egbert

***The Day Book* (Chicago, Illinois)**
1912 Sep 3   "Man Proposes, But—"   H. M. Egbert
1912 Sep 5   The Brent Inheritance   Harold Carter
1912 Sep 9   A Delayed Honeymoon   Harold Carter
1912 Sep 21   Wireless   H. M. Egbert
1912 Sep 28   Twixt Love and Duty   H. M. Egbert
1912 Sep 30   Father of the Regiment   Harold Carter
1912 Oct 10   Ephriam's Message   Harold Carter
1912 Oct 11   Snaith's Discovery   George P. Munson
1912 Oct 16   A Matter of State's Rights   Harold Carter
1912 Oct 19   Old Jennings   Frank Filson
1912 Oct 24   Wintergreen   Harold Carter
1912 Oct 26   A Marriage Arranged   H. M. Egbert
1912 Oct 28   A Scholastic Merger   George Munson
1912 Oct 30   At the Forge Fire   H. M. Egbert
1912 Nov 2   The Test of Fortune   Harold Carter
1912 Nov 5   Man Who Found His Own   Harold Carter
1912 Nov 6   A Role Repeated   Frank Filson
1912 Nov 9   The Heart of an Indian   H. M. Egbert
1912 Nov 11   Doctor's Sweetheart   Harold Carter
1912 Nov 16   A Bottle of Peaches   H. M. Egbert
1912 Nov 18   They Both Scored   Frank Filson
1912 Nov 20   Governor's Conversion   George Munson
1912 Nov 22   Grace Boyce's Sacrifice   Frank Filson
1912 Nov 23   The Flaw in the Title   H. M. Egbert
1912 Nov 27   Their Thanksgiving   George Munson
1912 Nov 30   Dolores   H. M. Egbert
1912 Dec 3   Two Prisoners   Frank Filson
1912 Dec 4   King's Ten Surgeons   Harold Carter
1912 Dec 6   Spinster's Island   Harold Carter
1912 Dec 10   The Supreme Test   Harold Carter
1912 Dec 12   Her Choice   Frank Filson
1912 Dec 14   Till Called For   H. M. Egbert
1912 Dec 21   Hewett's Reward   H. M. Egbert
1912 Dec 24   Johnny's Gift   Harold Carter
1912 Dec 27   Gurlick's Convolution   George Munson
1912 Dec 28   The Turn of the Page   Frank Filson
1912 Dec 31   Hubby's Love Letters   George Munson

1913	Jan	2	Uncle Takes a Hand	Frank Filson
1913	Jan	4	Simple Pete	Harold Carter
1913	Jan	6	Kane's Folly	Harold Carter
1913	Jan	8	Light on George's Past	Frank Filson
1913	Jan	9	Rensley's Return	George Munson
1913	Jan	11	Ten Years After	Harold Carter
1913	Jan	17	Brewster's Discovery	George Munson
1913	Jan	18	Sheila's Lovers	Frank Filson
1913	Jan	21	The Wolf and the Lamb	Frank Filson
1913	Jan	23	Hiram's Folly	George Munson
1913	Jan	24	The Wreck of the 10:10	Harold Carter
1913	Jan	25	The Blood Atonement	H. M. Egbert
1913	Jan	31	The Winning Battle	Harold Carter
1913	Feb	4	My Friends the Lins	George Munson
1913	Feb	7	Engine Driver's Story	Frank Filson
1913	Feb	8	The Bridge	H. M. Egbert
1913	Feb	11	The Saving Love	Harold Carter
1913	Feb	13	The New Letter	Frank Filson
1913	Feb	15	The Man in the Pit	H. M. Egbert
1913	Feb	18	Ben's Wedding	Frank Filson
1913	Feb	22	The Snow Bride	George Munson
1913	Feb	25	The Maid of the Mill	Harold Carter
1913	Mar	1	Gift of the Mountains	H. M. Egbert
1913	Mar	8	The Scapegoat	H. M. Egbert
1913	Mar	15	Lieut. Savard's Reincarnation	H. M. Egbert
1913	Mar	18	The Nurse's Miracle	Harold Carter
1913	Mar	22	Kemble's Compact	H. M. Egbert
1913	Mar	25	The Casting Vote	Harold Carter
1913	Mar	29	Lord Chancellor and Jones	Percy Keble
1913	Apr	3	The Hold-Up	Frank Filson
1913	Apr	5	An Eight-Year Nap	H. M. Egbert
1913	Apr	8	Aunt Mary's Gift	Frank Filson
1913	Apr	10	As a Thief in Night	H. M. Egbert
1913	Apr	17	The Coward	H. M. Egbert
1913	Apr	23	A Terrible Moment	Victor Radcliffe
1913	Apr	24	John's Mascot	Harold Carter
1913	Apr	26	Gardenias	H. M. Egbert
1913	Apr	29	Lady of the Manor	Frank Tilson (sic)
1913	May	1	The Serpent's Tooth	George Munson
1913	May	8	Five Seconds	Harold Charles (sic)
1913	May	13	The Master Touch	Frank Filson
1913	May	15	The Man in the Moon	George Munson
1913	May	22	The Toy Mouse	Harold Carter
1913	May	24	Ep's Emporium Fire	H. M. Egbert
1913	Jun	4	The Songbird	Victor Radcliffe
1913	Jun	7	Just Foolishness	H. M. Egbert
1913	Jun	10	Two in a Crowd	Harold Carter
1913	Jun	13	"All in the Family"	Victor Redcliffe
1913	Jun	17	A Woman's Sacrifice	Frank Filson
1913	Jun	20	A Double Intrigue	George Munson
1913	Jun	24	When a Man Marries	George Munson
1913	Jul	3	The Mystery of Om	George Munson
1913	Jul	8	Cousin Agatha	George Munson
1913	Jul	10	Grandma's Bluff	Frank Filson
1913	Jul	17	Flaherty at Bridge	Harold Carter
1913	Jul	28	Their First Quarrel	Frank Filson

1913	Aug	4	Jordan's Pilgrimage	Victor Redcliffe
1913	Aug	19	His Sweetheart	Harold Carter
1913	Sep	2	The Worth of a Man	H. M. Egbert
1913	Sep	9	The Eyes of Love	Harold Carter
1913	Sep	10	The Lost Will	Frank Filson
1913	Sep	16	An Experiment	Frank Filson
1913	Sep	18	The Serpent in Eden	George Munson
1913	Oct	2	An Angel in Glass	Harold Carter
1913	Oct	7	Johnny, Homemaker	Harold Carter
1913	Oct	14	Between Two Fires	George Hurson (sic)
1913	Oct	23	The Promised Land	Frank Filson
1913	Oct	25	Dead Man's Message	H. M. Egbert
1913	Oct	31	Belle's Problem	Harold Carter
1913	Nov	4	The Premium Bride	Frank Filson
1913	Nov	11	Her Cook-Book	Harold Carter
1913	Nov	13	Uncle Will's Legacy	George Munson
1913	Nov	28	A Question of Caste	H. M. Egbert
1913	Dec	9	A Double Intrigue	George Munson
1913	Dec	13	The Turning Point	H. M. Egbert
1913	Dec	16	The Evidence	George Munson
1913	Dec	18	Living and the Dead	Frank Filson
1913	Dec	23	The Spiranthea	Harold Carter
1914	Jan	13	A Sentimental Trip	Harold Carter
1914	Jan	15	The Runaway	George Munson
1914	Jan	20	The New Year Guest	Frank Filson
1914	Jan	29	Taming Miss Abigail	George Munson
1914	Feb	3	The Mill	Harold Carter
1914	Feb	12	A Puritan Girl	Harold Carter
1914	Feb	17	Art for Art's Sake	George Munson
1914	Feb	19	Two Kinds of Men	Frank Filson
1914	Feb	26	Getting Results	Harold Carter
1914	Mar	5	Three Generations	Harold Carter
1914	Mar	12	Flood at Blue Shank	Frank Filson
1914	Mar	19	Tony's Sweetheart	Harold Carter
1914	Mar	26	The Trap	Frank Filson
1914	Mar	31	Glen Cove's Surprise	Harold Carter
1914	Apr	2	Uncle Eustace	Frank Filson
1914	Apr	7	A Model Man	George Munson
1914	Apr	23	The Quick and the Dead	Harold Carter
1914	May	5	The "Squealer"	Harold Carter
1914	May	12	Miss Martha's Will	George Munson
1914	May	21	Bobby's Father	Harold Carter
1914	Jun	2	Phineas Kelly's Fortune	George Munson
1914	Jun	6	By the Peace River	H. M. Egbert
1914	Jun	9	Jim's Return	Frank Filson
1914	Jun	11	The Son Who Was Lost	Harold Carter
1914	Jun	16	The Poet's Corner	Harold Carter
1914	Jun	23	Old Michael	Harold Carter
1914	Jul	2	The Billiken Clock	George Munson
1914	Jul	9	Getting Even	Frank Filson
1914	Jul	16	The Lost Will	Frank Filson
1914	Jul	21	A Man of Faith	Harold Carter
1914	Jul	28	The Desert of Luxury	John Filson
1914	Jul	30	The Blended Strawberry	Harold Carter
1914	Aug	6	The Minister's Secret	George Munson
1914	Aug	8	A Woman's Will	H. M. Egbert

1914	Aug	15	The Trick Mare	George Munson
1914	Aug	27	Glass Vs. Bullets	Frank Filson
1914	Sep	1	The Girl in Green	George Munson
1914	Sep	10	The Shoe Partner	Harold Carter
1914	Sep	11	A Business Start	Victor Radcliffe
1914	Sep	12	First Love	H. M. Egbert
1914	Sep	15	Grandpa's Love Affair	George Munson
1914	Sep	16	A Little Schemer	Victor Radcliffe
1914	Sep	17	Blair's Plan	Harold Carter
1914	Sep	19	Hunting the Shoe	H. M. Egbert
1914	Sep	22	Aunt Jenny	Frank Filson
1914	Sep	24	The Hour and Minute	George Munson
1914	Sep	25	The Ne'er-Do-Well	Victor Redcliffe
1914	Sep	29	A Mental Twist	Frank Filson
1914	Oct	8	Johnson's Romance	Harold Carter
1914	Oct	10	The Colonel's Error	H. M. Egbert
1914	Oct	12	The Old Homestead	Victor Redcliffe
1914	Oct	15	Cache of Laughing Cloud	Harold Carter
1914	Oct	24	Miss Brown of Boston	H. M. Egbert
1914	Oct	29	The Laughing Box	Harold Carter
1914	Nov	3	Barton's Experiment	Frank Filson
1914	Nov	5	The Martyr's of Suburbia	Frank Filson
1914	Nov	6	At Holly Farm	Victor Redcliffe
1914	Nov	7	The Coup That Failed	H. M. Egbert
1914	Nov	10	The Moment's Indecision	George Hunson (sic)
1914	Nov	12	Art and Love	Frank Filson
1914	Nov	14	An Official Error	H. M. Egbert
1914	Nov	19	The Last Straw	George Munson
1914	Nov	21	The Peacemaker	Frank Filson
1914	Nov	28	The New Life	H. M. Egbert
1914	Dec	5	They Also Serve	H. M. Egbert
1914	Dec	8	A Widow's Strategy	George Munson
1914	Dec	10	The Moving Finger	Harold Carter
1914	Dec	21	A Real "Scoop"	Victor Redcliffe
1914	Dec	22	A Woman's Taste	George Munson
1914	Dec	23	The Lost Word	Victor Radcliffe
1914	Dec	26	The Last Message	H. M. Egbert
1915	Jan	2	Sold Out	H. M. Egbert
1915	Jan	5	Miss Raymond's Legacy	Frank Filson
1915	Jan	7	A Double Dream	Frank Filson
1915	Jan	14	Hard Luck in Nugget	Harold Carter
1915	Jan	16	The Wheel of Fate	Harold Carter
1915	Jan	19	Uncle Zeke's Millenium	Harold Carter
1915	Jan	23	The Doctor's Patient	H. M. Egbert
1915	Jan	28	The Presentiment	Harold Carter
1915	Feb	4	The Little Doc	Frank Filson
1915	Feb	6	Cupid	H. M. Egbert
1915	Feb	9	The Cabal at Rothstein's	George Munson
1915	Feb	10	The Old Love	Victor Radcliffe
1915	Feb	11	The Morals of Seacliff	Harold Carter
1915	Feb	13	Lemons—Orange Blossoms	H. M. Egbert
1915	Feb	16	The Honeymoon House	George Munson
1915	Feb	23	Jean's Reason	Harold Carter
1915	Feb	25	A Dress Rehearsal	George Munson
1915	Feb	27	Miss Mary's Indiscretion	H. M. Egbert
1915	Mar	4	The White Lie	George Munson

1915	Mar	5	Nobly Won	Victor Redcliffe
1915	Mar	11	John Smith's Theory	Frank Filson
1915	Mar	13	The Diamond Thief	H. M. Egbert
1915	Mar	16	The Vision of Love	George Munson
1915	Mar	23	Joe, the Bigamist	George Munson
1915	Mar	25	A Topsy-Turvy Proposal	Frank Filson
1915	Mar	27	The Visionary	H. M. Egbert
1915	Mar	30	The Traitress	Frank Filson
1915	Apr	6	A Wayfarer	Victor Redcliffe
1915	Apr	13	Mooney's Ghost Story	Harold Carter
1915	Apr	15	A Shy Man's Wooing	George Munson
1915	Apr	17	Where the Heart Is	H. M. Egbert
1915	Apr	22	A Ten-Dollar Phantasy	Frank Filson
1915	Apr	24	The Supreme Chance	H. M. Egbert
1915	Apr	28	A Freak of Fate	Victor Redcliffe
1915	May	1	Poor Uncle Thomas	H. M. Egbert
1915	May	4	The Machines	Frank Filson
1915	May	6	Nora Finnerty's Sin	George Munson
1915	May	11	A Happy Investment	Harold Carter
1915	May	13	The Catch in the Drawer	George Munson
1915	May	15	Shipwreck	H. M. Egbert
1915	May	20	The Man in the Swamp	John Edgerton
1915	May	22	Toodle's Discovery	H. M. Egbert
1915	May	25	The Air Battle	Frank Filson
1915	May	27	The Dead Man's Will	Harold Carter
1915	May	29	The Claim of Life	H. M. Egbert
1915	Jun	1	The Decoy Duck	Frank Filson
1915	Jun	3	The Nurse's Story	Harold Carter
1915	Jun	4	The Ordeal	Victor Radcliffe
1915	Jun	10	A Mutual Decision	George Munson
1915	Jun	17	A Woman's Faith	Harold Carter
1915	Jun	19	Jim's Chance	H. M. Egbert
1915	Jun	22	John's Opportunity	George Munson
1915	Jun	23	The War Baby	Victor Radcliffe
1915	Jun	26	Old Mark's Stratagem	H. M. Egbert
1915	Jul	1	The Secret Clause	George Munson
1915	Jul	6	A Jungle Meeting	Frank Filson
1915	Jul	8	Mollie's Mistake	George Munson
1915	Jul	10	A Man's Problem	H. M. Egbert
1915	Jul	12	The Legacy	Victor Radcliffe
1915	Jul	15	The Curate's Conscience	Harold Carter
1915	Jul	24	The Captain's Wishes	H. M. Egbert
1915	Jul	29	Two in Trouble	George Munson
1915	Jul	31	East and West	H. M. Egbert
1915	Aug	5	An Unfinished Story	Harold Carter
1915	Aug	7	Red Fox	H. M. Egbert
1915	Aug	10	An Old Man's Stratagem	Frank Filson
1915	Aug	12	The Blackmailer	H. M. Egbert
1915	Aug	13	Tender and True	Victor Radcliffe
1915	Aug	17	In Bohemia	George Munson
1915	Aug	19	A Trick of the Trade	Frank Filson
1915	Aug	24	Mistress and Maid	Harold Carter
1915	Aug	25	The New Mayor	Victor Radcliffe
1915	Aug	28	Maida's Wooing	H. M. Egbert
1915	Sep	4	The Blue Weed	H. M. Egbert
1915	Sep	8	Stanley's Return	George Munson

1915	Sep	9	Raphael	Harold Carter
1915	Sep	11	The Bond of Birth	H. M. Egbert
1915	Sep	14	The Laws of Commerce	Harold Carter
1915	Sep	18	The Power of Thought	H. M. Egbert
1915	Sep	24	A Girl's Wooing	Harold Carter
1915	Sep	25	The Point of View	Frank Filson
1915	Sep	27	Through Mischance	Victor Radcliffe
1915	Sep	28	Quarantine	George Munson
1915	Oct	1	The Temptress	H. M. Egbert
1915	Oct	5	Cynthia's Contract	Harold Carter
1915	Oct	9	Jim's Return	H. M. Egbert
1915	Oct	12	The Artistic Temperament	Frank Filson
1915	Oct	14	Ulysses	Harold Carter
1915	Oct	28	A Favorable Decision	Harold Carter
1915	Oct	30	Jim's Decision	H. M. Egbert
1915	Nov	2	My Love Story	Frank Filson
1915	Nov	3	Won By Waiting	Victor Redcliffe
1915	Nov	4	The Man and the Tiger	George Munson
1915	Nov	6	The Love Germ	H. M. Egbert
1915	Nov	9	The Peace-Maker	George Munson
1915	Nov	11	A Three Days' Holiday	Harold Carter
1915	Nov	13	A Forty-Dollar Husband	H. M. Egbert
1915	Nov	24	Good Neighbors	Victor Redcliffe
1915	Nov	27	A Ten-Cent Catastrophe	H. M. Egbert
1915	Dec	4	Mike's Job	George Munson
1915	Dec	7	The Girl in Gray	Harold Carter
1915	Dec	11	A Fool There Was	H. M. Egbert
1915	Dec	16	The Symond's Case	Frank Filson
1915	Dec	17	For Mother's Sake	Victor Redcliffe
1915	Dec	18	Night and Dawning	H. M. Egbert
1915	Dec	21	The Danger Point	George Munson
1915	Dec	23	Sam's Charge	Harold Carter
1915	Dec	30	Israel Reforms	George Munson
1916	Jan	6	The Happy Release	George Munson
1916	Jan	7	A Professional Optimist	Victor Redcliffe
1916	Jan	8	Letty's Garden	Harold Carter
1916	Jan	11	The Girl Downstairs	Harold Carter
1916	Jan	15	The God of Battles	Frank Filson
1916	Jan	18	Dorothy Butter-Fingers	George Munson
1916	Jan	22	Who Shot Col. Garrett?	H. M. Egbert
1916	Jan	26	A Clever Marplot	Victor Redcliffe
1916	Jan	29	Old Jim's Discovery	H. M. Egbert
1916	Feb	1	The Edelweiss	Harold Carter
1916	Feb	3	The Little Gentleman	George Munson
1916	Feb	5	Two in the Dark	H. M. Egbert
1916	Feb	8	A Father's Right	Harold Carter
1916	Feb	10	The Town Inventor	Harold Carter
1916	Feb	12	A Fool There Was	H. M. Egbert
1916	Feb	17	The Wolf-Pack	Harold Carter
1916	Feb	19	A Woman's Sacrifice	H. M. Egbert
1916	Feb	22	Only a Clerk	H. M. Egbert
1916	Feb	24	Best Man Out	George Munson
1916	Feb	25	The Fraternal Heart	Victor Redcliffe
1916	Feb	26	Horace's Mother	Frank Filson
1916	Feb	29	The Crystal	Harold Carter
1916	Mar	2	John's Deception	George Munson

1916	Mar	4	The Supplanter	H. M. Egbert
1916	Mar	9	The Bond	Harold Carter
1916	Mar	11	Judd Sees Life	H. M. Egbert
1916	Mar	16	Sim's Hoard	Harold Carter
1916	Mar	18	Requital	H. M. Egbert
1916	Mar	23	Ghosts	George Munson
1916	Mar	24	The Dumb Detective	Victor Redcliffe
1916	Mar	25	A Man's Choice	H. M. Egbert
1916	Mar	28	Old Bottle—Green	Harold Carter
1916	Mar	30	Mother and Child	Frank Filson
1916	Apr	1	The Angel With the Sword	H. M. Egbert
1916	Apr	4	A Change of Owners	George Munson
1916	Apr	6	One Sunday Morning	Harold Carter
1916	Apr	8	Old Grouch	H. M. Egbert
1916	Apr	12	The Window Washer	Victor Redcliffe
1916	Apr	13	The Baby Imbroglio	Frank Filson
1916	Apr	18	The Man Who Came Back	Frank Filson
1916	Apr	20	The White Feather	Frank Filson
1916	Apr	21	The Hidden Garden	Victor Redcliffe
1916	Apr	22	The Ring	H. M. Egbert
1916	Apr	27	A Dog With a Bad Name	George Munson
1916	Apr	29	Too Old For Dreams	H. M. Egbert
1916	May	4	The Second Generation	Harold Caster (sic)
1916	May	6	An Amateur Don Juan	H. M. Egbert
1916	May	9	A Woman's Past	George Munson
1916	May	11	Love and the Forceps	Harold Carter
1916	May	13	Twisted Leading Strings	H. M. Egbert
1916	May	15	The Practical Joke	Harold Carter
1916	May	20	An Old Man's Dream	H. M. Egbert
1916	May	23	Father's Conspiracy	George Munson
1916	May	27	A Double Stratagem	Frank Filson
1916	May	29	A Good Investment	Victor Redcliffe
1916	Jun	1	The Buddha's Eyes	Frank Filson
1916	Jun	3	The Eyes of the Blind	H. M. Egbert
1916	Jun	8	The Ride to Shiloh	George Munson
1916	Jun	10	The Stolen Treaty	H. M. Egbert
1916	Jun	15	Caldwell's Theory	Harold Carter
1916	Jun	17	The Great Prize Contest	H. M. Egbert
1916	Jun	20	His Father's House	Harold Carter
1916	Jun	24	The Traitress	H. M. Egbert
1916	Jun	28	The Hitching Post	Victor Redcliffe
1916	Jun	29	The Testimonials	George Munson
1916	Jul	6	Coningsby's Last Minute	Frank Filson
1916	Jul	8	Turned Down	H. M. Egbert
1916	Jul	10	Lost and Found	Victor Redcliffe
1916	Jul	11	The Airman's Story	Frank Filson
1916	Jul	13	Life	Harold Carter
1916	Jul	15	The Lead in the Ice	H. M. Egbert
1916	Jul	18	Their Wedding Eve	Harold Carter
1916	Jul	22	The Sheriff's Sweetheart	H. M. Egbert
1916	Jul	24	Gambler's Luck	George Munson
1916	Jul	29	His Own People	H. M. Egbert
1916	Aug	3	A Man's Mistake	George Munson
1916	Aug	5	On the Breast of the Waters	H. M. Egbert
1916	Aug	8	The Leading Witness	Frank Filson
1916	Aug	10	A Woman's Loyalty	George Munson

1916	Aug	11	The Shock of Peace	Victor Redcliffe
1916	Aug	12	The Coward of Regiment	H. M. Egbert
1916	Aug	14	The Magic of Duty	Victor Redcliffe
1916	Aug	15	Euchred	George Munson
1916	Aug	17	Old Man Colley	Harold Carter
1916	Aug	19	The Slow-Coach	H. M. Egbert
1916	Aug	21	A Loyal Love	Victor Redcliffe
1916	Aug	24	Young Mr. Burroughs	Harold Carter
1916	Aug	26	A Lesson in Matrimony	H. M. Egbert
1916	Aug	29	The Model Submarine	George Munson
1916	Aug	31	Jephson's Discovery	Harold Carter
1916	Sep	7	Angela's Marriage	Harold Carter
1916	Sep	9	The Blind Man	H. M. Egbert
1916	Sep	12	Big Ben	Harold Carter
1916	Sep	13	Mock Kisses	Victor Redcliffe
1916	Sep	14	Jocko's Diversion	George Munson
1916	Sep	16	The Luck of War	H. M. Egbert
1916	Sep	19	Co-Operation	Frank Filson
1916	Sep	20	The Abyss	Victor Redcliffe
1916	Sep	26	Jaspar's Experiment	Harold Carter
1916	Sep	28	The Real Thing	Frank Filson
1916	Sep	30	The Heart of an Actress	H. M. Egbert
1916	Oct	3	Denison of Shanghai	Harold Carter
1916	Oct	5	The Moment's Destiny	George Munson
1916	Oct	7	Killing No Murder	H. M. Egbert
1916	Oct	10	The Old Maid's Conspiracy	George Munson
1916	Oct	12	The Years of Faith	Harold Carter
1916	Oct	14	The Professor's Scheme	H. M. Egbert
1916	Oct	17	The Problem	Frank Filson
1916	Oct	19	A Rolling Stone	Frank Filson
1916	Oct	20	A Way Out	Victor Radcliffe
1916	Oct	21	Black Doe	H. M. Egbert
1916	Oct	23	In Fine Feather	Victor Redcliffe
1916	Oct	24	Uncle Truefitt	George Munson
1916	Oct	26	Sheer Luck	Frank Filson
1916	Oct	28	The Sacrifice	H. M. Egbert
1916	Oct	31	A Brotherly Proposal	George Munson
1916	Nov	2	Tuberoses	Harold Carter
1916	Nov	4	John Carey's Boots	H. M. Egbert
1916	Nov	11	The Plot	H. M. Egbert
1916	Nov	14	The Feat of Francois	Frank Filson
1916	Nov	16	The Governor's Dilemma	Harold Carter
1916	Nov	21	A Plain Man's Wife	Frank Filson
1916	Nov	23	The Veil	George Munson
1916	Nov	25	The Grafter	H. M. Egbert
1916	Dec	2	The Prophecy	H. M. Egbert
1916	Dec	4	The Mute Witness	Victor Redcliffe
1916	Dec	5	The Matron's Story	Harold Carter
1916	Dec	7	Uncle Jabez' Joker	George Munson
1916	Dec	9	The Drum	H. M. Egbert
1916	Dec	12	Doc Smith's Evolution	Harold Carter
1916	Dec	16	The Woman Hater	H. M. Egbert
1916	Dec	18	A Test of Endurance	George Munson
1916	Dec	23	The Decisive Moment	H. M. Egbert
1916	Dec	29	Seeing Life	Harold Carter
1917	Jan	2	Between the Lines	Frank Filson

1917	Jan	4	On the Mail Route	H. M. Egbert
1917	Jan	8	Bob White	George Munson
1917	Jan	9	A Trick of Imagination	H. M. Egbert
1917	Jan	11	The Empty Room	Harold Carter
1917	Jan	12	A Willful Maid	Victor Redcliffe
1917	Jan	13	The Trap	Frank Filson
1917	Feb	12	The Impersonator	Harold Carter
1917	Apr	6	His Partner	Victor Redcliffe

D. Chronological Index of Journalism and Articles

1906	Jan	21	Scenes in a Turpentine Camp	The Anaconda Standard
1906	Feb	25	The Orange Industry in Florida	The San Antonio Light
1906	Jun	10	Harvesters of the Seas	The Anaconda Standard
1907	Feb	3	A Ramble in Dickens' Land	Baltimore American
1907	May	5	The Romance of the Thames	Baltimore American
1907	Jun	16	The Season in London	Baltimore American
1907	Jul	21	The City of Gold	Baltimore American
1907	Sep		The Call of September	Every Where
1907	Oct		The Trail of October	Every Where
1908	Jan	25	Low Rent or No Rent	Harper's Weekly
1908	Mar	14	The Lengthening Bread Line	Harper's Weekly
1908	Mar	21	Wanted: Soldiers	Harper's Weekly
1908	Mar	28	Rex Beach and the Barrier	Harper's Weekly
1908	Apr	4	Hoop-la! The Circus	Harper's Weekly
1908	Apr	11	Unlocking $47,000,000	Harper's Weekly
1908	Apr	18	When Women Ruled	Harper's Weekly
1908	May	30	Court of Sorrows	Harper's Weekly
1908	Aug	23	Cupid and the Law	Harper's Weekly
1908	Oct	3	The Poor of London	Harper's Weekly
1908	Oct	3	The Puppet Play Which Lasts Two Months	Harper's Weekly
1908	Oct	10	The Doom of English Liberalism	Harper's Weekly
1908	Dec	19	Lawless New York—Part One	Harper's Weekly
1908	Dec	26	Helping the Filipinos to Fight Disease	Harper's Weekly
1909	Jan	9	Lawless New York—Part Two	Harper's Weekly
1909	Jan	23	Laura Jean Libbey	Harper's Weekly
1909	Feb	13	Bargaining with Criminals	Harper's Weekly
1909	Feb	20	Discovery of the Soul	Harper's Weekly
1909	Oct	2	Uncle Sam, Pickpocket	Harper's Weekly
1909	Oct	9	School for Souls	Harper's Weekly
1910	Feb	26	Pussyfoot	Harper's Weekly
1910	May	14	Britain's World-mourned King	Harper's Weekly
1913	Jun	7	Japan and the Philippines	Harper's Weekly
1914	Apr	19	New Writers: Mr. Harrison's View of Their Opportunities	New York Times
1923	Jun	10	Evolution	New York Times
1935	Jul	21	The Dies Bill	New York Times
1935	Sep	10	A Writer Defends the Pulps	New York Times
1936	Aug	21	Concerning Rabies	New York Times
1938	May	31	The Problem of the Alien	New York Times
1939	Jul	2	An Impenitent Alien	New York Times
1942	Jul	16	Old-Time Razors Preferred	New York Times
1942	Aug	26	Fashion Note for Men	New York Times
1942	Sep	17	Trials of a Shirt Owner	New York Times
1945	Mar	25	Japanese and Aztec	New York Times

RECURRING PROTAGONIST in a "SERIES"

Lead Character [Series Title] [NOTES]	Original Publication Source Publication Date, Month, Year	By-Line

Dr. Ivan Brodsky [*The Surgeon of Souls*]
[NOTE No. 1: Stories are listed in proper sequential order, not order of publication]
[NOTE No. 2: First Regional Rights to "The Seventh Symphony" not located; the Globe failed to print it]

The Case of the Jailer's Daughter	Globe and Commercial Advertiser, 5 Feb 1910	H. M. Egbert
The Woman With the Crooked Nose	Globe and Commercial Advertiser, 12 Feb 1910	H. M. Egbert
The Legacy of Hate	Globe and Commercial Advertiser, 5 Mar 1910	H. M. Egbert
The Tenth Commandment	Globe and Commercial Advertiser, 26 Feb 1910	H. M. Egbert
The Major's Menagerie	Globe and Commercial Advertiser, 12 Mar 1910	H. M. Egbert
The Fetish of the Waxworks	Globe and Commercial Advertiser, 19 Mar 1910	H. M. Egbert
The Seventh Symphony		
The Man Who Lost His Luck	Globe and Commercial Advertiser, 16 Apr 1910	H. M. Egbert
The Chairs of Stuyvesant Baron	Globe and Commercial Advertiser, 2 Apr 1910	H. M. Egbert
Homo Homunculus	Globe and Commercial Advertiser, 23 Apr 1910	H. M. Egbert
The Dream That Came True	Globe and Commercial Advertiser, 30 Apr 1910	H. M. Egbert
The Ultimate Problem	Globe and Commercial Advertiser, 7 May 1910	H. M. Egbert
The Cats That Looked at Cohen (solo)	Canada West Monthly, May 1911	H. M. Egbert

Captain Adams [*A King's Courier*; or, *Detective-Diplomat*]
[NOTE: the USA and UK jointly ran the series simultaneously; actual world first printings are noted]

The Peril of Magellan Strait	The New Magazine [UK] Jun 1910	H. M. Egbert
The Kaiser's Hairdresser		
as: The Toilet That Saved France	The New Magazine [UK] Jul 1910	H. M. Egbert
The Emperor's Double	The New Magazine [UK] Sep 1910	H. M. Egbert
The Affair of the North Sea	The New Magazine [UK] Aug 1910	H. M. Egbert
The Dinner at the White House	Globe and Commercial Advertiser, 10 Sep 1910	H. M. Egbert
The Left-Hand Wife	Globe and Commercial Advertiser, 17 Sep 1910	H. M. Egbert
The Amir's Move	Globe and Commercial Advertiser, 24 Sep 1910	H. M. Egbert
The Kidnaped King	Globe and Commercial Advertiser, 8 Oct 1910	H. M. Egbert
The Czar's Drive	Globe and Commercial Advertiser, 15 Oct 1910	H. M. Egbert
The Spanish Treaty	The New Magazine [UK] Oct 1910	H. M. Egbert
The River Rats	The New Magazine [UK] Nov 1910	H. M. Egbert
The Ingratitude of Kings	Globe and Commercial Advertiser, 12 Nov 1910	H. M. Egbert
The Flight of Abdul Hamid (solo)	Canada West Monthly, Aug 1913	H. M. Egbert

Nikolai, Independent Agent [*The King of Knaves*]

The Robinson Diamonds	Blue Book, Mar 1911	H. M. Egbert
The Treasure of Spandau	Blue Book, Apr 1911	H. M. Egbert
The Stolen Submarine	Blue Book, May 1911	H. M. Egbert
The Lighthouse of the North	Blue Book, Jun 1911	H. M. Egbert
The Essayan Statue	Blue Book, Jul 1911	H. M. Egbert
The Burning of Batoum	Blue Book, Aug 1911	H. M. Egbert
The Coronation of Nikolai	Blue Book, Sep 1911	H. M. Egbert
The Flight of the Princess	Blue Book, Oct 1911	H. M. Egbert
A Bid For a Throne	Blue Book, Nov 1911	H. M. Egbert
The Rubies of the Sacrifice	Blue Book, Dec 1911	H. M. Egbert
The Brother of the Moon	Blue Book, Jan 1912	H. M. Egbert
The Treasure of Egypt	Blue Book, Feb 1912	H. M. Egbert

Peter Crewe [*The Man With the Camera Eyes*]
[NOTE No. 1: Stories are listed in proper sequential order, not order of publication]
[NOTE No. 2: Sold entirely into the syndication market; this is the earliest known appearance]
[NOTE No. 3: First Regional Rights for the remaining 3 only found in small-town papers]

The Box of Borneos	Buffalo Sunday Times, 18 Jun 1911	H. M. Egbert
The Robbery at the Tower	Buffalo Sunday Times, 25 Jun 1911	H. M. Egbert
The Tell-Tale Glove	Buffalo Sunday Times, 2 Jul 1911	H. M. Egbert
The Champion of the Fleet	Buffalo Sunday Times, 9 Jul 1911	H. M. Egbert
The Record on the Screen	Buffalo Sunday Times, 16 Jul 1911	H. M. Egbert
A Matter of Mathematics		H. M. Egbert
The Whirl of Death		H. M. Egbert
The Crooked Seam	Buffalo Sunday Times, 13 Aug 1911	H. M. Egbert
The Misplaced Pigment	Buffalo Sunday Times, 20 Aug 1911	H. M. Egbert
The Face of the Clock		H. M. Egbert
The Broken Heel	Buffalo Sunday Times, 6 Aug 1911	H. M. Egbert
The Death in the Dirigible	Buffalo Sunday Times, 30 Jul 1911	H. M. Egbert
The Scar (solo)	Fiction Magazine, 9 Dec 1917	H. M. Egbert

Lord Richard Jocelyn [*Quest of Gentle Hazard*]
[NOTE No. 1: Stories are listed in proper sequential order, not order of publication]
NOTE: No. 2: First Regional Rights not found for the last tale. The Chicago paper failed to run it]

A Casual Champion	Chicago Daily News, 14 Oct 1911	H. M. Egbert
A Seaside Comedy	Chicago Daily News, 7 Oct 1911	H. M. Egbert
Master and Man	Chicago Daily News, 4 Nov 1911	H. M. Egbert
A Frustrated Alliance	Chicago Daily News, 28 Oct 1911	H. M. Egbert
[Story of] The Runaway Bride	Chicago Daily News, 21 Oct 1911	H. M. Egbert
The Diamond Tiara	Chicago Daily News, 23 Sep 1911	H. M. Egbert
A Family Reunion	Chicago Daily News, 18 Nov 1911	H. M. Egbert
A Midnight Elopement	Chicago Daily News, 30 Sep 1911	H. M. Egbert
A Matrimonial Disentanglement	Chicago Daily News, 16 Sep 1911	H. M. Egbert
Sauce and Gander [Sauce for the Gander]	Chicago Daily News, 25 Nov 1911	H. M. Egbert
Nelly of the Sluice Gate	Chicago Daily News, 11 Nov 1911	H. M. Egbert
A Wedding De Luxe		H. M. Egbert

Isabel Marston [*Isabel Marston, Star Reporter*]

The Kidnapped Cabinet Minister	Cassell's Magazine of Fiction, Sep 1912	Victor Rousseau
For the Honor of the Crown	Cassell's Magazine of Fiction, Oct 1912	Victor Rousseau
The Man on the Heath	Cassell's Magazine of Fiction, Nov 1912	Victor Rousseau
An Error of Longitude	Cassell's Magazine of Fiction, Dec 1912	Victor Rousseau
A Servant of His King	Cassell's Magazine of Fiction, Jan 1913	Victor Rousseau
Her Last 'Story'	Cassell's Magazine of Fiction, Feb 1913	Victor Rousseau

Paul Lane, American Millionaire [*The League of Lost Causes*]
[NOTE No. 1: Apparently were never found a First Rights publisher; syndicated in America]
[NOTE No. 2: First USA Regional Rights never found; below is earliest known small-town rights]
[NOTE No. 3: First world rights may be in an untraced UK Cassell publication; they purchased 7 tales]

The Woman from the Sea	Stevens Point Journal, 18 Oct 1913	H. M. Egbert
The Moroccan Treaty	Stevens Point Journal, 25 Oct 1913	H. M. Egbert
How the Kaiser Went to Paris	Stevens Point Journal, 1 Nov 1913	H. M. Egbert
The Misplaced Dream	Stevens Point Journal, 8 Nov 1913	H. M. Egbert
An Amazon of Tripoli	Stevens Point Journal, 15 Nov 1913	H. M. Egbert
The Prisoner of Hofberg	Stevens Point Journal, 22 Nov 1913	H. M. Egbert
The Pilot of the Fleet	Stevens Point Journal, 29 Nov 1913	H. M. Egbert
A Dutch Music Lesson	Stevens Point Journal, 6 Dec 1913	H. M. Egbert
The Séance of Nishikoff	Stevens Point Journal, 13 Dec 1913	H. M. Egbert
The Education of Edward	Stevens Point Journal, 20 Dec 1913	H. M. Egbert

John Haynes [*The Devil Chair*; or, *The Wheel*]
[NOTE: Released only into the syndication market, this is the earliest known appearance]

The Cripple of Prospect Park	St. Louis Post-Dispatch, 27 Sep 1913	H. M. Egbert
The Seven League Boots	St. Louis Post-Dispatch, 4 Oct 1913	H. M. Egbert
The First Victim	St. Louis Post-Dispatch, 11 Oct 1913	H. M. Egbert
An Involuntary Ally	St. Louis Post-Dispatch, 18 Oct 1913	H. M. Egbert
Roles Reversed	St. Louis Post-Dispatch, 25 Oct 1913	H. M. Egbert
The Arm of Justice	St. Louis Post-Dispatch, 1 Nov 1913	H. M. Egbert
The Shunted Man of Europe	St. Louis Post-Dispatch, 8 Nov 1913	H. M. Egbert
The Kingdom of the North	St. Louis Post-Dispatch, 15 Nov 1913	H. M. Egbert
The Man and the Maelstrom	St. Louis Post-Dispatch, 22 Nov 1913	H. M. Egbert
The Man in the Balance	St. Louis Post-Dispatch, 29 Nov 1913	H. M. Egbert
The God from the Pagoda	St. Louis Post-Dispatch, 6 Dec 1913	H. M. Egbert
By the Deep Sea Transit	St. Louis Post-Dispatch, 13 Dec 1913	H. M. Egbert

Dr. Phileas Immanuel, Soul Specialist [*The Tracer of Egos*]
[NOTE No. 1: Stories are listed in proper sequential order, not order of publication]
[NOTE No. 2: The 3 not in Holland's were nationally syndicated with the whole series]

The Amulet of Marduk	Holland's Magazine, Jun 1913	Victor Rousseau
Mary Rothway's Memory	Holland's Magazine, Jul 1913	Victor Rousseau
The Two Charioteers	Holland's Magazine, Sep 1913	Victor Rousseau
The Carfax Curse	Holland's Magazine, Nov 1913	Victor Rousseau
The Professor's Peach Trees	Holland's Magazine, Oct 1913	Victor Rousseau
Alf Barton's Princess	Holland's Magazine, Aug 1913	Victor Rousseau
Mr. Axel's Shady Past	Holland's Magazine, Dec 1913	Victor Rousseau
The Woman of Atlantis	Holland's Magazine, Jan 1914	Victor Rousseau
A Fisher for Souls	Illustrated Buffalo Express, 10 May 1914	Victor Rousseau
The Return of Claudia	Illustrated Buffalo Express, 17 May 1914	Victor Rousseau
The Wife of Ira Hopkins	Illustrated Buffalo Express, 24 May 1914	Victor Rousseau
Noureddin Bey's Sacrifice	Holland's Magazine, Feb 1914	Victor Rousseau

Pere Sebastian; or, Le Curé [*Tales of the St. Lawrence Riverway*]

The Keeper of the Light (unofficial tale)	Harper's Weekly, 10 Dec 1910	Victor Rousseau
The Voice in the Mist	Blue Book, Sep 1914	Victor Rousseau
The Evil Shore	Blue Book, Oct 1914	Victor Rousseau
The Wrath of Paul Dupuy	Blue Book, Nov 1914	Victor Rousseau
The Lie of Pere Sebastian	Blue Book, Dec 1914	Victor Rousseau
The Curé Goes Hunting	Blue Book, Jan 1915	Victor Rousseau
The Wooing of Fanchette	Blue Book, Feb 1915	Victor Rousseau
The Pacification of Anne	Blue Book, Mar 1915	Victor Rousseau
Big Pierre's Idol	Blue Book, Apr 1915	Victor Rousseau
The Desperation of St. Jean	Blue Book, May 1915	Victor Rousseau
Lafe Evens Up (solo)	All-Story Weekly, 11 Sep 1915	Victor Rousseau
The Gates of Rocky River (solo)	The American Patriot, Jan 1916	Victor Rousseau
The Curés Love Story (solo)	Everywoman's World [circa 1917]	Victor Rousseau
The House of Gingras (solo)	The Argosy, 22 Dec 1917	Victor Rousseau
Pierre and Paul (solo)	Extension Magazine, Jun 1918	Victor Rousseau
The Eyes of Pere Sebastien (sic) (solo)	Extention Magazine, Aug 1919	Victor Rousseau

Mr. X., the unnamed English agent [*The Revelations of an Ambassador-at-Large*]
[NOTE No. 1: Stories are listed in proper sequential order, not order of publication]
[NOTE No. 2: The UK printed many of these tales first, but they have yet to be traced]

The Bulgarian Papers	The Popular Magazine, 7 Jan 1915	H. M. Egbert
The Bookworm of Potsdam	Fiction Magazine, 13 Jun 1915	H. M. Egbert
The Montenegrin Ciphers	Fiction Magazine, 20 Jun 1915	H. M. Egbert
Count Berchtold's Party	Fiction Magazine, 27 Jun 1915	H. M. Egbert
The Bullet-Proof Mantle	The Popular Magazine, 23 Jan 1915	H. M. Egbert
The Golden Death	Fiction Magazine, 11 Jul 1915	H. M. Egbert
A Dead Man's Empire	Fiction Magazine, 18 Jul 1915	H. M. Egbert
A Patriot's Dilemma	Fiction Magazine, 25 Jul 1915	H. M. Egbert
The "X" Bacillus	Fiction Magazine, 1 Aug 1915	H. M. Egbert
The Wax Clavette	The Popular Magazine, 7 Feb 1915	H. M. Egbert
The Red Envelope	The Popular Magazine, 23 Feb 1915	H. M. Egbert
Kitchener's Coup	The Popular Magazine, 7 Mar 1915	H. M. Egbert

Francois l'Anglois, French aviator [*The Flights of Francois*]
[NOTE: Stories are listed in proper sequential order, not order of publication]

The Fair American	The Chicago Tribune, 31 Oct 1915	Victor Rousseau
Suzette	The Chicago Tribune, 7 Nov 1915	Victor Rousseau
The Bethune Charter	The Chicago Tribune, 14 Nov 1915	Victor Rousseau
The Phantom City	The Chicago Tribune, 21 Nov 1915	Victor Rousseau
Capt. Cholmunday's Monkey	Ainslee's Magazine, Sep 1915	Victor Rousseau
The Five Army Corps	The Chicago Tribune, 28 Nov 1915	Victor Rousseau
Alice of Chalons	Ainslee's Magazine, Oct 1915	Victor Rousseau
The General's Knave-Trap	Ainslee's Magazine, Nov 1915	Victor Rousseau
A Jest That Saved	The Chicago Tribune, 5 Dec 1915	Victor Rousseau
The Man With the Peaked Beard	Ainslee's Magazine, Dec 1915	Victor Rousseau
The Belfry Dawn	The Chicago Tribune, 12 Dec 1915	Victor Rousseau
The Eve of the Hospital	Ainslee's Magazine, Jan 1916	Victor Rousseau

Peggy Roche [*Peggy Roche, Saleslady*]

Adventure of the Three Georges	Photoplay Magazine, Mar 1917	Victor Rousseau
Adventure of the Town Pond Submarine	Photoplay Magazine, Apr 1917	Victor Rousseau
Torpedo Broker	Photoplay Magazine, May 1917	Victor Rousseau
The Road to Biskra	Photoplay Magazine, Jun 1917	Victor Rousseau
The Jungle Knights	Photoplay Magazine, Jul 1917	Victor Rousseau

Captain Acton Lake [*The Cloud Pirates*]

The Cloud Pirates	Chicago Ledger, 8 Jul 1922	H. M. Egbert
Contraband and Whiskers	Chicago Ledger, 15 Jul 1922	H. M. Egbert
Treasure of Cos	Chicago Ledger, 22 Jul 1922	H. M. Egbert
The Rubber Eagles	Chicago Ledger, 29 Jul 1922	H. M. Egbert

Dr. Martinus, Psychic Researcher / Detective

Child or Demon—Which?	Ghost Stories, Oct 1926	Victor Rousseau
The Doll That Came to Life	Ghost Stories, Jan 1927	Victor Rousseau
The Ghost of the Red Cavalier	Ghost Stories, Mar 1927	Victor Rousseau
Fire—Water—and What?	Ghost Stories, Jun 1927	Victor Rousseau
The Soul That Lost Its Way	Ghost Stories, Aug 1927	Victor Rousseau
The House of the Living Dead	Ghost Stories, Dec 1927—May 1928	Victor Rousseau

Jim Anthony—The latter 3 are not confirmed to by Emanuel

Dealer in Death	Super-Detective, Oct 1940	John Grange
Legion of Robots	Super-Detective, Nov 1940	John Grange
Madame Murder	Super-Detective, Dec 1940	John Grange
Bloated Death	Super-Detective, Jan 1941	John Grange
Killer in Yellow	Super-Detective, Feb 1941	John Grange
Murder in Paradise	Super-Detective, Mar 1941	John Grange
Murder Syndicate	Super-Detective, Apr 1941	John Grange
The Horrible Marionettes	Super-Detective, Jun 1941	John Grange
Border Napoleon	Super-Detective, Aug 1941	John Grange
Spies of Destiny	Super-Detective, Oct 1941	John Grange
I. O. U. Murder	Super-Detective, Dec 1941	John Grange
Cold Turkey	Super-Detective, Feb 1942	John Grange
Mrs. Big	Super-Detective, Apr 1942	John Grange
Needle's Eye	Super-Detective, Jun 1942	John Grange
Mark of the Spider	Super-Detective, Aug 1942	John Grange

M'Shane

Salvation of M'Shane	Speed Adventure Stories, Mar 1944	Victor Rousseau
Sea-Lubber M'Shane	Speed Adventure Stories, Jul 1944	Clive Trent
The Madness of M'Shane	Speed Adventure Stories, Apr 1945	Clive Trent
The Shaving of M'Shane	Speed Adventure Stories, Oct 1945	Clive Trent

Dr. Gabriel

House of Death	Speed Mystery, May 1943	Lew Merrill
Kenney's Stooge	Speed Mystery, Sep 1943	Hugh Speer
Sergeant Joe's Return	Speed Mystery, Nov 1943	Hugh Speer
Crossed Wires	Speed Mystery, Mar 1944	Hugh Speer
Beggar-Ticks	Speed Mystery, May 1944	Hugh Speer
Death in the Tank	Speed Detective, May 1944	Hugh Speer
Curse of the Tremaines	Private Detective Stories, May 1944	Hugh Speer
Unborn Terror	Speed Mystery, Nov 1944	Hugh Speer
Living Dead Man	Speed Mystery, Mar 1945	Hugh Speer
Terror by Night	Private Detective Stories, Nov 1946	Lew Merrill
Soul at Strife	Speed Detective, Dec 1946	Hugh Speer

Adam Somerville

The Tell-Tale Arm	Private Detective Stories, Dec 1944	Lew Merrill
Doubling for Death	Super-Detective, Mar 1945	Clive Trent
Typed	Super-Detective, Apr 1945	Lew Merrill
Proxy Murder	Private Detective Stories, Sep 1945	Lew Merrill
Corpse in the Car	Super-Detective, Sep 1945	Clive Trent
Rye and Die	Private Detective Stories, Mar 1946	Lew Merrill
Murder House	Super-Detective, Sep 1946	Lew Merrill
Brushless Cream	Super-Detective, Nov 1946	Lew Merrill

NON-FICTION SERIES

World-Famous Police Mysteries
[NOTE No. 1: Stories are listed in proper sequential order, not order of publication]
[NOTE No. 2: The Washington Post elected not to carry a by-line, but most papers used H. M. Egbert]

The Case of Madame LaFarge	Washington Post, 18 Dec 1910	
The Persecution of the Rector	Washington Post, 25 Dec 1910	
The Murder in the Rue Mazarin	Washington Post, 1 Jan 1911	
The Resurrection Men	Washington Post, 8 Jan 1911	
The Churchwarden Murderer	Washington Post, 22 Jan 1911	
The Last of the Bushrangers	Washington Post, 15 Jan 1911	
Inspector Denovan and Mackoull	Washington Post, 29 Jan 1911	
The Crimes of the Marchioness	Washington Post, 5 Feb 1911	
The Body in the Parcel	Washington Post, 12 Feb 1911	
The Mahratta's Revenge	Washington Post, 19 Feb 1911	
The Kidnapping of Charley Ross	Washingotn Post, 26 Feb 1911	
The Murder of Benjamin Nathan	Washginton Post, 5 Mar 1911	
Detective Anchisi and the Fort Wayne Gang (solo)	Detective Story Magazine, 23 Sep 1919	George Munson

Tales of 'Pussyfoot' Johnson [William Johnson, Prohibitionist]—unofficial series title
[NOTE No. 1: First Regional Rights never found; quoting small-town rights; never carried a by-line]

Exploits of 'Pussyfoot' Johnson in Cleaning Up Indian Territory	Stevens Point Journal, 21 Apr 1917
How 'Pussyfoot' Johnson Wiped Out the Monte Carlo of No Man's Land	Stevens Point Journal, 28 Apr 1917
Desperate Outlaws Put a Price on Head of 'Pussyfoot' Johnson	Stevens Point Journal, 5 May 1917
'Pussyfoot' Performs One of Most Daring Deeds in Frontier History	Stevens Point Journal, 12 May 1917
How 'Pussyfoot' Johnson Made Good Citizens of Indian Charges	Stevens Point Journal, 19 May 1917

Inside History of Famous Crime Cases

The Shooting of Colonel Fisk	Detective Story Magazine, 29 Apr 1919	George Munson
A Helen of New York	Detective Story Magazine, 6 May 1919	George Munson
The Wife and the Other Man	Detective Story Magazine, 13 May 1919	George Munson
The Man Who "Killed" A Corpse	Detective Story Magazine, 20 May 1919	George Munson
The Body in the Box	Detective Story Magazine, 27 May 1919	George Munson
The Doctor and the Wealthy Patient	Detective Story Magazine, 3 Jun 1919	George Munson
The Superfluous Husband	Detective Story Magazine, 10 Jun 1919	George Munson
The Case of Mrs. Wharton	Detective Story Magazine, 17 Jun 1919	George Munson
Birchall, the Canadian Murderer	Detective Story Magazine, 24 Jun 1919	George Munson
The Murder of Doctor Burdell	Detective Story Magazine, 1 Jul 1919	George Munson
The Alibi That Failed	Detective Story Magazine, 8 Jul 1919	George Munson
The Two Parricides	Detective Story Magazine, 15 Jul 1919	George Munson

MOTION PICTURES

Movie Title (Date Released)
Original Source / Date / Original Title

Devil's Tower (Jun 1928)
Ace-High, 2nd Dec 1923; The Devil's Tower
   Director: J. P. McGowan
   Cast: Buddy Roosevelt, Frank Earle, J. P. McGowan, Thelma Parr,
     Art Rowlands, & Tom Bay
   Produced by Trem Carr Pictures, black & white, silent
   Distributed by Rayart Pictures Corporation

Hi-Jacking Rustlers (Nov 1926)
Ace-High, 2nd Jan 1926; Hi-Jacking Rustlers
   Director: Bennett Cohen
   Cast: Jack Perrin, Josephine Hill, Buzz Barton, Leonard Trainor,
     Bud Osborne, Al Ferguson,
     Walter Shumway, Rex the Dog, & Starlight the Horse
   Produced by Ben Wilson Productions, black & white, silent
   Distributed by Rayart Pictures Corporation
   Length: 4935 feet

Lightnin' Shot (May 1928)
Ace-High, 2nd May 1925; The Lightnin' Shot
   Director: J. P. McGowan
   Cast: Buddy Roosevelt, J. P. McGowan, Frank Earle, & Carol Lane
   Produced by Trem Carr Pictures, black & white, silent
   Distributed by Rayart Pictures Corporation
   Length: 4797 feet

Prince of the Plains (Sep 1927)
Ranch Romances, V2 # 3 May 1925; Prince of the Plains
   Director: Robin Williamson
   Cast: Kermit Maynard, Betty Caldwell, & Walter Shumway
   Produced by Trem Carr Pictures, black & white, silent
   Distributed by Rayart Pictures Corporation
   Length: 4134 feet

A Ridin' Gent (Dec 1926)
Ace-High, 1st May 1924; A Ridin' Gent
   Director: Bennett Cohen
   Cast: Jack Perrin, & Starlight the Horse
   Produced by Ben Wilson Productions, black & white, silent
   Distributed by Rayart Pictures Corporation
   Length: 5027 feet

Trailin' Back (Mar 1928)
Lariat, July 1926; Trailin' Back
   Director: J. P. McGowan
   Cast: Buddy Roosevelt, Betty Baker, Lafe McKee, Leon De La Mothe, Tom Bay,
     Bert Sanderson, & Al Bertram
   Produced by Trem Carr Pictures, black & white, silent
   Distributed by Rayart Pictures Corporation
   Length: 4652 feet

The Truant Soul (25 Dec 1916)
Based on the script originally titled 'The Mask'
   Director: Harry Beaumont
   Cast: Henry B. Walthall, Mary Charleson, Patrick Calhoun, Anna Mae Walthall,
      Mary Parkyn, & Ullrich Haupt
   Produced by The Essanay Film Manufacturing Company, black & white, silent
   Distributed by K-E-S-E Service
   Length: 7 reels

Wanderer of the West (Dec 1927)
Ace-High, 2nd Oct 1924; A Wanderer of the West
   Director: Robin E. Williamson & Joseph E. Zivelli
   Cast: Kermit Maynard, Betty Caldwell, Frank Clark, Walter Shumway,
      Tom Brooker, Roy Watson,
      Allen Rogers, & M. A. Dickinson
   Produced by Trem Carr Pictures, black & white, silent
   Distributed by Rayart Pictures Corporation
   Length: 4200 feet

West of the Rainbow's End (13 Aug 1926)
Ranch Romances, V3 #3 Sep 1925; West of Rainbow's End
   Director: Bennett Cohen
   Cast: Jack Perrin, Pauline Curley, Buzz Barton, Tom London, Jim Welch,
      Milburn Morante, Molly Malone, Whitehorse, Rex the Dog, & Starlight the Horse
   Produced by George Blaisdell Productions, black & white, silent
   Distributed by Rayart Pictures Corporation

When Dreams Come True (15 Jan 1929)
Ranch Romances, V14 #3 1st Jan 1928; as Sunburst Valley
   Director: Duke Worne
   Cast: Helene Costello, Rex Lease, Claire McDowell, Danny Hoy, Ernest Hilliard,
      Buddy Brown, George Periolat, Emmett King, Ranger the Horse, & Rags the Dog
   Produced by Trem Carr Pictures, black & white, silent
   Distributed by Rayart Pictures Corporation
   Length: 6242 feet

STORY ADAPTATIONS of PHOTOPLAYS by the Universal Film Mfg. Co.

Movie Title, Release Date Date Printed, Newspaper, Town or City, State	By-Line
The Blood of the Children (16 Mar 1915) 19 Mar 1915, Akron Weekly Pioneer Press (Akron, Colorado)	H. M. Egbert
Changed Lives (16 Feb 1915) 15 Mar 1915, Elyria Evening Telegram (Elyria, Ohio)	H. M. Egbert
The Dancer (18 May 1915) 31 May 1915, The Victoria Daily Advocate (Victoria, Texas)	H. M. Egbert
The Duchess (30 Mar 1915) 2 Apr 1915, Brandon Bell (Brandon, Colorado)	H. M. Egbert
The Faith of Her Fathers (4 May 1915) 19 May 1915, The Victoria Daily Advocate (Victoria, Texas)	H. M. Egbert
The Girl of the Secret Service (2 Feb 1915) 17 Feb 1915, The Victoria Daily Advocate (Victoria, Texas)	H. M. Egbert
Haunted Hearts (23 Feb 1915) 26 Feb 1915, Akron Weekly Pioneer Press (Akron, Colorado)	H. M. Egbert
The Human Menace (23 Mar 1915) 5 Apr 1915, The Victoria Daily Advocate (Victoria, Texas)	H. M. Egbert
The Heart of Lincoln (9 Feb 1915) 8 Mar 1915, Elyria Evening Telegram (Elyria, Ohio)	H. M. Egbert
Life (unknown) 25 Mar 1915, Chaffee County Republican (Buena Vista, Colorado)	H. M. Egbert
Matty's Decision (27 Apr 1915) 30 Apr 1915, Brandon Bell (Brandon, Colorado)	H. M. Egbert
The Mysterious Contragrav (27 Mar 1915) 15 Apr 1915, Chaffee County Republican (Buena Vista, Colorado)	H. M. Egbert
The Phantom [of the] Violin (Oct 1914, re-released 9 Mar 1915) 12 Mar 1915, Akron Weekly Pioneer Press (Akron, Colorado)	H. M. Egbert
Scandal (19 Jul 1915) 2 Sep 1915, Pella Chronicle (Pella, Iowa)	Victor Rosseau
Shattered Memories (25 May 1915) 28 May 1915, Akron Weekly Pioneer Press (Akron, Colorado)	H. M. Egbert
Smugglers' Island (19 Jan 1915) 15 Feb 1915, Elyria Evening Telegram (Elyria, Ohio)	H. M. Egbert

The Sun God (possibly "The Fair God of Sun Island," 19 Oct 1915)   H. M. Egbert
   13 Nov 1915, The City Times (Galveston, Texas)

Their Hour (2 Mar 1915)   H. M. Egbert
   5 Mar 1915, Akron Weekly Pioneer Press (Akron, Colorado)

The Torrent (11 May 1915)   H. M. Egbert
   24 May 1915, The Victoria Daily Advocate (Victoria, Texas)

The Whirling Disk (20 Apr 1915)   H. M. Egbert
   23 Apr 1915, Brandon Bell (Brandon, Colorado)

A Wild Irish Rose (13 Apr 1915)   H. M. Egbert
   9 Apr 1915, Brandon Bell (Brandon, Colorado)

A Woman's Debt (2 Jan 1915)   H. M. Egbert
   9 Feb 1915, Elyria Evening Telegram (Elyria, Ohio)

FOREIGN TRANSLATIONS

ARGENTINA:

La Maldición de la Momia [The Curse of Amen-Ra]
>Publisher: Géminis
>Argentina, 1968 (128pp)
>Translated by J. Marieges
>Narraciones Géminis de Terror # 11

BELGIUM:

Quand Veillent les Dieux Morts [When Dead Gods Wake]
>Publisher: André Gérard
>Anthology: 13 Histoires de Sorcellerie
>Edited by Albert Van Hageland and Jean-Baptiste Baronian
>Verviers: 1975 (207pp)

FRANCE:

L'Œil de Balamok [The Eye of Balamok]
>La Valette-du-Var: Antares, L'Or du Temps 1, April 1991 (p 119)

Le Femme de Jackson [Jackson's Wife]
>Wendigo # 1, 2010

SPAIN:

El Campamento Infernal by Victor Rousseau [original title unknown]
>Publisher: Prensa Moderna
>Collection: Aventuras # 85
>Madrid: circa 1930s (94pp)

La Maldición de la Momia [The Curse of Amen-Ra]
>Publisher: Valdemar
>Anthology: Gótica # 65
>Edited by Antonio José Navarro
>ISBN: 84-7702-546-0
>Madrid: 2006 (656pp)

La Muerte Invisible by Victor Rousseau [The Invisible Death]
>Publisher: Presna Moderna
>Collection: La Novela Fantastica # 3
>Madrid: circa 1932 (108pp)
>Illustrations by Máximo Ramos
>Digest: 5 x 7 inches

Dentelladas de Lobo by Victor Rousseau [Loot of the Wolf]
>Publisher: Prensa Moderna
>Collection: La Novela Fantastica # 20
>Madrid: circa 1932 (96pp)

El Diamante Escondido by Victor Rousseau [original title unknown]
>Publisher: Prensa Moderna
>Collection: Aventuras # 26
>Madrid: circa 1930s (79pp)
>Illustrations by Máximo Ramos

El Ojo de Balamok by Victor Rousseau [The Eye of Balamok]
> Publisher: Villanueva de la Torre: Rio Henares Producciones Graficas
> Collection: Pulp Ediciones # 6
> Translated by Francisco Arellano
> Guadalajara: 2004
> Combined with El Planeta Loco by Murray Leinster (p 200)

El Rayo Invisible by Victor Rousseau [The Invisible Death]
> Publisher: Editorial Bruguera
> Collection: La Novela Fantastica # 4
> Madrid: circa 1944-1945 (32pp)

SWEDEN:
Djävulstornet by Victor Rousseau [The Devil's Tower]
> Detektivmagasinet # 9, 1962

En Cowboy Slår Knockout by Victor Rousseau [A Wanderer of the West]
> Publisher: Romanförlaget-Göteborg, 1961
> Collection: Wild West # 553

Ensam Varg Går På Jakt by Victor Rousseau [original title unknown]
> Publisher: Romanförlaget-Göteborg, 1962
> Collection: Wild West # 559

En Virvel av Pistoler by Victor Rousseau [A Ridin' Gent]
> Publisher: Romanförlaget-Göteborg, 1962
> Collection: Wild West # 560

Fredlös i Texas by Victor Rousseau [Hi-Jacking Rustlers]
> Publisher: Romanförlaget-Göteborg, 1962
> Collection: Wild West # 563

Månplaneten by Victor Rousseau [Moon Patrol]
> Jules Verne-Magasinet # 44, 1941

THAILAND:
ผีมัมมี่คืนชีพ (by) และ มิติผวา [The Curse of Amen-ra]
Nonthaburi, Thailand, 2535 (year: 1992)

FACSIMILE EDITIONS

Golden Fleece 4-1939 (by Girasol Collectables)
Jungle Stories Fall-1939 (by Adventure House)
Spicy-Adventure Stories 4-1936 (by Girasol Collectables)
Spicy-Adventure Stories 11-1935 (by Girasol Collectables)
Spicy-Adventure Stories 1-1936 (by Girasol Collectables)
Spicy-Adventure Stories 2-1936 (by Girasol Collectables)
Spicy-Adventure Stories 3-1936 (by Girasol Collectables)
Spicy-Adventure Stories 4-1936 (by Girasol Collectables)
Spicy-Adventure Stories 5-1936 (by Girasol Collectables)
Spicy-Adventure Stories 6-1936 (by Girasol Collectables)
Spicy-Adventure Stories 7-1936 (by Girasol Collectables)
Spicy-Adventure Stories 8-1936 (by Adventure House)
Spicy-Adventure Stories 9-1936 (by Girasol Collectables)
Spicy-Adventure Stories 11-1936 (by Girasol Collectables)
Spicy-Adventure Stories 1-1937 (by Girasol Collectables)
Spicy-Adventure Stories 7-1937 (by Adventure House)
Spicy-Adventure Stories 9-1937 (by Adventure House)
Spicy-Adventure Stories 12-1937 (by Girasol Collectables)
Spicy-Adventure Stories 8-1939 (by Adventure House)
Spicy-Adventure Stories 11-1939 (by Adventure House)
Spicy-Adventure Stories 12-1939 (by Wildside Press)
Spicy-Adventure Stories 12-1940 (by Adventure House)
Spicy-Adventure Stories 2-1941 (by Odyssey Publications)
Spicy-Adventure Stories 4-1941 (by Adventure House)
Spicy-Adventure Stories 5-1941 (by Adventure House)
Spicy-Adventure Stories 9-1941 (by Adventure House)
Spicy-Adventure Stories 11-1942 (by Adventure House)
Spicy Mystery Stories 12-1935 (by Girasol Collectables)
Spicy Mystery Stories 2-1936 (by Girasol Collectables)
Spicy Mystery Stories 3-1936 (by Girasol Collectables)
Spicy Mystery Stories 4-1936 (by Girasol Collectables)
Spicy Mystery Stories 6-1936 (by Girasol Collectables)
Spicy Mystery Stories 7-1936 (by Girasol Collectables)
Spicy Mystery Stories 7-1936 (by Odyssey Publications)
Spicy Mystery Stories 8-1936 (by Girasol Collectables)
Spicy Mystery Stories 9-1936 (by Girasol Collectables)
Spicy Mystery Stories 11-1936 (by Girasol Collectables)
Spicy Mystery Stories 12-1936 (by Girasol Collectables)
Spicy Mystery Stories 2-1937 (by Wildside Press)
Spicy Mystery Stories 3-1937 (by Girasol Collectables)
Spicy Mystery Stories 6-1937 (by Girasol Collectables)
Spicy Mystery Stories 10-1937 (by Adventure House)
Spicy Mystery Stories 2-1938 (by Adventure House)
Spicy Mystery Stories 7-1941 (by Adventure House)
Spicy Mystery Stories 10-1941 (by Adventure House)
Spicy Mystery Stories 7-1942 (by Adventure House)
Spicy Mystery Stories 10-1942 (by Adventure House)
Spicy Mystery Stories 11-1942 (by Adventure House)
Spicy Western Stories 12-1936 (by Girasol Collectables)
Spicy Western Stories 1-1937 (by Girasol Collectables)
Strange Tales of Mystery and Terror 9-1931 (by Girasol Collectables)
Strange Tales of Mystery and Terror 11-1931 (by Girasol Collectables)
Strange Tales of Mystery and Terror 10-1932 (by Girasol Collectables)
Weird Tales 1-1927 (by Girasol Collectables)

INTRODUCTION TO SELECTED SHORT STORIES

The stories in this volume were chosen for inclusion for a number of reasons. I could elaborate, writings pages of introduction, but a quick synopsis and an I'll-let-you-read-the-tales-yourself should suffice.

"The Last Cartridge," simply because it is Emanuel's earliest known tale printed in a magazine. He also credits the vignette as his first professional sale. It is a drama of love and betrayal in the frozen realms of the North.

"Picked Off" has been mentioned in past introductions of other Spectre Library collections and is Emanuel's first fiction story printed in *Harper's Weekly*. The tale is a poorly constructed pastiche to "An Occurrence at Owl Creek Bridge" by Ambrose Bierce.

"Youth the Conqueror" is his first weird short story, predating the Dr. Ivan Brodsky tales. The plot is lifted and rewritten to form "The Fetish of the Waxworks" in *The Surgeon of Souls* series.

"Jackson's Wife" is beyond a doubt one of Emanuel's best efforts in the weird-realm and a damn fine yarn, involving a soul-devouring vampire.

In order to exemplify Emanuel's humorous writings, "The Jam God" has managed to squeeze into this volume. During his first decade of writing, many of his vignettes were of a humorous nature, and this was among the first purchased by W. G. Chapman.

Many colorful stories were supplied to the Sunday syndicates, and "A Man's Birthright" mirrors Emanuel's frustration over that only a strong man can prevail in a cruel world.

A King's Courier is undoubtedly the most well-written of all the political series during the 1910s decade, in which this genre, up through the first World War, was most popular amongst the magazines. "The Peril of Magellan Strait" is the first title in the series.

"Five Aces" was a prize winner in the *Associated Sunday Magazine* contest. The tale is marginal, but it marks the only instance in which Emanuel succeeded in crashing this syndicated publication.

This next tale [sadly] will probably be the number one reason most people will acquire a copy of this book. It is a thirteenth hitherto unknown and recently discovered Dr. Ivan Brodsky tale from *The Surgeon of Souls* series. Originally titled "The Broken Scroll," Chapman outright rejected this tale from the series due to it not being weird or ghostly at all. In fact, it is humorous. However, Chapman liked the story and purchased it for future use. Read here, for the first time since its last publication nearly 100 years ago, "The Cats That Looked at Cohen."

Emanuel was very adept at writing tales concerning Canada and her kindly residents, whom he often refers to as the *habitants*. "Jean of the Silence" represents the best of these tales. This story and "Keeper of the Light" in *Harper's Weekly* would both come to form the basis for the *Tales of the St. Lawrence Riverway* series.

Mesmerized by the uncanny abilities of William Sheridan to recall every incident in his life visually, Emanuel lifted Sheridan's nickname to form the Sherlock Holmes pastiche *The Man With the Camera Eyes*. The series, for the most part, hardly played up the "camera eyes" to any level of importance, but is Emanuel's first foray into the detective genre. The series begins with "The Box of Borneos."

Yet another Northern tale is "The Girl at Three Mile Fork." Its inclusion marks one in which a female plays the predominant leading role.

After the abysmal sales on *The Man With the Camera Eyes*, Emanuel realized that what makes a series sell better is a romantic interest. His *Quest of the Gentle Hazard* not only included a romantic-byplay, but also loosely revolved around international scenarios. The series launches with the introduction of Lord Richard Jocelyn in, "A Casual Champion."

A couple of years earlier, Chapman had sent Emanuel a cut-out from a magazine, an article and image depicting a gyroscope, in hopes that Emanuel could effect an ingenious plot. Finally, Emanuel settled down and wrote *The Devil Chair*. The series has already been compiled as a collection by the Spectre Library. The first installment—"The Cripple of Prospect Park"—is included here for first-time readers.

Returning to the romance plot, Emanuel churned out an international affair entitled *The League of Lost Causes*. The series was imaginative, but, oddly enough, sold poorly. Offered here is the first installment, "The Woman From the Sea."

It had been nearly four years since *The Surgeon of Souls* sales debacle in 1910, yet, reincarnation was a huge to-do in America and abroad. Realizing Emanuel was best suited amongst his small coterie of writers, the cleanly written *The Tracer of Egos* was born. This series has also been fully collected and printed by the Spectre Library. The first installment—"The Amulet of Marduk"—is offered again for first-time readers.

While the *Revelations of an Ambassador-at-Large* series is hardly anything new, what with five tales printed in *Popular Magazine*, the truth is that Emanuel had created 12 tales in the series. Once *Popular* was done with the series, Chapman resold the whole series in his syndication field. "The Golden Death" is of a more fantastic nature, bordering on the scientific and strange.

Rounding out the selection is the first Emanuel tale I ever read, "The Wolf Trap." It takes place in the cold frozen reaches of the North, and employs the psychological wiles of a determined widow upon a man whom loves her daughter, played up against the man whom she believes to have murdered her husband.

Read all, and enjoy!

THE LAST CARTRIDGE
Munsey's (September 1907)

All through the night the bear had been heard scratching upon the walls, testing now one side, now another, searching for entrance, maddened by hunger. From time to time there came an interval of silence; then the scratching commenced again and continued persistently.

No voice could have been heard through those hard-frozen snow-blocks. A strong man, perishing in the cold, might have shouted for help in vain through the long winter night and remained unanswered. Only the crepitation of those restless claws was audible, though once the occupants within seemed to hear the sound of a half-human wail.

The woman gripped her companion's arm with a shudder.

"Did you hear anything?" she whispered, with wide eyes. "A cry?"

Both listened intently.

"No, it was nothing. Hush, dear, you are trembling!"

"If it should get in!"

He patted her arm assuringly.

"A legion of bears could never force these walls. Take courage, dear; tomorrow you will hear the pattering of the dogs' feet across the snow, and he will be back, with food and cartridges."

"If we had only one!" she said. "Strong as you are, it would be death to face those furious animals—even with that."

He had pulled from its sheath a rusty knife.

"For you," he whispered, "I would succeed even with this knife. Be calm, dear—there is no danger."

One grows accustomed to whispering in those solitudes. The loneliness is too profound for sound.

Inside the hut it was almost warm. The moisture had frozen the snow walls into opaque ice-blocks, and from the roof icicles hung everywhere. Above the flame of the large candle water dripped imperceptibly, hissing on the hot tallow.

But for their voices the sex of the two inmates might have been indiscernible. Their hair was hidden under great hoods of fur; from feet to waist they were wrapped in their loose sleeping-bags.

"It has stopped now," she whispered presently. "It must be growing light outside—it is eleven o'clock. Yesterday one could almost have read at midday. Soon the sun will appear again. Ah. This desolate winter!"

"Be brave, dear. To-morrow he should return with the dogs, and we will start for the vessel. We will sail southward, after the sun."

She shivered in the gloom. He had placed his arm round her, and their dancing shadows, enormous in size, mocked them grotesquely from the walls. In the silence the slow drip-drip of water from the roof was heard.

"Yes, to-morrow," said the woman. "And then—the end. Well, it had to come. He will return, and then—ah, I love you!"

She flung her arms round his neck and laid her head upon his shoulder. He raised her fur cap and patted her hair.

"Oh, how I hate him!" she whispered fiercely. "I wish I might never see him again. He drives me mad with his grave, questioning looks, his silence. He is old and selfish. He thinks nothing of me. He brings me here, into these terrible solitudes of ice and snow, and leaves me—with you. Well, he is a fool; let him suffer and learn!"

"They say you love him devotedly. The papers—"

"Yes," she sneered mockingly, "always the papers! When I was a bride I first went north with him. I was only a girl, and he a middle-aged man, and I thought it heroic; my imagination was fired with romantic notions of duty. And now I have to accompany him every journey, to live up to my reputation. I did not care, till I met you; but now—oh, I hate him, I hate him!"

He remained quite silent, and presently she bent to look into his face, under the candle-light.

"I believe you—love him," she murmured.

"Yes," said the man, quietly and hopelessly, "I love him. I love him more than any man in the world—or any woman, excepting you. And I know that I am doing him the greatest wrong one man can do to his friend. You know how he saved my life upon the ice-floe."

"His reputation," she said sneeringly. "He was paid in fame. He got a good advertisement."

"You wrong him," said her companion gravely. "He is incapable of self-seeking. I think he is the simplest, noblest character I have ever known."

She twined her arms round his neck until she felt him respond to the intensity of her ardor.

"Do you love him, then, more than me?" she whispered.

"No!" he cried with sudden passion. "I need you more. Listen—will you come with me after the voyage is over?"

She nodded, nestling down into his furs.

"We will go south together, to Florida, to Cuba, to lands of perpetual sunshine, and leave these horrors behind forever. We will lie in the sun and watch the blue, open sea and the palmetto groves."

"Oh, if this voyage were over!" she answered. "If he might never return! Yes, I am wicked enough to wish the ice might engulf him, or that he might perish in the snow."

Outside the scratching commenced again. It persisted, low down toward the ground, beside the loose ice-blocks which were piled up at the entrance, as if the bear sought to scratch through by tireless persistence.

"Ah, that terrible sound!" the woman cried. "I cannot endure it." She stepped out of her sleeping-bag and crossed the floor. Presently she stooped quickly, with a little cry.

"See," she exclaimed, "I have found a cartridge!" She came over eagerly and handed it to her companion. "Now you can shoot the bear," she whispered, opening the rifle-breech. "I will scrape the snow from the loophole, and you can pass your barrel through."

She took the knife and began to dig between the two of the loose ice-blocks. The soft snow crumbled easily. A faint light filtered through the orifice.

"It is dawn," she whispered. "You can just see, distinguish—ah!" She dropped the knife; then stooped suddenly and picked it up. "Stop!" she cried in excitement. "No, shoot now, shoot! Quickly, before it goes!"

In the dim dawn a shaggy form was discernible, crouched upon the snow, ten paces distant. The man took careful aim. As he did so the figure rose, and, rearing itself, seemed to stretch out its limbs as if in supplication. Then, as the shot rang out, it fell, and a stream of bright blood spurted into the snow. The mournful howling of a dog was faintly audible.

The man inside gave a wild cry.

"Down with the ice-blocks!" he shouted to the terrified woman. "Quick, help me!"

Heedless of her bewildered words, he began lifting down the great blocks with frenzied movements, working with super-human energy, till he had cleared a space wide enough to admit of exit. Then, leaping over, he ran toward the prone figure. The dog howled dismally beside it, and licked the blood that came from the wound.

"My captain!" he cried, flinging himself upon his knees; and, overcome by grief, he wept unreservedly.

The dying man opened his eyes and sought unavailingly to raise himself. His furs were frozen into a stiff matting of ice; his hair and beard, uncovered by any hood, were stiffer than steel, and his features had the bloodless aspect of a face of wax. Exhausted, emaciated, his dogs all dead but one, his sleigh abandoned, he had struggled homeward alone.

"Take care of her," he whispered. "The ship—is safe. Andersen—will be here with the—second sleigh—to-morrow."

He closed his eyes and shuddered slightly. Then the limbs relaxed and the eyes opened.

Slowly the man rose from beside the body of his captain. The woman stood by his side, white with fear, raising her eyes dubiously in supplication.

"Ah!" she said, "this is terrible. I—"
He read her eyes.
"You knew!" he answered bitterly. "Murderess! I never want to see your face again!"

PICKED OFF
Harper's Weekly (4 January 1908)

Corporal Herring flattened his stomach against the ground. He had shifted his ammunition pouches onto his haunches, so that he might embrace his Mother Earth more closely, and the cartridges had dribbled out into a small metallic pile on either side of him. He had lost his pull-through, and his shoulder ached vilely from the kick of his foul rifle. With bleeding nails he scratched at a small mound of earth in front of him, which he had made compact with stones. "If one of them things 'its me, it'll 'it me in the 'ead," reflected the Corporal.

Corporal Herring's world consisted of a fiery ball, burning in a zone of blue, some distant boulders, horrid with rolling rifle fire, and the long yellow grass wisps that bent under the fitful wind. Through these he could distinguish, on each side of him, familiar profiles: Dutchy, the squarehead; Scotty; and Orseguard Baynes. Coarse pleasantries were bandied between them.

Overhead the bullets were humming like honeybees. At times one whistled past him, or a little spurt of dust arose close by; then Corporal Herring's stomach turned to water, and he shouted some jest coarser than the rest. It was his first general engagement.

"Did you hear that one?" quavered Orseguard Baynes, with simulated interest, as something louder than the rest went booming by.

"Shet up, you fool!" said Corporal Herring. "Thet's a pompon shell."

Five miles from flank to flank, unseen by their invisible foes, five thousand men lay prone, held to the ground by that unceasing shower which hooted over them. They knew that somewhere some directing mind controlled them, and they lay there, eager, as all recruits, to charge. Two hundred yards in front was a safety zone, from which, once gained, they might advance uninjured almost up to the enemy's trenches. Many had tried this perilous passage; it was strewn thickly with corpses, which made strange, irregular depressions in the waist-high grasses.

High overhead, mere specks in the blue, the vultures waited. They had followed the trail of dead transport animals which marked the progress of the column. Corporal Herring shuddered as he squinted up at them. He had seen flocks of these sable scavengers, clustered on dead horses, too gorged to rise, their bald heads whiter than leprosy, their curved beaks indicative of horrible repletion.

The sun's hot trail blazed in the zenith of the brazen sky. Mirages danced over the staring plain—houses where there had been rocks, boulders where trees had grown, rivers of gurgling water.

Ah, those waters of the mirages! How they longed for them as they flattened themselves beneath that pitiless glare, the swollen tongues lolling from their panting mouths! They almost envied the dead who, with open jaws and clenched fingers, lined the long slope behind them.

Dust whitened their gaunt, unshaven faces; dust had caked the moist necks of their drained water bottles; dust clogged their eyes, their matted hair, and their sweat-stiffened shoulder straps.

One man, shot through the brain, twined and untwined his fingers ceaselessly, winking away the flies that clustered upon his staring eyeballs. Under its chocolate stains his face was whiter than a clown's. Some sucked the sweet roots of grass-blades to relieve their intolerable thirst; some, rendered ravenous through fear, crunched their emergency rations of beef and chocolate in their dry mouths, and could not swallow them. And everywhere Fear reigned, fear that would have driven them in headlong flight but for that sweeping sleet of nickel above them; fear that increased as the slow hours went by while they lay helpless.

A hare leaped through the grass toward Herring and sat, poised on her haunches, watching him. He saw her little heart thumping tumultuously. "Hey, puss!" he yelled, and flung his hat at her. "Benk! Benk!" shouted the soldiers, as she sped swiftly down the line into the distance. "Benk, Benk, Charing Cross, Cheapside; all aboard, lydies, penny all the way." The hat twirled through the air and floated back, with a hole through the brim no wider than a lead pencil. "If my 'ead 'ad bin there," the corporal murmured, as he crowned himself.

The wounded man suddenly began to choke and hammer on the ground; then his head dropped and he rolled backward. The flies descended on him. Orseguard Baynes stared at the corpse one moment and then sprang to his feet. "Advance," he yelled. "Follow me, boys; to hell with them!" A storm of protest rose.

The corporal pulled him down. "Easy; don't funk, lad; easy," he shouted. Orseguard Baynes sat down and burst into tears. He felt up his sleeve for his handkerchief, but before he had found it his head went down on his arms, and he was snoring.

Far to the left cheers arose, which were taken up along the line. "Hooray!" they cried. "'Ere come the guns! Now we sharn't be long." The batteries rolled past in splendid alignment, the yellow muzzles of the guns black against the skyline. Suddenly a distant boom broke the deep silence, and with a roar a shell spun through the air and dropped among the horses. The batteries wheeled and disappeared through smoke wreaths, the drivers lashing their mounts furiously. *Boom!* sounded again; and with the slow roar of a train a shell plunged into the ground not fifty yards away, scattering a circle of steel fragments, and splashing up a shower of smoking earth. Another fell nearer; the enemy were getting the range. And now heaven was filled with them. They shrieked and howled on their long journey; they fell right, left, in front, behind; escapes appeared miraculous. Some-times the acrid fumes hung overhead in a yellow, sickening cloud. Men rose up, shaking their fists at the mute sky. "Lie down, you blarsted fools!" cried others. "You're droring the fire of their 'ole blooming battery."

"If one of them things 'its me, I'm a dead 'un. Gord syve me and get me out of 'ere," prayed Corporal Herring.

"If this keeps up we'll orl be corpses, myte," said Scotty, moistening his cracked lips with his swollen tongue.

"Oh, I dunno," the corporal responded. "A bloke's a juggins if 'e gits 'isself killed in 'is fust fight, thet's wot I say."

"Ah! And wot abart thet bloke there?" asked Scotty, sneering. "And wot abart Fagin at Paardeburg? Nice wy to die, thet, ain't it? It's a public noosance, thet's wot it is, myte. A nearse and fevvers for mine, thet's my tyste."

"Ho! Wot's the difference?" asked Corporal Herring. "It's orl one, ain't it? 'E didn't feel nuffink."

"'Ow d'you know 'e didn't feel nuffink?" Scotty persisted. "'Ow do you know wot it feels like at orl?"

The chorus of a song came rolling out of the distance:

"Brike the news to muvver,
Tell 'er that I love 'er,
Kiss 'er dear, sweet fyce fer me,
    and sy I am no more;
Brike the news to muvver,
Sy there is no other . . ."

On the flank a bugle pealed. "Advance—advance!" it called. Instantly Orseguard Baynes, who had snored through the shellfire, was on his feet, with a thousand others, stumbling forward over the uneven ground. Their lips were blue with fear, but the habits of the parade ground held them and drove them on. Most of their rifles were still sighted to fifteen hundred yards. Fear verged upon fury; they leaped from among the scattering shell splinters, cursing the enemy and one another.

Sometimes a knot would bunch, and then the bullets hissed past them like hailstones; and all the while shells whined out of the distant sky and plunged, roaring, into the ground beside them. Orseguard Bayne's rifle stubbed Corporal Herring in the side, and he turned on him furiously.

"Fer tuppence 'alfpenny I'd bash yer blooming fyce in!" he screamed, as they raced neck and neck together toward the safety zone.

Men began falling thickly. Some, shot through the brain, would spin round and round, their features horribly contorted, their fingers clutching the air. Others, who had fallen down and could not get up again, stared wide-eyed at their wounds, in stupid resentment and astonishment.

"Git out of my wy, damn you!" Corporal Herring screamed to Dutchy, as they lay down to breathe. An instant later the sky seemed to fall in on them, and everything was lost in a choking fog. A shell had dropped between them. As the smoke thinned the corporal saw Dutchy grinning at him. "Git out, you grinnin' swine!" he howled. Dutchy's grin widened, and his eyeteeth showed in the corners of his mouth like fangs. "Wot's the matter, Dutchy?" asked Corporal Herring. "I don't know," Dutchy whimpered. "My eyes hurts. I think I'm going blind." He stood up uncertainly, spreading his arms, and tottered forward.

"Lie down, you blarsted fool," Corporal Herring shouted. "Lie down, I sy." And Dutchy lay down obediently, but all his members reached the ground at the same instant, and he doubled upon himself like an acrobat. He was only the shell of a man.

"My Gord!" the corporal whispered, trembling.

"My Gord!" screamed Orseguard Baynes, pointing and gibbering at him.

"Watcher all staring at me fer," asked Herring resentfully. "Wot's hup? Were 's all these flies come from? I fell down over a stone." He tried to rise, but his legs sank under him, and looking down, he saw a crimson stain widening upon his tunic. His mouth opened, and he looked at it in foolish amazement.

"I wonder where I'm 'it?" he thought. "I'll 'ave to lie 'ere till they pick me up, I suppose. They'll send me down to the bise 'orspital, and then wot O fer beer!" It was very comfortable there in the soft grass, and he could have gone to sleep but for the thirst which tortured him. There was another thing disturbed him, too, and that was the grinning face of Dutchy, lying in the grass, ten paces distant.

"Stop that. Keep your fice strite!" shouted Corporal Herring.

"Pore beggar, 'e carn't 'elp 'isself," he added, reflectively. "They'll 'ave to spide 'im under pretty quick, or 'e'll swell 'orrible. Thenk Gord, I'm out of it."

Then it occurred to him that he might as well possess himself of Dutchy's water-bottle; but when he tried to crawl toward it an agonizing pain shot through him. He essayed to rise himself upon his hands and knees, but his hands turned sideways, and his feet had no more sensation than horseshoes. The distance seemed tremendous.

"I'll 'ave a bit of a nap, and proceed when it gits cooler," thought Herring, sinking back into the grass and watching a vulture circling over him.

But a few minutes later his strength returned. He clambered over the corpse and seized the water-bottle, draining it eagerly; then sprang to his feet and hastened after his troop. Bullets whined overhead, but none touched him. "To hell with them!" he shouted, waving his arms. "Follow me, boys!" The whole line leaped up with a roar.

"Fix bay'nits!" the corporal screamed, and led his men right into the trenches. A giant Boer, with a patriarchal beard, leaped up with a pistol. The corporal had lost his rifle, but he seized his antagonist round the waist and grappled with him. The Dutchman's hat fell off, and his bald head looked exactly like a vulture's. They swayed backward and forward, until the corporal stumbled and fell full length into the burning sand. He gasped and spluttered, and opened his eyes; he was back where he had been lying, and the hideous leer of Dutchy confronted him. Overhead there passed the shadow of wings.

"Stop thet, I sy. Stop it!" he screamed, shaking his clenched hands at Dutchy. "You bloomin' squarehead, will you stop grinnin' at me?" He meant to take him by the throat and choke him, but Dutchy disappeared, and in his place stood the white tents of the encampment bellying in the wind. The company cooks were boiling bully beef with compressed vegetables over a fire of wet wood. "Silly fools," yelled the corporal, "you've fergot to put in the pertyers." The cooks threw down their utensils and advanced with threatening gestures, but the corporal was not afraid. He knew that they were only phantoms. Something that he knew very well, had always known in the most intimate manner, was lying upon the veld, thirsting with an unquenchable thirst, winking

away the flies, and Dutchy was back again and grinning at him.

"'Ow did you git back, Dutchy?" he thought he said, but only the rattling of air came through his open jaws.

A vulture swooped down from the blue, and now hung poised directly over him, as though some hand had nailed it to the firmament. Then, one by one out of the distance, pinpoints appeared, at equal intervals, grew larger, and hung poised in their places, motionless against their background of cloudless sky.

"You'll 'ave to wite a long time for your dinner, myte," thought Corporal Herring, mentally apostrophizing the leader. As if in answer one simultaneous movement seemed to communicate itself to each. They swept downward and circled over him, their wings outspread, their claws contracted tightly against their breasts. He quivered in abject fear.

"My Gord," he whimpered, "what will I do? Suppose a snike should bite me?" The rustling grass seemed to betoken a snake's stealthy approach, and in anticipation he could feel the smooth contraction of the sleek coils about him. From where he lay he could perceive the mud-colored felt covering of Dutchy's water-bottle, which had been torn from its supporting strap, and rested between the corpse's knees. Only ten paces distant! He heard his breath hiss through his swollen lips as he strained his avid eyes toward it; but not a muscle would respond to his mind's promptings, and the corpse still lay, facing him with its deriding smile.

Slowly, after unaccountable epochs, his fears subsided. And now he no longer suffered from that torturing thirst. His mind was clearer than crystal, but he could no longer reason inductively, for the sentinel of his consciousness had fallen at his post, and ideas, no longer ushered in with sequence, poured through his brain with quick, fantastic imagery. "Wy are my 'ands so wet?" he thought. "It must be ryning—and I fergot to arsk the ole woman fer 'er umbreller."

Presently he was aware of companies that moved toward him. With them were prisoners, and all gazed at him mournfully as they passed by. "Wy, there's Fagin," he whispered. "I saw 'im killed at Paardesburg." But nobody noticed him; only Fagin, as he passed, indicated two empty places in one file of fours. The corporal rose. Before him lay a hideous thing that writhed and twisted, beating out a tattoo upon the ground with hands and heels. "My Gord," he thought, "thet's me!" The tattoo ceased suddenly, the thing fell backward, and, with a swoop, the vultures alighted.

YOUTH THE CONQUEROR
Young's Magazine (March 1909)

Two men were talking together in the smoking room at the annual reunion of the club.

"So Cassel's dead?" said one. "He was engaged to be married, too; wasn't he?"

"Yes," said the other, in a non-committal tone, drawing steadily at his cigar.

"Do you know, I often wonder at that," said the first man. "Of course, Cassel was a good fellow, but Mary Lovatt—"

The other raised his eyebrows inquiringly.

"Well, she was good, of course—thoroughly good and honest and simple, but she wouldn't have understood Cassel; and, if she could have, she would have shrunk from him with loathing."

"'*De mortuis*,'" the second man began.

"Yes, I know. He wasn't bad, as men go. Which of us could throw the first stone at him? But Mary!"

The second man threw his cigar away.

"Broome," he began, "I came to know Cassel pretty intimately during the last few months of his life. I think he realized his responsibilities toward her more than any of us can imagine. He had not gone through life unstained; and yet he had that intense longing for righteousness which is possessed by many whose sins and errors have been rather the result of circumstances than of instinct. It was a perpetual wonder to him that Mary, with her high, untried ideals, her lofty dreams, should have entered her life on him.

"He told me so one dreary February day—one evening when the harsh cold had yielded to that sticky warmth that is an occasional feature of winter in this latitude. We were waiting in his studio on Fifty-seventh Street, while he ran his fingers and thumbs over his model of Youth—the statue that killed him.

"That was about six weeks after a reputation had come to him through his Baseball Pitcher, and he was being acclaimed as one of the greatest of contemporary modelers. It was pretty to see him shaping the plastic clay, which gradually took on a more and more life-like appearance under his touches. It was the figure of a noble Greek, nude, the face immobile in his severity, and yet portraying in every characteristic, in the firm, nervous poise, the beauty of the soul within. The left arm, which was upraised, carried a shield, heavy and square, as though to ward off some unknown evil that impended.

"Remembering his Baseball Pitcher, which could not have been compared with this masterpiece, I praised his work unstintedly. Cassel flushed with pleasure at my words.

"'It is Youth indeed!' I had cried, carried away. 'It stands as the type of the youth of all the world, with its noble thoughts and high, unshattered aspirations.'

"'Yes,' he said quietly. 'It is the youth of all, that nobler part that never dies, is never stained nor degraded.'

"Then, sitting beside me, he began to talk about Mary. If I had ever feared for her he dispelled those fears.

"'I'm not worthy of her, I know, Garrett,' he said, leaning forward, with his head on his hands. 'I suppose you realize that, too. No'—for I had uttered some faint protest—'it is true. We all know it. But she doesn't. And the worst of it is, she wouldn't be capable of understanding. If I should try to tell her, I should pass out of her life, her thoughts, her dreams.'

"I could make no reply to that. She had been brought up sheltered from the world; whole tracts of common experience were beyond her imagination.

"'But I've put all that behind me,' he cried. 'Yes, Garrett, I've come to recognize that the man worthy of the name must shield the woman he loves from any knowledge of his past. And, then, is it in reality his past? When youth is gone—at thirty say—do we not, in a measure, stand at the opening of a newer life? Would it be fair to hold one culpable for the acts of his days of immaturity?

"'And that is how the inspiration for the statue came to me,' he continued. 'It is my nobler self, all the best that is in me, drawn, so to speak, to the surface of my personality and externalized in the clay, to be my good angel and guardian.'

"And, looking from Cassel to the statue, and back again, I could detect now a certain faint but none the less significant resemblance under the immobile features of clay, as though the modeler had in very truth delved into his soul to find its most secret qualities.

"I did not see Cassel for some time afterward. Mary was abroad; the wedding was to take place on her return, which would occur in about a month. I had expected that Cassel was busy finishing his statue, or making those little preparations for his marriage which one would naturally expect to engross his attention. Judge, then, of my surprise when he called at my lodgings unexpectedly one blustery night toward the end of March. He came in, wet with rain, his clothing disordered, his eyes bloodshot. He was not drunk, and yet he had been drinking deeply.

"'I want you to come and stay with me through the night,' he said hoarsely.

"I tried to brace him up. I think I even took the liberty of lecturing him on his conduct. I know I mentioned Mary. He seemed like a man who had been on a prolonged debauch.

"'No, it's not that,' he muttered. He came nearer and whispered. 'God! man, do you know what fear means? If you don't know, go down upon your knees and pray to heaven that you never may. I have been drinking to banish it and I dare not go back alone. Come with me.'

"I accompanied him to his studio, in one corner of which was a lounge on which he slept frequently when the fever for work was upon him. As I preceded him into the room, the statue seemed to loom in a menacing manner through the dark shadows. For one instant I started backward in alarm. Then, with a laugh, I turned up the gas and the ocular hallucination vanished.

"'Do you see any difference?' Cassel muttered, coming in behind me. He was breathing heavily; his lips were blue and his face chalky white.

"And, looking at the statue carefully, I did detect a difference. The immobile face seemed to have taken on an aspect of anger, and the shield, no longer carelessly raised, was grasped in a minatory fashion above the arm.

"'You've changed it!' I exclaimed.

"'Yes, I had to change it,' he whispered, going over to a table on which stood a decanter of water and a bottle half full of Scotch whiskey. Then he sat down beside me.

"'Garrett,' he began, 'you think me crazy. But I must tell you. Do you remember what I told you about the statue—how I had meant to incarnate in flesh-like clay all that was noblest in my nature?'

"I nodded in sympathy. I still believed that overwork and overdrinking had set his nerves on edge.

"'I thought I could externalize in visible form all that was best in me, to be a permanent inspiration,' Cassel went on. 'But what remained? The evil—the sleeping, deadly evil that lies, like a chained, sleeping hound, in all our natures. I am rotten all through, Garrett, and there stands all that was best of me.'

"'My dear fellow,' I said, 'without pretending to believe a word of what you say, I think you've worked yourself up to the border line of insanity. Cassel, you must destroy that statue or the statue will destroy you.'

"'I know it,' he answered quietly. 'Garrett, it's angry with me. As sure as I live, it will kill me when it has grown stronger. My God! Garrett, there's a living soul in the thing! Tonight, when I came in and shut the door, it moved—'

"'Oh, wake up, man!' I cried, pinching him violently. 'Now, see here, Cassel, I'm going to stay with you tonight, and you're going to take a long, strong drink and go to sleep. And then tomorrow I am going to take you away with me for a week in the country.'

"He was almost persuaded. 'You're sure it's nothing but my imagination?' he asked dubiously. 'Well, for God's sake, promise you won't leave me!' he went on, glaring with haggard eyes into the corner.

"I quieted him at last. I poured out a liberal potation—it's no time to haggle about temperance when a man's upon the verge of delirium tremens—undressed him like a baby, and put him to bed. Then I sat in a rocking chair to pass the night there.

"It must have been long after midnight when I awoke. A slight sound roused me. Through the skylight of the studio, a long, thin moonbeam, a finger of light, fell full on the statue's face. Broome, it was twitching; no longer inanimate clay, it born an expression of uncontrollable, noble anger. And on the floor, crouching and cowering at the Thing which he had made, under the upraised, minatory shield, was Cassel, babbling and muttering incoherent words.

"I tried to move, but the most hideous terror chained me to my chair. I tried to speak; I could not utter a sound. For suddenly the face of Cassel came into the path of the finger, which, like a search-light, lit up each separate feature. And it was the face of a demon, indescribably old and vicious and evil, and stamped with the insignia of sin in every furrow and line. And he crouched, praying at the feet of his good self, that nobler self which is at war perpetually with the lower instincts. Broome, even while I looked, I saw the figure straighten itself. It towered aloft, it raised the mighty shield.

"*Clang!* The great shield fell to the ground, hurled as though by an athlete. The babbling ceased; one hideous scream broke through the night. You know the rest. When they burst in and lit the gas, they found me fainting there and Cassel upon the ground, under the shattered fragments of the shield."

JACKSON'S WIFE
The Smart Set (May 1909)

When Hale entered the dining room of the boarding house on Washington Square upon that first evening after his return he found it difficult to realize that he had been away at all, much less for fifteen months. As he walked automatically toward the table which he had formerly occupied he noticed that everything—almost everything—was exactly as it had been before. There was the fat Colonel, snorting over his soup; there was Miss Hallett, of the good heart and shrewish tongue, and Madame Oberhaus, placid, fat, smiling, beringed, unchanged.

Mrs. Crewe, the landlady, showed Hale to his old seat, and he sat down, instinctively shifting his chair in order to avoid the leg of the table which, fifteen months previously, had habitually annoyed him. The Colonel looked up, growled, snorted and wiped the soup from his mustache; Miss Hallett permitted her acidulous features to relax and Madame Oberhaus beamed all over her face.

"Welcome back, Hale," she said, stretching out her plump, bediamonded clean hand.

Hale scrutinized the diners. Those fifteen months seemed more than ever like a dream. All—almost all were known to him; and they sat in their accustomed places and interchanged the same banal platitudes. There were the same chairs and tables, the same, it almost appeared, fruit stains on the cloths; and Miles, the stately colored servitor, was handing Hale the *menu* as formerly.

"Where have you been all this time, Hale?" asked Madame Oberhaus.

"Oh, Europe," Hale answered vaguely. "Paris at first, then Florence and Rome. But I didn't do much painting—just drew in inspiration from the picture galleries."

"What is your craze now, Hale?"

"Madonnas," he answered. "I caught it in Florence, after looking at the Madonna by the unknown painter."

"The unknown? That sounds fascinating. Who was he? Tell me about him."

"Oh, it's only a guide's story," answered Hale carelessly. "After I'd been there a few times they got to know me and stopped pestering me, but there was one old fellow who wouldn't let up until I had hired him out of desperation. Most of his talk was the conventional guide's patter, and as full of inaccuracies; but this story he told me was new, though no doubt he invented it. It seems that there was a very beautiful woman who lived in Florence in the early Middle Ages, for whose love scores of men had killed themselves. According to him she was a sorceress, a kind of spiritual vampire. She had no soul, but when anyone kissed her she drew his soul through his lips, which gave her a new lease of life, while he, having no soul, promptly went off and committed suicide. This unknown artist was hopelessly in love with her, and when his love was rejected he begged as a last favor to be allowed to paint her, to which she consented. Then there was a cardinal whom she favored, of whom the painter was jealous. The story gets a little mixed up here; some say the two men killed one another in a duel, some that both committed suicide. Anyway, it appears that the soul of the cardinal, who was presumably a man of good works, proved too strong for her, and so she died too."

"A kind of spiritual indigestion," said Miss Hallett.

"That legend of the *Belle Dame Sans Merci* runs through all medieval literature," said Madame Oberhaus. "But you don't require the vampire explanation. Death is incarnate in all beauty—everywhere."

"Why, what is your religion now, madame?" asked Hale, laughing. "Christian Science?"

"No, Maeterlinck," answered madame, respiting a large morsel of chicken upon a fork, which was on its way to her mouth. "Last month it was Pragmatism. Before that I was a Jain."

"You haven't altered a bit," said Hale. "And I, too, have the most curious sensation, as though these fifteen months of my absence had been blotted out of my life and I had just come back from a day's jaunt in the country. Nothing seems to have changed at all."

"Nothing ever does change," said Madame Oberhaus. "You are like the child in the railroad carriage who thinks the scenery flies past him. Really it is standing still. You rush hither and thither, you 'make time fly'; and then some day you wake up and understand that it is you who fly. We go out of the door called 'Death' and come in at the gate called 'Birth' and see much the same scenery as before, and we go groping round blindly for old associations and acquaintances, not knowing them or our destiny. We are like blue flies buzzing under a small, inverted tumbler."

"What an unpleasant simile!" said Hale. "I think I liked you best when you were a Theosophist, madame. Your auras and haloes used to appeal to my sense of color. You always insisted that my halo was snow white, didn't you?"

"Death white," said Madame Oberhaus. "You are a spiritual albino. But I believe in all that still. All my religions really amount to the same thing. Everything is true. It becomes true by thinking it's true—or perhaps that's a remnant of my Pragmatic days. But that's the beauty of it: when one understands the essential details one can have one's religion fresh every day, like rolls."

"Well, you're right in one respect; nothing seems to have changed here," said Hale, looking around the room once more. "I don't see a single face that is new to me. There's Bryant; and there's old Mr. Jones, getting red in the face over his soup; and there are Mrs. Burns and those two daughters she was always bothering me to paint. Oh, by the way, where's Jackson? I am to have his studio on the top floor next to the empty room that Mrs. Crewe used to occupy. I forgot Jackson had gone. I never thought he'd leave Washington Square, but I suppose he's grown rich and sold out in favor of Philistia."

Madame Oberhaus spread out her plump hands in deprecation. Miss Hallett's thin face lit up; she opened her mouth and closed it again irresolutely. The Colonel snorted and poured out some claret from his bottle.

"I can't imagine this place without Jackson," Hale went on. "He never used to miss a meal—and Bryant's sitting in his place, too. Isn't he coming back?"

"Jackson is dead, Hale," said Madame Oberhaus.

"Dead!" exclaimed Hale in astonishment. "Jackson dead? Why, he was the healthiest old bachelor going, the sort of fellow that never

dies. It made one feel ten years younger to shake hands with him. Was is sudden?"

"It was last June," said Madame Oberhaus evasively. "He wasn't a bachelor; he had been married—"

"Two day," Miss Hallett interposed acidulously.

Their voices dropped, for a hush had fallen over the dining room. The conversation died; the clank of cutlery on plates became more and more monotonous. Hale felt that somebody was coming in alone the corridor behind him. She entered and went past.

She was small, slight and thin. Her hair was of a pale brown, strained back. Her eyes were gray. She was attired in black, and as she walked she bowed her head slightly forward, as though she had been broken once and must always go delicately.

"By George!" Hale muttered, white as the tablecloth. "Who's that?"

Madame Oberhaus paused in the act of conveying a tumbler to her lips. She had not turned her head.

"Hush!" she said. "That's Mrs. Jackson. Who did you think she was?"

"The—the Madonna in the gallery at Florence," stammered Hale in confusion. "What color is her aura?" he continued foolishly, not knowing why.

"Blood-colored," said Madame Oberhaus. "Her husband shot himself with Mrs. Crewe's revolver."

Hale went upstairs to his new room, once Jackson's, on the top story, over-looking the tumble-down Italian rookeries of Bleecker and Thompson Streets. It was a quaint, old-fashioned apartment, built, apparently, before the science of architecture had standardized its houses by dividing their spaces into parallelograms. In length it extended along the entire width of the house, and the low, sloping roof formed numerous eccentric angles with the irregular walls. Jackson had occupied it as a studio for several years. It was not meant for a living room; the bed and bureau had been relegated to an obscure corner adjacent to a single faucet, and hidden behind a screen, leaving a large and empty space of blue-washed walls and uncarpeted floor.

The boarding house, which stood on the south side of the Square, was one of a row of ancient and unprofitable tenements, whose rooms were leased unfurnished to impecunious painters, sculptors, modelers in clay, workers in stained glass and the kindred arts and literary endeavorers. In sharp contrast to the squalor of the adjoining houses, it had been renovated by Mrs. Crewe, refurnished, and was conducted with a modicum of profit and tolerable enterprise.

The bed behind the screen was neatly made, but outside Hale was conscious that the dusty lay thickly everywhere. Melancholy and desolation seemed to cling to the worm-eaten rafters, the creaking boards, the rattling window frame; the very atmosphere of the place was infected, as though by the mentality of the dead man who had once lived there. An old, charred pipe of Jackson's rested upon one corner of the mantel, the dust-white ashes still in the bowl and crumbling at its side. There were match scratches upon the walls, whose pale blue surface was disfigured by numerous indentations in the crumbling plaster.

Hale flung the window open and looked out. Over his left rose the high tower of the Judson, dominating the frowsy courtyards opposite, from which the wrangling voices of uncorseted Italian women, the squalling of infants and howls of chained and neglected dogs rose in a series of shrill crescendos, accompanied by the rumbling bass of the elevated trains rounding the curve out of Sixth Avenue. Four feet beneath him was the flat roof of an extension, which stretched toward the window of an apartment in the adjacent house, falling short of it by a space of two feet or thereabouts that formed an alley leading from the Square into a back courtyard.

As Hale stood there the window of the room in the house opposite was opened and a girl appeared. She wore a blue dress, which was partly concealed by a great, paint-stained apron. A brush was in her hand. She leaned forth, resting her arms upon the window sill. When she perceived Hale she started.

"Good evening, painter man!" she cried, waving the brush gaily. "So you've come home again!'

"That you, Blue Girl?" Hale called.

"Me, sure enough," she answered, poising herself in the window frame and swinging her feet unconcernedly over the alley beneath her. "Where have you been all this long time? I thought that you were never coming home again."

"Take care you don't fall down. I've been in Europe for the last year or so—Paris and Italy."

"Paris and Italy? My, but you must have been having a good time!" she mocked. "You didn't say good-bye to me before you went," she continued petulantly, wrinkling her eyebrows. "Your friend in there had to apologize until I forgave you. Really, you have been extremely rude to me. Mr. Jackson was ever so much nicer than you. And are you going to have his room and live here now?"

"Yes, for the present," said Hale abstractedly.

The girl ceased swinging her feet and looked over toward him curiously.

"You certainly are not nice any longer," she said emphatically. "Here I've been pent up in little New York this year and more while you've been traveling, thinking about the good times we three had together, and wondering whether you were ever going to return, and whether I should forgive you or not when you did return—and now you don't seem a bit pleased to see me, and I don't believe you'd care whether I forgave you or not. Would you? What are you painting now? I've gone back to still life. I'm coming over on to your roof like I used to. Look out!"

She poised herself as though for a spring.

"Take care," Hale cried. "Don't fall. I wouldn't try to get over; it's dangerous."

She stopped short as if struck, looking at him defiantly.

"Well," she said, "Europe certainly hasn't improved you. I wasn't coming; you needn't be so afraid of me. I think you're hateful. I don't want to see you any more or speak to you."

She leaped down backward inside her room and closed the window with a rattling slam. It had grown dark, and with the brooding of twilight came renewed that sense of melancholy and fear. And all through that night Hale dreamed of Jackson, as he tossed and tumbled in his strange bed, unable to sleep. He saw him in a thousand guises, in quaint, medieval Florentine dress, pacing the room, pistol in hand. And he was always angry, and ever striving to hurry him along some secret corridors and dark, mysterious passages toward some unknown purpose.

She spoke to few people in the boarding house and was not popular; but she paid well for the two rooms she occupied on the second story, and Mrs. Crewe, smiling, parried the attacks of calumniators.

"There's something uncanny about her," Miss Hallett declaimed. "She gives me the creeps."

"She has an altar in her inside room," said Mrs. Burns. "The housemaid snooped in one day, and Mrs. Jackson slammed the door in her face. Mary was crying about it. She keeps the door locked night and day. There must be more in there than is supposed, or she wouldn't be ashamed to let anyone see—that's what *I* say. And the incense she burns! The other night I was as sure as anything the house was on fire. I could smell burning as plainly as I see you. So I put on a wrapper and went out to see, and what do you suppose it was but that disgusting stuff floating out in clouds!"

"I must say I dislike that priest she had to dinner last week," said Miss Hallett. "He walks so softly and is so sly and has such a sinister, creepy look. I've almost knocked into him on the stairs two or three times of an afternoon, just as it was growing dark. He makes me shudder, positively."

Hale had once met the priest outside her door, a meager, pale-faced man, in somber black, pursing his lips and pressing his thin finger tips together above the wooden crucifix which hung from his breast. He would have bidden him good afternoon, but the priest had passed him with a perfunctory, hurried gesture of salutation.

"I tell you one thing," Miss Hallett said, tossing her head, "that priest's in love with her. You can't fool me; I knew it the first minute I saw them sitting side by side at the table."

The Colonel looked up with a snort.

"Shows his good sense," he growled. "I'd be in love with her myself if I were twenty years younger and she had a little more meat on her bones."

"Horrible man!" said Madame Oberhaus playfully, tapping him on the knuckles with her dessert spoon.

"And what I say," Miss Hallett concluded, "is this, and I don't care who hears it: It isn't the thing for any man to spend hours at a time inside her room, and the door shut, priest or no priest. If she wants spiritual consolation she can get it in the drawing-room."

"Hale pushed back his chair and walked abruptly from the table. The conversation disgusted him; the more so in that he knew this elderly spinster only voiced certain suspicions of his own which he had not ventured to put into thought even. He remembered how he had seen the priest's smooth hand—he detested smooth, white hands in men—laid for an instant caressingly upon Mrs. Jackson's shoulder as he passed up the stairs, and what an unreasoning jealousy the action had awakened in him. That evening he betook himself to Madame Oberhaus, determined to secure an introduction.

"But, Hale, it won't do you any good," she insisted, as they sat in the drawing-room. "She really does not care to form acquaintances; and besides, you really do not want to be introduced to her. You only imagine you do. It would be much better that you should not be. She goes her way and molests no one. Go yours. You are aware that you would be disappointed?"

"Of course; but I am prepared to be disappointed."

"Foolish painter! I have already told you that there is nothing in the least mysterious about your Madonna; that her life is commonplace and eminently practical. That she goes to church on Sundays and puts something in the collection, reads novels infrequently, hates all advanced notions, such as divorce and women's enfranchisement, turns faint at the smell of tobacco smoke, leads a useful, sequestered life of little duties and practical interests, and is, withal, much broken up by Jackson's death and occupied with the consolations of her religion."

"That may be true," said Hale. "But if I discern in her that alluring quality which I saw in the Madonna at Florence, her replica, then it exists, so far as I am concerned. I believe that Da Vinci's Gioconda was a more commonplace personage in her everyday life; but that did not prevent the painter from immortalizing her in such a way that she has become the type of the Woman of Sorrows. I've got to search out this baffling, maddening quality, whatever the consequences may be, to analyze it, to label it, to be able to say 'It is this,' and 'It is not this.'" He went on earnestly. "I must discover it or I shall lose my reason. I can't work. I can't think of anything but the realization of this intangible and elusive thing that is perplexing me."

"Ah, intangible!" said Madame Oberhaus. "That is the word, Hale. Because you are an artist you want the pot of gold under the rainbow and the bloom on the butterfly's wing. So you would fix the rainbow in the sky and hunt for the gold, and you would catch the butterfly in the net; and when you had succeeded you would find nothing. These things are not to be obtained in life. Haven't you really learned yet that when one catches the butterfly the color fades?"

"But I am ready to lose the color to catch the butterfly."

"Rather than have its inspiration? Think, Hale—suppose you should never speak to her. Well—you see her three times a day. She bends her head forward in walking, like that little angel of Botticelli you told me about. She has a rapt air, like that woman of Raphael. These are perpetual joys to you, three times each day; and from the place where you sit you can watch her without staring, as you would look at a picture. And do you really mean to say you wish to destroy these things for the sake of finding out what they mean, like the child that takes a watch to pieces to find out why it ticks?"

"Yes, I do. As you say, they are not real, I know—"

"Pardon me, Hale, I didn't say that. They *are* real—they are the most real things in the world. They are so real that they transcend the perceptions of all but the few." She leaned forward and laid her plump, bediamonded hand upon his sleeve. "Hale," she continued earnestly, "people are not meant to meddle with such things. They are not for our poor, three-dimensional world at all. People who have them are like dynamite lying in a ditch, harmless only so long as it is not meddled with. Don't meddle with her. Jackson meddled, poor man. He hadn't your sensibility, but he had glimmerings; and he tried and tried and tried to understand her, and then—"

"He killed himself for that?" Hale asked hoarsely.

"Yes," answered Madame Oberhaus, nodding her head slowly. "I tried to warn him, as I am warning you, but he wouldn't listen to me. He tried to understand till he was nearly mad; then he took Mrs. Crewe's revolver out of the bureau drawer in her empty room and blew his head to pieces. Give it up, Hale."

He shook his head.

Someone was coming into the drawing-room. They rose up simultaneously.

"Mrs. Jackson," said Madame Oberhaus, "allow me to present to you Mr. Hale, our artist."

"The strength of the Catholic Church," said the priest thoughtfully, pressing his thin finger tips together, "lies in her intimate comprehension of the imperfections of humanity. Is it not in her doctrines, nor in that she forces upon our acceptance that which may be repugnant to common sense and credibility. Those burdens of doubt we leave to her, who bears them upon her shoulders. Her strength lies in the re-cognition of the elemental forces of evil, a devil real to each one of us, who must be combated. We know that human nature is too weak to fight him unassisted; and it is in our recognition of this that we have weathered the storms of nearly two thousand centuries—of Aristotelian skepticism and medieval scholast-icism, of Jansenism, and of the so-called Reformation—just as we shall weather that of the speculative philosophy which you call Science today."

He was sitting in Hale's room toward the close of a wintry afternoon, apparently in no haste to brave the bluster of the blizzard that raged outside. Hale had encountered him unexpectedly as he was mounting the stairs. The priest was taking leave of his *protégée* at her door; he held her face between his hands and stroked her hair paternally. Of a sudden they had perceived him, and she darted away, closing the door swiftly and leaving the two men face to face together alone.

With sudden determination the painter invited the priest up into his room, the latter accepting, evidently under some embarrass-ment and anxious to justify himself by his restored composure before departing. He had succeeded perfectly. The exchange of con-versation, desultory at first, had become animated, and it was now Hale's turn to feel at a disadvantage in the presence of this bland, confident prelate.

"You mean that we are liable to obsession by these particular powers of which we speak?" he asked.

"I mean," the priest replied, "that the struggle with evil is a real warfare which is being waged unceasingly through life within the soul of each of us. Why, I myself, unfortified by my faith, would often fail to withstand them. The powers of evil and good are so nicely balanced that only the utmost steadfastness and fortitude, coupled with the divine aid, can rescue man. Remember, for His inscrutable purposes, God has created Satan only a little less powerful than Himself, and man is only a little below the fallen angels. I know a soul," he went on musingly, "that has been peculiarly tried; yet, steadfast in faith and never wavering, she has endured the utmost of affliction in resignation."

Hale knew of whom his companion was speaking. He knew, too, that the priest knew that he knew.

"She is a woman of the most noble nature," the priest continued, with something of unctitude. "She married as a mere girl and lost her husband by accident on the morning after the ceremony. Seven years later she married for the second time. Again her hopes and life were blighted by a horrible catastrophe. He husband killed himself—"

"She was already a widow when Jackson married her?" cried Hale in horror.

He stopped and blushed hotly, conscious that he had betrayed himself. The priest waved his interjection aside.

"Contrary to what one might expect," he continued, not heeding the interruption, "this only softened her. She is one of those souls who belong naturally to God. Her suffering drove her back into the seclusion offered by the Church to all such natures, from which she ought never to have emerged. Thenceforward she shunned all men. Ultimately I hope to be able to induce her to take the veil."

Was it a threat or a warning? Hale's anger rose.

"At least, she may consider that carefully when her grief subsides," he answered. "It is the world, with all its beauty, and not the cloister, that she requires."

"I think not," said the priest, smiling softly. "Well, the storm seems to have stopped, and I must be on my way." He went out with his soft, stealthy tread, leaving Hale sitting alone, musing and pondering.

Why had the priest uttered his subtly conveyed, but unmistakable warning? Why, too, had he undertaken to save this stranger from the priest's designs—he, who knew nothing of either? Some force seemed to control and urge him along unknown paths to unguessed purposes.

In no wise had his introduction aided him. He had asked for permission to call on her and had been refused. She was at home to none except her spiritual adviser, she told him. She did not care to entertain callers so soon after her husband's death. Her life was broken. And the door of her room closed relentlessly behind her.

Thus he could obtain only chance, fragmentary conversations with her upon the stairs, in the hall, at the front door, whenever they met by accident.

Sometimes, conscious of the silent scrutiny of Madame Oberhaus, he thrust the thought of her away for a few hours. But he could paint no longer; and always, three times a day, after the horrible jangle of the loud bell had drawn the boarders into the dining-room, he saw her facing him across the table adjacent, silent, with bowed head and piteous, Madonna's face.

She haunted him and held him, as though invisible, fine chains restrained him. It was about this time that his dreams of Jackson took more coherent form; and he began to feel in some dim fashion as though he were an actor in some portentous tragedy that was being renewed each night among three players—himself, the woman and the dead man.

It was always Jackson who played the leading part in these long, drawn-out pieces, from which he awoke with a parched throat and burning fever. He came, convulsed with jealousy and hatred for the sake of the woman whom his incorporeal substance could not possess. And Hale would awake with pulses madly throbbing and outstretched arms, to find himself upon his feet somewhere, at door or window, as though about to set out for some mysterious regions upon some unknown errand.

Upon one thing he was resolved: he would fight the priest on his own ground. He would allow no threats to scare him away. So he asked Mrs. Jackson's permission to paint her, pleading his cause and art manfully.

"Mr. Hale, you are so persistent," she replied petulantly. "One does not—no self-respecting woman could entertain company so soon after such an affliction as mine." Tears came into her eyes. "Besides, in my position it wouldn't be altogether the thing; and Mrs. Crewe would talk—perhaps ask me to leave. I have been so contented here—" She withdrew, leaving him baffled and conscious of a sensation of final, utter defeat.

To his astonishment she came to him of her volition on the following day.

"Mr. Hale," she began, "I have been speaking to Father Darragh, and he has advised me to accede to your quest. He thinks it might be good for me, some little relaxation from the monotony of my life." She smiled at him for the first time, and Hale felt his pulses leap. "I will give you an hour each day—each afternoon."

Hale grasped at the opportunity eagerly, conscious, however, of a strange perplexity. What could be the motive of the priest in thus granting him as a gift what he had contended for unsuccessfully, in yielding to him after he had already beaten him? Was it in scorn, to demonstrate the security of the clutch with which he held his victim?

She was expecting him on the following afternoon, when he carried his easel into her apartment. Hale looked around; it was his conceit to gather something of his sitters' mentality through the medium of their environments. The room was furnished plainly, though certain feminine adornments, in the way of cushions and draperies, were not absent. Upon the shelves were a few books, in the main of a devotional nature. An enlarged photograph of Jackson hung from a wall. The *ensemble* was drearily conventional.

The door which led to her inner room was locked; he could see the tongue clinched into its frame of steel.

"Sit so," he said, placing her against a background of drapery. He knew instinctively the attitude which he desired: how the head must be bowed, the shoulders stooping, the hands folded. Of a sudden the explanation dawned on him. He wished her in the pose of the Madonna of the unknown painter.

That was the first of several sittings. Under his brush the picture grew into life unsurpassed by that of his imagination. He felt the creative ardor consume him with so intense a flame that the sheer ecstasy swept all doubts and troubles aside. She was his! He loved her! He could communicate to her that divine spark of passion that should win her from her morbid, secluded fancies and cloistral meditations, from the narrow sway of the priest into the broad, free sunshine of love. Beneath that spell that hovered round them her own insensibility seemed to relax. It seemed as

though her heart, frozen so long, were about to yield up its treasured secret to him. He cast his brush suddenly down and caught her by the hands.

"I want to understand you," he blurted out. "Tell me your secret." They had joined issue at last; and they stared into each other's faces. Hale was aware of the presence of some intense and overpowering emotion. He bent toward her, seeing only her eyes, like stars, and the redness of her mouth. Another moment—and her face froze, her eyes widened in fear and she looked fearfully over her shoulder behind him. Hale turned. The priest was standing in the doorway.

"Go!" she said, pointing into the passage. The spell had snapped; she was imperious in her resentment. On the priest's features was an expression of triumphant scorn.

Hale picked up his easel and went out wearily.

An hour later he was seated before the easel in his own room. He was not conscious how he had gone there; he had known nothing of the lapse of time. It was a soft voice that roused him from his meditation. Two arms were laid on the window sill and a face looked in over them.

"May I look in?" the Blue Girl called.

He started up in confusion, turning on her a look of distress, profound and abysmal.

"I've been watching you from my window for the last three-quarters of an hour," said the Blue Girl. "I called to you twice, but you didn't seem to hear me. So I made the jump you told me not to make and came over to your roof to see if I could help you and to find out what you were painting."

He did not answer, but gazed at her irresolutely, piecing together the disordered fragments of his thoughts.

"I'm sorry I was so hateful to you the other evening," said the Blue Girl remorsefully, picking at her paint-stained apron. "But I'm desperately sorry now." She cast a glance at the easel. "O-oh!" she cried, clutching at the window sill.

He glanced involuntarily at the picture. There she was, the heavenly Madonna of the gallery of Florence, glowing in her beauty and youth, bearing in her eyes the immortal secret that wrung the hearts of men.

"What is it?" he muttered.

"Who is she?" cried the girl. "Who is she?"

Hale laughed.

"Who is she?" he asked. "I'll tell you, Blue Girl. She stands for the type of eternal goodness and loveliness. She is the embodiment of all in women that is noble and pure. She appears upon this earth rarely, from century to century, to portray that divine light of the soul that shines like a lamp through the flesh. But why she is this, or how is it that she wrings the sinews of the heart in agony and ecstasy and worship, Blue Girl, I can't tell you."

She stared at Hale in terror. Her lips parted; the breath came heavily between them.

"Lovely and beautiful, did you say?" she cried. "Oh, painter, what have you created? What has possessed you? Don't you see that she is devilish? I cannot look at her; she frightens me."

"What?" he cried.

"Can you not see what you have made? It is a fiend, a lost soul that knows its own intolerable, eternal woe. And you think it divine?"

She turned her quiet blue eyes upon his own in mute appeal. He gazed for one moment into their placid depths, then turned his own upon the picture. And for one instant, briefly, but certainly, something seemed to be rolled away from him before his sight, as one rolls up a curtain. Then an odd fancy came to him. He thought that the pictured face took on the semblance of a skull; through the thin features he could trace the outlines of the bones, and the rictus that widened under the fleshless cheeks into the hollows of the jaws. Suddenly

the secret was made clear to him. This piteous Madonna guise, this flowerlike face, was but the mask and the lure of death, that gate toward which converged all avenues of life. It was that death incarnate in all beauty, everywhere, as Madame Oberhaus had said.

He dropped heavily into a chair. He passed his hand over his brow. And then, glancing once more toward his picture, he saw her again, the Madonna of the unknown painter in all her matchless loveliness.

The Blue Girl's lips tightened at the corners. She clasped her hands. There was infinite pain in her blue eyes, in the slow, sorrowful cadence of her voice.

"Oh, if I could help you!" she said brokenly. "How could you have created such a dreadful thing, painter man? I know her and I know you are in love with her. It isn't that I care; don't think I care. But she's not good, or else you couldn't have painted her in such a way as that. How could you paint and love such a thing, when every line of it is evil? And there are others—" She checked herself and stretched one arm through the window frame. Hale rose and took her hand in his.

"I know that this is good-bye," she said quietly. "I can't come here any more or call on you as I used to. It isn't that that's making me cry. But you're in trouble—I've seen that for a long time, ever since you came back—and I can't help you. But I will help you, when you most need it, painter. That picture means terrible things to happen to you, and when they come think of me for a minute, and my thoughts will go out to you and I shall help you, and perhaps save you."

Hale felt a shadow behind him. The girl freed herself with a little cry and disappeared. Hale turned. The priest was standing behind him.

"That girl loves you," said the priest quietly.

"What business is that of yours?" demanded Hale fiercely. "You stand too much upon the rights of your cloth, it seems to me.

That last occasion was sufficient for my self-restraint; this goes beyond it."

"That girl loves you," the priest repeated, eying Hale steadily. "Are you blind that you should spurn it and rush to your ruin?"

"Ruin?" sneered Hale contemptuously.

"Ruin," the priest repeated. "I tell you," he went on with rising tones, "I tell you that the woman you seek is not for you, can never be for you. Will you men never take warning?"

"I thought at first you wanted to get her into a nunnery," replied Hale with dangerous calmness. "But now I am tempted to believe that you are in love with her yourself."

To his astonishment the priest showed no resentment. He sank down heavily into a chair and bowed his head silently upon his breast. Shame and humiliation showed on his face.

"I am," he replied simply after a while, looking up at Hale calmly. "Yes, I have loved her ever since I have known her. But I call Christ to witness that I have fought this passion unceasingly, night and day, year after year, stifling it, throttling it, conquering it, by the divine aid. If it were not for that, God knows it would have mastered me long since. I love her, Mr. Hale.

"And if I did not love her I should never have come to you, to make this confession of my own weakness and to appeal to all that is best in you. I hardly know how I am to speak. You have misunderstood me, thought me an enemy, an interloper, when all the while, by all that I hold sacred, my thoughts have been for her alone. If I were to attempt to tell you of what we priests have seen, know beyond a doubt, of the immanence of evil, of the terrific forces of evil that move and have their being in and around us, you would set me down as a madman.

"I will say this only, that I am fighting for her soul. You cannot dream of her predictament. I have fought for her daily, from year to year, gaining, losing, gaining, losing, yet never faltering, conscious of the never failing assistance of my Divine Master. And you," he went on bitterly, "you think of yourself alone, your love, your happiness.

"I let you paint her, rather than seem to her too meticulous in my guardianship. What did you do? What would you have done if by the aid of Providence I had not entered at that moment? You would have snared her soul in human bondage once more and turned her from the Church. Nor would it have helped you. Do you suppose the Powers of Evil would have been tolerant of you—that you would have fared better than Jackson fared?

"You think it love that you feel. It is not love. It is a devil's snare. Your love means death to you, and death to her own soul. That girl loves you. Go to her, Mr. Hale, in her kindness and purity and goodness, and don't try for what you can never attain."

The sun had sunk; one star was shining in the sky. Hale turned. Against the darkening east the deathless beauty of the Madonna's face flamed like a fire. He turned on the priest furiously.

"Curse you and your windy words!" he cried, not knowing what speech poured from his lips. "I'll have no interference. Fight your own battles, but don't come whining to me to help you disgrace the uniform you are wearing."

The priest rose.

"I'll save you yet, in spite of yourself," he answered. He bowed coldly and went softly out of the room. Hale sank into a chair. Night came. The hours were tolled from the town clocks. He did not move.

Was it indeed death, this secret? And must he pass through that door before he could attain its mystery and understand? Better death, then, than this unquenchable desire that ran like ichor through his veins.

He knew that he was asleep. It seemed he stood in the void, striving to reach her through some maze of passages whose secret he had forgotten. And Jackson came to him, but furious no longer. There was a hopeless sadness in his eyes. He took him by the hand and led him, but cautiously, lest he should awake.

Pale faces glared at them as they passed by—the faces of her dead lovers. "Join us. Be one with us," they seemed to say. There were the dukes and lords of ancient Italy, and the cardinal, in his Papal uniform, with the face of the priest. And there, a little apart from the others, was a beautiful boy's face, the eyes closed in death, a gaping wound in the temple—the face of the unknown painter—*his* face!

Then they passed on for centuries, down dim stairways and secret passages till they came to a half-open door. There he saw her at last, his Madonna. The old fire leaped into her eyes; she stretched her arms toward him. He leaned forward.

Then, like a clear bell, something rang through the darkness. It was the Blue Girl's voice.

He awoke with a shock, his heart hammering in his breast heavily. He was upon his feet and fumbling in a bureau drawer. He was in Mrs. Crewe's empty room, and the pale moonlight that filtered through the window fell upon something in his clenched hand—something heavy and cold, of shining steel.

He dashed it to the floor and ran downstairs, heavy with sleep, his heart leaping with some intolerable fear. Her outer door was ajar; she was not in her room. He entered and stood reeling like a drunken man, helpless, spurred on by something inexplicable that seemed to direct his footsteps. Then for the first time he saw that the door of her inner room stood open. He entered.

He saw nothing but the altar of her devotions. The rest of the apartment was in darkness, but the light of six candles of wax illumined the figure of the saint and the great crucifix that hung over it. There was something peculiar about the crucifix. Hale looked more closely. It was upside down. And the saint—was this the object of her devotion, this horned and leering figure behind the candles?

Then in a flash he knew. He had once been inside one of those places in Paris where atheists, in mockery of God, celebrated their devil worship in sickening jest. But this was real; this was no jest, this costly altar, these candles, these evidences of worship about and around him. A horror came over him; he shook; his knees trembled, and in physical nausea he turned to fly.

But he stood rooted to the place, for through the outer door the woman came, the priest close on her heels. They stood upon the mat, arguing—she pleading, the priest in expostulation.

"I tell you," Hale heard her murmur, "it is no use. You cannot save me. I have struggled too long. For a little ease, a little happiness, a little of that peace which other women have, I have prayed, I have wept, I have fasted. Now I am tired to death of it."

Hale heard the priest's murmured expostulations. He could not distinguish the words, but he seemed to plead, eloquently at first, then brokenly. Cautiously he crept to the door. He saw the priest stand as though hypnotized; he saw his hand fumble with helpless effort at the wooden crucifix that hung from his breast; he saw him subside, motionless now, his face transfigured with ecstasy. And upon hers was the light that was upon the face of the Florentine Madonna.

"Come," Hale heard her murmur. "Come, and I will show you why your prayers are unavailing. I have found a sweeter God than yours. For too long a time I have struggled against Him, and He has punished me."

She took him by the hand and led him toward the inner door. Hale drew back hastily into the darkness. His feet shuffled upon the floor, but neither heard him. They stopped before the altar.

"Here is my God," she said, bending her gaze on her companion's face.

A look of mortal agony and anguish transfixed the features of the priest. He struggled to cry out, to move. Three times he lifted his arm, and three times it fell back to his side helplessly. The woman stretched out her arms. Slowly the priest drew near—he bent his head and pressed his lips to hers.

Then the spell snapped. She raised her head and laughed, clearly and loud. Was it imagination, or even in that brief moment's space did her thin form expand, new life blood flood her pale lips and cheeks and brows?

The priest spun around, staggering drunkenly, clutching at his head. Then, with a groan that seemed to rend his being, he swung out his arm and dashed the candles from their sconces with one blow, so that they sputtered and hissed on the soft carpet and the illuminated face of the saint suddenly went out. And, breathing heavily, he stumbled out of the room.

Hale sprang from his concealment and followed him, caught him, plucked at his sleeve. But the priest shook him away, possessed by an almost superhuman power, and went on to the ground floor, Hale following, as though in a dream. At the street door he seemed to hesitate for an instant; then he opened it and went out.

It had been snowing and the ground was white with the fast falling flakes. They went on side by side through the maze of alleys that lead through the Italian quarter toward Bleecker Street. At the street corner the priest stopped for a moment, tore from his waist the wooden crucifix and snapped it in two. He threw the pieces into the snow.

"There is no God," he muttered as he strode away.

He repeated these words over and over in reverie. Hale kept at his side, catching at his arm often, but vainly. He might not have been there for all that his companion knew. In this manner they passed into Bleecker Street. The rumble of trains on the elevated railway now became audible. As they reached the Bleecker Street station the priest turned, and, with slow deliberation, began to ascend the stairs. He dropped a ticket into the box and moved to the platform on the downtown side. Hale halted one instant to purchase a ticket from the sleepy attendant and hurried after his companion to where a southbound train was approaching, sweeping away the snow before it in white clouds.

Then suddenly, as though impelled by some invisible power, with a convulsive movement the priest sprang upon the metal road, directly in front of the approaching train. The motorman saw him and pulled frantically at his lever. It was too late. As Hale stood on the platform, he saw the great bulk of the monster reared aloft, saw it bear down upon the black garmented body in its path, saw it catch it up, play with it, tear it and hurl it away, a crumpled, tumbled, lifeless heap of inert flesh and shreds of clothing, dabbled and stained.

Hale turned. A gleam of light shot upward into the sky before him.

He never knew how he got home. For at the very moment when the train dashed the life out of its plaything his spell fell from him, the old glamour of evil died and in his heart rose up a passionate love and worship for the Blue Girl with her pure heart and quiet eyes. And the next moment he was dashing down the elevated platform and down the steps and through the snow homeward.

As he ran he saw flames shoot into the sky, sending out showers of sparks, roaring, engulfing the upper stories of the old house on the Square. He ran on desperately, with labored breath and desperate fear. Now he had reached the place. They caught at him and tried to restrain him, but he shook them away.

"They are all safe," they cried. "All but one, and she was dead when the firemen reached her. You cannot save her."

But it was not of her he thought.

Into the house, up the stairs, through the hot flames and stifling smoke he ran, up steps that crumbled under him and along passages that crashed down beneath his feet.

Now he had reached the top story and the fire fanned him with its burning breath. He broke into his room—one moment's respite before the flames reached it. He shattered the window with one blow.

"Blue Girl!" he called with sickening fear.

But the house was safe; the menace was not there. The wind, which blew from the west, had turned the path of the conflagration.

"Blue Girl!" he called again.

He heard her voice; he saw her arms stretched out; he saw her face before him over the roofs.

"Come!" she said, placing her hands in his.

THE JAM GOD
Short Stories (May 1909)

Lieutenant Peters, of the Royal Nigerian Service, was lying upon the ground face downward, under a prickly tree. The sun was nearly vertical, and the little round shadow in which he reclined was interlaced with streaks of hot light. As the sun moved, Peters rolled into the shade automatically. His eyes were shut, and he was in that hot borderland which is the nearest approach to sleep at noontide in Nigeria.

The flies were pestering him, and he was thirsty—not with that thirst of the mouth which may be quenched with a long draught, but with the thirst of the throat that sands and sears. He felt thirsty all over. He had been thirsty, like this, ever since he struck the bend of the Niger. What made it worse, every night he dreamed of fruits that were snatched away, like the food of Tantalus, as he approached to grasp them. Two nights before he had been wandering knee-deep in English strawberry beds; the night before he had been shaking down limes and oranges from groves of trees set with green leaves and studded with golden fruit. Once he had dreamed of a new fruit, a cross between a pear and a watermelon; but when he cut into it he found nothing but hard, small seeds, with a pineapple flavor, which he detested.

Peters was dreaming now, for he twined his fingers in the long grass and tossed uneasily.

"I'll pick them all," he muttered sleepily. "All mixed together, with ten or twelve pounds of damp, brown sugar, and boiled into jam."

He woke and felt his teeth for the hundredth time, to note whether any untoward looseness betokened the advent of the dreaded scurvy. Reassured, he stretched his limbs and rolled over into the shade of the tree.

"When I get back to a white man's country," he murmured—"when I get home to England what is it I am going to do? Why, I shall go into a restaurant and order some rich brown soup. Then I shall have *pâté de foie gras* sandwiches. Then scrambled eggs, chocolate, and muffins buttered with whipped cream. Then half a dozen cans of jam. I shall either begin with strawberry and conclude with apricot, or else I shall begin with apricot and wind up with raspberry. It doesn't matter much; any kind of jam will do except pineapple."

He opened his eyes, brushed away the flies that swarmed noisily round him, took out his hard-tack, and opened a small can of dried beef. He munched for a while, sipping occasionally from the tepid water in his canteen. When he had finished he put the can-opener back in the pocket of his tunic and rose, his face overspread with a look of resolution.

"I believe," he cried, "I believe that I could eat even a can of pineapple!"

He rose, the light of his illusion still in his eyes, and began staggering weakly under the blazing sun in the direction of his camp. He was weaker than he had thought, and when he reached the shelter of his tent he sank down exhausted upon the bed. Through the open flap he could see, five hundred yards away, the round, beehive-shaped huts of the native village and, in their centre, the square palace of King Mtetanyanga, built of sticks and Niger mud, surrounded by its stockade, the royal flag, a Turkish bath-towel stained yellow and blue, floating proudly above.

Lieutenant Peters had been sent by the Nigerian Government along the upper Niger to conclude treaties with the different kings and sweep them within the British sphere of interest. The French were out upon a similar errand, for in this region the two nations possessed only a vague and very indeterminate boundary line. Peters had been successful until he came to the village of King Mtetanyanga, who had balked at affixing his cross to the piece of mysterious parchment on the ground that it was unlawful to do so during the festival of the great Ju-Ju, whose worshipers could be heard wailing and beating tom-toms nightly in some unknown part of the jungle. What this Ju-Ju fetish was nobody could tell; it had come into the village recently, from the coast, men whispered; it possessed awful and mysterious potency; was guarded zealously by some score of priests, who veiled its awful vision; and it was the greatest Ju-Ju for hundreds of miles along the Niger, tribes from distant regions frequently arriving to sacrifice pigs to it.

However, Lieutenant Raguet, the French commissioner, had been equally unsuccessful in inducing the dusky monarch to affix his signature to the French treaty, and the ambassadors of the rival nations were both encamped near the village, waiting for the Ju-Ju festivities to reach their plethoric conclusion before the king sobered up and attended to business.

Raguet, strolling into his rival's camp that evening, found Peters in his tent, flushed, and breathing heavily.

"*Tcht! tcht!* You are seeck," said the Frenchman sympathetically. "That ees too bad. Have you quinine?"

"Quinine be hanged," cried Peters huskily. "I've taken the stuff until I've floated in it. There's only one thing can cure me, Raguet. I've been living on crackers and canned beef for over a month, and I'm pining for jam. Have you got any jam?"

"Dsham, dsham?" repeated Raguet with a puzzled expression.

"Yes, les preserves—le fruit et le sugar, bouilli—you know what I mean."

"Ah, ze preserve!" said the Frenchman, with an expression of enlightenment. "Ze preserve, I have him not."

"I tell you what, Raguet," said Peters irritably, "I've got to get some jam somewhere or I shall kick the bucket. I'm craving for it, man. If I had one can of the stuff it would put me upon my feet instantly, I can feel it. Now it's ten to one I'll be too sick to see the king after the ceremonies are over, and he'll sign your treaty instead of mine. And I've given him three opera hats, a phonograph, and a gallon of rum, curse the luck! What did you give him, Raguet?"

"Me? I give him a umbrella with ze gold embroider," the Frenchman answered.

"My government won't let me give the little kings umbrellas," said Peters in vexation. "It makes the big chiefs jealous. I say, Raguet," he rambled on, sitting up dizzily, "what is this Ju-Ju idol of theirs?"

"I know not," said the French lieutenant. "Only ze king and ze priests have seen him. If zey tell, zey die—ze idol keel zem."

"I suppose they'll be keeping up these infernal tom-toms for another week," grumbled the sick man, lying back and half closing his eyes from weariness. "Well, I'll have to try to get well in time."

The Frenchman resisted the impulse to leap back in surprise, but his eyes narrowed till they were slits in his face. So! This Englishman did not know that this had been the last day of the sacrifices, that at midnight a hecatomb of pigs was to be killed and eaten in the bush in honor of the Ju-Ju. Nor that the king, when he had broached and drunk the cask of rum, would be in a mood to discuss the treaty. Peters evidently was unaware how much his majesty had been affronted by his failure to present him with an umbrella. La! La! Fortune was evidently upon his side. All this flashed through the Frenchman's mind in an instant. A solitary chuckle escaped him, but he turned it into an exclamation of grief, sighed deeply, seated himself upon the bed, and kissed Peters affectionately on either cheek.

"My Peters, my poor friend," he began, "you must not theenk of leaving your tent for ze next two, t'ree days. Ze fever, he is very bad onless you receive him in bed. I shall take care of you."

"You're a good fellow, Raguet," said Peters, wiping his face surreptitiously with the backs of his hands. When his visitor had left he turned over and sank into a half-delirious doze that lasted until the sun sank with appalling suddenness, and night rushed over the land. Tossing upon his bed, all through the velvet darkness he was dimly conscious, through his delirious dreams, of tom-toms beaten in the bush. His throat was parched, and in his dreams he drank greedily from his canteen; but each time that he awoke he saw it hanging empty from the tent flap. Presently a large, bright, yellow object rose up in front of him. Greedily he set his teeth into it; and even as he did so it disappeared, and he awoke, gasping and choking under the broiling blackness.

"I'll have to take that canteen down to the stream and fill it," he muttered, rising unsteadily and proceeding toward the bank. To his surprise he found that rain had fallen. He was treading in ooze, which rose higher and higher until it clogged his footsteps. He struggled, but now it held him fast, and he was sinking slowly, but persistently, now to the waist, now to the shoulders. Frantically he thrust his hands downward to free himself, and withdrew them sticky with—jam! He scooped up great handsful greedily; and even as he raised it to his mouth it vanished, and he awoke once more in his tent.

He flung himself out of bed with an oath, took down his canteen, and started toward the river. The noise of the tom-toms was louder than ever, proceeding, apparently, from some point in the bush a little to the left of the king's palace. Scrambling and struggling through the thorn thickets, he reached the sandy bed of the stream, filled his water-bottle at a pool, and drank greedily.

It was that still hour of night when the many-voiced clamor of the bush grows hushed, because the lions are coming down to drink at the waters. The rising moon threw a pale light over the land. The tom-toms were still resounding in the bush, but to Peters's distorted mind they took on the sound of ripe mangoes falling to the ground and bursting open as they struck the soil. He counted, "one, two, three," and waited. He counted again. There must be thousands of them. Peters began to edge his way through the reeds in the direction of the sound. After a while he came to a wall of rocks perpendicular and almost insurmountable. He paused and considered, licking his lips greedily as the thud, thud continued, now, apparently, directly in front of him. All at once his eyes, curiously sensitive to external impressions, discovered a little, secret trail between two boulders. He followed it; a great stone revolved at his touch, and he found himself inside the sacred groves. He went on, gulping greedily in anticipation of the feast which awaited him.

Suddenly he stopped short. He had seen something that brought back to him with a rush the realization of his whereabouts. Seated in the shelter of a cactus tree, not fifty yards away, was King Mtetanyanga, wearing his three opera hats, one upon another, in the form of a triple crown, and drinking his own rum with Raguet, under the shade of Raguet's umbrella. Prone at their feet crouched Tom, the interpreter.

"His Majesty say, 'How you fix him Ju-Ju?'" translated Tom.

"Tell His Majesty, my Ju-Ju stronger than the Englishman's Ju-Ju," answered the Frenchman. "My Ju-Ju eat up his Ju-Ju. He very sick. If I choose, he die."

"Ugh!" grunted the king, when this explanation was vouchsafed, apparently impressed.

"Tell His Majesty my Ju-Ju stronger than his own Ju-Ju. If he no sign treaty, eat up his Ju-Ju," Raguet went on.

A flow of language came from the king's lips.

"His Majesty say, he bring his Ju-Ju, see whose greater," said the interpreter.

Vaguely aware that treachery was impending, but crazed now by the falling mangoes, Peters left them palavering and followed the trail. All at once he emerged into a tiny clearing and stood blinking at a fire, round which a group of men—priests, as he knew, from their buffalo horns and crane feathers—were reclining, hammering upon tom-toms and shouting in various stages of intoxication. The firelight blinded their eyes. Peters stood still uncertainly. Then his eyes fell upon a sawed-off tree-trunk, in the hollow of which lay something wrapped in a white cloth, surrounded with snake-skins. He had come by this secret road into the actual presence of the great Ju-Ju.

Curiously he inserted his hand, lifted the object out, and examined it. Inside was something of a strange, yet familiar shape, oval, and flattened at the ends. He lifted it out of its wrappings, and there, in his hand, he saw a can, bearing the legend:

GREENAWAY'S BEST JAM.

He looked at it in solemn and holy meditation; then, sitting down, he drew the can-opener from his tunic and wiped it clean upon his sleeve.

After awhile a babble of sound broke in upon his ears. Men had come running up, brandishing spears, stopped, flung themselves upon the ground prostrate in front of him. The priests were there, frantically abasing themselves; Mtetanyanga, his opera hats rolling, unheeded, on the ground. Their cries ceased; they veiled their eyes. Then from the dust came the feeble tones of the interpreter.

"His Majesty say, you eat him Ju-Ju—yours greatest Ju-Ju, he want to sign treaty."

But Peters, waving the empty can over his head, shouted:

"I've eaten jam, I've eaten jam! It's pineapple—and I don't care!"

A MAN'S BIRTHRIGHT
Literary Magazine Section (9 May 1909)

Cain stirred upon his narrow cot in cell 360 of the Mills Hotel in Bleecker Street. He opened his eyes. In his recumbent posture he could just see the reflection of his face in the small mirror on the opposite wall, at the foot of the bed. It was the face of a man nearing forty—though Cain was nearly ten years younger than that—abject, thin, pale, the hair grizzling over the ears; the face of a bookkeeper. In his nightgown of coarse flannelette, however, Cain saw that there attached to him some of that elemental human dignity that was lost inside the shabby clerk's clothes by day.

From the adjoining cells came that medley of sound that announces the day: wheezes and groans, and old limbs pressed in protest against a cold stone floor. Cain blinked his eyes. Something stirred at the back of his mind. Presently he remembered and was glad: on the preceding evening he had talked with a man.

With a free man, no desk slave toiling for a miserable pittance and cringing before his master. A free man such as he used to read about in books, a hunter from the north woods, the oldest settled section of America, left forgotten and deserted in the mad rush westward. He had come to New York for the first time in his life upon some business connected with his son; and he had spoken of a wonderful free life when Cain encountered him, hilarious ands slightly tipsy, in Washington Square.

The hunter asked to be directed to a hotel. Cain looked at him doubtfully, timid and shy because of the unexpected greeting, while some wretched remnant of the clerk's pride of station suddenly grew rampant. This man's clothes had surely never seen the inside of any tailor's shop. The cap upon his head was—coonskin. His shoes were rawhide. In his pockets, he said, were ninety-five dollars in bills.

"I've been drinking a spell, but I can trust you, friend," said the hunter.

"How do you know?" Cain blurted out sheepishly, half ashamed that a stranger should read in his face that nervousness that had constrained him, with no fixed principles, in the path of integrity.

The hunter took him by the sleeve and pawed at the stained coat. "Know?" he roared. "Why, friend, doggone it, look at your clothes."

"I live at a sort of hotel," said Cain, after a pause, "but I can't recommend you there. It's for poor men. It's clean and very comfortable, but you'll have to wash in public."

"Why, hell, friend," answered the hunter, "haven't I washed in God's public streams this fifty years?" So Cain led him to his hostelry; and there, when they had drank coffee, they sat till the lights went out in the great, spacious smoking room with the floor of green glass, where patriarchs played chess.

"What's your business, friend?" the hunter asked. And somehow Cain found himself telling him.

Cain was the poor New York son of a poor New York father. He had been a bookkeeper. Just why, only God knew, save that he had learned no trade and was fit for nothing else. Did it not cramp him, sitting on a book-keeper's stool, did not his eyes ache, poring over columns of figures, till he obtained no pleasure in his work? Why, certainly; but who found pleasure in work? That was a man's daily portion and lot, which made his evenings and Sundays blessed to him. He had worked his way up, with painful slowness, from five to fifteen dollars a week, spending his income freely, never thinking of putting by. Presently he was engaged to be married. Then he lost his job somehow, and when he failed to get another the girl threw him down. That was five years ago. Cain was thirty-one now, too old to begin life on five dollars a week again—and nobody wanted to hire a bookkeeper at fifteen. Besides, after he had been out of a job six months his credentials became less than so much waste paper. After a while he came to acquiesce in his condition; he disappeared from the ken of that world that wore collars of linen and attached cuffs; and the underworld swallowed him.

"How do you live now, friend?" asked the hunter wonderingly.

Cain addressed envelopes. It was quite a profession, he explained, and when one knew the ropes one was seldom unemployed more than a few days at a time. There were perhaps three hundred men in New York who had taken to addressing envelopes as a permanent occupation. It was hard on the arm and shoulder when you began, but after the first couple of months the work became mechanical, and the hand wrote automatically, the eye following the list, each movement adjusted with the nicety of a machine, so that one came to like to work. The body toiled, while heart and mind were heaven only knew how many years away. And then, when the day was at an end, behold, one had unconsciously addressed from ten to fifteen hundred envelopes, according to whether they were three line addresses or four. Again, since one was paid by results, there was an incentive to turn out large quantities. Moreover, there were bonanzas, for sometimes one received the same rates for merely signing the name of the firm to mimeographed copies of letters. Cain followed the rounds. Before Christmas, for instance, he went to the big publishing houses which would then be getting out their seasonal books and circularizing the subscribers to their magazines. They paid best: they paid a dollar a thousand. Ten years ago, older men said, it had been a dollar and a half—then men could earn as much as ten dollars a week—but too many had been attracted into the field, and rates had fallen. Before the holidays there was work at the big stores. Then there was election work and directory work, at ninety cents; and there was generally employment at a dozen or more offices where they paid from seventy-five cents to eighty.

"What did it cost to live," the hunter asked.

"Four dollars a week," said Cain, explaining. A bed at twenty cents a night was one dollar forty; two meals each day at fifteen cents brought the total up to three fifty. He walked to his work, washed his clothes Sundays in the hotel's free laundry, and retained fifty cents for tobacco and small extravagances.

Then, somehow, he found himself telling of his dreams, those dreams that are permitted even to addressers of envelopes. A year previously he had awakened to a sudden realization of his servitude and the hopelessness of it. He had heard that in parts of the country the government gave away farms. He had had dreams of a free life sometimes in some place where men owned homes and were their own masters. So he had begun to save. After a year of systematic scraping and starving he had amassed nine and seventy dollars. Three dollars a week was the limit of his saving capacity—but that assumed continuous occupation. When he was out of a job his store disappeared alarmingly. Three times, too, he had broken his eyeglasses, and every breakage meant an entire week's savings eaten up at a crash. That was his hope—just freedom, a man's birthright.

Cain stopped, ashamed, that he had said so much; and suddenly the hunter was telling him in his melodious, ringing voice, of his own life in the far north, in the hut which he had built with his own hands in the great forests where he hunted and trapped, ready with ever-loaded rifle to defend his home alike against wild beasts and lawyers who might show deeds to claim it. He had never paid a tax and never meant to. His garden kept them in food, he shot and fished for meat. They were very happy, his wife and he—she was a Frenchwoman, but a good mother to the children. But he had a grown son, very apt at figuring, and he had come to New York to see what chance a boy might have in the great city. That was the point at which Cain gripped him by the arm with all his puny strength.

"For God's sake don't send the boy here to be a bookkeeper," he gasped. "Do you understand what it will mean for him—to be at one man's beck and call, his very existence, and perhaps his wife and children dependent upon his humors? He will learn to cringe and skulk and lie. He will know what it means to be deprived of a man's birthright, some woman's love, and to feel less than a man because he cannot make her a home. Why—why—" he panted, "they give the cheap work to girls nowadays. A cheap man hasn't a chance, and even the girls can't live on their wages. There's one at the place I'm at now, a lame little thing—she gets three dollars a week for sealing envelopes, and lives on it—if she wasn't lame perhaps—God knows but it's her safeguard—"

He broke off, breathing as hard as one who has run some desperate race, and sank back exhausted, huddled up into his chair.

"Go back to your woods," he said, "and tell your son sooner than become an unskilled laborer with the pen it would be better for him to dig ditches his whole life long, and carry stones on his back for foundations."

Presently they parted; the hunter was to leave the city at dawn. Cain heard his voice still ringing in his ears as he said good-bye, half convinced, pressing upon him an earnest invitation to visit him some time and live with him till he grew tired. Perhaps, he hazarded, he might keep him there in the woods.

Cain had been dreaming on; now he started up swiftly and began hurriedly to put on his clothes, for he was due at eight o'clock at the offices of the mailing company, where envelopes could be addressed at sixty-five cents a thousand. It was the cheapest place in the town, presided over by one Jackson, a bully who shouted and swore and slave-drove his cringing employees. At one table the addressers sat in two lines, facing each other, and as fast as the envelopes were ready they were sealed and stamped by the girls at another table—cheap girls who, nevertheless, instinctively despised the cheap men that worked there, and uttered scornful comments on them. But then, when one is an addresser, one does not seek the admiration of women.

As Cain parted his hair with his broken comb, the hunter's words came over him as a revelation. He looked back across the past, down the barren vista of wasted years.

"By God!" he said slowly. "By God, I'm going to live like a man!"

A hasty breakfast and the long daily tramp, up Bleecker Street, down Broadway, past Houston Street, Grand and Canal, Great Jones Street with its intolerable name, into the purlieus of Greenwich Avenue and East Broadway, where the roaring elevated shuts out half the sunlight and paper scraps litter the greasy sidewalk, Then the climb up the long flights of stairs, and so to work, beneath the scowl of Jackson and the cheap badinage of his fellow slaves.

"Say, if youse fellers can't git to work on time youse can git to hell out o' here," stormed Jackson as Cain entered; and the girls looked up tittering as he slunk into his seat. He noticed that the lame girl had been moved, so that she sat back to back with him.

"Git busy now an' give your envelopes to Bella," cried Jackson. "Mame's gorn an' got married."

The girls tittered again, snuffling and whispering as they adroitly shuffled their piles. Across the table the addressers, toiling at their tasks, ogled them on occasion and made audible comments upon their looks.

It was during the half hour's recess for luncheon, while Cain was still writing, that he realized the lame girl was still seated behind him. He turned round. She was bent over the table, working away desperately. Then something caught Cain's attention, something that splashed down on a heap of envelopes—a tear.

He had never looked scrutinizingly at the girl before. She was a little, fair thing, pretty in a rather child-like way; her lameness had protected her against the advances of the addressers and shielded her from ill-treatment. Now for the first time Cain saw that here, too, was one who had had the upbringing which he had known, who was as different from those who worked at her side as a lily is from the noisome water weeds among which it springs up.

"What's the matter?" he asked awkwardly, as one who has not spoken to a lady for five years.

She looked round swiftly, clasping her hands together with an impulsive gesture.

"O please will you give me your envelopes in small lots as soon as you've finished them?" she faltered. "Don't wait till you've finished a whole box; it keeps me idle, and that pleases Jackson."

"Pleases him?" whispered Cain, some unaccustomed emotion stirring at his heart. He felt his whole body grow cold. "Has he got his knife into you?" he demanded.

She nodded. "Since yesterday evening."

"What did you do?"

"O, nothing much," said the girl. "I was the last to leave and he wanted to kiss me and I wouldn't let him."

Cain sat perfectly motionless. The room seemed to rock, the bright sunshine without, the twittering sparrows, the rumbling trains, the cries in the street combined in a large symphony of hate. Something in Cain's appearance startled the girl. She caught at his arm.

"Please don't say anything," she said eagerly. "He'll take it out on me. He's put me here to punish me because I can only get your envelopes instead of two men's like I used to. It'll mean two a week now instead of three fifty as I used to make. Thank God, I've nobody else to care for. If I had time I'd look for another place. But I can't afford to lose a day, and Jackson knows it. So give me your envelopes as fast as you can write them, won't you?" she concluded, looking up and smiling through the tears that brimmed her eyes.

Cain's heart began hammering suddenly, like a runaway horse. Before he could answer, Jackson, who had seen them talking from across the room, advanced toward the table. His swollen, unhealthy face had become crimson.

"Look at 'em," he shouted. "Spooning. Spooning, by God! Say, if youse two ain't the limit—the limit—" he stuttered. The men and girls were returning; they came up smirking and tittering, fawning upon Jackson's words.

Over Cain's face there passed the ghost of a smile. He could afford to smile. Red rage had beaten at the portals of his heart, and he had opened them. The habit of years had fallen away. The bully was more than a man—he was the type of the whole, merciless world that drove the weak to the wall, stripped and oppressed them, lashing them with the two-thronged whip of poverty and scorn. He did not know what he was going to do: he waited.

He wrote—how he wrote that afternoon, trying perhaps, to keep time with the galloping of his heart. He wrote with aching wrist till it grew numb, till the numbness descended from wrist to finger tips and he no longer felt the pen. And as fast as he built up a little heap of addressed envelopes he turned and handed them to the lame girl behind him. Once their fingers touched, and in her cool clasp was something that renewed his energy, repressed his maddening fever of rage that burned in him.

At half-past five Jackson came over to the addressers' table. He was smiling jocosely and a little uncertainly. He unfastened his collar and the thick veins stood out upon his purple throat.

"Boys," he began, "it'll be sixty cents a thousand today and in future."

They stared at him incredulously; then a storm of protest arose.

"You hired us at sixty-five, and that's the cheapest in town, God knows," one man cried desperately. He was a little, weazened, gray-haired man, with a paralyzed left arm. "I can't work for less than sixty-five, Mr. Jackson," he screamed, becoming more and more excited.

"Youse can't, hey?" cried Jackson, his humor changing to rage.

"Git out o' here, then, and stay where you belong. Hey, youse, did youse hear me? I said git out o' here. I can hire fifty bums like you for half the price. Hey, Jobbins!" he called to his assistant, "pay this guy for his envelopes at sixty cents—and if I see your face in here again, God help me if I don't mark it."

He advanced with threatening gestures; and the little old man, terrified into silence, gathered his work together and shuffled away, Jackson's shrill taunts pursuing him to the door.

"God!" said the bully when he had gone, wiping his brow with a dirty handkerchief, "some of youse bums have a nerve and no mistake. Why, I can hire all the men I want at fifty and forty-five." His eyes wandered over his slaves uncertainly and fell upon Cain. "You git too, d' you hear?" he shouted. "Go and git your sixty cents, if you've done that much. What d' you think the place is anyway—a spooning shop?"

The lame girl winced as though she had been struck. Jackson laughed coarsely and the girls began tittering. Cain rose to his feet. There was something ominous, threatening, in his face.

"If you insult this lady, by the Lord, I'll—" he began.

"Hell!" said the bully, retreating two steps in astonishment. "What have we here? What is it, boys, what is it?"

He stopped short. Some years before Jackson had had a fight with a man and had been hammered into insensibility. It had been a little man; Jackson had thought that he could safely oppose him, and he had always remembered afterward how the man's face went pale and the nose and nostrils seemed to emerge and stand out upon the sunken flesh. Such was the look on Cain's face now. The men were close up on one another. Jackson tried to bluster.

"Git out o' this shop and take that—" he began. The next instant he was reeling back under the force of a blow, weak, but well planted, which struck him between the eyes. Then he came staggering forward again with wildly waving arms.

One well directed blow would have completed his discomfiture. But Cain was no boxer. His blow fell harmlessly upon Jackson's chest, and the next instant the bully's arms were round him and he was thrust backward helplessly over the table. Jackson was striving to work his hands upward to clench Cain by the throat, while the addresser struggled and strained and panted in a vain attempt to release himself. Suddenly his hand came in contact with an overturned ink bottle. He grasped it and brought it down with all his force upon Jackson's mouth. Blood spurted from the wound. For a moment Jackson released his hold; then Cain was upon him, one arm around his enemy's neck, while with the free hand he pummeled the imprisoned face with short, thudding uppercuts. He felt the flesh quiver beneath the blows. Somebody cheered; in Cain's heart was a new, fierce, primitive delight in battle, and everything swam dizzily before his eyes. "Kill, kill!" shrieked voices in his ears. And all at once, with a deep groan, Jackson slipped from his grasp and fell to the ground in an inert, motionless heap. Then Cain came to himself and looked round in astonishment.

Jackson lay, frightfully mauled, under the table. His eyes were closed by the discolored and swollen flesh, his breath came stertorously from between his lips. There was blood upon Cain's coat, his sleeves and hands. As he strode down the room all shrank from him upon either side, giving him passage. They recognized the birth of something terrible and new.

It was the birth of a man, a free man, coming into the inheritance of his own. Cain saw the lame girl and stopped in front of her.

"Come!" he said, holding out his arm.

He was bloody, bedaubed, ragged and stained with grime. One upward glance into his face and she took his arm unresistingly and went out with him. For he had found his birthright. His mate had recognized him; and what did it matter if she was lame of limb when he was crippled of soul?

A KING'S COURIER
Being the Narrative of Captain Adams, Detective-Diplomat

THE PERIL OF MAGELLAN STRAIT
The New Magazine [UK] (June 1910)

I had left the foreign office in deep dejection after an unhappy hour spent in the company of the secretary for foreign affairs. In vain I had pleaded, in extenuation, that I had only obeyed the orders which another had issued. A diplomatic scapegoat had to be obtained in order to save England from humiliation at the hands of a powerful neighbor—and I had been chosen. Upon the threshold of my career, the diplomatic service seemed to be forever closed to me.

"I'm sorry for you, Adams," said the foreign secretary, Sir Edward Grey, to me, "heartily sorry. But the element of luck has evidently deserted you. If you are really anxious to continue to serve your country, however, I might be able to make use of you at some time in the secret service, which constantly requires the air of gentlemen having a certain social status, with training in the legitimate branch. And, to facilitate matters—since you are in favor with his majesty in spite of your misfortune—I will ask him to appoint you as one of his couriers-at-large."

Who has not heard of the king's couriers—that small band of private gentlemen who carry his majesty's private dispatches among crowned heads and statesmen? A king's courier often bears the peace of Europe in the little black leather wallet which, whether he sleeps or wakes, must never leave his person until its contents have been delivered in safety to their destination. He is the unofficial, as the ambassador is the official, representative of his sovereign; deeds of the most hazardous nature often fall to him to perform; and never, by any chance, whether he fail or succeed, does he receive public acknowledgment.

A few days afterward I received notice of my enrollment. The salary was small, but sufficient to enable me to continue to keep on my bachelor apartments in Half Moon Street, Piccadilly, where I resided with Talbot, my ex-soldier servant, who had attended on my wants when I held a captaincy in the Fourth Lancers, and now refused to be separated from me. Six years in exile in the Far East as a legation attaché had made me practically a stranger in London; the friends whom I had formerly had, had married or moved elsewhere or forgotten me. So I remained week after week, held to the capital by the terms of my engagement, which required my constant attendance upon his majesty's pleasure, yet confident that I had long since been cast, along with other failures, into oblivion.

And then one afternoon I received an official document requiring my presence at the foreign office immediately. I jumped into a hansom and lost no time in presenting myself. Sir Edward Grey himself came out of his private office to receive me, led me in and motioned me to a chair.

"Captain Adams," he began abruptly, "you are, I believe, the hero of a certain desperate adventure in Afghanistan, for which you received the Victoria Cross?"

I murmured something. Of course those things come by luck. I am sure all our officers are equally brave.

"His majesty's government is in need of a man with dauntless courage and inexhaustible resources of will and ingenuity, in order to carry out a difficult and momentous duty," Sir Edward continued. "His majesty has been pleased to indicate yourself. How soon can you be prepared to start for Tierra del Fuego, via New York?"

I thought. "In four hours," I answered.

"Good," replied Sir Edward. "Then I will recount, as briefly as possible, the situation." He sat down at my side, handed me a cigar and lit one himself, which he consumed in his rapid, nervous way.

"As you know," he began, "ever since Lord Pauncefote died, England has been unfortunate in the matter of her American representatives. In some subtle way they have not seemed to hit it off right, either with the president or with the American people. Now, my dear Adams, you are aware that to preserve the best possible relationship with America is the cornerstone of both British and German policy, and, since the rivalry between us and our neighbors across the North Sea is intense, the alliance of America with either would be a fatal blow to the other.

"What has sorely strained amicable relations between England and America has been the Anglo-Japanese Alliance. That it is directed against American interests seems to be the opinion in Washington. This ill feeling has been increased by the bellicose Japanese attitude toward America over the schools questions, which has culminated in the dispatch of the American fleet round South America through the Straits of Magellan, to the Pacific Ocean. Somehow or other, Mr. Roosevelt has got the notion that England is privy to the attitude of Japan. In short, we are face to face with a three-cornered quarrel.

"Now I come to the climax. There exists a certain group of international financiers, mainly of German origin, who would have everything to gain by the outbreak of hostilities between Japan and America—in which England would be compelled to join, as Japan's ally, by the terms of the treaty. The influence of this group, though powerful, is not sufficient to bring about a war. They intend, therefore, that the voyage of the fleet shall be attended by such incidents as shall kindle the anger of America to the explosion point and bring about the results that they desire. Remembering how the destruction of the Maine precipitated the war with Spain, it is their intention that the flagship of Admiral Evans shall be destroyed by Japanese treachery during the passage of the fleet through the Straits of Magellan. More than one

vessel they will not injure, lest their loss leave America too weak to fight Japan. This act will force America to declare war, and England will be compelled to take up arms against her. Hence it is of the utmost urgency that this murderous scheme be foiled."

"But how is it to be accomplished?" I inquired.

Sir Edward Grey threw away his cigar and continued in hurried, agitated tones.

"We received information this morning. An order, to which the name of the Mikado has been forged, has been placed in the hands of a Japanese military attaché at Rio de Janeiro, by name Kitachi. It states that he will consider himself responsible only to his emperor; that he will proceed immediately to Punta Arenas, the little Chilean town upon the Straits of Magellan, and the center of the sheep-farming industry. Thence he will proceed to a tiny harbor, known only to the Japanese survey, that lies like a cleft among the frowning cliffs which rise sheer from the waters. There he will set up his camp and make his preparations, and, at the precise moment of its passage, he will destroy the flagship of the American admiral by means of the new secret Japanese torpedo, which can be controlled and guided during its flight by means of wireless telegraphy. There will occur one moment of panic; then the great ship will rear herself and plunge to her grave, through the almost fathomless waters, carrying all her crew to destruction. Captain Adams, the future of England lies in your hands." With the concluding words he dismissed me.

The American fleet was preparing to set sail from Hampton Roads that very afternoon. On the following morning I could reach a Cunard steamship which would land me in New York on the sixth day. Thence a fast passenger ship would carry me to Rio close at the heels of the squadron. Every day she spent in that port would be a clear day's gain thereafter. I hoped to reach Punta Arenas a full week ahead of the fleet, allowing for delays and coaling; and this I actually succeeded in accomplishing. It was about one month later when Talbot and I, standing side by side upon the deck of the little sheepboat which brought us southward from Rio, perceived, through a drenching rain, the fearful heights that bordered either side of the Straits of Magellan, and the little town looming up white against a background of barren hills, bordered with dripping forests.

"Begging your pardon, sir, might I arsk whether our stay in this burg is liable to prove a long one, sir?" asked Talbot.

I could not but smile at the faithful fellow's misery. After the long sea voyage our terminus certainly did not appear very attractive—and Talbot was a cockney of cockneys. But the thought of the work on hand quickly reduced me to a condition of seriousness.

"Talbot," I said, "you and I are going into a hard game." I saw his eyes brighten. Talbot was with me in Afghanistan, when for three days we two and a wounded lancer kept 50 Afghans at bay. "Henceforward," I continued, "until the danger is over, you will kindly address me as an equal."

"All right, old man," said Talbot easily, instantly falling into the spirit of his instructions. It was, in fact, an ancient understanding between us. So soon as we passed beyond the boundaries of the conventional, in which fortune had made us master and servant, Talbot would show himself the fine comrade that he is, by my request.

"Hidden somewhere among those cliffs," I said, "is a little bay. There's a man there, playing with dangerous toys. We've got to get him and break his toys. Savvee?"

Talbot grinned. "What ho!" he answered, in his inimitable cockney dialect.

It was arranged that I should pass as a sheep purchaser, or as a wealthy Englishman who desired to look over the sheep runs with a view to making an investment. Talbot was a gold prospector whom I had met on the voyage. In this way we calculated that we could best make our investigations of the surrounding country. Upon our arrival good news cheered us. The fleet had just sailed from Rio, where it had been delayed overtime. It would not enter the straits for several days. This allowed us additional time to make our plans.

A visit to the English consulate gave scanty information. To my question whether there were many Japanese around Punta Arenas the consul answered that it was impossible to answer.

"The territories are quite unorganized," he answered. "There may be ten, there may be fifty, scattered all the way between the mainland and the Horn. The land is most imperfectly known, and inhabited by tribes of hostile savages who make periodical raids upon the sheep-runs. There's sheepmen and prospectors scattered over 20,000 square miles of forest and bog. And, talking of bogs, let me warn you not to stray off the beaten paths, or you'll be trapped sure."

Then he unexpectedly added something which made my heart leap.

"There's a little Chink or Jap fellow passed through alone last week. Said he was going gold-washing along the straits, but he had a curious outfit—some kind of patent machinery, he claimed."

And this information was worth a gold mine to me. For, now that I knew the direction in which Kitachi had gone, it was obvious that, by following the general contour of the land, I must come upon the secret cove.

So far neither Talbot nor I had noticed any signs of espionage. This seemed strange. Sir Edward Grey had informed me that the syndicate which was backing Kitachi in his murderous plot was of vast wealth and ramifications. It seemed incredible that they had permitted us to get this far in safety; that they had not suspected an attempt was being made to frustrate their scheme. Or had they mercifully tolerated our approach thus far in order to make the more sure of our destruction?

The question was soon to be answered. Talbot and I had engaged a single, large room at the top of the little mining hotel that looks out over the waters. We retired to rest that night early, having taken the precautions to close the window and bolt it. Under my pillow I had placed my loaded Colt automatic pistol. Fatigued by the day's work, I fell quickly asleep, and dreamed that I encountered Kitachi under all sorts of impossible conditions, but principally engaged with him in wrestling matches upon the summit of those fearful cliffs, while the American squadron hove into view, miles down beneath us. I remember Kitachi got his arm under my neck and was about to throw me over the brink—when suddenly I awakened with a start to find one part of the dream real. An arm was certainly coiling under my neck, but ever so softly, the fingers worming their way down deep beneath the pillow. The habits of ten campaigns had taught me one essential of the adventurer's life—to wake noiselessly. I opened my eyes the least possible amount—enough to see that dawn was breaking in the customary eternal fog and rain. And at my side I saw a tawny figure that squatted there, while the fingers worked toward the pistol which was but two inches further on. I measured the distance, and suddenly shot out my arm from under the bedclothes. The guess was accurate. My first caught the intruder beneath the ear and bowled him over. Instantly I whipped out my pistol, which he had so nearly obtained; but not before the figure, pulling itself together, vanished with a bound through the window, from which the glass had been carefully dissected. I discharged the magazine into the darkness, but without effect, except to rouse the other occupants of rooms in the hotel.

"One of those thieving Ona Indians," was the general comment. Such events, it appeared, were far from uncommon in Punta Arenas. The natives were expert "second-story men." I listened skeptically, being more concerned in attempting to soothe Talbot, who was reproaching himself bitterly for having been sunk in "stinkin' slumber," as he described his sleep, while my life was endangered.

On the next day we were to start upon the trail—Talbot ostensibly to prospect for gold, I to consider a choice location for a sheep-run. We busied ourselves the remainder of that day securing four stout little Shetland ponies, which we loaded down with our impedimenta, intending to adopt the customary method of the country and to walk beside them, since riding over the yielding bogs is almost impracticable for man and beast. It had been our intention to go alone, trusting to our campaigning experience. Now, however, we determined to engage an escort. Three ex-miners, who had flung away their hard-earned gains in a week of debauchery at Punta Arenas, were easily persuaded for money to accompany us as a protection against anything we might encounter. We started off on the next afternoon through dripping undergrowth, following, so far as was practicable, the line of the shore. At nightfall we camped upon the borders of a stretch of open land, and arose after a period of sleeplessness and general dampness to find the pale sun struggling through the fog drifts and the eternal line of the cliffs still firm and unbroken. Now ensued a dreary tramp across a spongy bog, in which horses and men sank to their fetlocks and ankles.

Suddenly a naked, bronzed figure ran out from the trees, lifted a bow at us, and began fitting an arrow to the string. He drew the string. The distant twang floated across the still air, and an arrow buried itself in the ground 100 yards in front. The Indian, having missed his mark, began to run aimlessly in the direction of the wood.

"Catch that fellow!" I shouted, leaping upon my pony. The others followed suit, and, spurring the beasts, we galloped in pursuit. All at once my pony tripped and fell under me, throwing me heavily. I was stunned for the moment; when I recovered my senses I found that his leg was broken. I attempted to rise, but my feet sank into the bog.

All were in the same plight. Knee deep, they labored painfully toward each other from where their horses stood, mired to the thighs. With infinite difficulty Talbot made his way to my side; the rest were 50 yards away—they might as well have been three miles.

"Well, old chap, they've copped us good," said Talbot.

Wh-ee-ee-ew!

It passed over us in answer with a whistle and a scream, and the detonation of the rifle followed it. Talbot and I had heard that sound many times before. We flung ourselves upon our faces and began to adjust the sights of our rifles.

Spit! Spit! Whiz! The air was alive with bullets. They plunged overhead, they shrieked and screamed. We began firing back at our unseen enemies in a desultory way, to save our cartridges.

"How many rounds, old man?" asked Talbot presently.

"Twelve more!" I groaned, piling them in a little heap in front of me. Meanwhile the firing continued unabated.

"Adams," said Talbot presently, when we had both ceased, "'ave you noticed anything strange about them beggars, old boy?"

"They're damned bad shots," I answered.

"They ain't trying to hit us, Adams," Talbot retorted. "All their shots 'ave gone 'igh. Noticed anything more?"

"It's no rifle I've ever heard fired," I answered.

"You're right, old man. It's a rifle of tiny caliber. It might be our Lee-Metford, if it was a little shriller, and it might be the Yankee Krag, if it had more of a tang to the whine. But it's something well under .300."

"It's the Jap Murata," I cried; and suddenly a sick feeling came over me. For, on the morrow, if all went well—or ill, rather—the battleships would enter the Magellan Straits. And somewhere near was the devilish engine of Kitachi. And I, upon whom rested the fate of two nations, blundered helplessly and hopelessly, into this trap. Suddenly I saw a look of fury pass over Talbot's face. He half raised himself.

"Gawd, Adams, they've killed 'em all!" he muttered.

"Well, Talbot," I said cheerfully, "there's only one thing to be done. Your shirt's older than mine—give me a piece."

"Not while I can fire another shot, Adams," replied Talbot sulkily. "Surrender? What for?"

"Because our position's hopeless," I retorted. "We can't get away, and if we could they'd catch us again. Talbot, they'll release you. It's me they want. Make a flag out of your shirt."

"You be damned," retorted Talbot sulkily. "Say that again and I'll bash yer blarsted fyce in."

"Silence!" I shouted. "I'm commanding officer here, my man. I order you as your officer to hoist that flag."

"O, orl right," said Talbot sullenly. I heard the *z-z-z* of linen in the tearing. And then, slowly, Talbot hoisted the white flag on his rifle barrel.

A moment later a little squint-eyed Japanese tripped out of the wood and beckoned to us.

"This way, gentlemen!" he shouted, pointing to a line of coarse tussock grass that grew near and, as I now perceived, formed an excellent pathway through the morass. "Fling down your rifles!" he added. "Now your pistols! So!"

At a signal from him three Indians stepped forward from among the trees and bound us, after which we were led along a narrow trail that seemed to disappear right over the face of the cliffs. In places the path was so narrow that we literally clung to the side of the precipice. Presently it widened out; we were descending a wooded chine that led to the little cove, on which already we could hear the booming of the sea-rollers. A turn disclosed it to us. A neat little military house, the encampment of the Indians, and a large shed, surmounted by a high pole for wireless transmission, stood just at the boundary of the high tide, fringed with coarse seaweed and almost washed by the spray. At the encampment we were halted.

"What are you going to do with us?" I asked Kitachi.

The little man turned round and looked at me quizzically.

"Do you know why I spared your lives?" he asked.

"And murdered our companions," I retorted bitterly.

Kitachi shrugged his shoulders. "I obey my emperor," he said, saluting at the word. "Their lives are nothing, my life is nothing, and yours are nothing, to be weighed in the balance with his command. I spared yours because, gentlemen—you are to be the torpedoes!"

"What?" I cried.

"Since you will never leave this spot alive, I will explain the matter gladly. The principle of the new dirigible torpedo is different entirely from that of any other. It is not only directed, but is set in action from the shore; in other words, instead of being discharged at a high rate of velocity, it proceeds at a constant and leisurely speed through the waves, until within aiming distance of its target. Then, and then only, does the operator on shore detonate the charge and hurl the missile into the vitals of the ship. Now you will readily see that, proceeding at such a slow rate of speed, a torpedo of metal would simply sink below the surface of the waves. We must make use, therefore, of something of the same relative gravity as water—in other words, the human body. Now, when you are encased in a hollow shell of aluminum, and discharged at a constant speed of some ten miles per hour, you will make your course half submerged, and, when the charge is detonated, you will hit the flagship betwixt wind and water—exactly on the water line."

"What, make a torpedo out of me?" cried Talbot, advancing upon the Japanese with whirling fists. I pulled him back with difficulty from the Japanese's revolver.

"While there's life there's hope, Talbot," I whispered. Kitachi heard.

"You have until tomorrow morning at ten, gentlemen," he answered briefly. "At that hour the flagship will be passing abreast of our station. They are now nearing the entrance; you see, I am picking up their position by means of wireless.

"Will you be paroled until tomorrow, or will you be tied?" he asked. We gave our parole. Apparently Kitachi had entire confidence in it, for he merely indicated a tent in which we were to sleep and went into his house.

I shall never forget the horrors of that night. At ten in the morning we were to die, to fulfill the forged communication to Kitachi. And, this being so, and escape impossible, he had placed us upon our honor as soldiers and servants of our king, knowing that he held us thus more securely than if ropes bound us. All night we heard the thunder roaring in the sky, and saw the lightning flashes, and heard the heavy downpour of the rain. It seemed eternity before the darkness yielded to the diffused grayness of dawn and an Indian brought us our breakfast of the Japanese army ration of rice and fish. We swallowed it with an effort.

At nine Kitachi came for us and announced that our parole was ended. At a signal, we were seized by Indians and, before we understood what was occurring, our arms were bound to our sides and ropes were fastened round our knees. A futile struggle and we stood trussed and helpless. Kitachi entered the shed and threw open the wooden wall on the shore side, disclosing a complicated arrangement of batteries and, prominent among the machinery, two huge, coffin-like oval structures of aluminum, each about the length of a man.

When I come to die my last memory will be of standing there, beside Talbot, bound, on the beach, listening to the waves, and straining my eyes for the thin wisp of smoke that would indicate the approach of Admiral Evans' flagship and announce our imminent death.

Ten o'clock tinkled from a clock in the Japanese officer's house. We looked hard out to sea. The mists lifted; now we could see the frowning cliffs opposite and, in the distance, the white houses of Punta Arenas. But no ship came. The clock tinkled 11 and then 12. A wild hope throbbed in my heart. Suddenly the electric instrument began to click. Kitachi turned impassively to the machine. It was not Morse, but the secret Japanese method of communication, and neither of us understood, though we concluded it was the signal for the ships to enter the Strait.

As Kitachi stood reading I saw his body stiffen gradually, until he seemed to be a figure of wood. When the last click ceased he came to us and stood watching us with a peculiar smile.

"You're very lucky!" he said, and turned aside to mutter to the chief Indian. Immediately the ropes were taken off our limbs, and we remained looking at Kitachi in amazement, free, yet hardly daring to hope.

"These Indians will escort you as far as the sheep trail where they met you yesterday," he added. "Go—you are free."

"Free?" I stammered.

"Yes, gentlemen," said Kitachi wearily. "The vessels of the American fleet passed through the Straits last night. The magnetic storm, unusual for this time of the year, was caused by an event which only occurs once in long periods—and last night it happened and luck overthrew all my plans. There was a shifting of the south magnetic pole, due to some unknown combination of heavenly bodies, which caused my instruments to pick up the fleet in a wrong region of the compass. But my emperor does not permit chance to overcome his will. I have failed; all is over." He threw up his hands and walked slowly into his house.

I whispered to Talbot to wait and ran after him. My heart was touched with pity. After all, he was merely obeying what he fancied were his emperor's commands; and he had treated us as an officer and a gentleman should do. Now, perhaps, he would believe me if I told him the truth about the conspiracy.

I knocked at the door twice; then, as no answer came, I opened it and entered. Kitachi was sitting, Japanese fashion, upon the floor, wrapped in a rug, his shoulders curiously bowed. He looked up at me patiently as I entered, but made no sign.

Gradually, however, as I unfolded the story, an expression of horror came over his features. He groaned; he tried to rise. As he did so the rug fell from him and I saw that its underside was stained with blood and that a short sword lay between his knees, hilt down, point upward. Even as I looked, Kitachi's features composed themselves, his eyes closed, and he fell forward, transfixed upon the weapon with which, in the old feudal style, he had performed the sacred rite.

Sick with pity, I ran out, to find Talbot at the door.

"All right, old boy?" he asked. Then, seeing the answer in my eyes, he saluted me, soldier fashion.

"Begging your pardon, sir," he said, "I think we ought to be moving."

FIVE ACES
Associated Sunday Magazine (30 April 1911)

I have heard men who have been wounded on the battlefield say that the swift shock of the bullet stuns and benumbs and bears with it its own anodyne, so that it is only afterward that pain comes, and remembrance of the wounding. So it was with the blow that fell upon me. It fell so swiftly that only recently, after the passage of years, have I been able to piece together my fragmentary recollections of it. For a long period I could remember only that at one moment we were all seated together at the card table in the Crown Prince's quarters, brothers in arms, and that an instant afterward I was standing alone, confronting them, an outcast, denied, by every honorable code, further acknowledgment from my brother officers.

Americans have said to me that affability is the price Princes pay for their sinecures. That was not so with Prince Lothair at any time. In those days, when, although Crown Prince, he held not more than a Major's commission in the Fifth Imperial Uhlans, he was as a brother to all of us, from stern old Colonel Heller, who had been peppered with shrapnel at Gravelotte, and whose temper had ever since been like a pepper caster with a loose lid, to young Graf von Obersee, the youngest subaltern. And if a divinity hedged him, as Shakespeare would say, by reason of the fact that some day, when God should please to recall to Himself his father, the reigning Prince Lothair would become ruler of Thüringen-Gotha, it was not for the office that we showed reverence, but for the man merely love and comradeship. In barracks or out, with us Lothair was no more than a brave officer and a good friend, and many a young sprig from Essen or Berlin or Hamburg could spend money more freely, for his debts always curtailed the Prince's means.

Of late this fact of Lothair's indebtedness had been discussed in no veiled language among the baser newspapers. The bride whom he had chosen, and was soon to wed, a Princess of a landless, mediatized line, would bring him little dowry; nor could he cumber the scant revenues of his father with his obligations. But, though rumors were rife, and even we shared in the speculations that were hazarded, Lothair bore himself as though no creditor had ever thrust his shadow into the sun of his nobility.

On this evening we were to play poker, a game but recently introduced into our part of Germany, and still novel to many of us. I recall how the Prince held up one of the new packs of cards that he had had sent from America.

"They say that only with Yankee cards can one enter into the spirit of this game," he said, laughing, and we all sat down at the baize table, joking like schoolboys.

Old Colonel Heller had the first deal, and when I looked at my hand I found that fortune had given me two aces, the ace of hearts and the pictured ace of spades. I drew three cards; but gained nothing.

Then the betting began, and one after another they dropped out—the Colonel, young Graf von Obersee, Captain Schmidt, Adjutant Sonnenberg—leaving only myself against the Prince. I bet five marks; he raised me five; I made it fifteen. He called my hand, at the same time laying down his own—two aces, clubs and diamonds. As he did so, his sleeve dislodged the top card of the pack, which slipped to the floor.

I felt my heart leap and begin pounding like a runaway nag. A white haze crept up from the floor and blinded me; but through it I could still discern my hand dimly—the ace of hearts and that terrible ace of spades—terrible because there were five aces in the Prince's American pack; for the card on the floor was the ace of spades also.

I think no one had seen it fall. I stooped and picked it up. I rose out of my chair. I remember seeing the clear blue eyes of the old Colonel turned on me in surprise. A ring of smoke curled upward out of his pipe and floated toward the ceiling. Graf von Obersee was whispering to Captain Schmidt, and Adjutant Sonnenberg was tapping the ashes out of his pipe into a tray. Then I saw the Colonel's smoke ring break into a volute and the fog hid everything.

"I have three aces," I said, and laid my hand on the table. "Your Highness, Gentlemen, my resignation will be received for posting tomorrow morning."

I clicked my heels, bowed, and backed out toward the door. I recollect with what slowness all their expressions changed; then I had closed the door and passed into the barrack yard and so to the street. For in Thüringen-Gotha one does not let gossip accuse the Crown Prince of cheating at cards.

There remained two hours before the night train started for Hamburg. I went to see Elisabeth. Though her parents and she inhabited only a small house in an unfashionable district, she bore sixteen quarterings. American do not understand what aristocracy means. You think that it is pleasure and wealth and the power to command. Truly; but how are these gained? What are the rights and duties that accompany them? First, then, it is our right to be the first to die for our country in time of war. Then, again, it is our duty never to lie for gain, never to betray, nor to do any dishonorable thing. Otherwise we become cowards in the presence of danger. So, because of these things, we must keep truth with honor; and, because of them, I must needs face her scorn.

The old folks were abed. Our engagement had been of long standing, and in a year I should have attained my captaincy, and then—well, that dream was ended.

"Elisabeth," I said, "I have come to bid you goodby. Tomorrow my resignation will be posted at the barracks. Tonight my life comes to an end. If it begins again overseas, that is a new life, you understand, not this one."

She did not flinch; but just put out her hands to me. "You have refused to fight a duel, Karlchen!" she said. "You told me once that if ever—Have you considered well?"

"No," I replied. "I was caught cheating at cards."

"You—cheating?" she said, and, leaning back against the edge of the door, she began to laugh softly. "No, Karl, you did not cheat," she said.

Then I broke into a wild torrent of words. I had cheated, I cried; for I had been wretchedly in debt for years, I had been tempted and had succumbed; for otherwise I saw no means of marrying her. It was for her sake I cheated. That hardened her, as I had meant it to do; for the first time she began to believe me, and I saw her press her hand to her bosom and peer into my eyes, as though to read them. Gradually, as I stumbled through my premeditated story, I saw her own eyes darken. When I concluded they were full of scorn and disdain.

"And you came here to tell me this?" she questioned.

"Only to say farewell," I answered.

She softened somewhat at these words. "Yes, yes, I begin to understand," she said. "But you should not have come. It was for me to go to you. When I looked into your dead face I should have forgiven you. Death wipes out all stains, Karlchen."

"But I am not going to die; I am going to America," I stammered.

The blood receded from her face and left her white as a dead woman. She stretched her hand forth, feeling for support, and found my shoulder. "Karl," she said, "when—a certain officer—ran away in battle, he blew his brains out, and they buried him from a gun carriage among the heroes."

"I am afraid!" I whispered, and sank into a chair and hung my head in shame. I heard her come softly toward me; I felt her breath in my hair. Then she was gone, and I knew that the kiss was but a valediction.

You do not understand. But if your land, America, had been for centuries a prey to foemen who had harried and drained it, if your women had been conquerors' spoil and the courage of your men broken, then, if one stock had welded you with steel and blood, so that your bodies were your country's living walls and your leaders' honor yours—do you not understand?

I wrote my resignation on a sheet of paper and posted it. I left for Hamburg, still in my undress uniform, concealed only by my overcoat, which I had mechanically taken from its peg when I walked out of the barracks. At Hamburg I purchased a steerage ticket for America, vaguely remembering that a friend of my father, whom he had forgiven a debt, had settled and prospered there. I reached New York with twelve dollars in my purse, and they held me at Ellis Island for a special board.

"How comes it, Herr von Mesenrath, that you have no more money?" asked a white haired official who presided. "Have you no means, no profession?"

I looked at him and saw that he too had been a soldier. His trade was in his bearing, his blunt and courteous speech, his searching eyes.

"I have two hands to work," I said, and, flinging back my overcoat, displayed my uniform. "I shall not beg," I said.

I saw him whisper with the board, and they nodded their heads.

"We will admit you, Lieutenant," said the presiding officer. "I myself will stand sponsor for you; for I fought at Sadowa in your own regiment, as a trooper, under your father. Remember only this, Lieutenant; here all service is honorable."

I should have become a soldier, but for the need that I should renounce my country. That I would not do. So, since I was debarred from all association with my own people, and could neither apply for aid at the Consulate nor for work to any of the mercantile firms of my own nationality, I joined a gang of workmen who were building the aqueduct that was to bring water to New York from the mountains.

At first the strain was almost unendurable. But soon I grew accustomed to the work; afterward I came to love it and the fatigue for the respite they brought me. For I learned that the body can become master of the soul, and physical stress can cast oblivion over the preoccupations of the mind. After some months I became able to remember the past calmly. I even took pleasure and pride in the reflection that God have given me a part to play for my country, surely no less a one than that of my father, who fell at Mars-la-Tour, leading his regiment, even though I played it in silence and solitude, cheered by no comradeship or trumpet call. I came also to think of Elisabeth as one who had died, or as one whom I had loved in some past life, dimly remembered. She was the power that nerved me to endurance.

After six months I was made foreman.

Often at night I would sit beside the card players in the laborers' tent, smoking and watching them. But I never touched a card.

You remember the accident at Grays Bend Tunnel? A wall of rock caved in after a premature dynamite discharged and killed and injured twelve. I was one of those hurt—an arm and a leg were broken, and I lay for weeks in a hospital. When I was well there was no work for me. As foreman, I had to bear the blame for the catastrophe. I was discharged, and was too weak to wield a pick as a laborer again.

I returned to New York and walked the streets, penniless. Frightful were the temptations that assailed me now. I could go to my Consul, or to my father's friend, a merchant on State St., whom he had forgiven the debt. In the end I remembered my sponsor's words,

"All service is honorable." I became a waiter in a German restaurant on 14th St.

Two years went by. When I look back on these I can comfort myself with the assurance that they were wholly good for me. I, who had commanded men, now learned to serve them; I ran to obey; I received monetary doles, who in past times had been prodigal of them. But ever before me stretched away that black vista of future years, and ever my heart went back to Germany.

When my grief healed, the memory of Elisabeth became a beacon light which lifted me above the mire and bore me through the sordid battles of the day. And gradually I came to see that in the materialism of this new country there lay dormant other ideals than ours, destined some day to bear abundant fruits when this new nation quickened and grew responsive to them—ideals of civic right-eousness, of a democracy for whom our own poor, narrow code of honor, the property of a small caste, should expand to be that of a nation.

I had served nearly three years when the Crown Prince of Thüringen-Gotha and his suite came to visit America. In the metropolis I fancied myself secure. There was room for both of us here, and it was the most unlikely thing that the heir to a principality would betake himself to this obscure 14th St. rest-aurant to eat those German dishes that our good master supplied to a small group of lovers of the Fatherland's cookery.

Fate is more sure than that. For that was just what occurred. One evening, from where I served across the room, I saw Lothair enter in evening dress, and with him Adjutant Sonnenberg and Graf von Obersee.

"Mesenrath," said the proprietor, hurrying to me after had had bowed before his visitors and sent the waiters scurrying in all directions, "do you know who those gentlemen are? It is the Crown Prince of Thüringen-Gotha who has come to dine here. You will wait on his Highness," he continued excitedly; "but you will not show him that you know who he is; he is to be treated only as an ordinary guest—such are his instructions. You will do credit to us, won't you, Mensenrath?"

I had been trained to obey commands, whether from a Captain or a hotel manager. There was no reason why I should flinch from facing Prince Lothair. So I went to his table, and, though my heart beat faster, I served him tolerably well, as a waiter should, and for a long time they did not recognize me. Then, as I was drawing the cork of their second bottle, I saw Adjutant Sonnenberg staring at me through his eyeglasses, and saw the Graf whisper to the Prince, who turned round in his chair and looked quickly in my direction. All this I saw while my eyes were glued on the cork; for a waiter learns to do things like this. When I came back they were seated in silence and their eyes were on the tablecloth.

I served the sweets and cheese and brought coffee, and if my heart was breaking, their own buoyancy of spirits had gone. There was but little change in them. The Prince looked more mature, and Graf von Obersee had sprouted a long, fair mustache; but otherwise they might have stepped out of the barracks together, as though those three years had been yesterday. And long forgotten memories stirred in me, and in imagination I heard the bugles blown and saw the long cavalry lines sweeping down the field proudly in review before the Prince's father, the ruler of Thüringen-Gotha. Then I looked down at my black coat and my stiff shirt, a little spotted with grease, with a napkin tucked into one corner, and—I went on serving.

When I would have assisted them with their overcoats they waved me aside and each helped his comrade. As they turned to go Graf von Obersee approached me and, flushing with shame, pressed a bill into my hand.

"From his Highness, Lieutenant von Mesenrath," he said.

But the title seemed then only a courtesy.

When they had left the restaurant our master came up to me, wearing a most woebegone expression.

"Did you see how glum they were, Mesenrath?" he asked. "Now I wonder why they did not like my cooking."

"It was not that," I said. "The Prince was sad because he recognized a former friend among our waiters here."

The proprietor rubbed his chin some moments in perplexity; then the meaning was made clear to him. "*Hein?*" he said, scrutinizing me sharply. "You?"

It was no bill that Graf von Obersee had handed me. It was the resignation I had written out that night before I left for Hamburg. And in one corner was a penciled scrawl:

> His Highness will see Lieutenant von Mesenrath at his hotel at nine o'clock tomorrow morning.

A hundred times that night I swore I would not go. When I awoke, early, after an unquiet sleep, I renewed my resolution. At nine o'clock I found myself at the door of the Prince's apartment.

Lothair was seated in a chair, reading a German newspapers; but when he saw me he rose to his feet and came forward, bowed, and pointed to a chair. But I remained standing before him.

"Lieutenant, you have been absent from your regiment without leave nearly three years," he said.

"My resignation, your Highness—"

"Colonel, if you please, Lieutenant. Your resignation had not yet been accepted by his Serene Highness, my father; whereupon you have put me to the inconvenience of carrying it in my cardcase ever since you made your rash journey to this country."

And, as I stood still, staring at him, trying to understand the portent of his words, he continued more lightly:

"Of course there is no means by which I can compel you to forsake this foolish whim of yours, Lieutenant; but—" He stepped toward me and, placing a hand on each shoulder, gazed very earnestly into my face. "There is one in Thüringen who waits for you," he said. He placed a photograph in my hand.

Then I could restrain my grief no longer. Through tears I saw the face that had been with me ever through those three years. I forgot honor and the task of duty to which I had set myself, and with clasped hands and trembling lips besought Lothair wildly that he would remove the stigma that rested on me. When I ceased and looked at him I saw that his face was set into the same stern, deeply carved lines as those of his father, the soldier Prince, as he appears in the great picture of the crowning of the old Emperor William at Versailles, which hangs in our barrack hall in Thüringen. He answered slowly:

"Lieutenant von Mesenrath, your court martial will convene in my quarters at the barracks four weeks from today." Then, as I turned to go, he added, "Karl, is this how you guard the honor of your Prince?"

Then I saw tears in his own eyes also.

That I had made myself the victim of some terrible blunder I could no longer doubt. The prospect of absolution filled me with an intensity of emotion; yet not so keen as the anticipation of vindication in the eyes of Elisabeth. I followed Prince Lothair on the next steamer, and timed my movements so that I should reach Thüringen on the morning of the court martial.

How poignantly the familiar environment oppressed my spirit! The sight of the horses in their stalls, our soldiers on fatigue, the thousand and one smells of the barracks rushed into my consciousness like an irresistible tide. Then the scenes and events of the last three years became only a memory to me.

But when I entered the Prince's quarters to present myself before the court martial, to my astonishment I found that those who were to judge me were the same company that I had left there on the evening of my departure. There was old Heller, no longer in regimentals now, but wearing the dress of a citizen; there were the Prince, Adjutant Sonnenberg, Schmidt (a Major now), and Graf von Obersee. They even occupied the same positions round the table—the same card table, on which, face downward, lay the cards just as they had been left there. But the room had remained unswept and untenanted; for everything was white with dust—the mirrors, the furniture, even the cards, themselves, which lay half buried in the accumulation of the years.

"Take your place, Lieutenant," said the Prince, motioning me to my seat. "Gentlemen, our game is resumed."

Heller lit his pipe and puffed out a great cloud of smoke. "I pass," he said quietly.

"You have all passed, Gentlemen?" asked the Prince. "I think you bet fifteen marks, von Mesenrath. I'll see your hand." And once again Lothair laid down a pair of aces on the dusty baize.

I spread my own cards out before his eyes. Then, without a word, the Prince turned over the top card of the pack from which we had drawn, and, as I gazed at it, the monstrous blunder that I had made came home to me.

For my third ace was the joker! I had confounded it with the ace of spades; for I had never seen a pack containing it in Germany.

I recollect that I was upon my feet and they were flocked round me, pressing my hands. I saw their faces through darkness, heard their voices, far off, amid the wild sounds that reverberated through my ears. Then, one by one, they filed out, leaving me with the Prince alone.

"You see, von Mesenrath, your court acquits you," he said. "So it becomes my duty to inform you that in your rotation, you are entitled to your captaincy."

And, as I did not respond, he added, smiling:

"You bear the news with wonderful equanimity. But doubtless your mind busies itself with weightier affairs. Permit me to present you to my wife, the Crown Princess."

And he led me, still walking as a man in a dream, to the Crown Princess' house, set into the north angle of the huge barracks inclosure. We passed into the hall, and then he opened a door and closed it softly after me; but did not follow me.

I knew not whether he was with me or no; for there, before me, I saw Elisabeth at last. And in the fullness of our happiness all else was forgotten.

THE CATS THAT LOOKED AT COHEN
Canada West Monthly (May 1911)

When Dr. Ivan Brodsky first began practising in the New England country town which was my home, there were many who looked upon him with disfavor, and even actual dislike. This was not surprising in a community where to the present day there lingers a dread of the powers of Darkness which may be traced back to the influence of Puritan ancestors who firmly believed in witches, sorcerers and others of that ilk, and visit with the severest penalties of the law all such unholy dealers in black art. For Brodsky, it soon became known, did not confine himself to the surgical and medicinal limits of his profession. The man was indeed a scientist of the highest order and extraordinary intellect, and from the start made a great impression on me. We became very friendly, in fact, our acquaintance ripened into the closest intimacy, and I was thus enabled to witness some convincing examples of his skill in handling certain psychic phenomena. That his investigations had resulted in his acquiring an almost uncanny knowledge of the workings of the spiritual world and its reactions upon the realms of physical life could not be denied. Yet the clever Polish physician was not gifted with mediumistic powers, nor did he advance any such claim. Nevertheless, it is certain that his unusual attainments enabled him to cure obsessions and overcome the powers of evil in many cases where distinguished, but conservative, members of his profession had failed.

In the course of time, however, much of the opposition which had grown against Dr. Brodsky passed away, as people became aware of the really wonderful cures he wrought—cures for which the physician's sound reasoning faculties and common sense were as much responsible as the exercise of any occult power. One morning, going to Ivan Brodsky's office outside the hospital, I found him listening to a little man who was jabbering in an excited manner. Seeing me, the Doctor cut his interlocutor short peremptorily.

"There is a humorous aspect even to psychical affairs," he said, waving back the little man, who was upon his feet again, pouring forth a flood of what I, from my German studies, recognized as Yiddish, a mediæval corruption of that language. "I'm afraid there will not be much more medical work for me to do now that my fame as a necromancer has spread broadcast up and down the land. What do you think this fellow wants me to do? To cast out cats!"

Recognizing the familiar word, which appears to be much the same in all European languages, the little man was upon the scene again instanter.

"Sit down!" roared Brodsky, turning upon him.

"I will not sit down," cried the little man. "These cats—they come from everywhere, they eat my wife's sausages she had fried—all, all our supper was gone yesterday and to-day—"

Ivan Brodsky advanced toward him, took him by the shoulders, and looked into his eyes intently. "You will not sit down, my friend?" he asked gently. "Then stand!"

Actuated by the same spirit of contrariness the little man moved back to his chair and seated himself. An instant later he was upon his feet with a howl of dismay. He looked at the chair, he searched as though for a pin, once more essayed to seat himself, and sprung up again with a scream of anguish.

"Stand, now," said Brodsky, laughing heartily. "And be silent, or I will take your speech away."

Thoroughly scared, the little man remained standing, shifting from one foot to the other, and gazing at Brodsky much as a whipped spaniel might regard its master.

"A very simple principle of hypnotics," said the Doctor to me with much amusement, "but it adds not inconveniently to my prestige among these folks. It is the same principle as is used by the Indian juggler who makes the mango seed apparently sprout into a tree before the eyes of his audience. But, as I was saying, I've come down in the world. It's a far cry from casting out spirits to casting out cats."

I waited in patience for the story.

"I must tell you," said Dr. Brodsky, "that I am in some repute as a necromancer among the Jewish population of this place on account of a little experiment I once performed—well, never mind that. But you've heard of the Kabbalists?"

"The Jewish miracle-mongers who undertook to practise magic by means of the Kabbala?"

"Their book of secret rites. Yes," said Brodsky. "They were greatly feared for their knowledge of certain simple tricks of psychics, such as calling in the services of those elemental spirits, or Jinns, as the Arabians name them. As a matter of fact, any modern necromancer could give those old fellows points. Well, you may not know that there still exist Kabbalists among our Russo-Jewish immigrants. There seems to be a famous miracle-worker in this town, by name of Solomon ben Yankel, whom, in a moment of misguided zeal, these people expelled from their synagogue as a wizard. Naturally, being human, he wants his revenge, and he appears to be working a modern version of the ten plagues of Egypt upon our friend here, who is president of the congregation. Now," he added to the visitor, "sit down and tell us what he has down to you."

Very gingerly the man seated himself, and then, delighted to discover that his normal powers had been restored to him, he burst into voluble exclamation.

"My name is Gershon Cohen," he said, "and I am president of our synagogue, which consists of nearly fifty members, the most Orthodox in town. We never fail to fulfill all the commandments of the law. We wear broad phylacteries upon our arms at prayer and we celebrate each festival on two successive days instead of one, and we fasten small scrolls containing the Ten Commandments upon our doorposts to drive away spirits of evil, as Moses commanded."

"Continue," said Ivan Brodsky.

The ghost of a smile hovered upon his features, and I thought I could read what was passing in his mind. Brodsky was the son of a Jewish father and a Polish mother; he was thinking of his own early days in the ghetto of Warsaw, and recalling the, to him, meaningless, yet not to be forgotten, ceremonies of the past.

"This Solomon ben Yankel is the cause of all our misfortunes, curse his red hair!" cried the little man excitedly. Then, glancing at Brodsky's own head-covering, which was of a decided auburn tinge, he stopped short in confusion.

"You see, the prejudice against red hair exists everywhere," said the Doctor to me. "One day I shall write a treatise explaining its origin. Go on, Mr. Cohen."

"This Solomon ben Yankel is a maker of praying shawls, phylacteries, and mezuzoth, as we call the door scrolls," said the little visitor. "As you may know, these scrolls, upon which the Ten Commandments are written in a microscopic hand, are enclosed in hermetically sealed glass tubes and nailed to the tops of the doors. I have built a new house recently, and so, wishing to throw business in the way of a member of the congregation, I went to this Solomon ben Yankel and asked him his price and what reduction he would make upon a dozen—there being twelve doors in my home. 'Three dollars apiece,' he had the impudence to answer.

"'What?' I exclaimed angrily. 'Impudent one, I can get them for fifty cents. Moreover, on twelve the reduction must be great.'

"'There will be no reduction,' answered Solomon ben Yankel. 'Are you the president of the synagogue, and do you not know that it is written, "Thou shalt not add to nor diminish one jot or tittle from any of my Commandments"? How, then, can I make any reduction? I will let you have the twelve scrolls for thirty-six dollars, and cheap at the price, considering that I write them myself, and certify that they are correct.'

"At that I lost my patience. 'There is a poor traveling peddler in town, seeking communal relief,' I replied, 'and he will make scrolls, tubes and all, for fifty cents apiece. He seeks alms to take him on his way to Jerusalem, where he hopes to lay down his bones. From him I will get my scrolls.'

"At this, the red-haired one became purple with wrath. 'Go, then, and buy from your traveling peddler, if you think his work is better than mine,' he shouted.

"Dr. Brodsky, I am naturally a man of quick anger. I should have laid him low with a blow of my fist. But just as I was about to strike, my good angel whispered in my ear. 'Hold, Gershon Cohen,' he whispered. 'Art thou not president of the synagogue, and the most Orthodox in the town? Remember how slow to anger Moses was. It would ill become the president of the synagogue to use violence upon the body of such as one.' So I replied slowly and scornfully.

"'It ill becomes you to disparage such a holy man,' I replied; 'you, a wizard, who are reputed to make use of enchantments for raising the dead.'

"He put his flaming head against my own.

"'Thou hast spoken rightly, Gershon Cohen,' he answered. 'And I will raise spirits against thee so that thou shalt curse the day thou wert born.'

"At that I went away and laid the matter before the members of the congregation. 'Thou shalt have no wizard nor necromancer among thy people,' said Moses in the Commandments. So we cast him out until such time as he shall repent. Moreover, he was forbidden to make further scrolls or phylacteries or prayer shawls. He was present while we debated and walked out laughing, putting us to shame. The very next day thieves broke into my store and stole two sacks of potatoes. When I met Solomon ben Yankel I taxed him with working witchcraft upon me in this, and he laughed again. But nobody would purchase his scrolls or prayer shawls, so by and by he came to ask that we remove the ban, and, when this was removed, for lack of evidence in his repentance, he vowed a speedy vengeance upon me. Next morning he walked right into my store, bold as brass, followed by three cats.

"His aspect was so terrible that I dared not molest him, and he walked through my house, from door to door, laying his hands upon the lintels, and smearing his palms against them and muttering imprecations. Before I had recovered from his appearance he was gone—but the cats remained. My wife chased them away. Next morning she found seven in her kitchen, rubbing themselves against the door. They had stolen the dinner and were devouring it. And so it has gone on three days," said the little man, spreading out his hands hopelessly. "There is an army of cats around my house; we find them in every room, rubbing themselves against the doors under the holy mezuzoth, and I know they are spirits of evil. So I have come to ask you to banish them, lest worse befall us."

"To-morrow be here at the same hour," said Brodsky, "and I will direct you what to do. Go home and rest in peace. If any cat accost you, say nothing."

When the little man was gone, with some reluctance, Dr. Brodsky turned to me, laughing till the tears rolled out of his eyes.

"This Solomon ben Yankel is evidently a man of fine humor," he gasped. "Of all the things he might have done, to send a plague of cats! Fancy the good housewife beset with them in her kitchen!"

"Do you suspect him of having charmed them there from their homes?" I asked. "Or has he created them?"

"The act of creation is the ultimate power of the occult to be acquired," said Brodsky. "It can only be done in the dark, and for a few moments, as in rarely authenticated cases at séances. No, to create life and send it about its business away from the creator is practically an impossibility. I strongly suspect we have the working of some simple charm such as is known to many primitive folk and recorded in folklore. Well, this is a humorous interlude in our investigations."

I shuddered involuntarily, remembering more gruesome experiments which had fallen to Dr. Brodsky's lot to perform.

"Now," he said, "when two medicine men get together the first thing that they do is to measure each other up. I must pay a visit to this Solomon ben Yankel."

I was considerably disappointed that Dr. Brodsky did not invite me to accompany him on his mission, but, knowing that he did not care to be questioned, I made no sign of my chagrin. He had requested me to call for him half an hour before Gershon Cohen's arrival on the following morning. Arriving there, he plunged promptly into the subject.

"Well, I've seen this Solomon ben Yankel, this terrible, red-haired demon," he said with a hearty laugh, "and I must confess my sympathy is largely with the necromancer. You see, for all that Gershon Cohen pretends it is a religious quarrel, the matter is really economic at bottom. For years Solomon ben Yankel had enjoyed a harmless reputation as a dealer in white magic. Young folks consulted him about their love affairs; old people went to him with their marital troubles. He eked out a harmless existence by the manufacture of implements and accessories of prayer. Now this Gershon Cohen goes to him and calmly demands that he reduce the price of his mezuzoth from three dollars to fifty cents apiece, at the same time threatening him—this I learned yesterday—with the loss of all the community's trade unless he acceded. Naturally Solomon loses his temper. As for the cats, the explanation is a simple and, like all simple things, a surprising one. It is one of the commonest of all spells. But here comes Gershon Cohen to the door. Now my friend, by the exercise of a little diplomacy, I hope to cure him of his cats and to restore to Solomon ben Yankel his occupation."

"You told me to come at this hour," cried our excitable visitor, bursting into the room. "I may sit down, what?" Gingerly he seated himself with many comical expressions reminiscent of his experience of the preceding day. "And now you will come round and cure me of my affliction? Ah, all night they howled under my front windows. I have not slept—"

"Gently, friend," said Ivan Brodsky. "These things are not remedied in a day. It takes time."

The little man's face fell. "Time? How much time?" he muttered. "I tell you I am sick from want of sleep, and—Ach, Gott! Last night they got into the ice-box, and when my wife went after them with a broom they flew at her and drove her from the kitchen. First they take our food, then they take my house away—"

"Yes, yes, but all that will soon be over," said Brodsky sympathetically, though I could see by his shoulders that he was shaking with suppressed mirth. "To-night is the third night after the full moon, is it not? Good. Otherwise you would have had to wait a month longer. Do you know the Lutheran cemetery at the north end of the town?"

"Yes," said Gershon Cohen eagerly.

"To-night you will go there alone toward the hour of twelve. You will enter by the large gate and proceed to the open space of ground by the north wall. There, under the tall pine tree, you will perceive a cluster of wild herbs. Pluck as many as you can between the beginning of the first stroke of the hour of twelve and the end of the last. Take them home secretly, make a distillation of them over a fire, and bathe in the concoction, allowing yourself to dry by the process of evaporation. Then shut yourself up in your own room until I arrive in the morning, and above all else, say not a word to your wife as to the purpose of your actions, or the spell will be broken."

The little man's face had been lengthening visibly, until it was a study for a painter.

"Never since I was married have I been out at night alone and not told to my wife where I went," he cried. "She will give me no peace hereafter. And if I shall tell her afterward that I went to the graves of the dead Lutherans she will think I lie to her."

"Very well, my dear sir, then keep your cats," said Brodsky suavely.

"No, I will go," cried the little man. "There is no other way?"

"No other way," said Brodsky, shaking his head sympathetically.

The little man arose and stumbled out of the room, his hands clapped to his head despairingly. When he was gone Brodsky sank into a chair and went into an ecstacy of silent laughter.

"Your instructions savor of *Macbeth* and the witch scene," said I, much mystified. "What is this herb that must be plucked in the churchyard at midnight?"

"A secret remedy," said Brodsky, chuckling. "Patience, my friend, and by and by I will explain everything. And now, while Gershon is pondering upon his bath, let us get busy on that section of the brain of our orangoutang."

On the following morning we set out together for Gershon Cohen's new store, which was located at the end of the town, just where the wider intervals between houses and plots of unoccupied building ground indicated the approach of the country. At the door a woman, evidently the little man's wife, encountered us.

"Help me, help me, Doctor," she cried, clinging to Brodsky's arm. "My man is mad, stark, raving mad."

"What's the matter, Mrs. Cohen?" asked Brodsky.

"Last night he disappeared from the house, the first time he has been gone in fifteen years. Just as I was about to call up the police department and ask them was he murdered, he comes back, at half past twelve, and tells me he has been walking for his health. Then what think you he does? He lights the furnace and makes hot the water and takes a bath. A bath, at one o'clock in the morning! So I waited at the bath-room door. 'Gershon, Gershon,' I pleaded, 'say you are not mad!' There was nothing but the splashing of water. All at once he opens the door, dashes past me, and locks himself up in the bedroom. I have not slept all night. He will not answer me. Save him, Doctor, save him!"

"He'll be all right soon," said Brodsky cheerfully. "Where are the cats?"

"They've all gone into the bathroom," shrieked Mrs. Cohen. "Hundreds of cats—red cats, blue cats, yellow cats, black cats, white cats—all, all there, sitting on the bathroom floor. I locked the door. I dare not go near them. I have driven them away and they come back, they fill the house. It is the work of Solomon ben Yankel," she concluded, bursting into tears. "Curses on the wizard!"

"We'll soon rid you of your cats forever, Mrs. Cohen," said Brodsky kindly. "And as for your husband's insanity, I may tell you that he is acting under my instructions. The cats are all in the bathroom and cannot get out?"

"See," cried Mrs. Cohen, leading us to a small window at the rear of the house. "Stand on that water-pipe and look!"

We climbed up and peered in. I had never seen such a sight in my life before. The room was swarming with cats; there must have been some two dozen of them, and they were acting as though possessed by those spirits that the red-haired Solomon ben Yankel was accused of calling from their abodes. They scrambled about the bath tub, they rolled on the floor, they rubbed themselves against the walls, biting and snarling and acting as though under the influence of some over-powering emotion. Brodsky rubbed his hands.

"It's working; the charm's working," he said. "Keep the door locked, Mrs. Cohen, and meanwhile I will go to your husband."

The woman led us to the bedroom, knocked, and called loudly:

"Gershon! Gershon! The Doctor is here to cure you from being mad. Gershon, open the door. Answer me, Gershon!"

There was a sudden noise inside and, a moment later, the door flew open, Gershon Cohen, very white and terrified, standing at the entrance.

"Thank God you have come, Doctor," he cried. "Ah, the cats! They waited at the bath-room door; when I came out they flew at me as though I were the arch-enemy of all cats in the world. They want my life. I am doomed, unless you save me. They are evil spirits from hell."

Ivan Brodsky looked up meditatively toward the top of the door. My eyes followed the direction of his own. Just where the door set into the framework at the top I caught sight of a small tube of glass, enclosing a minute fragment of white paper.

"Gershon Cohen," said Brodsky solemnly, "what is that?"

"The scroll of the Commandments," cried the little man. "The scroll which I bought for fifty cents from the poor peddler who is now on his way to lay his bones in Jerusalem, and the cause of all my calamities."

"Gershon Cohen," said Brodsky, more solemnly still, "how can spirits of evil enter a house where there are mezuzoth fastened upon the doors?"

The little man stood stock still, his eyes dilating.

Ivan Brodsky reached up with his stick and knocked the tube from its fastenings. It fell, the glass splintering on the floor. Gershon Cohen staggered back, amazed and horrified at the sacrilege.

"See," said Brodsky, taking the scroll from the broken tube. He held it out. In place of the neatly written, microscopic Hebrew characters was a series of dots and crosses.

"Gershon Cohen," said Brodsky, "you are the author of your own troubles, and your avarice has caused them. You thought to save a few paltry dollars by buying your scrolls cheap from some wandering peddler. You might have known no scholar capable of writing them would sell them at the price he named. More than that, you have wickedly taken the bread out of the mouth of Solomon ben Yankel. You have sinned and you must suffer for it."

"What shall I do?" cried Cohen miserably.

"You will confess your crime to-morrow before all your congregation. Then you will readmit Solomon ben Yankel to the community. Lastly, you will purchase from him a dozen new scrolls at three dollars apiece."

"Yes, yes, I will," cried Cohen. "But take away the cats."

"You yourself have brought them here, and you alone can remove them," said Brodsky solemnly. "They are the sins you have committed; they are sins of avarice. Each cat represents fifty dollars that you have deprived other men of."

In spite of his terror Cohen's thoughts wandered. He was estimating the value of his sins in terms of cats at fifty dollars apiece.

"You will go to the front door of your house," continued Brodsky, "and wait there while I open the door of the bathroom. The cats will run out and follow you. You need have no fear; they will not hurt you. You will walk at a steady pace toward the place in the Lutheran cemetery where you plucked the herbs. There you will burn this scroll"—he picked the parchment from the ground and handed it to Cohen—"and pronounce the prayer for forgiveness of sins. Then turn round quickly and return home. The cats will remain in the churchyard. Come!"

He led the trembling man to the door of his house and left him there. He opened the bathroom door. Instantly, with a leap and a scramble, a huge white cat flew from the room, hesitated one instant, and made for the little man, followed by a score or two of others—tawny and grey, black, white and tabby. There must have been cats from all sections of the town. The little man saw them coming, a wild shriek burst from his lips, and he flew for the churchyard, his little legs twinkling over the ground, while cats of all shapes, colors and sizes followed beside him. Then Brodsky collapsed into speechless laughter.

"Was it necessary to go through all those ceremonies and rites?" I asked him, when we had got back to his house.

Brodsky turned upon me, his eyes twinkling.

"Don't look a gift horse in the mouth," he cried. "Haven't I rid his house of his cats?"

"Dr. Brodsky," I said, "I am beginning to suspect you of being a humbug."

"Pshaw!" said the Doctor. "If I had assisted him without the elaborations he would never have appreciated the work I had done for him. And besides, he deserved to be punished for his attempt to take away Solomon ben Yankel's means of livelihood."

"Then you confess that you are a fraud," I said. "And I strongly suspect that this is a put-up job between Solomon and you."

"What was it Cicero said the Roman augurs did when they met each other in the streets?" asked Brodsky irrelevantly.

"They were supposed to wink," I answered.

"Just so," said Brodsky.

"But how did you get rid of his cats, and how did Solomon bring them there?" I asked, still baffled.

Brodsky looked at me amusedly. "Catnip," he answered.

JEAN OF THE SILENCE
The Smart Set (June 1911)

The bird whose soul goes forth in song at mating time knows no such happiness as that which filled the heart of Jean Dupuy as he strode up the last hill caroling. Upon the crest he paused, shook the accumulations from his snowshoes and made a hollow of his hands through which to peer.

Out of the gulf uprose the orb of the sun, piercing and rolling back the mists that clung to the land. Like ghosts of night they fled through valley and cleft, disclosing the long reaches of the shores. He knew each pin point in that home country of his: Mont Ste. Marie, Mont St. Siméon and the white sands of Baie du Caribou; further, St. Joseph, where the fierce maskinonge lurked in the brown weeds, Ste. Anne des Matelots, lastly St. Boniface, his goal, six hours away. Six hours, twelve miles—what did they matter to him, who had covered a thousand in the white North and crossed the lower gulf in a *chaloupe* through drifting ice floes, rich with his spoils of winter furs? He shouted and sang from joy, jingling the gold pieces in his pouch and crinkling the paper plasters in his bulging belt. Thus he stood, looking now seaward, now to the land, its white snows glittering beneath the first

March sun, that brought the first warm south-born winds with their promise of spring. His long blond beard, unshorn since his adventuring began, swung to the breeze; his hair, of woman's length, he had bound back over his shoulders with a deerhide thong. With his lean arms outstretched he gloried in his man's strength and all the hopes of life.

For he was returning to his wedding with Marie Lavergne.

For six years he had wooed her, since that memorable day when, ceasing to raise her as a child in his strong arms and toss her skyward, he had grown suddenly abashed at sight of her and consciousness of his love awoke in him. His wooing then became worship; nor had her shy consent kindled it into flame and fire until the rigors of the wilderness had steeled and strengthened him and taken his youth's heart and dowered him with a man's. They had been betrothed before Father Sebastian; and when he should return in earliest spring, with gold for slaughtered ermine and the rare arctic fox, she was to be his. The spirit of adventure should stir in him no more. He dreamed of quieter years and the maturer joys of life that they should garner—they and their children.

He was a week too soon, yet even now he could endure no longer. Stark as a Viking he strode on, with his fur coat flung back that the cold air might chill his blood pulsing too fiercely. He called welcome to each familiar tree, each bowlder on the bleak hillside.

But when toward evening the bending road disclosed the village of St. Boniface, he became silent and newly shy. Though the sun lacked yet some spans before he dipped to the hills, the settlement was still; all were ensconced by fire and chimney nook. He saw his house, the first in the long street, before him, and with a strange eagerness to prolong the delicious agony of that suspense, he entered, passed into the small sleeping chamber, opened the window wide that the fresh air might enter, and flung himself upon his bed. He lay there, dreaming still.

Some moments afterward came the awakening.

Two farmers, passing from their cattle sheds, halted near by. He knew them, babbling old men, gossips of the settlement.

"'Tis time that Jean Dupuy returned to his nuptials," said one to his companion. "Yestere'en I saw Marie Lavergne sewing her bridal dress behind her open door."

"'Twill be a sad day for the chit when Jean comes back," the other answered.

"How so, neighbor?"

"Hast thou not heard it said how sore her heart was set on Edouard Smith when he came here last fall to take our strongest fellows for his Maine lumber camp?"

"I heard him boasting in the store, but I thought him a liar."

"Liar he is, and yet he swore that, should he speak the word, she would set shoe on his sleigh step when he departed."

They cackled and moved onward. But Jean lay still upon his bed. In the reaction from his love, rage choked him, and he struggled and gasped and moaned in doubt and miserable pain.

He knew the man, Edouard Smith, a Yankeefied Frenchman, the boss of the Maine lumber camp, who came to St. Boniface and the gulf villages for recruits each autumn. He

himself had spent one season with him in the spruce forests. He was a man well matched in strength with himself, fearless and reckless, a practical joker, well liked by his men, but a scoffer at women and a teller of brave tales of his prowess with them by the night camp fire to the fascinated Canadians. Jean had listened among the rest and the stories had passed through his head lightly; now they came back to him.

Their tenor was that woman was light as the wind, unstable, false, liar and trifler always. Jean had laughed openly, thinking of his own. But if those tales were true—what then?

As he stumbled toward the door he saw his answer in a rusting knife on a shelf, and picked it up, hiding it in his sleeve. Then he walked down the street until he came to Marie's door. He opened it and went in. Marie was seated at the table, stitching, stitching; over her gown a garment of white hung down, and she hummed as she hemmed it. But when she looked up hastily and perceived Jean standing there the garment dropped unheeded upon the floor, and she ran to him with a low cry, clasping him round the neck and looking up into his eyes. Jean's head hung down.

"It is thou, really, Jean?" she murmured incredulously. "Thou hast returned! Art thou not glad to see me, Jean?"

Slowly he raised his face, dark with angry blood. On either slender shoulder he placed one clinching hand and he looked hard into her face. Then with her child's strength she drew him toward her; he bent his lips to her and the knife clattered upon the floor.

He went into the parlor and sat down, while Marie ran to bring her mother from the byre. "It is a lie!" he thought as he sat there. "God help the liars if I meet them before my blood has cooled!"

He looked round him. He knew each nook of the small house, each object in the small room, bright with chromos from the Quebec trading firms, with pictures of the Virgin and the village patron, St. Boniface. Here were the horns of the great caribou he had killed, there the lace curtains, tied with ribbons of blue, the missal there, there the black walnut table with its photograph album, on the first page of it his photograph and Marie's. He had given the girl a newer likeness of himself before he left for the North, to wear in a small locket that he had purchased for her. This was an old one and not well liked by either. The plush binding was thick with dust. Jean raised it idly, then slammed it down and sprang to his feet with a choked cry.

At Marie's side a photograph of Edouard Smith stared up at him—Smith, bold and complaisant, in stiff collar and white tie, and inset so neatly into the stiff paper that both seemed to form one picture.

He composed his features hastily as he heard Marie returning with her mother.

"Thou hast become so silent, Jean," said Marie, presently. "It seems as though the cold of the North woods has frozen thee. And I—I have longed for thee."

He felt helpless as a fish, trapped in the nets that swims in its narrowing space of water before the sides close in. Why had she this photograph in place of his? Would he have found it there if he had not arrived earlier than was expected?

The old hate surged back into his heart again tenfold, hate of a heart betrayed, of a wrong long beyond redemption. But mingling with it was the craft of a slow, murderous vengeance. He would match guile against guile. It was not for nothing that he had opposed his cunning against that of the crafty beasts of the North woods.

Afterwards Jean was gayer than any man among the throng that gathered to welcome him.

He watched their eyes and seemed to see the knowing looks that passed. He longed to take each by the throat and wring the truth from his lips. But a stronger motive held him. From Smith's own lips, while she stood by, truth should be wrung, in fair fight, eye against

eye and knife to knife. But he should never possess her. He would fulfill the betrothal contract. Afterwards let the shame of a repudiated wife be hers.

That night, when Jean confessed, Father Sebastian discerned the heaviness of his heart.

"Thou hast told all, my son?" he asked gravely. "Thou knowest unless thou confess all it is a mortal sin. If death should overtake thee so—"

"I have told all," said Jean.

The wedding was to take place on the sixth day. That night he announced that he had a journey to make, a matter of trading in Quebec which would not wait. By sleigh he could make it and return within five days.

Marie looked up, wonder in her blue eyes. "Thou must leave me again, Jean?" she said, tremulously.

She felt his lips like ice upon her own. "'Tis the last time," he said. "It is true that there will be a second journey a week hence, but we shall make it together, thou and I."

She was overjoyed then. She had never been further west than Tadoussac. Next morning he harnessed two horses to the sleigh, and he drove all that day and all of the next over the frozen trail. Winter had returned, more fierce for its eclipse; the trees cracked under the frost like guns discharging, and the keen winds searched out his breast beneath his furs. But keener was the ache in his heart, which, no longer stirring to simple passions, seemed to respond to some furious demon that watched there and strove with him.

He did not enter Quebec, but stopped at Ste. Anne de Beaulieu and passed at night into the famous shrine. Kneeling before the altar rail alone, between two piles of crutches that the devout had cast away, he made his vow to the saint:

"From his own lips, Blessed One, I will wrest truth; and as he answers me in one word, 'yes' or 'no,' when death is at his throat, swearing by thee, so I will deal with him."

All the next day he drove back again, and the next, while the snows whirled and tempests blew and winter raged about him, and all the while the devil within his heart grew more insistent, so that his purpose became quite clear to him in every detail. On the third morning he stood up with Marie before the priest and they were made one.

"And they start upon a wedding journey to Quebec," the gossips whispered. "What if the snows begin once more? He must have a mint of money at stake to make the venture."

"Easy come, easy gone," others replied.

Jean had harnessed the horses and placed the cushions in the sleigh. Under the seat he laid a pack such as guides carry, then turned to help his wife who, with one foot upon the step, bade adieu to the villagers. As he approached her, holding the bearskin robe, a vague unrest showed on her face; for the first time some premonition of impending sorrow beset her. She leaned toward him as he enveloped her; he felt her heart fluttering.

"If ever I wronged thee, Jean, tell me thou hast no shred of malice in thy heart for me, as I have none for thee," she whispered.

He trembled so that he caught at the sleigh side to steady himself. The devil within his breast prompted him with mocking words. "Guard thyself, Jean," it sang. "Guard thyself; wait." Her words awoke no pity in his heart. He turned abruptly away, untangled the reins and sprang into the sleigh without a word.

She watched his face as they drove on. She knew now that he was in the grip of some mighty emotion, but, daring to think it love, nestled against him, drawing the robe round them more closely so that it covered both and only his gloved hands emerged. She watched him again, furtively. His lips were firmly clenched over his teeth and his eyes shone with somber fires. She grew afraid. She caught his free hand in her own trembling ones; it was ice cold and unresponsive to that least timid pressure of hers. At last she summoned strength to speak. He did not answer her. Only

the hoofs of the horses answered and the song of the runners. At last, terror-stricken, she desisted and sank back against the cushions, looking at him with anguished eyes. This was not he who once had been so tender to her; this was some dreadful dream, not the reality of their love's fulfillment. She clutched at his arm. "Jean, what is the matter?" she pleaded. "Art thou ill? Have I offended?" He answered nothing, but stared at the snow, and his face was convulsed with conflict.

At the fifth mile the road divided, one path running parallel with the shore toward Quebec, the other turning inland among the country villages. Jean turned the horses' heads.

"This is not the way, Jean!"

He looked at her so menacingly that she began weeping hysterically; as she did so he drew further away, so that the robe no longer enveloped him. This guile should never soften him. This was the power of girls, Smith had said laughingly. To man, the fist and the knife; to woman, tears. He lashed the horses furiously and they bounded over the frozen road. So they drove on all day, only halting at noon to feed and rest the animals, while Marie wept and pleaded in alternation and he answered never a word.

Sometimes, drying her tears, she made believe that he jested. At others she became cold, seeking to respond in kind. He was not moved. Only once when, overcome by panic, she sought to spring from the sleigh, he put forth a restraining hand and forced her back into the seat again.

By afternoon the road had dwindled to a mere cart track through the snow. The settlements had been passed; they were approaching that vast interior forest belt that still covers the eastern portion of Quebec Province, extending south through Maine. Now their path was a mere woodman's trail, a trapper's way trodden among the trees. Jean had taken it two years previously when, with his fellows, he had accompanied Smith to his lumber camp in the heart of the woods. At last they stopped;

neither wheeled vehicle nor sleigh could proceed farther. Jean sprang down and swung Marie to the ground.

Still his heart was stirred momentarily when he saw her wan face and beseeching eyes. But the violence of the man's love had found its own equivalent in hate. He led the horses round, and, cutting one from the harness, smote the other upon the flank. It bounded forward and stopped; he struck it again and it broke into a gallop back along the homeward path, dragging the vehicle behind it.

"Jean, where art thou taking me?"

He answered for the first time. "To thy lover," he said.

She sank into the snow, knelt to him with clasped hands and hair unhooded. "Jean—tell me my sin—pardon me! How have I erred? What have I done against thee?" she prayed. She clutched at her throat. "It is little that I can give thee, Jean, except my love, and that thou hast always. See, here is thy picture; night and day my heart has beaten against it. Forgive me—love me—my heart is breaking!"

Then, since his heart was breaking, too, he poured it forth in such a torrent of furious speech that she rose up from where she knelt and faced him, a new dignity in her eyes. Love, wounded unto death, had made himself a little shield of pride. "I have vowed to obey thee, Jean. I will go whither thou leadest me. Do what thou wilt with me," she said.

"No prayer shall turn me from my resolve," Jean cried wildly.

"I shall beseech no more," she answered.

"Then mount this horse and ride, and I shall lead him. And see that thou say no word to me thenceforward, for I shall make no answer until I learn the truth."

He lifted her as easily as when she was a child and placed her on the beast's back, wrapping her in the bearskin robe. He took the pack on his back, thrust an axe through his belt and, reins in hand, followed the forest path, only pausing from time to time to lop some overhanging branch that obstructed it. At last,

when the way was too dark for them to proceed farther, he scraped a resting place among the snows, set loose the beast to find what sustenance he might and felled dead trees for fuel. He ringed her round with fire, and when she left the food untasted, covered her with the robe, then, lying at her feet, watched all night that the flames might not burn low and the wild creatures that moaned mournfully from afar creep in on them. Yet once he heard a panther cry, and, later, starting out of a doze, leaped to his feet and hurled his axe at a lean form that slunk into the shadows of the trees. The wind woke and shook the burden of their snows from the dark hemlock branches and the frost groaned in the trees. When, after she had sobbed herself into unconsciousness, Marie awoke, it was dawn; a soft pillow rested beneath her head and Jean stood furless over the embers. Over her and around the fallen snow was piled, but she was warm and dry.

So they passed nights and days, and neither spoke. On the fourth morning the horse stumbled as she mounted him; he had found no sustenance among the snows, and now, with gaunt and heaving flanks, rested upon his knees and watched the preparations for departure. He struggled to his feet and stumbled after them, whinnying—fell, rose and sank in the snows again. Jean went back with the axe.

The third morning after should bring them to their destination. But that night, when Marie waited while Jean gathered wood for the fire, she heard a tree crash, heard him cry, and, running in the direction of the sound, discovered him lying unconscious upon the ground, blood on his face. As the tree fell a stout projecting branch had struck him on the head and knocked him senseless. She raised him in her arms, and with all the strength at her command, dragged him into an open space, where she sponged his face with her skirt and washed away the blood with snow. At first she thought him dead, but presently he stirred. Then, leaving him, she hunted in the pack for matches with which to light a fire.

The food was all but gone and he had not stinted her; she looked into his thin face and tears sprang into her eyes. When she got back she heard him murmuring. She listened—it was her name he spoke.

He woke to find his head pillowed upon her knee and her bending over him with compassionate gaze from which all else had disappeared but love. He thought that her lips moved as though she meant to speak, but no word came from them; he was glad, for he must learn the truth before their silence was broken. Yet something melted in the breast of the man and all at once the flood of his fierce hate dissolved. What if she had been faithless? Even so, had not men been the same?

With this lowering of his esteem came a more human judgment, mingled with a great pity. Surely some madness had possessed him that he had dragged this little creature through the deep snows upon that desperate mission. And he had wronged her beyond all redemption, for so long as life endured they were indissolubly bound. But he must know—he must know.

Although it seemed but an hour, three days had really passed while these thoughts possessed his mind. When at last his brain was clear he seemed to have awakened in a world of silence. The demon voices that had rung through his ears were gone, and, with this internal peace, external quiet seemed to wrap him about so closely that he might have moved in a dream world. Though it was cold the great trees crackled no longer; the very fall of his snowshoes was muffled, and he was vaguely conscious of a vast peacefulness into which he had entered. That healing calm renewed his strength and he strode forward fiercely and eager as before.

That afternoon, halting to adjust his shoe, he allowed Marie to precede him for a few paces; and when he followed after her to resume the lead he saw a thread of blood upon the snow. Her shoes were ribbons and her feet cut and bleeding. He caught her in his arms, raised her to his shoulder and, holding her with both hands, struggled on with pace hardly diminished.

Their food was gone; they had not eaten since the preceding morning. The next day he found her weight increased perceptibly; by noon she was a burden. At last, gasping, he set her down and, rendered desperate by hunger, set forth, axe in his hand, to seek for meat. Fate favored him; three hundred yards from the resting place he saw the white underside of a deer's tail flash warning through the brush. A large herd, huddling nose to nose, had stalled themselves against the bitter wind, and now, bewildered and terrified, came breaking through the gnawed trees in his direction. As they flashed past, with a true aim he sent his axe against the neck of a fawn, and as it stumbled to its knees he ran forward and killed it. He returned laden with meat; afterwards, scraping and salting the raw hide to make it pliable, he fashioned a pair of moccasins for her.

And twice that day, watching her secretly, he saw her lips begin to move and cease, as though she meant to plead with him.

He was glad she desisted, for the weight of his remorse had grown too heavy for him to endure speech with her. His plans were matured. With knife at throat he would force the truth from Smith; but, if the word were what he feared, he would turn the weapon against his own breast, not his enemy's, thus saving her from a long life of bondage.

On the third morn they came into a place of blazed trees and felled timbers. Here was Smith's land, spread through five thousand acres of virgin spruce and pines; near by the river ran; through the trees curled the smoke of the camp kitchen. And suddenly a tall, blond man, bare of arm, shaggy of beard, strode out of the woods.

For an instant Smith looked at the pair in amazement; then a grin spread over his cheeks, wrinkling the corners of his mouth and eyes. Never had he expected such a consummation of his jest. What a tale to tell! And a woman was at the bottom of it. But as Jean advanced menacingly his smile became more sheepish, until at last, when they stood face to face, it had faded into a dogged stare, wherein anger was fast enkindling anger.

Immovable, feet wide apart, they sought to measure each the strength of his adversary, and only their arms were engaged as each sought for a vantage hold. Then suddenly Jean knew that he was no match for his antagonist. Fever had weakened and hunger wasted him, and he had not reckoned with these enemies. In a trice Smith had pinned his arms and forced him backward against a tree, where he held him and stood grinning at him.

Shamed, humbled, Jean found his speech.

"I have come here," he said tremulously, mumbling like one not fully awakened; "I have come here to learn whether you be her lover or no.

"I have sworn by Ste. Anne of Beaulieu that you shall tell me," he went on, his voice now choking. "But I should not have harmed you. I only sought to know. Take her, if she is yours. But I must know. Set my hand free."

Smith's grasp relaxed; some pity moved his heart. His jest had had a difficult finale.

As he released Jean's left arm the Frenchman drew the knife from his belt and cast it into the snow. Then, looking up, he saw Smith's lips moving, but no sound came from them. It seemed that he mocked him.

"You will tell me," he cried. "For, see, if she is yours, I shall never molest you. You shall not see me again to trouble either of you. And I have brought her to you."

As nobleness kindles a flame in others' breasts no less serene, so pity leaped in the breast of the lumber boss and shone out from his eyes. Again his lips moved; still Jean could hear no sound. He thought Smith mocked him; and now he turned away and, leaning against the pine, wept helplessly. He had lost all; he had lost love and manhood, honor and pride; he bowed himself to the snows—then saw the knife and stooped for it.

But small hands clasped his own, and his wife's arms formed a soft, impenetrable barrier about him. Her face was raised to his; he looked into it and once again saw her lips moving. And he heard nothing. And as in bewilderment he looked from face to face, still hearing no sound, it was borne in on him that neither did he hear the sough of the pines nor footsteps nor the drip of the snows. Ste. Anne had answered him.

He knew that miracle of her love now, love that she had given back for hate, faith for unfaith, trust for disloyalty, love stronger than broken pride and honor shamed, yet softer than the warm airs that breathed on them as they passed into the sunlight.

THE MAN WITH THE CAMERA EYES
An Adventure of Peter Crewe

THE BOX OF BORNEOS
Buffalo Sunday Times (18 June 1911)

It was a rough passage, and though we were already half way between New York and Tilbury, our destination, few of the passengers had found their sea legs. I sat on the captain's right; upon his left was a pleasant, florid, gray-haired man, rather slow of speech, who was introduced to me as Mr. Peter Crewe.

"Do you find that this Atlantic breeze agrees with you better than the air of Plainfield, N.J., Mr. Langston?" asked Mr. Crewe politely.

"It certainly does," I answered. "But may I ask you how on earth you know that I am a resident of Plainfield, N.J.? To the best of my belief I have told nobody; in fact, as a lawyer, I am naturally secretive about such matters."

"I only know," replied Crewe, "because on two occasions I have seen you hurrying to the boat from the New Jersey terminal at nine o'clock in the morning. You carried a newspaper and a suitcase and your shoes were red with Plainfield clay. Is not that reason enough?"

"Quite," I replied. "But how in the name of conscience do you remember me?"

"Why, I saw you," returned Crewe. "Everybody within a twelve mile radius of New York has seen everybody else—or at least, ninety per cent of all other citizens, at some time. Need I remind you that on August 12, 1910, you took a small party to a roof garden on Forty-second Street? Or that, the previous February, you rendered first aid to a child who had been knocked down by a street car on Sixth Avenue?"

Later in the day, discovering Mr. Crewe alone in the smoking room, I showed him the photograph of a young man in cowboy attire and asked him if he could give me his history. He took the photograph and studied it intently; then closed his eyes in mental concentration.

"I have only seen this young fellow twice," he said. "Seven years ago he strolled up Broadway from the Battery in a suit of English clothes, carrying a 'Gladstone' bag. Three years afterward, while visiting New York from the west, he was arrested at the corner of Twenty-third Street and Fifth Avenue on a charge of intoxication."

I leaped from my seat. "For the love of heaven, explain your secret to me," I exclaimed. "You may be the man I am most in need of."

Crewe smiled in a self-depreciatory manner. "It is very simple," he explained. "You are, no doubt, aware of the discovery of psychologists that every mental image remains permanently impressed upon the brain?"

"Yes."

"Unfortunately, when the average man sees a thing he straightway forgets it. Similarly with what he hears. When you and I hear a passing sound—the scrape of a wave against the ship, the fall of a twig in the park—the impression is so faint that it is at once lost and never recurs to us throughout life. But when I receive an image through the eyes I never forget it. In my earlier days it caused me much inconvenience. Now, having acquired a modest competence and retired from business, I derive considerable amusement from this power. I travel, I study, I try to turn my advantage to the good of humanity. Already I may say that I know practically every inhabitant of New York City by sight and can recall every occasion on which I have ever seen him. I could tell you strange stories in this regard. I know half London and two-thirds of Paris. Not a day passes but I meet a dozen old acquaintances, all of whom are blandly unconscious of having ever encountered me before."

"But why should you not help me?" I exclaimed. "You are just the man I need to help me in unraveling a painful mystery."

"I shall be delighted to be of service to you," said Crewe. "Let us be perfectly frank—that is all I ask."

"I will be entirely frank," I answered. "I am traveling to England to investigate an affair which threatens the life of a man whom I believe to be innocent. Here is the story:

"Upon a small estate in Surrey there lived two brothers, retired Anglo-Indian officials. Both were widowers. Sir George Bamwell, the eldest, a baronet, had a daughter. His brother, William Bamwell, to whom the baronetcy would in due course descend, had a son, a ne'er-do-well, who, after a rather profligate career, went off to America, where he became successively a sheep-herder, prospector, and cowboy. The boy was cast off by his father, a martinet of the old English school, and it was understood that the bulk of his money would go to Selim, an Indian servant, whom William

Bamwell had brought home with him, and who had served the brothers faithfully for twenty years."

"The boy, I take it, is the original of the photograph you showed me," said Crewe.

"Yes, and your statements in regard to him were perfectly correct. He did land in New York seven years ago, and he was arrested upon a charge of intoxication at a subsequent date.

"Last year Claude Bamwell, the son, returned home unexpectedly. He had tired of his roving life. He asked his father to give him another chance to redeem himself and to let him remain with him. The cousin, Lydia, the daughter of Sir George Bamwell, who had conceived a romantic attachment for her graceless relative, was instrumental in effecting a reconciliation between the father and son. Claude was given his chance and seemed to make good use of his opportunity. Within six months father and son were on friendly terms. William Bamwell, who was perhaps seventy years of age, had a passion for amateur photography. Claude humored his father and never tired of helping him in his hobby. Father and son began to appreciate each other better than they had ever done before.

"This increasing intimacy was not looked upon favorably by Selim, the Hindoo servant, especially since William Bamwell contemplated altering his will in favor of his son, Claude, and greatly reducing the legacy which Selim had come to look upon as his own reversionary right. However, Selim was inscrutable and kept his own counsel.

"The Bamwell brothers were very set in their ways. One of the characteristics common to both of them was their fondness for a certain East Indian cigar that came from Borneo. These they imported direct from the manufacturer. Claude, however, discovered a similar brand on sale in London, and gave a box to his father for a Christmas present—at Selim's suggestion, as he declares. In fact, according to Claude, Selim discovered the existence of this brand and induced him to purchase the box. Selim, however, denies that he ever heard of these cigars and ascribes the entire scheme of purchasing and presenting them to Claude.

"Now we come to the crux of the situation. Three months ago Sir George Bamwell was discovered dead in the library early one morning. He had been sitting up alone the night before, and had taken one of his brother's cigars—the first of the box. He was found dead, the half-smoked cigar upon the table before him. A post-mortem investigation disclosed the presence in the body of a minute portion of a powerful poison allied to prussic acid. The cigar was analyzed, but nothing was found wrong with it.

"In spite of a rigorous cross-examination of all persons concerned, no motive or clue could be discovered. Sir George was buried in the family vault, and William Bamwell became Sir William.

"Not three weeks afterward the tragedy repeated itself. Sir William Bamwell was found dead in precisely the same manner. Again the presence of the prussic acid variant was disclosed at the post-mortem; again the cigar was analyzed and found to be entirely harmless. Yet Sir William, like his brother, had undoubtedly died after smoking half of the Borneo cigar.

"But in this case several new facts were brought out at the inquest. In the first place, Claude had been with his father until a few moments before his death. The two men had been smoking together. Sir William was a very rapid smoker; Claude preferred cigarettes and barely burned away an inch of his cigars, which he smoked merely to humor his father. Again, it was proved that Claude had recently purchased prussic acid at a drug-show in the village. When interrogated, he acknowledged this fact, but asserted that his father used this deadly compound for intensifying the images upon negatives that had been under-exposed. It is perfectly true that a certain compound of prussic acid is used for this purpose, and Sir William had always compounded his own photographic chemicals.

"To cut the story short, Claude, or Sir Claude, as I must now call him, was arrested upon a charge of murder and is now awaiting trial at the assizes."

"And the motive?" Crewe queried.

"Fear that his father, who was becoming a little senile, and was largely under the influence of Selim, would again disinherit him."

"But did Claude know the contents of the will?"

"No. It had actually been changed in the son's favor, but so far as is known Sir William had kept his own counsel."

"Then that works either way," said Crewe. "Selim might have committed the murder, fearing lest the will would be changed in the son's favor, and not knowing that this had actually been done. And that very open purchase of prussic acid is not compatible with guilt. And the cigars—how do they come into the story? You say that analysis showed them to be harmless?"

"Entirely so; and to my mind, whoever was the murderer, it was not Claude. But the young man had a bad name, and Selim appears to have made certain statements which greatly increased the feeling against him. However, all that is now sub judice.

"It was the cousin, Lydia, who, at the instigation of Claude, telegraphed to me to gather all material I could tending to show that the young man's life in America had not been so bad as is currently rumored in England, and to hurry across the water with this material to aid the defense. I may say that Claude Bamwell has never been convicted of a felony, and only once of a misdemeanor. I am the attorney who defended him on the charge of intoxication."

In this manner Crewe and I came to be associated in this first of our many enterprises.

I passed many an anxious moment until the boat docked at Tilbury. But all my speculations and impressions were killed abruptly when, at the moment of docking, a messenger rushed up and thrust a telegram into my hands. I tore it open and read:

"Claude Bamwell found guilty willful murder. Godalming assizes. Judge refused postponement till your arrival, on ground your evidence not material. Come to Fairview instantly."

Crewe shook his head dolefully when I showed him this missive. Although he would not say so, I could see that he had scant hope in our ability to save Claude Bamwell's life. We took the train to Fenchurch Street and, half an hour later, were speeding southward in the Godalming local. At four that afternoon we arrived at Fairview, a small and unpretentious place, but in good taste and a typical English gentleman's country seat.

We found Mr. Clayton in charge. Lydia, the cousin, was prostrated and under medical care. Hardly had we taken our seats for a conference, however, than she appeared dramatically before us, arrayed in black, her hair disheveled, her eyes tear-stained.

"You must save Claude, Mr. Langston," she pleaded. "Indeed he never killed his father. Tell me that you have not come all the way across the ocean fruitlessly."

Slight as my hope was, I could not wholly cast it out.

"I will do my best," I said. "I understand an appeal is to be taken to the court of criminal appeal. I can testify that the stories as to Claude's wild life in America are fabrications. I will save him if he can be saved."

Mr. Clayton took Lydia by the arm and led her to the door. "We will spare no effort," he said.

She seemed to collapse. Mr. Clayton led her to her room, while we waited in painful doubt. I saw Crewe cast his eye upon a photograph that stood upon the mantel.

"That is Selim, the Indian servant," I explained to him. "I had a duplicate copy of it, but unfortunately left it at home in the hurry of packing. Pleasant-looking fellow, isn't he?"

Crewe made no answer. His eyes were closed; he seemed to be calling up some memory. At this juncture Mr. Clayton returned and seated himself.

"Now, gentlemen," he said briskly—I had already introduced Mr. Crewe to him as my confidential assistant—"I must confess that matters look very black indeed. In our English courts a conviction for murder is practically never reversed and justice moves with appalling swiftness. Let me say, however, that I am assured a hideous wrong has been done, and that the real criminal is the Indian. But for his perjured evidence, a very different verdict would have been returned.

"What most impressed the jury was the fact that a prussic acid compound was found in the bodies of both Sir George and Sir William, while it was proved that Claude had bought prussic acid at the village drug store. Then there was the motive—fear that the will would be revoked. But what clinched the jurors in their decision was Selim's evidence that Claude had approached him with the project of destroying his father and sharing the money that might be left, irrespective of the will. Selim had been a faithful servant for many years; Claude was reputed to have been a man of vilest character in America. The judge, who is old and testy, refused to wait until you could put in evidence in rebuttal of this, on the ground that it was immaterial in law. Perhaps it was—but in fact it undoubtedly decided the jury's verdict."

"And where is Selim?" I asked.

"Living at the village hotel," said Mr. Clayton. "Living there brazenly. Says he will remain on the spot until his dear master has been avenged, and is the object of universal solicitude, as Sir Claude is of execration."

"And now," I said, "what part did the cigars play in this mystery?"

"None whatever," answered Mr. Clayton.

"Have you the rest of the box?"

"No," Mr. Clayton answered. "Oddly enough, it cannot be found. It disappeared on the day of the murder, together with the bulk of the prussic acid supposed to have been purchased, and with a few other little articles having relation to the crime. But none of these is material. The prosecuting attorney suggested that Claude had hidden these in an effort to destroy all evidence of his crime."

"Can we see this Selim?" asked Peter Crewe.

"Well," said Mr. Clayton, "if you think it will do any good, we can undoubtedly find him at the village hotel."

At Crewe's urging we started out for the village. It was a small country town of one main street, flanked by little laborers' cottages, with, here and there, a tradesman's residence of more imposing type. At the inn we learned that Selim was out walking.

"What time does the next train come in from Godalming?" Crewe asked.

"At 5:07," the landlord answered.

"And departs?"

"There is a 5:12 local running clear through to Charing Cross."

"We have just time to catch the local," said Crewe, looking at his watch. "Mr. Clayton, we leave you here and shall see you tomorrow." Then, disregarding the lawyer's look of surprise, he took me by the arm and, without further explanation, urged me to accompany him. I saw that something important must have transpired.

"This fellow Selim does not know you by sight?" he asked.

"No," I said.

"Still, it would be as well not to let him perceive two strangers when he arrives upon the down-platform."

"But where are we going?" I asked.

"Tilbury," said Crewe shortly. "There is no time to lose. With your permission I will defer explanations until later."

We reached the station with three minutes to spare. As we panted up the inclined pathway toward the train Crewe pulled me aside into the shadows of a cluster of box cars. An instant later I saw Selim pass stealthily by in the direction of the village. He had evidently arrived on the down train.

Still amazed, I entered the up train, and, as soon as we were settled in our compartment, Crewe turned to me.

"I think, Mr. Langston," he said, "that we shall find that box of cigars in that rag and bone shop along the waterfront of Tilbury. Doubtless you remember it."

"But—" I began.

"Did you not see this Selim entering it this morning as we came to anchorage?" Crewe asked.

"I remember an Asiatic with a parcel entering some shop."

"You could not distinguish the face? It was rather faint. Nevertheless that man was the original of the photograph upon the mantel at Fairview, and the parcel was a box of cigars wrapped in a dirty cloth. Selim must have learned of our coming and determined to remove all evidence from the scene of the crime. Not daring to burn or bury the cigars, he resolved to go to London secretly and dispose of the box to some one of his compatriots who frequent the Wapping and Tilbury purlieus. By great good fortune his visit synchronized with our arrival."

At Crewe's suggestion we purchased cloth caps and threw away our felt hats; we turned up the collars of our coats and made ourselves appear as much as possible in our role of ship's officers ashore. To find the junk shop was easy. As Crewe had surmised, it was kept by an East Indian, a swarthy, ill-favored fellow who eyed us with no very great appreciation.

"Mate," said Crewe, "we want some smokes to take aboard with us in the morning."

Without a word the East Indian produced a handful of vile-looking cheroots. Crewe tossed them roughly aside.

"What d'ye take me for?" he said, somewhat thickly, as though slightly under the influence of liquor. "Gimme a box. Got any split boxes?"

Leaning over the counter I saw a small package wrapped up in a dirty cloth, which disclosed the end of a cigar box.

"Gimme those," I said, pointing.

The East Indian looked at me furtively. He took up the box, unwrapped the cloth—and suddenly darted through the back door of his shop. Instantly Crewe leaped upon him.

"Hold him," he cried to me, as the Indian twisted himself adroitly out of Crewe's grasp. I saw his hand go down to his side and, with a fortunate blow, knocked him sprawling. His head came in contact with the edge of the door and the fall stunned him. The box fell from his clasp. Picking it up hastily I saw upon the cover the word "Borneo."

"Come on," cried Crewe, and, holding the box under my coat, I darted after him down the alley. We reached the main road panting, and, finding that we were not pursued, set off at a rapid pace toward the station. On the way we recovered our hats, which we had thrown behind some boarding.

It was five o'clock on the following morning when we reached Fairview, after many hours of waiting at junctions for trains which either did not run or did so with exasperating unpunctuality. We went straight to the house and called Mr. Clayton out of bed. Crewe held up the cigars.

"Now, Mr. Clayton, we must act quickly," he said, "or you will find that the quarry will have flown. Can you bring Selim to the house as soon as possible?"

"I will do so at once," said Mr. Clayton, much mystified.

"If he refuses to come—" I said.

"He will not refuse. I can procure a warrant from Mr. Tighe, our nearest magistrate. But may I ask—"

"I would rather say nothing," Crewe answered. "It is a desperate hope, and yet it seems built upon something of a foundation. At any rate it will do no harm. May I be allowed the setting of the little drama?"

"By all means," Mr. Clayton answered.

He set off as soon as he had snatched a hasty breakfast of bread and milk, and, after two hours of waiting, Crewe and I saw him reappear with Selim. The servant came in blandly; he was as suave in his demeanor as he had been pictured; nevertheless I thought I could discern an uneasy glance in his eye.

"Sit down, Mr. Selim," said Mr. Clayton. "These gentlemen are friends of Claude Bamwell's and wish to interrogate you."

"I shall be delighted to do everything in my power to assist them," said the Indian, seating himself easily at the table. "If only I could believe that the unhappy young man was not guilty of my dear master's death—"

"Do you smoke, Mr. Selim?" asked Crewe abruptly.

The Indian started violently; then, recovering his composure, replied:

"I am not much of a smoker, sir."

"But you have smoked? Will you oblige me by smoking a cigar with me?" And he produced the box of Borneos.

I never saw such a change come over a human countenance as came over the Indian's. For a moment he gasped like a fish out of water. Before he could regain his self-possession Crewe had placed before him a sheet of paper and a pencil. Upon the paper was written:

"I swear that I and I alone am responsible for the death of my master, Sir George Bamwell."

"As an alternative to smoking, perhaps you will sign this," said Crewe. "You may do both," he added.

The Indian collapsed into his chair with a ghastly smile.

"No, I will smoke," he said, pushing the paper away.

Crewe calmly lit a cigar, and then applied a match to the Indian's. And there they sat, smoking in perfect silence, while we others gathered around in strained expectancy.

"Come, throw away your cigar, Selim, and sign that paper," said Crewe, after a pause. The Indian's cigar now had an inch of ash on it; Crewe's was hardly rimmed.

Suddenly, as if inspired by some invincible determination, the Indian began smoking furiously. The smoke came from his mouth in puffs. His cigar was half consumed. The silence deepened. Some dreadful tragedy seemed to depend upon the issue of that smoking match.

"Selim," said Crewe, laying down his cigar, "sign that paper." And he removed the cigar from the Indian's mouth.

I saw the Indian shoot out a trembling claw. He grasped the pencil and wrote his name almost illegibly beneath the paper. Then he glanced into our faces with a pitiful smile. "It is finished," he said, and picked up the cigar again.

Crewe leaped toward him and tried to wrest the cigar from his mouth. But the Indian, with a grip of steel, held Crewe's wrists, all the while drawing in and puffing out the smoke in thick clouds. The ash was lengthening. Still none of us stirred. We were fascinated into inertia by this strange drama.

All at once the end came. I saw an ashen pallor overspread Selim's swarthy face. He choked; he beat the air with his hands; then, without a sound, he toppled over to the ground. Mr. Clayton raised him quickly, but one look into Selim's face was sufficient to tell us all that life was ended.

"You see, gentlemen," said Crewe, "as I suspected, those cigars were highly charged with a volatile poison, a variant of prussic acid. Selim had given the box to Claude to present to his father, or, rather, had cunningly contrived that Claude should purchase the box at the store in Tilbury, where he had it placed on sale. The reason why no poison was found in the cigar butts was that it had already been drawn out of the cigars into the lungs of the victims.

"You know that as one smokes a cigar toward the butt the stump constantly becomes warmer and damper, the fluids being driven back by the flame. There was no danger in the cigars until they were half smoked down, for the poison did not vaporize. After they were half smoked, however, the acid became sufficiently heated to pass into vapor, which was inhaled into the smoker's lungs and caused immediate death. It was a diabolical trick, and could only have originated in the cunning mind of an East Indian, a race notorious for its vendettas and vengeances."

"And if you had not so opportunely seen Selim entering the shop at Tilbury?" I suggested. "The coincidence was almost an impossible one, according to the laws of chance—and yet it saved an innocent life."

"There are not laws of chance," Crewe answered. "Believe me, Langston, somewhere or other lies the clue to every crime, if only one has sense to discern it."

THE GIRL AT THREE MILE FORK
MacLean's Magazine (August 1911)

When the Canadian Transcontinental put a girl in charge at Three Mile Fork, the newest survey camp for the line that was to run north to tap the wheat territories, the settlers shook their heads dubiously.

"Women's all right for home stations," they admitted. "But here—"

Sergeant Ralph Hay, of the Mounted Police, completed the sentence for them.

"Margaret Royce has as good a head on her shoulders as any man in the Provinces," he said. "She'll make good at the job."
She did. The "job," indeed, was not a difficult one. It consisted for the most part in making out freight bills on the typewriter and transmitting telegraphic messages along the branch line that was being strung out northwest of Edmonton. Meanwhile the surveyors packed up and moved on to Friar's Hole, seven miles nearer the expected terminal, paying out its telephone line as it went. Margaret had charge of the telephone local also, and after their newest camp was pitched the engineers would call her up and have an after-supper chat over the wire.

That was, until Sergeant Hay was detailed by the government to accompany the expedition along its route. Thenceforward all others who called up Margaret must needs have urgent business with her. For the Sergeant and Margaret had known each other back in Toronto, years ago, and after winter had gone they were to take up a grant together in the Northwest. Margaret wore a ring.

"It's hard to feel each evening takes me further from Three Mile," he called to Margaret, when they left Friar's Hole and started off along the survey route. "I'll try to ride over Sunday." But when Sunday arrived the engineers were carrying their theodolites through swamp lands ten miles further to the west, and the visit was postponed.

Nor did it come for months afterward. For on the following Wednesday Zere Buck held up the freight train as she came puffing up to the water reservoir at Hatmetack, twenty miles southward, on the main line, and Hay was sent posthaste to bring him in. Zere Buck gave Hay a good run for his money, forcing his beast southward over the boundary line and into the Bad Lands. There he went into hibernation for the winter and the Sergeant let up perforce until the following spring. He knew that when the suns warmed the prairie country the badger would come out of his hole again and cross the border, and he preferred to await him rather than move for extradition. The Plains Police never let up for long. Sooner or later every fish comes into their nets. The arm of the Canadian Government is one of the longest in the world, and its fingers have the sinews of a Paderewski. Finally Sergeant Hay hoped to take in Margaret on his return northward, but even then an imperative call brought him hurrying back to Friar's Hole. The Transcontinental had established a new base depot there, and the theodolites were working fifty miles north-westward. He called up Margaret.

"How are things going?" he asked.

"Fine," she answered with a queer little laugh. Hay hung up his end with an oath. He knew that laugh: his girl was lonesome, so was he. "If this wasn't my last year I'd leave the depot to the coyotes and go," he swore. But he was the only Policeman within a radius of fifty miles, and messages came piling up, both telegraph and 'phone, each hour of the day. Perhaps he would not see Margaret until spring. And yet Three Mile Fork was but seven miles distant as the surveyor sights!

He grew vastly uneasy when he heard that the monthly pay train was stalled at Three Mile station. The permanent line ended there, and the light rails, temporarily laid down to connect with the new Friar's Hole base had buckled under a heavy freight. That meant a stall of several days before the men could be upon the scene, and there was seven thousand dollars and a trifle more lying upon the platform. The French fireman and engineer went off and fuddled themselves with whisky. Margaret was in sole charge of everything.

She caught the men as they came staggering out of a dive and forced them to carry the boxes of bullion into her room. Then, while they ambled off to complete their libations, she cleaned and polished the Service revolver which Sergeant Hay had left with her

for any emergency. For three nights she slept in her clothes behind two bolted doors.

On the morning of the fourth day Zere Buck and another came riding into Three Mile. They were tired: even the spare horse Buck led was tired, for he had ridden forty-eight hours direct for Three Mile after the news reached him as he came creeping out of his winter quarters. A late Chinook had cleaned up the snowbound prairies and the March sun had thawed out every ice-bound swamp, which made traveling difficult. But Zere had sized up the situation with ample vision. The farms were strung out over a wide area; from Three Mile station to the dive in which the engineer and fireman were now nursing their heads, was a full quarter-mile; nothing but a girl stood in his way, though Hay had been frantically wiring from Friar's Hole for leave to go. But Government business takes precedence of all else, and they were Government stores he guarded, the company owning nothing except the line, the rolling stock, and the pay-money. Discipline held him at his post, but he never left the zone of the telephone's call.

Zere Buck had picked up a fellow, Pitman by name, along his route and the two made Three Mile on this fourth morning, riding in under a damp fog. They broke down the outer door easily. It was Margaret herself who opened the inner door to them. Zere saw her stand confronting him, pistol in hand, across a twelve-foot room.

"One step and I fire," she said. There was no tremble in her voice, but Zere saw how the heavy pistol wavered in her fingers. He took the step and Margaret fired—and missed, fired and missed, fired and missed again; flung the weapon into Zere's face and missed. Next moment Zere had her arms pinioned.

"I ain't a-goin' to hurt ye, Missy," he said with a laugh. "It ain't you I want, Missy, it's the coin. B'y'r leave."

He left her to his assistant and entered the inner room. One glance sufficed to show him the location of the pay-chests, under the couch.

Zere lifted the seven of them in turn and took them out, leaving Pitman to keep guard over Margaret. He poured the money into the gunny bags that he had slung across the saddle pommel. When he came back he found Margaret standing before Pitman, scolding him while he was shuffling under her gaze uneasily.

"That's the way, Missy," said Zere chuckling. "Take it easy; you won't come to no harm from us." He was good-natured over his success. "Write out a statement on your machine, Missy," he said, "and I'll put my fist to it. That'll save you from being suspected; I guess Sarge Hay knows my signature."

Margaret went to her typewriter and sat down. Then the queer thing happened; as Zere leaned over she moved the telephone and, unobserved, displaced the telephone receiver, so that, the receiver propped itself upon the edge of the desk, and to the casual glance appeared to be in position. A wild scheme had flashed into Margaret's brain. She placed her fingers on the keys and waited.

"I got the money out of the young lady's room," dictated Zere. *Tap-tap* went the typewriter keys. "She kept it there for safety. Got that? For safety. She put up a game fight and fired three shots at me. I alone am the guilty party. Hoping to see you all when I'm at home. Now hand it here and I'll put my scrawl to it."

Hay, seated at his table moping, heard the telephone "click!" He was so lonely that he noticed it and wondered.

"That you, Margie?" he called.

Click-click, click-click. It was the telegraph call. He shot a glance towards his telegraph instrument. The needle remained motionless. As he stared at it in bewilderment, he heard his name spelled out, faintly but clear, over the telephone. Then he recognized the sound of the typewriter keys.

"C-o-m-e," the message ran. "B-u-c-k h-a-s p-a-y m-o-n-e-y." She repeated the word," Come! Come! Come!"

Zere Buck scrawled his uncouth signature to the typewritten declaration which Margaret handed him. He left the room, returning shortly with a pair of nippers.

"I'll slit a piece out of them wires, Missy," he said, leering wisely, and then, to his companion, "come on, Pit. Say good-bye. We got to make the dry lands before the Sarge gets too curious."

Sergeant Hay rode out before his feet were fixed in both stirrups. He buttoned his tunic as he rode, and adjusted the carbine in the saddle bucket as the horse settled into its steady lope. He went directly to Three Mile. The station was deserted. There was no Margaret, but ample evidence of the robbery. Of Margaret he dare not think, but mounted again and rode off, due south across the marsh country. He knew what would be Zere Buck's place of refuge, and he knew the route. He hoped to head off his man before he could reach the dry lands with his booty, and perhaps Margaret!

Three hours later he perceived a solitary horseman ahead of him. The figure stood out indefinitely, perhaps a thousand yards ahead of him. The horse and rider seemed to be going through strange movements. The rider directed the animal now this way, now that way, and seemed at times to crouch low in the saddle, as though following some one. Suddenly the figure disappeared completely. Peering ahead to watch for his reappearance, Hay neglected his horse, and it came to a standstill in a patch of the marsh land which had been thawed by the March sun. He urged the horse, but the ground was impossible. He dismounted, and leaving the animal, went ahead on foot, choosing the hillocks of solid ground.

The thousand yards which had appeared to separate him from the figure before it disappeared, seemed to grow into a terrible distance. He floundered in the mire. His feet became clogged. He began to wish that he had not left his horse, when suddenly, as he reached the foot of a small rise in the ground, and where the footing was dry, he saw a small figure lying prostrate at the top of the rise, peering down into the depression which lay beyond.

"Margaret!" he cried, drawing closer.

"*Hush!*" she replied, repressing the relief and gladness she felt. "I followed them. Look!"

There, in a deep swamp lying behind this hill he beheld three horses and two struggling objects which might have been men.

"It is Zere Buck," she said, "and Pit. The third horse carried the pay. They rode too quickly up the hill and over it, and they were into the muskeg before they knew it. Their guns must be gone. They—do you think we can get them out?"

Hays went down closer, revolver drawn.

"You've got us, Sarge," said Zere Buck. "Only git us out quick, or we'll sink for good."

"All right, Buck," drawled the Sergeant. "Just toss a fellow your guns, so's you won't have the extra weight . . . What? . . . Lost! Or you'd have plinked us? Oh, no, Buck. You knew you'd rather get out of the hole first, anyway."

Two hours later, as the prairie sunset faded out of the sky, a strange little procession ambled into Three Mile. First came two horses with two bound figures swaying to the motion of the animals as they sat in the saddles. Beside them, but a little in the rear, was a red-tunicked mounted policeman, and a girl, mud-bedraggled, white and haggard. Behind them, led by a tether came a third weary horse, stumbling under the weight of the company's pay.

An hour later they sat on the station platform.

"So you followed them?" muttered the Sergeant.

"Yes. And they thought it was you, and took a hurried short cut from the trail. They rode over the little hill too quickly, and were into the mud before they could stop. The horses fell before they knew it."

"And it was you I saw following them, Margaret?"

"Of course, silly."

"*Hmph!*" snorted Hays, apparently brooding over some very weighty matter. "*Hmph!* What kind of a weddin' shall we have? Church or—or here at the station?"

THE QUEST OF GENTLE HAZARD
Being the Adventures in Love and Chivalry of Lord Richard Jocelyn

A CASUAL CHAMPION
The Chicago Daily News (14 October 1911)

Lord Jocelyn yawned. He had chosen an unsuitable locality for this relaxation, being, in fact, upon the curb at the northeast corner of Forty-second Street and Broadway at eight o'clock in the evening, and, in pausing to give vent to his feelings, he narrowly escaped being run down by a taxicab which skidded past, the wheel not five inches away. But the truth is he was horribly bored. He had not met with an adventure worth speaking of for several days and had decided to return home to his apartments on Madison Avenue, play a game of solitaire and go to bed.

He had already arrived at this admirable decision when his attention was attracted toward a young woman of remarkable beauty who went hurrying past. Instinctively he turned—not, of course, with any design of addressing her or in any way molesting her, but to follow her with his eyes until she rounded the corner and was lost to view among the crowds of upper Broadway. For beauty was to Lord Jocelyn a lodestar that attracted him irresistibly, and the beauty of this particular young woman was as that of—a peach, let us say, among a basketful of nectarines.

And then an incident occurred which changed all his intentions and resolutions. For, as she was about to round the corner, a flashily attired man, whom Lord Jocelyn had observed hurrying after her, caught up with her and planting himself in her path made some remark to her.

Lord Jocelyn felt his blood tingle. He saw the girl shrink back, saw the fellow pursue her with the evident intention of commencing a flirtation, and strode through the crowd in hot anger, an angel of avenging chivalry. A dozen steps and he was at her side.

"Is this fellow molesting you?" he asked, doffing his hat.

The girl raised her eyes to his appealingly; Lord Jocelyn swung round upon his heel and, as the first sneering words broke from the man's mouth, he let drive his fist with his full force and caught him between the eyes. The man fell like a log and, striking his head upon the curb, lay as though stunned. Before Jocelyn could guide his protégé through the crowd that instantly assembled, a policeman was at his side. He looked at Jocelyn's evening attire, then at the rough clothing of the fellow, whose consciousness was slowly returning.

"No need to explain, sir; I saw the whole business," he said. "Giddup and come," he added, addressing the street loafer. "Station house for yours."

"Do you want me to come with you as a witness?" asked Jocelyn.

"No need of that, sir," answered the policeman. "I'll take your name, and that of the lady's, and you can be at the Jefferson Market court at ten tomorrow morning."

"My name's Jocelyn," said the involuntary hero of the episode, adding his address. "And this lady is—"

"Miss Murray—Clara Murray, 462 West Ninety-first Street," said the lady promptly.

The policeman noted down these facts in his pocketbook, keeping one eye warily upon the ruffian, who was now rising to his feet and looking round him with a dazed expression. He snapped the book shut and jerked him to his feet. Then the man seemed suddenly to realize his predicament.

"Lemme go!" he shouted, struggling in his captor's grasp. "I gotter speak to the lady. I will speak to her—"

He fought himself free and, with a blow of surprising force, sent the policeman reeling backward. The latter, recovering his balance, drew his club and brought it down with his full force upon the man's head. For the second time he dropped.

Meanwhile, catching the young woman by the arm, Lord Jocelyn forced his way through the crowd to a street car, which they boarded.

"You must let me see you to your home," he insisted. "Ninety-first Street is not far out of my way, Miss Murray."

She turned on him a look of intense scrutiny. Then she faltered:

"I don't live there. I gave that address to the policeman, but I live on Fifty-first Street. And here's where we get off," she continued, a moment later.

And, when they were on terra firma again, she added:

"And here is where we part, Mr.— *Jostling*?"

Lord Jocelyn bowed. "But I must at least insist on being permitted to accompany you to your door," he protested. "Really the streets are not safe for you—on account of your attractions," he was going to add, but decided that the acquaintance was too short to permit of such an expression.

She hesitated for an instant. "Well, come along, then," she said, finally, and led the way along a deserted street to a small, old-fashioned house. Drawing a key from her wrist bag she unlocked the door.

"Why, it's all dark," she said, peering into the vestibule. "Alf isn't home yet. Mister

Jostling, I don't want to send you away empty—would you like a glass of wine before you go?"

"I should, immensely," answered Lord Jocelyn, wondering who Alf might be and what relationship he bore to Miss Murray.

"Then you shall have one," the girl answered, leading the way into a dark parlor and lighting a gas jet. She produced wine and glasses from a cupboard, and filled them. "Here's to—to—" she said, laughing.

"To our meeting at the police court tomorrow morning," answered Lord Jocelyn, draining his glass and looking round at the well-furnished but rather gaudy room.

The next moment they heard the sound of a key in the lock of the front door. Its effect upon the girl was electrical. She set down her glass with trembling hands, and looked round her in terror. "O, what shall I do? What will you say?" she gasped. "It's Alf and he'll kill you. He'll kill you, Mr. Jostling. Quick, hide! Anywhere!"

But before Jocelyn could even look round for a refuge a man, heavily built, and having unmistakably the appearance of a prize-fighter, came striding into the room. At the sight of Jocelyn his brows contracted into a scowl and he clenched his fists menacingly.

"Who—who the devil—" he began.

"It's Jake, Jake McGee," cried the girl desperately, looking at Jocelyn sidewise.

The man's brow cleared as if by magic. He strode forward and clenched Jocelyn's hands in a grip that nearly crushed them.

"I'm glad as thunder to meet you, Mr. McGee," he said. "How did you find the house?"

"He got the address from Barney," said the girl promptly. "He just came in a second before you did."

"Just in from Chicago, eh?"

"Last night," said the woman promptly.

"You know we've changed the meeting place?" said the man, turning to Jocelyn. "It's ticklish work, but I think we've outwitted the cops for once. But if you hadn't struck Barney, why I don't know how we'd have got word to you. The inspector swears it won't be pulled off—but he doesn't know we've got Bill's stable on Thirty-second Street."

"O, that's where it is?" asked Jocelyn, feeling his way in the dark.

"Sure. Didn't Barney tell you? He must have been crazy. You won't feel strange, McGee, seeing you'll have to introduce yourself?"

"I suppose there was no other way," Lord Jocelyn answered.

"Well, let's have a whisky and talk things over," said the man, bringing out more glasses and a bottle of Scotch. "Sit down. You stay here, Lizzie; you're in on this deal. Where did you get that English accent, friend?"

"I've just come back from a six months' visit to London," said Jocelyn, watching the girl intently for some cue.

The other poked him in the ribs. "Quit joshing and come to business," he said. "You've bin back a whole year now and you've had time to get rid of it. Honest, McGee, you mean business, don't you? I'd hate like thunder to hurt you, and I'm in the pink of form," he added, frowning at his huge wrists.

"I certainly do mean business," answered Lord Jocelyn.

"Then don't try any monkey games, or it'll be the worse for you. It's a couple of thousand apiece, share and share alike, and you're to drop in the third."

"So I understand," answered Lord Jocelyn, still without a glimmer of understanding.

"Then here's luck to both of us," answered the man, becoming suddenly hilarious. "Barney said I was a fool to do it—said I could whip you easy and take the whole amount, and from the looks of you I guess he's right; but Alf Orme never went back on a deal yet and he ain't going to begin. Here's how!" And he drained his glass, an example which Jocelyn followed. Then he rose to his feet.

"I'll have to be going," he said, apprehensive that Orme might attempt to detain him. But to his surprise the latter agreed.

"Best thing you can do," he answered. "Turn in and get a good night's sleep. And remember, Jake, eight-thirty to the minute at the stable, and go in through the back of the saloon on the other side of the block."

He shook him by the hand, but this time Lord Jocelyn was prepared and returned the grip hard enough to make Alf Orme wince. As he passed out of the door the woman followed him.

"You'll be there?" she whispered in an agitated voice. "You won't go back on me?"

"Not if you wish," answered Lord Jocelyn, more mystified than ever. "What is it?" he added. "A gambling game?"

"Gambling game?" she repeated scornfully. "No, a prize fight. And you're Jake McGee and you're going to meet Alf Orme for a purse of four thousand dollars."

Lord Jocelyn felt decidedly foolish at that moment.

"But—won't they know I'm not McGee?" he faltered.

"Not on your life. It's your first visit to town, and you were unknown until you beat the Blarney Kid in Chicago last month and made a reputation. Nobody here has seen you, and the thing's got to be kept mute as the grave because the police have got wind of it. Say," she continued, grasping him by the arm, "you won't throw me down? Heavens, if Alf learns you aren't McGee he'll kill me sure."

"But what'll I do if the real McGee turns up?"

"He may not learn that the place has been changed. We've got to take chances. If he comes, bluff it out. At the worst you'll clear me all right if only you show up. Alf'll think I was deceived like him. But you've got to be there. Promise me?"

"I promise," answered Jocelyn solemnly; and he passed out of the house and took a taxicab home. Then, since his mind was in a whirl, and he had to meet Alf Orme upon the morrow, he went to bed and was soon wrapped in dreams.

He awoke at nine o'clock, but for several moments he could not quite recall what had happened on the preceding evening. Then as memory slowly came back to him he sat on the edge of his couch and groaned.

"First I've got to give evidence in the police court," he muttered. "And then I've got to fight for four thousand dollars, and run the risk of being half killed as a 'faker,' even if I don't give myself away." He felt the muscles of his arms and took several imaginary punches in the air. At college Lord Jocelyn had been a famous boxer; he was not really afraid of the battle, though his chances of winning seemed infinitesimal. Something else was troubling him, but for a minute he could not discover what it was. Then the recollection came to him, and he groaned out loud.

"And she's married," he cried, in a voice that was half a sob. "She's Alf Orme's wife."

There came a tap at the door and the face of Talbot, his servant, appeared, peering round the jamb. "Did you call, sir?" he asked. "I thought I heard a sound."

"No—yes," Lord Jocelyn answered. "Talbot, what would you do if you made an ass of yourself for a girl and then found that she was somebody else's wife?"

"I'd clear out, sir," answered Talbot. "There was a young woman as lived down Epsom way—"

"Drat your young woman, Talbot. I can't clear out. The police have my address."

"Then, sir, I'd see the thing through," said Talbot sagely.

"You're right, by George," his master answered. "Talbot, my dressing gown. And look alive; I've got to be bathed and dressed in 30 minutes."

"Which you shall be, sir," Talbot replied—and proved his contention.

But the young woman was not at the police court. The case came on at eleven, and her aggressor, now very much the victim, came into the dock a miserable object, his head swathed in bandages. Briefly, Lord Jocelyn gave his evidence, which corroborated that of the policeman.

"Where's the young woman in the case?" the magistrate asked.

"Can't be found, your honor," the policeman answered. "And she don't live at the address she gave."

"Where does the young woman live?" asked the magistrate, turning a suspicious gaze on Jocelyn.

"Your honor, I never saw her in my life before last evening," he answered.

"And the prisoner don't live at the address he gave neither," the policeman continued.

"Well, what have you to say?" the magistrate asked the prisoner, who had been scowling at Jocelyn vindictively. "Why did you stop that woman?"

"I wanted to talk to the lady," he answered sullenly. "I knew her an' I wanted to talk business."

"Then you will tell us where she is to be found."

"That's what I wanted to ask her," the prisoner shouted excitedly. "It's an outrage to knock me down and club me. Why, I could settle both them guys with one hand tied. I—" He broke off and turned a glance upon Jocelyn in which hatred and fury were equally combined.

"Three days in the workhouse," said the magistrate. "Next case." And the man was hustled away, growling and shaking his fists at Jocelyn vindictively.

This part of his duty concluded, Lord Jocelyn walked out of the courtroom moodily. This was only an incident; the hardest part would fall to his lot that evening. A dozen times the plan flashed through his mind not to go, but he dismissed it on each occasion as an unworthy one. If he did not appear Orme's suspicions against his wife would be re-awakened, with what consequences he could

not foresee. But it was better that he should continue with his deceptions now than prove perhaps the innocent cause of a tragedy.

"I wish the silly business were over," he growled, as he entered his apartment.

"Pardon me, sir—a letter," said Talbot, handing him a missive on a salver. Lord Jocelyn took it and broke the envelope. Inside he found a scrawl signed "Elizabeth Orme."

"Forgive me for writing," it said, "but I remembered the address you gave the policeman last night, and I implore you, as the gentleman I know you are, not to turn me down. Alf was drinking last night and grew suspicious. He doubted you were McGee. He hasn't trained, and if you'll only be brave you can put up a good appearance before he knocks you out in the third."

Lord Jocelyn tore the letter to pieces and laughed.

"I wouldn't go down in the third if I were standing up to Johnson himself," he said; and, with the words, a new spirit entered his breast. He would fight, not merely to keep up appearances, but to conquer.

Punctually at the time appointed he made his appearance at the saloon door, and pushing aside the janitor without a word passed through a maze of passages into an anteroom, the office of the stable, in which he found a number of men clustered together. Among them was Alf Orme, in fighting attire, re-clining in a chair, while his second rubbed his limbs. When he saw Jocelyn he bounded out of his chair in delight.

"Here's Jake, boys," he shouted. "Good old Jake, I knew you'd make it. Mr. Barney Jones—Mr. McGee. Barney's your second and you'll find him A1. Come, get your togs off."

Lord Jocelyn stripped and assumed his fighting gear, while Barney looked at him in approval.

"You'll last three rounds," he said, approvingly. "Tell you what, boy, I shouldn't be surprised if you couldn't whip him if you wanted to."

"Hello, Jake, me boy," put in a man in a silk hat, evidently the master of the ceremonies, who had just entered. "Glad to meet you," he said, grasping his hand warmly. "Say, Jake, you don't look as if you'd done much work with them mitts," he added, looking with disapproval at Jocelyn's well-manicured hands.

"He'll do," said Barney. "Jake's the dude all right. How's the house?"

"Fine," said the manager. "Full up and no standing room. Ready, boys? Time, gentles—in with you."

Jocelyn arose lightly out of his chair and followed Orme into a large circular stable, already hazy with tobacco smoke, through which he could dimly descry row upon row of heads surrounding the dais on which he trod. Men were shouting and yelling to him and his opponent from behind the ropes.

"Remember," whispered Barney in his ear, "you fall in the third."

"Unless he falls in the tenth," said Jocelyn, laughing.

Barney stared at him, then nudged him in the ribs. "Go 'long with you, kid," he said. "See here, you'll play fair? The boys would kill you if you didn't, Bo."

"I certainly shall," said Jocelyn; and a moment later he found himself confronting Alf Orme across the ring.

"Time boys," shouted the manager, dancing around inside the ropes. Jocelyn advanced to meet his adversary, felt his hand grasped, and, an instant later, went staggering back under a violent body blow which propelled him against the ropes. As he hung over them for an instant he heard yells of delight from the crowd. "That's sharp practice," he muttered, setting his teeth angrily, and ducked just in time to escape a knockout blow which Orme aimed at his jaw. He dodged under Orme's arm and regained the center of the ring, where he parried several more vicious thrusts until his breath came back to him. Then the round ended and he was led back to his seat.

"Ye'll have to show more fight," whispered Barney, "or they'll think something's crooked. Go into him, Bo. Soak him in the ribs with that right of yours. Time—time."

And now Jocelyn, recovered, faced his enemy with something of the confidence that he had felt at college on many an occasion when, the novelty and stage-fright wearing off, he had aroused enthusiastic plaudits with his science and skill. Orme was fighting viciously, but his blows were wild and his muscles sluggish. Toward the end of the round Jocelyn saw an opening and lunged. He felt his fist thud into Orme's flesh, realized that his adversary was out of training, and found himself standing over a prostrate man, while the crowd howled and yelled.

"Say, that was a good punch all right," Barney whispered as he fanned him. "You drop this time—remember! He'll hit you in the jaw and you take the count—see?"

Jocelyn laughed at the prediction, for he knew now that he was going to win. Orme came up puffing like a motor and there was no force in his blows. As he drove for Jocelyn's chin the latter fell upon him with the force of a cyclone. *Thud, thud, thud,* the blows fell right and left upon his antagonist. Orme staggered back to the ropes, hung there a moment, facing Jocelyn with an expression of astonishment and injury, and slowly rose to receive a blow upon the point of the jaw delivered with all the victor's strength. Alf Orme fell backward and lay with closed eyes like one dead.

The manager bent over him. "One—two—three," he counted, and Orme lay still. "Four—five—six—seven," he continued. Orme's second was dancing round him, screeching at him to rise. Slowly Orme's eyes unclosed. He stared up at the faces vacantly, and the audience shouted itself wild.

"Eight," said the manager. "Nine." There was an almost imperceptible pause. "Ten. I declare Jake McGee the winner."

And Jocelyn, standing in the corner of the ring, was suddenly overwhelmed by his admirers, who burst through the ropes and crowded round him. "Good boy, Jake, bully for you," they shouted. "You got him good. Three cheers for Jake McGee!"

Jocelyn forced his way through to the dressing room, sponged himself and began to put on his clothes. His second seemed to have deserted him. But, as he was completing his toilet, the manager came up, looking black as thunder, and flung a purse into Lord Jocelyn's lap. "Here's your money," he growled. "If you got what was coming to you—"

Lord Jocelyn looked at him inquiringly. "Anything wrong?" he asked.

"Anything wrong?" the manager echoed. "O, no. I'm only ruined, that's all, and serves me right. Ask Barney here."

Barney, white as a sheet, came up to him and shook his fist in his face. "You damned cur," he howled, almost weeping with rage. "To sell us all out like that! To sell us out— and Alf untrained, and as true a man as ever breathed. You got to face Mrs. Orme before you quit, you loafer. If you're ready you can git, and let me tell your fighting days are over."

Jocelyn, too astounded by this tirade to answer, stepped through the door—into the arms of Mrs. Orme.

"So this is how you keep your word to your friends, is it?" she sneered. "Cheap way to make a little bit more, isn't it? And Alf and me with the rent to pay and every coin gone through trusting you."

"Madam," said Jocelyn, "I am wholly at a loss to understand you. Do you suppose that I came here to fight for the pleasure of it, or to oblige you?"

"You robber!" she hissed. "Didn't you know you were fixed to lose? Didn't I hear Alf tell you himself and you say you'd play fair? And that was to have meant two thousand to us, and Alf not to trouble to train; and you've bin and trained and hogged the whole kitty."

Then for the first time Jocelyn understood the meaning of Barney's insinuations about the third round. He drew the purse from his pocket. Inside he found eight bills of the value of five hundred dollars apiece.

"Madam," he said, "let me assure you that the whole thing was a misunderstanding." He counted out four bills. "Here is your share," he said, and thrust them into her hand. Then, while she stood, stared open-mouthed at him and at the bills alternately, he made his way into the street, eluding the mob that sought to follow him, and made his way home.

"That'll keep me going for a few days," he said, putting the remainder of his winnings away. "And now for a game of solitaire before I got to bed."

Jocelyn was so stiff the next day that he kept to his bed. On the second he was limping around his room. The unwonted exercise of the muscles, disused for several years, had painfully affected him, and he was grateful enough to be able to prop himself up in his chair and play solitaire. By the third evening, however, he was sufficiently recovered to think of taking a stroll, and he had just found his cane and hat when there came a ring at his bell.

"There's a man wants to see you, sir," said Talbot, entering. "Looks like a tramp. Shall I say you're not at home, sir?"

"Why, I love tramps," answered Lord Jocelyn. "Ask him in by all means." And presently there entered, dirty, unshaven, scowling, the man whom he had knocked down and afterward seen sentenced to the workhouse.

"Sit down, sir," Jocelyn said, handing him a chair. "To what am I indebted for the honor of this visit?"

"Aw, don't hand me none of that," his visitor growled. "You put the job through on me and I ain't got no more to say about it. What I want is Lizzie Orme's address."

"If you mean the lady whom you so grossly insulted the other evening," said Lord

Jocelyn, "I certainly shall not give it to you unless you can show just cause."

"Just cause?" shouted his visitor indignantly. "What? Me just in from Chicago, and not knowing where to find no one, and sighting Liz in the street—and then to get knocked down in the gutter by a guy as I could settle with one hand behind me back? Ain't that just cause? If I hadn't have seen her and recognized her from her photograph, I'd a trod the streets till Doomsday and never known where the fight was to be pulled off."

"Your name?" gasped Jocelyn.

"Is Jake McGee, if it's any satisfaction to you," answered the man.

Jocelyn arose and went to his desk. Unlocking a drawer he pulled out four bills of the value of five hundred dollars apiece and thrust them into his visitor's hand.

"Her address is 666 Fifty-first Street," he said, "and she will tell you why these belong to you. Don't say a word, please," he continued, urging his visitor out. He closed the door on him and then turned back and opened it. McGee was standing in a sort of trance at the head of the stairs. "Tell Mrs. Orme I'm through with all of you and I don't want to see you again," he said. "Now, in the expressive vernacular of this country, beat it."

And McGee obeyed.

Lord Jocelyn stretched himself out upon his lounge and yawned.

"I certainly did spend that four thousand quickly," he said, groaning as the cramp seized his aching limbs. "No more adventures in the lower world for me. Talbot! Bring me a whisky and soda and a new bottle of liniment!"

THE DEVIL CHAIR
A Chronicle of the Strange Adventures of John Haynes and His Gyroscope Vehicle

THE CRIPPLE OF PROSPECT PARK
St. Louis Post-Dispatch (27 September 1913)

Patrolman Daniel O'Sullivan, standing on the west side of Prospect Park, Brooklyn, twirled his club and yawned. It was mid-day and the end of his period of duty was approaching. In ten minutes, he reflected, he would be hurrying homeward to snatch a rest in the bosom of his family within the six-room flat which he modestly sustained in the region of Flatbush.

He yawned again, not so much from weariness as by reason of a happy state of complete mental relaxation. At that moment Patrolman O'Sullivan felt at perfect peace with all the world. If at that instant a member of the Clancy gang had assailed him with an outburst of profanity against the land of his nativity,

Patrolman O'Sullivan would have tapped him mildly across the hat and bidden him go home.

"By the powers!" he ejaculated joyfully, seeing a brother officer approaching him, "there's Mulcahey at last. Hey, Mul, git busy on the patrol. I'm for Klapperkopf's joint and a schooner of beer to wash the dust away!"

Mulcahey approached leisurely and relieved him; the two men engaged in a friendly joust of words, and Patrolman O'Sullivan turned his face resolutely eastward. The thought of the schooner smoothed out the wrinkles in his forehead and an anticipatory grin made itself visible about his mouth and extended its purview into the neighborhood of O'Sullivan's ears. Suddenly he paused and turned round, extending his right arm in the direction of the roadway.

"Holy saints, Mul, what the divil would yez call that?" he asked.

Moving slowly along the curb there came a cripple in a chair, which he was laboriously propelling by means of a hand-wheel. But as the patrolman walked in a leisurely fashion to intercept it, they perceived that it was like no other cripple's chair which had ever come within range of their vision. To begin with, it was shaped like an old-fashioned infant's "perambulator;" that is to say, it was broad at the back and tapered in front to a wedge, tipped with a rim of steel, which gave it the forcible aspect of a miniature battering ram. It moved, apparently, by some hidden mechanical power, for under the seat was a steel-cased receptacle of considerable size, from whose hidden interior proceeded a faint humming sound exactly reminiscent of that made by a top whirling at full speed. O'Sullivan, as he bent low to examine the nature of this contrivance, knew immediately that the mechanism concealed within the case was not only extremely powerful, but was working at full speed, though it was in some way disconnected from the motive power of the chair, so that the latter could move forward at its pace of two miles an hour, propelled solely by the cripple's arms. So fast came the separate explosions of the gas engine, which was evidently a part of this complex arrangement, that they were merged into a single rolling sound.

"What the divil's thot, Jack?" exclaimed O'Sullivan profanely, rising slowly from the exertion of bending his comfortably covered body beneath the chair.

From the cushions a strange figure raised itself and regarded him. The occupant was a man of perhaps forty years. He was evidently a gentleman, although the blue suit that he wore was cheap and frayed and his wrists were innocent of cuffs. Mulcahey, whose mind did not turn toward mechanics, as did that of his friend, observed the peculiar pallor of the occupant's face. "Prison pallor," he thought immediately, and the closely cropped hair and stubble of a new beard confirmed in his own mind the last awakening suspicions that he was forming. His glance turned toward the man's limbs. The legs hung limply as a paralytic's, and were evidently powerless. But what struck him most strangely were the arms. For while the left was, if anything, rather under-developed, the right was that of a Samson. Under the frayed sleeve Mulcahey could trace the outlines of the great muscles, rippling up from the wrist, and then the protruding biceps, and under the arm, the triceps, rigid as steel. The man perceived his gaze and withdrew his right arm, flushing slightly as he did so.

"Now, who is he?" pondered Mulcahey. "I'd like to know. There's something queer about that fellow." His intuition struck home with the conviction of a fact. He determined that he would keep him in sight so long as he was on his post, but without awakening suspicions.

Meanwhile the cripple was answering O'Sullivan's questions.

"This is my chair, sir," he said courteously, and in well bred tones which at once lulled the patrolman's suspicions to sleep. "I have been injured, as you can see, and have come here to meet Mr. Staples at one o'clock, when he returns to his house."

O'Sullivan was impressed. Mr. Staples, the multi-millionaire, who had begun his career as a poor lawyer and was now director of numerous western land companies, was a name to be respected. He did glance for a moment at the cripple's shabby coat, but reflected that many queer people came from all parts of the country to interview Mr. Staples, and so dismissed all further thought of the matter.

"Well, Mul, I'll see yez again," he said, and started off, twirling his club joyously, his mouth watering as he thought of that foaming schooner in which he was so soon to plunge it. But something about the chair was worrying him, and he had hardly proceeded three paces when it grew clear to him. He swung around. It seemed incredible, but—the chair was actually supported upon a single wheel!

O'Sullivan had worked as a mechanic before he joined the "force," and was never satisfied until all manner of mechanism was made clear to him. That he had failed consciously to notice this astonishing phenomenon before was simply because his mind had never conceived the possibility of its existence. He looked again; yes, the chair stood bolt upright upon a single wheel.

"Mul! Mul!" he shouted. "Look here, me lad. Did yez iver see a chair that ran on one wheel before?"

Mulcahey looked again. Surely enough, his friend was right. O'Sullivan placed his powerful hands upon the side and tried to tilt the apparatus. His effort was as useless as though he had attempted to tilt St. Patrick's cathedral. The chair did not budge in the least, but remained still upon the sidewalk, perfectly motionless, and, as it seemed, busily humming itself to sleep.

"Hey! Beat it!" shouted Mulcahey, turning upon the curious crowd that had begun to assemble round the uncanny vehicle. He drove them away and then turned to the cripple again, scowling crossly. "You'll have to move on, young feller," he said. "Keep her a-moving and don't collect a crowd, or I'll run you and your chair into the station house."

The cripple returned no answer, but began slowly propelling his strange vehicle along the road that borders the park in the direction of Mr. Staples' house. He moved at his two-mile gait, and a small crowd followed him; but as he made no answer to their badinage, they tired of worrying him and dispersed, with the exception of a few small boys, who ran alongside, jeering. Officer O'Sullivan remained standing beside his friend in an attitude of indecision. At last he drew the back of his hand across his mouth with a gesture of finality.

"Mul," he said, "they say as it's a wise cop knows when he's off duty—but that gets my goat. Something's going to happen. I feel it in me. And I'm going to stay and see it through."

Much as he needed the liquid refreshment which had presented its mental picture so alluringly to his mind, O'Sullivan felt that he could not go home until he had solved the mystery of that chair. He could think of no mechanical law which would enable it to balance itself upon a single wheel with such tenacity that, with the exertion of his utmost strength, he was unable to disturb its equilibrium. What was the hidden mechanism which gave out that buzzing sound? Suppose this were to be connected at will with the running gear! Suppose, for example, that, hidden under the seat of the chair, was a powerful gas engine, capable of exercising sufficient force to convert it, with a sharp wedge-like front, into a battering ram and hurling it at thirty miles an hour through the crowded streets of the metropolis! A vista of possibilities stretched before O'Sullivan's mind. Muttering uneasily, he left Mulcahey and started in pursuit of the cripple, with the intention of questioning him further.

"Aw, it's only a bicycle chair!" exclaimed the other in disgust at his friend's curiosity, which he felt, in some vague way, to be a reflection upon his lack of interest. "What's biting you, Danny? Come back!" But O'Sullivan was already out of hearing and crossing the road in the cripple's wake, pausing only long enough to shoo away the pestilential small boys that dogged the trail of his quarry. A glance back showed that Mulcahey had changed his mind and was coming after him.

But to the disgust of both patrolmen the cripple's chair seemed to take on a sudden acceleration of motion. O'Sullivan walked faster. Yes, there was no doubt of it. Although to his eye the wheel did not seem to be revolving more rapidly, yet the distance between himself and the peculiar vehicle was materially increased. Then, remembering that the man would undoubtedly stop at Mr. Staples' house, he proceeded more slowly and permitted Mulcahey to catch up with him.

They were about five hundred yards behind when the chair came to a stop outside the millionaire's residence. They saw the crippled figure leave it and move painfully up the steps with the aid of two crutches. Long before they had come up the door had closed on the man and, when at last they arrived, the empty chair was buzzing amiably upon the curb.

"I guess this story was straight enough—there's no use waiting, Mul," said Patrolman O'Sullivan. Mulcahey shook his head doubtfully. He was not sure; he was not by any means sure that, even if the cripple's exit were orderly and peaceful, he would not arrest him on the chance of having picked up an ex-convict. But even while he debated, the front door flew open and the cripple came hurrying down the stairs with the aid of his crutches, while from within the hall resounded the screams of the maids, mingled with the shouts of the financier.

As the patrolman dashed to seize the fellow, Staples came bounding down the steps.

"Arrest him!" he yelled, purple with fury. "He's an escaped convict and he's got five thousand dollars of mine, damn him, in his coat pocket. Held me up with a pistol and made me open my safe. Hold him!"

"We're holding him," answered Mulcahey grimly, as he clutched the man by the collar, while O'Sullivan extracted from his pockets a bulging wallet and a revolver. "Loaded in every chamber!" he exclaimed, inspecting it. "Hey, youse must be mad, young feller. This ain't no wild west show—this is Brooklyn!"

The cripple's face remained entirely impassive as the policeman bundled him back into his chair. Followed by the wrathful cries of the financier, they prepared to wheel him to the station house.

"My money!" cried Mr. Staples. "I identify that! He stole it from me a minute ago."

"Sorry, Mr. Staples," replied Mulcahey respectfully, "but you'll have to get it from the sergeant, sir. That's the law, Mr. Staples, and I'll have to take it with me. You can reclaim it any time, sir," he continued. "Or if you care to come along now—"

He had turned his back on the chair as he began to speak, while O'Sullivan, holding the pistol and the wallet, was pushing back the crowd which had instantly assembled, his arm resting upon the hand-wheel in order to keep the vehicle motionless. Of a sudden, quick as a flash, the cripple's mighty right arm shot forth and clutched him as in a vise; an instant later, and the chair had shot down the street with the force of a tornado, the wedge-front scattering the mob right and left, hurling them upon the sidewalk and into the street. As O'Sullivan went down he felt the wallet torn from his clutch; before he could recover self-possession enough to fire, the vehicle was nowhere in sight; only far down the road a spiral column of dust showed the course it had taken.

The two patrolmen stared dismally at one another; Mulcahey from the road, where he lay, dusty and torn. From the steps above, Mr. Staples stormed for his money.

O'Sullivan held up a bleeding hand. It looked as though it had been torn by pincers of steel.

"It's gone, Mul," he said in hollow tones. "He got it away from me. My God, he must have been traveling at fifty miles an hour."

Mulcahey laughed derisively. "Fifty miles, eh?" he said, sneering. "Don't you suppose I'd hit him if he'd been going at fifty? Why, that was two hundred if it was one; the fellow was out of sight before I could draw me gun."

Then, dashing through the immense crowd which had blocked the roadway, he ran into a nearby telephone booth.

"Hello! Mr. Frank Staples has been held up and robbed at No. 3742 Prospect Park West by a man in an auto, wedge-shaped, running on a single wheel. Got that? Yes, a single wheel. Machine is making for Fulton Street down Flatbush, meaning, of course, to cross into Manhattan and gain the country. Telephone all stationary posts and branch offices; call the bridge, Manhattan side, and have ropes stretched across the carriage road and footway or he'll get free. You've got less than three minutes to do it in."

He hung up the receiver and slouched back like a broken man, as indeed, he felt himself to be. This meant the finish of his career as a member of the police force. "Three minutes!" he muttered viciously. "Three seconds, more like. I'll bet he's over the bridge already. Unless—" he added, with a glimmer of hope— "he's had a collision."

But the man in the chair was too sagacious to collide with any vehicle that afternoon; the slightest jar of wheel against wheel would have plunged him, traveling at that fearful rate to immediate death. And it was by reason of this sagaciousness that in point of fact the police actually were enabled to stretch ropes across the middle of the Brooklyn Bridge before the strange vehicle arrived.

As soon as he had shaken off his pursuers and passed from the quiet residential section into the traffic-haunted region of Flatbush Avenue the cripple displayed a singular indifference, as though he were supremely confident of his ability both to outwit and to outrun his enemies. He had sped toward Flatbush Avenue at the rate of a hundred and fifty miles an hour, whirling so fast that he was completely hidden from sight in the clouds of dust flung up by the wheel. But when he reached that artery of traffic he had slowed down to not more than fifty miles. He whizzed past the traffic policeman who attempted to stay his progress, turned into a maze of small side streets, constantly diminishing his speed, and finally emerged upon Court Street, gliding no faster than a man on a bicycle. He looked right and left for the fraction of a second as he neared Fulton Street. It had been his intention to return across the Brooklyn Bridge to Manhattan, but he had not calculated upon the presence of the two policemen, and it occurred to him that others might be waiting for him at the other end. But that risk was smaller than the one which would ensue should he become isolated upon Long Island in a cordon, and so

he swung into Fulton Street and headed toward the East River, traveling at about twenty miles an hour. The wheel glided upon a rail of the car tracks, to which it adhered immediately without a single guiding motion of the driver's arm, and the pace began automatically to increase immediately. But the route became obscured by the approach of an up-town car, and the cripple swung his chair off the line again, upon which he had run merely as a test, and proceeded in a leisurely manner past Clark and Pineapple streets and so to the bridge entrance, where he disconnected his running gear and began to move by hand power toward the passenger track that crosses the center of the bridge.

None of the crowd was idle enough at that hour to examine the strange-looking vehicle closely, and it was obvious from the lack of interest which the wayfarers displayed, that the news of the robbery had not yet become public property. The cripple patted his pocket as he moved deftly through the crowd toward the bridge footway. There, snuggly ensconced in the leather wallet which he had taken from Mr. Staples lay five thousand dollars in bills—his money, long overdue, of which he had been robbed when Staples had aided the land gang to railroad him to prison five years before. But he would not let his mind dwell upon that for the present, lest his anger invalidate his judgment; just now he must concentrate all his forces upon the endeavor to escape. And, once across the bridge and safe in Manhattan, he knew that nothing could prevent his progress.

He had threaded the crowds and was moving toward the footway when he heard shouts behind him. The news had just been telephoned to the stationary policemen on duty at that point, one of the fat elderly policemen who are detailed in their last years of duty to the lighter offices. The man was racing after him, puffing heavily as he ran. His tunic was unbuttoned and in one hand he held a heavy revolver, which he pointed as he ran, with no sure aim.

"Stop!" he yelled. "Stop right there or I'll fill you full of lead."

In the depths of the chair the cripple had another revolver, but he did not attempt to seize it. He had no quarrel with the officers of the law—only with the men who had leagued together to obtain his inheritance and put him away in the penitentiary at Nokomis Falls. He heard the hiss of bullets pass his ear and, with a turn of his wrists, connected the running gear of the chair with the top-like mechanism within. The chair shot forward with a bound. Ahead of it lay a flight of steps, a formidable obstacle for the best auto-bicycle to have attempted to surmount. The policeman ran on, waving his revolver, reloading hastily as he proceeded, certain that the cripple would come to grief if he attempted to negotiate that obstacle. He had him fairly trapped. On either side lay the parapet of the footway, there remained nothing but surrender. He stopped to recover breath; and two brother officers from the Adams Street station, who had received the summons a few minutes before, came panting up to join him. Then all three gasped in wonder.

For with a series of light, curveting plunges, resembling those of a graceful colt, the chair leaped upward on its single wheel and, surmounting the steps, began to run easily at about fifty miles an hour across the bridge.

The way seemed clear. But, even as the chair gained the summit and raced forward, the cripple saw a body of police come running across the bridge toward him. They were from the Manhattan end, and, not content with stretching ropes to bring him to grief, had resolved to intercept him and gain the credit for his capture. On they ran, five abreast, thrusting the pedestrians aside, their revolvers to their hands, and barely a hundred yards distant.

The cripple stopped the chair dead and looked back. Behind him, not more than sixty yards away, the three Brooklyn policemen were in pursuit, led by the stout, elderly fellow who had fired at him ineffectually. As the chair stopped, with grinding and jarring of brakes that flung the cripple forward against the wedge front, the three men aimed again. But they did not dare to fire, for fear of hitting the policemen who were approaching from the opposite direction, and so ran forward, yelling to their quarry to surrender.

The cripple hesitated. To charge full tilt into the advancing men would undoubtedly kill them; but it might kill him. Besides, a chair is not an easy mark to miss, when it is advancing immediately upon one, whatever its speed, especially by five policemen, each firing a number of rounds, and each presumably practiced in the use of the revolver. The man looked upward. The immensely long loops of the steel cables, enclosed in their chilled steel casing, which held up the gigantic structure, lowered themselves here to a point barely five feet above the ground. Without further hesitation the cripple skipped nimbly out of the chair, clinging for support to the ironwork of the structure. Then, stretching forth his powerful right arm, he hoisted himself upon the cable, clinging there like some disabled monkey upon perch. The policemen yelled in triumph and precipitated themselves toward him from before and behind. The nearest was barely five and twenty yards away. The last was less than forty.

The cripple laughed shortly, and, clinging now by the left hand, reached down and grasped the chair firmly with his right. Then, when his pursuers were almost upon him, they saw the muscles of his right stand out like loops of rope, saw him pick up the chair, and deposit it upon the narrow six-inch cable in front of him. It stood there, buzzing like a top and motionless, and, while the policemen stood still in amazement, the cripple climbed in, not budging the chair by a fraction of an inch, and was speeding away.

And looking at him, they did not even fire.

Not that they could have hit him even if they had tried. But awe, and something as nearly akin to terror as a New York policeman can feel restrained them. For this crippled man in the crazy car was soaring away, far over their heads, climbing to the very summit of the high structure along that six-inch cable, till at last he seemed no more than a black spot against the blue sky, running with security at the rate of an express train, with a drop of hundreds of feet into the river on one side of him, and, on the other, a fall to certain death upon the structure of the bridge.

He seemed to soar like an eagle; he reached the topmost tower, and then, seeing the pathway under him heavy with stalled cars, and the roadway black with cheering, gasping spectators—seeing, too, the ropes which had been ineffectually stretched forth to hold him, he laughed, waved his hand genially, and, at a tremendously accelerated pace, began to glide down the cable line that stretched to the Manhattan entrance.

He reached the end of it, traveling as steadily as a bicyclist, hit the asphalt with a gentle jolt twelve feet behind the little group of police who had idly gathered there, staring across the bridge, not thinking to glance upward; shot over the loops of the street car lines, and dashed into Park Row. Across the City Hall park he raced, crossed Broadway

under the horses' noses, reached the river front, where nothing but slow-moving wagons blocked the wide street, and dashed northward at a rate of a hundred miles an hour. He reached the extreme limits of Manhattan, crossed into Westchester, and, like a streak of light, he entered the suburban districts, passed them, and so gained open country and was lost to the knowledge of all.

Ten minutes later he stopped the chair under a tree, descended, and bathed his face and hands in the water of a gurgling brook. That was the first of his exploits and there was much yet to be done. Vengeance on all who had banded against him, broken up his home, thrust him for five lonely years into the western jail—this must be meted out. But now, having regained a tiny fraction of his own, he had funds with which to start on his immediate quest, the discovery of his daughter Eleanor. She had been fourteen when he last saw her; now she must be nearly twenty. The thought of seeing her again gave him new hope. He entered the chair, and at the leisurely pace of fifteen miles an hour, set off toward the north, along the old post road.

THE LEAGUE OF LOST CAUSES
Being the Romantic Adventures of Paul Lane, American Millionaire

THE WOMAN FROM THE SEA
Stevens Point Journal (18 October 1913)

Paul Lane felt utterly dispirited as he ascended the front steps of his cottage on the Long Island shore that Friday afternoon in mid-autumn, with two days of leisure in front of him before he should resume his daily labor with its monotonous toil.

It was not that he hated work or craved a life of ignoble ease and pleasure. Philosophically inclined, even before he left college he had discerned the futility of the search after happiness. Contentment, he knew, must be the reward of work. But this—this eternal toil in a New York office, adding millions to millions for the aggrandizement of the monopoly which his father had built up—this was what appalled him. In other lands a man situated as he was might enter politics, devote his life and fortune to his country; here—well, his country could get along very well without his assistance. In the vast and varied public life of America his efforts would be lost, his ambitions crushed out by daily disappointments and the sordid strife of the political world. He saw no future of contentment for him in the land of his birth; he, with his millions, looked forward to fewer opportunities than the poorest and most illiterate immigrant passing beneath the Statue of Liberty.

Many times a millionaire at the age of thirty he had succeeded to the control of his father's enormous business. He fulfilled his duties punctiliously, sedulously, but without heart. And his weekends he spent alone in his cottage on the northern Long Island shore, among his books, reading, dreaming, or wandering by the barren, desolate marshes and the surf-swept shores of the Sound, while his magnificent town house remained closed and his automobile rusted, unused in his garage.

Half a mile from his isolated house he stopped, awaking out of his meditations to discover that he could no longer see his way. A death-white fog, one of the sea-borne fogs of November, had shrouded the land, blotting out all the familiar landmarks. Lane drew in great breaths of it greedily. It reminded him of London, with its mystery and its charm, of melancholy France, when the leafless poplars glisten with white frost beside the Seine. His years abroad had been too few though vivid in incident. Something of his dejection fell from him as the pictures stirred in his mind and painted themselves upon his memory in vivid colors anew. Some day, when he decently could, he would shake off the cares of his life, resign the business into other hands, and withdraw to that life of leisure which he loved in other lands.

Suddenly he heard the booming of a gun over the waters. It sounded like the signal of some ship in distress. That was a treacherous shore near the east end of the Island, and one on which ships often came to grief, for the long, oily billows hid the menacing rocks which threatened vessels. Although it was far less than a hundred miles from the metropolis, this region might have been a remote part of the New England shore; it was out of the track of passing ships; a little, forgotten space devoted to sea birds and hunters.

Then over the waves came something strident and shrill, hooting like a steam siren and shrieking like an approaching cable car. And out of the void fell something not fifty yards away that plunged into the sand and flung up a smoking hillock. Lane walked quickly toward this object; as he approached he heard the booming sound once more.

When he came up he saw that it was a fifty-pound shell from a man-of-war's gun that had burst asunder there and buried itself in the sand. The shell had fallen before the booming began; sound traveled slowly; he calculated that the warship must be about three miles in the offing. She was evidently some vessel that had lost her bearings in the fog and was attempting to target practice notwithstanding.

That might be a rational explanation, but— suddenly the thought came to him: was ever target practice held in the waters of Long Island Sound before? Though that especial region was out of the track of ships, numerous small craft traversed the waters, to gather oysters or lay them down on the marine oyster farms. Surely no man-of-war ever engaged in target practice in that populous, landlocked sea.

Again a distant scream rose into a clangorous din, and, as the boom of the gun followed, a shell ploughed up the sand, this time falling further away, but scattering more widely. Lane might have hastened from the spot without imputation upon his courage; and so he would probably have done, but at that moment the fog lifted.

He stared out at a stretch of undulating, gray sea, rippling away toward the horizon. Half a mile out, just where the crests of the Rip Rocks emerge from the waves, a small steamship lay on her side, grinding to pieces slowly under the incessant pounding of the waters. And, further away, a hulk low down on the horizon, were the black outlines of a man-of-war.

The warship was evidently shelling the steamship. This much was evident, for the trajectory of her shells was immediately over the latter. And it was equally clear that the steamship was no abandoned target destined to be battered by navy guns, for Lane could distinguish tiny figures that moved hither and thither upon the decks, swarming toward the boats, which they were frantically endeavoring to lower over the side. All was confusion aboard. Another shell hurled forth, falling short of the shore; another, and a pillar of smoke rose out of the steamship's sides. Then, even as Lane watched, he saw that one of the boats was lowered at last; and the fog descended again.

It was incredible that such an episode could occur off the Long Island shore. Where were the warships of the United States, to avenge her outraged majesty? Had war broken out, and was this warship one of a hostile battle fleet already engaged in ruining the shipping of the country and devastating her ports? Lane stood peering out through the blank mists, vainly endeavoring to penetrate the mystery.

He must have stood there fully five minutes when he heard the splashing of oars, the shout of voices, challenging cries. Then the sharp crack of a rifle whipped the air, and through the opacity of the fog a boat's nose bore in toward the land and the keel grated upon the sandy bottom. Two men and a woman leaped to their feet, sprang into the sea, and began wading through the shallows. The men were sailors, roughly clad; the woman, who was heavily veiled, was dressed in costly clothes. From her ears hung loops of gold, set each with a single pearl of brilliant luster, and her fingers were encircled with rings. Lane sprang into the sea and offered her his hand; when she took it he saw that it was the hand of a lady who had never done any manual work in her life.

"Save me, Monsieur!" she gasped, in French, and, seeing that he understood, she added, "Take me ashore—to some place of safety. I can pay anything!" She clutched at a little purse strapped inside her belt. The two men stood by, a little sheepishly, though casting alarmed glances from moment to moment out through the fog.

Cries were heard again, and through the murk the sharp nose of a ship's cutter appeared. It was manned by a half dozen sailors in uniform, commanded by a bearded officer, evidently of high rank. The woman looked at them, turned suddenly, and began running across the sand. Lane, intensely curious, but more concerned for safety, did not stop to parley. He took her hand in his and ran with her, leaving the two sailors to their own devices. In a moment the two were running alone in the fog, which closed in a damp, dripping cloak, on every side. They heard the shouts of their pursuers as they spread out and stumbled blindly through the mists in search of them. But the strangers were ignorant of the shore. They did not know that wall of heaped up stones that separated the farming land from the sand's encroachments. That was their stumbling block; before they could regain their feet and ascertain how the land lay Lane and his charge had gained the level road and were running toward the cottage under the hill.

The shouting died away. They had eluded their pursuers. Once in his own demesne, Lane felt that the girl was safe, and anger replaced curiosity. He had been made to run as though he had been a schoolboy stealing fruit. The one servant whom he kept in his little waterside retreat of his was away for the afternoon and there was no human habitation within a mile or more. He was alone with this strange woman from the sea, dramatically alone with her, and feeling uncommonly perturbed and foolish. She, meanwhile, calmly took off her veil. When Lane turned toward her he found himself face to face with a young woman of not more than two or three and twenty years. She was beautiful—but that was the least of her charms. There was on her face an expression of high breeding, of dignity, something of hauteur, but everything that was altogether fine. She smiled as he gazed frankly into her eyes; her own scrutiny of him seemed to have been equally satisfactory.

"If you will pardon me, Mademoiselle," said Lane, "I will get my fowling gun. Those robbers, those pirates—"

She sat down, laughing. "Robbers!" she exclaimed. "That officer, Monsieur, is a captain in the Imperial Austrian navy."

"Then you, Mademoiselle—" Lane began, and checked himself. Her features seemed to have frozen. She looked through him as though he had been an underling. He understood that they could not meet on a common footing in her opinion; she must be at least of noble birth, and probably looked on him merely as a convenient medium of assistance.

"Sit down, Monsieur, and let me speak," she said coldly. "As for those sailors, they will not dare to lay a finger on me, nor Captain von Holzrath either." She pulled the little purse from her belt, opened it, hesitated, and then replaced it. "I was about to offer you money," she said, "but I see that you are a gentlemen. I appeal to your goodness instead."

Lane remained standing. He bowed gravely at her words but attempted no answer.

"I am a person of rank in my country," continued the girl with a faint smile, "of very high rank. I found it necessary to visit America upon a certain errand. My government objected to this mission of mine and sent a battleship in pursuit of the steamer on which I had taken passage. You know the rest. Happily I succeeded in reaching land, and I have no doubt that the warship is now speeding away seaward, for even the audacity of Captain von Holzrath would go no further than the firing of a few shells in American waters. I do not think he will molest us. So now I want you to put me in touch with the person whom I have come to see."

"If that be possible, Mademoiselle, I will do so," said Lane. "What is his name?"

"His name," answered the girl slowly, "is Paul Lane."

"I am Paul Lanc," answered her companion.

The girl made no reply but looked at him scornfully.

"Evidently you disbelieve me, Madam," Paul said. "May I inquire the reason for your disbelief? Will my visiting cards suffice to prove my identity?" He opened his card case; it was empty. He stared at it in chagrin and then hung his head like a schoolboy. Over the girl's features a faint smile spread once more.

"If you are Paul Lane," she said, "you are undoubtedly acquainted with Monsieur Rosny, of Paris?"

"Rosny!" exclaimed the other. "The agent of the Orleans family? Jean Rosny, of Breton-sur-Marne?"

The girl looked at him in consternation.

"You are really Paul Lane?" she murmured in embarrassment. "A thousand pardons, Monsieur. But—are you not rich, a millionaire? If this is your house, where are your automobiles, your servants?"

"Ah, Mademoiselle, not every American cares for those things," he answered. "I have, I believe, seven automobiles in the garage of my city home. But I have not seen them for seven months now."

The girl sprang to her feet and extended her hands impulsively.

"Veritably, you are Paul Lane, just as he was described to me," she said. "Monsieur Lane, how can I express my regrets for my mistrust of you? You knew Monsieur Rosny two years ago," she resumed. "You spoke to him of your desire to devote your millions to certain causes; he had not forgotten. Your name had been a familiar one among our circle during all the time that has elapsed since you last saw him. And so I have come to you to petition that you follow the former impulse of your nature, Monsieur. If riches have not corrupted you, you will obey that inner call that you have heard."

Lane looked out through the window at the drifting fog clouds, the low, sandy shore, growing more visible each moment, the long deserted stretches of desolate country; and suddenly there revived in him the impulse to taste that fullness of life when, for three months, he had been closer than a brother to Jean Rosny, the leader of the Orleans conspiracy which was being formed against the government of France to re-establish her ancient kings and renew her greatness. He felt shaken to the depths.

"I will obey that call," he said in a low voice, and raised her hand to his lips.

"Then let me speak quickly," said the girl, "for at any moment we may be interrupted. He cannot hurt me now, but assuredly Captain von Holzrath will not leave these shores until he has talked with me. You are agreed with Monsieur Rosny that certain things are true; that the history of the last century has been one of gigantic blunders. We have reversed the traditions of our fathers, and all the ills of the modern world are due to them." She spoke like a prophetess; her bosom heaved and her eyes flashed as the words poured from her lips. "You are agreed, Monsieur, that it was only under the rule of their ancient kings that the peoples prospered, that democracy, with its drab equality, has removed all purpose, all poetry, all happiness from life. We have formed a league, then, the League of Lost Causes, for the re-establishment of the ancient orders, and our adherents are numerous in every country of Europe. But we need money to finance our appeal. Will you assist us, Monsieur Lane? Will you venture your wealth and offer us your personal aid? The reward is danger, such as a man should love, and hardship, and perhaps a shameful death; but there are also other rewards awaiting one courageous enough to venture all in such a cause."

The heart of Paul Lane leaped in his breast and his soul went out in answer to her appeal.

"Yes, I will venture all," he answered. "And now—"

"One moment," said the girl. "There are certain traditions of chivalry which we believe in and in which you must believe. We live in different ages, you and I; nevertheless we must meet on this common ground. The man who serves our cause must give everything and ask nothing; he must obey orders until he has proved his fitness to serve. You must serve without question; you must ask nothing, not even my name."

"Your name!" exclaimed Paul. "But, Mademoiselle, how am I to meet you again, how—"

"You will go to Paris, to Jean Rosny," she answered. "There you will learn much that is now unknown to you. Our League has grown incredibly strong during the past two years. Kings are members of it; other kings are united against us. Someday, perchance, when we have succeeded you shall know—"

Steps sounded on the graveled walk outside. Paul Lane ran to the window. The officer of the boat was coming toward the house, but alone. There was no sign of any of his men. The fog rolled away and the sea lay blue under the declining sun. There was no trace of the battleship. But for the deserted steamer, pounding away her life upon the rocks, Paul Lane might have thought that all had been a dream—but for these things and the approach of Captain von Holzrath.

He went to the door and knocked; he stood there until Paul admitted him. Neither man asked any questions of the other. The officer entered the room in which the girl was standing, Paul at his heels.

Captain von Holzrath bowed very low, clicking his heels, and addressed the girl in German. Paul did not understand that language; he noted however, the deference of the officer and the girl's scorn of him. He seemed to be pleading with her, spreading out his hands as he spoke in a deprecatory fashion, while her replies were as those of a mistress to a servant. Their conversation was animated and prolonged. At last the girl turned to Paul.

"Tell him," she said scornfully, and speaking for the first time in English, with a slight and pleasant accent—"tell him that this is free soil and that he cannot drag me hence with all the battleships of the Austrian navy."

Paul told him. He added:

"Perhaps you do not know, sir, that by firing upon a peaceful steamship in these waters you have violated international law. You can be hanged as a pirate. I hope you will be."

The officer stared at Paul coldly but did not deign to respond. He turned and addressed himself to the girl again. He pleaded earnestly and volubly with her. She shook her head and stamped her foot angrily, pointing to the door and bidding him be gone. At last he desisted and turned to Paul again.

"I hope that we shall meet again some day, sir, under different circumstances," he said threateningly, and flung his card down on the table.

"There is no time like the present," answered Paul angrily, and tore the scrap of cardboard into fragments. The officer laid his hand upon his sword; he seemed about to draw on the other, but after a moment's pause, turned instead and made his way toward the door. Paul watched him silently as he went down the graveled path toward the seashore. He disappeared beneath the wall of stone, to reappear a little later upon the marge of the sea, where now the ship's cutter lay, manned by the sailors.

He stepped in and, very rhythmically, the oars began to propel the boat from the shore. It rounded the point of rocks and disappeared. The sea was very still. When Paul turned back into the room the girl had disappeared.

She had gone silently from his presence while he, in a day-dream, stared through the window; gone like a wraith, leaving behind her only a little glove and the faint essence of some perfume. Paul ran to the door. She was not in the hall. She was not in the house. He ran to the back.

There, in the distance, he saw a little figure making its way carefully over the rocks and roots that strewed the branch road toward Farmingville, the nearest station on the Long Island Railroad. His first impulse was to run after her. Next, remembering the injunction which she had laid upon him, he desisted. This was evidently her wish, to depart thus; and evidently she knew her purpose.

She was gone like a wraith—but how different now life seemed to him. This old dejection, his uncertainties, had fallen away. Life had become fair once more and the beacon light of hope flashed out again, calling and luring him to new adventures. Very thoughtfully he strolled back along the shore, and he paced it till the sun sank and once again the white fogs rolled round him, blotting out all but his memories.

THE TRACER OF EGOS
Chronicles of Dr. Phileas Immanuel, Soul Specialist

THE AMULET OF MARDUK
Holland's Magazine (June 1913)

I remember vividly the conversation in Doctor Immanuel's library, because that evening was the beginning of my association with him, and the conversation was, so to say, the starting point of my own investigations.

There were five of us there, Dr. Phileas Immanuel, Doctor Maine, Paul Tarrant, the millionaire whose priceless art collections passed to the nation recently under the terms of his will, and another man whose name I have forgotten. We had been discussing the case of Helen Blythe, Mr. Tarrant's governess, who had been dismissed for stealing, after the court had passed a suspended sentence upon her by grace of a defense of kleptomania.

"You say," said Doctor Maine, the eminent neurologist, "that you believe in reincarnation upon the analogy of the plant—the lilac plant, you used for an example. The lilac, as I understand you to say, flowers during some two weeks in the year and, having faded, reviews its earthly experiences in some paradise of dreamy somnolence until, in due season, the soul of the flower incarnates itself in another cluster of petals. So, you say, man comes to birth again after he has passed through the gates of death. That's not a bad simile, Immanuel, but that's not biology. How do you justify your belief biologically—or, let us say, by any laws of inductive reasoning?"

"You are, of course, acquainted with the researches of Freud?" asked the Greek of Doctor Maine.

"Well, I should say so," the other responded. "A big man—one of the biggest in his line of today."

"How would you sum up his discoveries?" asked Doctor Immanuel.

Doctor Maine did not hesitate for an instant. "Freud's great work," he said, "has been the proof that our subconscious or dream life is continuous, that every dream accurately corresponds to some ungratified physical or mental need and is, one may say, its fulfillment. For instance, take the man who has always wanted, but never owned, a motor car. His dreams will show a more or less continuous experience—not of motoring, for they will be veiled under some symbol, but of flying, or aeroplaning, or holding the throttle of an engine. He may even be a fly on a wheel, or a swimmer clinging to an upturned boat in a whirlpool; but in some manner the dream life will reflect the waking wish."

"Precisely," answered Doctor Immanuel. "Well, now, let us carry the simile further. The condition after death represents to the full

this dream life, magnified to the nth power. There, in that paradise of bliss, every ungratified wish that was ever experienced in life comes true—generally. But suppose that the impulse to rebirth cuts short the experiences of heaven prematurely. What then?" He paused and, looking round at us, raised his hand impressively. "Then, gentlemen, you have a soul reborn on earth which, instead of holding these past memories securely tucked away in the innermost recesses of its being, flowering as gifts of character and natural ability, is built upon shifting sands. The submerged consciousness of these unsatisfied needs of its past life haunts it and drives it to unlawful deeds. All our criminals, for example, are merely persons who failed to fulfill their destinies; and, in proof of my contention, are not all criminals—criminals by instinct, of course I mean, not the starving beggar who snatches a loaf—are they not all physically unstable, mentally unbalanced, and easy subjects for the hypnotist? Yes, my dear Maine, and I believe that when hypnotized they can be made to yield up these past memories."

The subject was changed soon afterward by Doctor Maine. Like many medicos of the old school, he held opinions rooted in the barren sands of materialism. Such theories as Immanuel's savored to him of the charlatan. But for the eminence of the Greek physician he would, I am sure, have broken forth in angry protest. He took his leave soon after, and the fifth man also departed, leaving Paul Tarrant, the Doctor and myself alone.

"Now, take the case of Helen Blythe," said Mr. Tarrant, when we had settled ourselves in our chairs again. "Do you suppose that you could prove your contention in her case?"

"I didn't read the account," answered Doctor Immanuel. "All reports of crime distress me exceedingly. When I think how futile it is to put these unhappy creatures in prison, instead of treating them medically, I become enraged at the world and disgusted with my own inability to convince penologists of their mistake. But tell me about her."

"Helen Blythe," said Mr. Tarrant, "is a well-bred, good-looking, modest young woman of, I should say, seven or eight and twenty. She came to me with excellent recommendations, to be a nursery governess for our children. Mrs. Tarrant took a great fancy to her and trusted her fully. Needless to say, neither of us was aware that Miss Blythe had been dismissed from a former situation for theft. As we discovered afterwards, she had stolen four valuable rings, which, in spite of the threat of prosecution, were never recovered. The girl claimed that she had forgotten where she had hidden them, but fully acknowledged her offense and repaid the value of them out of her savings. In spite of careful investigation of all the pawnshops in the city, however, the rings were never found.

"A few weeks after we had engaged Miss Blythe my wife began to miss valuables of hers. Rings seemed to be the young woman's penchant. An opal, a diamond and sapphire, and a magnificent emerald in a fifteenth century setting disappeared successively. We changed our servants without result. At last, by force of a constantly dwindling number of hypotheses, the suspicion came to rest upon Miss Blythe's shoulders.

"However, as Mrs. Tarrant locked away her valuables, nothing more was taken, and we should probably have kept the young woman in our employment but for what happened. The governess was a great student of antiquities; in fact, she had a knowledge of Hittite and Babylonian archaeology which astonished me and was a primary factor in the securing of her position. She had a half day's leave every week, and invariably spent it at the museum. She became a well-known figure there, for she always haunted the Assyrian room, in which, as you may know, are a number of engraved gems, of immeasurable value, brought from Babylonia by the expedition which I sent there for the purpose of excavating the mounds of

Nineveh. Some ten days ago the watchman, who had somehow become suspicious of the young woman, discovered her with the half of a sacred amulet in her hand—a ring supposed to have been worn by the high priest of Marduk. As you may know, that half amulet is one of the most cherished possessions of the Assyrian department. The watchman arrested her and summoned the curator. When he came it was discovered that the half amulet still reposed in its place inside the case. The half which Helen Blythe held in her hand was mine—the other half, and willed by me to the museum. The young woman made no resistance, but suffered herself to be led away, as if in a comatose state. She was brought to my house, I identified the half of the charm, and the girl was placed under arrest, to be released under a suspended sentence yesterday."

"Where is the girl?" asked Doctor Immanuel.

"Why, Doctor," said Mr. Tarrant, flushing, "I am ashamed to say that I have taken her back."

"Good!" ejaculated the Doctor, puffing vigorously at his cigar. "But she will steal again."

"Indeed, no," answered the millionaire with conviction. "We had a very serious talk with her, Mrs. Tarrant and I. We told her that we felt, under the circumstances, which we had not fully understood, that we ought not to turn her adrift into the world. We thought that by the force of example, perhaps, we might cure her of her unfortunate propensity. And so she was re-engaged—not, of course, as governess, but as a sort of aid to my wife."

"And she was penitent?"

"Entirely so. She protested that she would conquer her weakness; she vowed never to touch jewelry again, or to look at it. She pleaded earnestly for our confidence, said it was only rings which she felt an irresistible temptation to take, and—"

"And she will steal again," said Doctor Immanuel.

"Well, Doctor, you have a poor faith in human nature, considering your humanitarian profession," said the millionaire.

"I tell you, Mr. Tarrant, she will steal again," persisted the Doctor. "You cannot eradicate the instincts derived from a former incarnation with kindness only. Doubtless she was a wealthy gem collector in Rome or Athens—or Alexandria, more likely—about the year 100 A. D."

Paul Tarrant smiled skeptically. "Will you tell me how you arrive at your date so exactly, Doctor?" he asked.

"By the analogy of the lilac tree," replied Doctor Immanuel. "The lilac blooms for two weeks in every fifty-two—is that not so? Then we may say its sleeping life is twenty-six times as long as its life in physical form. Now, if we take the normal human life to be seventy years, each human item will reappear after an interval of about 1,820 years—shorter or longer according to the individual idiosyncrasy, but more or less upon time. Hannibal, for instance, whose discarnate life must have been peculiarly rich in memories, and therefore prolonged, was reborn as Napoleon after a little more than 2,000 years. Cicero reappeared as Gladstone after some 1,850 years; the fabulous Queen Semiramis after 2,000 years as Cleopatra, and after some 1,750 more as Catherine II of Russia. Those mighty figures appear and reappear through history with the regularity of comets, and, like them, are recurrent phenomena which flash through a wondering world. Well, then, some 1,820 years ago your Helen Blythe was a gem collector or lapidary or something similar in the classic world, and it is the ungratified desire for jewels which has made her a kleptomaniac today."

"Perhaps you would like to see her, Doctor?" the millionaire suggested tolerantly. "I confess I am not convinced as to the truth of your theories, but I should immeasurably like to know just how the ancient Romans set their rings."

Doctor Immanuel accepted this seriously, and before we parted it was arranged that we two should visit Mr. Tarrant at his house after dinner on the following evening. So we separated, upon terms of the utmost good will and both Mr. Tarrant and myself, I am sure, politely skeptical as to Doctor Immanuel's claims.

Doctor Immanuel was staying at my house at this time. He had been sent to America, where he had been educated, by the Greek government, as her most distinguished medical representative and publicist, to attend the International Congress of Penologists at Boston. But the first few days' sittings had so disheartened the Doctor, convincing him that his own theories would never gain him a hearing, and would, in fact, seriously prejudice his country, that he had withdrawn from the congress and was making my home his headquarters during the period occupied by some special researches, about whose nature he had not enlightened me.

On the following morning we received two letters from Mr. Tarrant, in which he apologized for his inability to ask us to dinner on account of the death of a near relative of Mrs. Tarrant, and reiterated his desire that we visit him that evening. Accordingly, about eight o'clock we found ourselves in his library and received a cordial greeting.

"Before we see Miss Blythe," said Mr. Tarrant, "perhaps you gentlemen would care to inspect my antiquities?"

We knew that such an invitation could not be refused without the possibility of seriously affronting the millionaire; furthermore we were both interested, in a limited way, in such matters. We did anticipate a lengthy and somewhat tedious round of the museum, but such proved not to be the case. Mr. Tarrant's collection consisted mainly of works of art of the Middle Ages; the Assyrian room was quite a small chamber at the back of the house, enclosed by concrete walls and approachable only by the door leading out of Mr. Tarrant's library. We entered, he switched on the electric lights, and we found ourselves looking up into the faces of bull-headed kings with wings, broken-faced goddesses, and colossi of black marble and granite. At one end of the room were a number of packing cases, forming a barrier across one-third of its length; down the center were the customary glass cases filled with gems, stones of all sorts, fragments of clay inscriptions, etc. We made the round slowly, Mr. Tarrant expatiating upon his trophies.

"And now," he said, "I must show you the gem of my collection in its literal sense—I mean the half amulet whose other part is in the museum. I don't keep it here," he added, smiling. "It is far too valuable, and my one experience of losing it has made me resolved to run no more risks. It is—" he paused and continued in a stage whisper which certainly carried as far as his natural voice—"under the Persian rug behind my desk, in a tiny piece of false parquet works in the floor. Simple, isn't it? Yet I am sure it is safer there than in any of these cases—or, for the matter of that, in a steel safe.

"First, let me tell you something about this treasure," he continued, waxing enthusiastic. "The amulet is supposed to have been made for the high priest of Marduk, at Babylon. According to the cuneiform inscription, it was kept by the priestess of Ishtar pending the completion of Marduk's colossal temple, and it is believed, since it was discovered in the ruins of the temple of Ishtar, that for some cause the priestess never delivered it. Perhaps it was hidden, perhaps the city was destroyed before the transfer could be made. At any rate, it was a most sacred object and, from the fact that it was made in two halves, it is certain that the highest value was placed upon it. But I am wearying you, gentlemen. Come into the library, and I will show it to you."

We passed into the library. Mr. Tarrant switched off the lights in the museum and, carefully closing and locking the door,

switched on the library lights. As the room became illuminated we heard the door at the other end close softly. There was the swishing of skirts.

I was not prepared for what followed. With a yell the millionaire leaped across the room, burst open the door and reappeared, dragging with him the figure of a woman. Of course it was Miss Blythe. She stood staring at him, looking like a sleepwalker. Her hands were tightly closed.

"Open your hands!" yelled Mr. Tarrant. "What have you got there? Open them, I say!"

But the frail woman seemed to have the strength of an athlete, for Mr. Tarrant, powerful man though he was, could not open her hands. All the while she stood and stared at him, and she seemed to be utterly unconscious of our presence.

Doctor Immanuel walked over to her; he placed one hand on either shoulder and looked into her unwinking eyes.

"Helen," he asked quietly, "open your hands!"

There was a moment of uncertainty, then the hard eyes closed and the hands opened obediently. With a cry of exultation, Mr. Tarrant pounced upon an object held in one of them—a massive ring containing an enormous engraved stone which looked like a sardonyx.

"Here it is!" he shouted. "Now, then, will one of you gentlemen go for an officer?"

Doctor Immanuel turned round and held up a finger in warning.

"She doesn't hear you," he said quietly. "She is hypnotized."

"Nonsense!" exclaimed Mr. Tarrant, angrily. "How could you hypnotize her in that minute."

"She has hypnotized herself," answered Doctor Immanuel. "She came to you in a hypnotic condition, and in her normal condition would be totally ignorant of what she had done. Helen," he added, softly, "you are in the hands of your friends. Go over and sit down on that sofa and sleep until I waken you."

The girl crossed the room obediently, walking just as a normal person would have done. She found the sofa and sat down; but all the while her eyes were closed. Mr. Tarrant stood by, still fuming.

"Have I your permission to proceed?" asked Doctor Immanuel. "I believe you invited us here for this very purpose, Mr. Tarrant."

"Oh, yes, by all means," Tarrant answered. "But you'll have to convince me before I allow her to leave this house except under police supervision."

"I hope to," answered the Doctor. "But first let me assure you that this young woman could never be convicted of theft in any court. Ignorant as our police magistrates are, the understanding that there is such a thing as alternating personality has finally entered into the public mind. If you will remember, you yourself told me that when Miss Blythe was arrested in the museum she suffered herself to be led away as though she were in a comatose condition."

"Yes—yes."

"The fact is, Mr. Tarrant, that Miss Blythe the governess is not in the least the same personality as Miss Blythe the kleptomaniac, and has no knowledge of her. She doubtless realizes that, when these periods of forgetfulness come on, she commits actions of which she has no waking knowledge, and it is the impossibility of explaining this to an incredulous world that had led her to suffer in silence rather than attempt to vindicate her reputation. Now, with your permission, I shall proceed."

Tarrant and I sat down. All this while Miss Blythe had not moved a muscle.

"Give me the amulet, please," said Doctor Immanuel, and Mr. Tarrant handed it to him with obvious reluctance. Had the situation been less dramatic it would have been amusing to see the intense gaze which the millionaire kept upon the gem.

"Helen," said Doctor Immanuel, holding the gem before her, "can you read the inscription on this?"

"No," she answered in a voice which seemed disappointingly natural, "it is in Assyrian cuneiform, is it not?"

"Oh, yes, you can read it," said the Doctor coaxingly. "You are not half asleep yet. Go to sleep completely, now."

He stroked her forehead caressingly, and when he held up the amulet and asked the question again, it was a totally different voice that answered him—a woman's voice, but harsh and nasal and strident.

"Why should I read it?" it asked protestingly.

"Read it!" said Doctor Immanuel. "No, read it in English"—for the voice had begun to talk in a sort of gibberish totally unlike any language that I had ever heard spoken, and bearing a distant resemblance to what I imagine Chinese to be.

"To the high priest of Marduk in Babylon," whined the voice. "Made for and donated by Asshur—Tiglath—Pileser, king of Nineveh—"

Paul Tarrant leaped out of his chair.

"That solves it!" he shouted, and sank down again and stared round him like a man thoroughly bewildered.

"Solves what?" asked Doctor Immanuel quietly.

"That word Nineveh, Doctor. The translation read 'King of Bel's slave,' and were utterly meaningless. If that is correct—it must be, but the stone was so rubbed none of us could decipher it—why, it places the date back to the thirty-fifth century, B. C., instead of the twenty-seventh. And that explains why the old cuneiform was used by the engraver."

"Who has this stone?" asked Doctor Immanuel, and we all gripped our seats more tightly at the snarling monosyllable "*I!*"

"Why did you not deliver it to the high priest of Marduk?" the Doctor asked.

"I did. He would not receive it," shrilled the woman on the sofa. "Instead, he sent soldiers to arrest me. It is his. He does not know. He—"

Her voice ceased, her eyes were open, and she was clinging desperately round Doctor Immanuel's neck and deathly pale. She shuddered and quailed as though in tolerable fear; and she would have screamed but that she could not find her voice again. Then she collapsed, a dead weight in the Doctor's arms, and he placed her in a supine posture upon the sofa.

"Call your housekeeper and we will help carry her to her room," said Doctor Immanuel. "No,"—for Mr. Tarrant was protesting—"it will be all right now. The strain was too intense for her; the awakening too sudden, but she will sleep peacefully and, but for a little nausea tomorrow, she will be quite herself again. And she will have no recollection of what has occurred."

"I don't want to let the housekeeper know," Mr. Tarrant answered. "Help me, Doctor, and we will take her upstairs. I'm glad my wife is not at home tonight," he added, grimly. "She mightn't approve of this."

But Mr. Tarrant took good care to secure and pocket the amulet before he took Miss Blythe's head and shoulders into his arms and led the way out of the library. I sat there for three or four minutes, wondering. I could not quite understand just what had occurred.

The two men came back arguing violently. Doctor Immanuel's voice rose high and shrill above that of his friend.

"She told you the inscription of the stone and set you right some six centuries," he cried. "What other proof do you want, Tarrant?"

"Oh, well, it's all rubbish, you know," answered the millionaire. "Of course, now that I have the amulet, I don't want to have the girl sent to jail. But I can't keep a thief in my house—now can I, Doctor?"

"She need not be a thief," Doctor Immanuel answered. "It all depends upon you."

"How so? Didn't you yourself tell me that she would steal again?"

"Yes. As long as she was looking for the opportunity to restore the lost amulet to the high priest."

"Well, I guess she'll have to go on looking for him," said Mr. Tarrant. "What do you want me to do—take her to Babylon and look for the incarnation of the old fellow among the desert Bedouin?"

"Why, my dear Tarrant, you don't suppose you'll find him there, do you?" the Doctor asked quizzically. "More probably in this city. Do you suppose a man of that intelligence is condemned to be reborn as a camel herder? The civilization of Babylon passed on to Rome, and thence to England and America, just as the Hindus became the Egyptians and the Greek republics, the republics of Florence, Genoa and Pisa and Venice in the Middle Ages.

"Now look here, Tarrant," he continued, as they sat down, "here is the situation as I size it up. Believe me or not, as you please—it doesn't matter. Your Helen Blythe was once the priestess of Ishtar. It wasn't a position that called for any high intellect; it was a semi-servile position, in fact, and the priestess was chosen mainly for her appearance and birth. We may suppose that in her former birth she had merited her good fortune by generous deeds, but, once the reward had been enjoyed, she sank down to the grade of governess again—or its equivalent in the ancient world. She had the care of this amulet. She was bound under the most sacrosanct of oaths to deliver it to the priest of Marduk. For some cause she failed to fulfill her task, and the omission so profoundly affected her that it lay like an incubus on her soul during her next incarnation. She stole rings, obsessed solely by the desire to discover the lost amulet again. At last she found it. She took it to the museum—still in her entranced condition—and was on the point of pinching it with the other half when she was arrested, or, as she rather confusedly interpreted the occurrence when on the borderline between sleep and waking, 'the king sent soldiers to arrest her'—probably the police and watchmen at the museum. Now, Tarrant, send the half amulet to the museum and you will find it perfectly safe to keep Miss Blythe in your house henceforward."

"Well," said Mr. Tarrant, "to be frank, I have intended to present it to the museum shortly, and after my experiences of the past few days I'll follow your advice. But as for keeping her in my employment—"

"Try it, Tarrant," pleaded Doctor Immanuel.

"Suppose she steals—"

"She won't steal any more, when once the amulet is in safekeeping."

Mr. Tarrant drummed his hands on his knees.

"Oh, all right, have your way," he said shortly. "But, by the way, Immanuel, do you mean to insinuate that Doctor Faust, our curator, is a reincarnation of the high priest of Marduk? He would be horrified to hear you say that. Why, he is a director of two Sunday schools and contributes liberally to foreign missions in—" He paused.

"Yes, where?" asked Doctor Immanuel.

"In Assyria and Mesopotamia," answered Mr. Tarrant sheepishly.

And Doctor Immanuel forbore to press his advantage home.

"But look here," said Mr. Tarrant, presently, "how does your 1820 year period work out, Doctor? The amulet, according to our revised estimate, was made in the thirty-fifth century before Christ."

Doctor Immanuel began to estimate.

"Our period takes us back to the year 100, does it not?" he asked. "The birth before that, then, would have been about 1750 B. C., probably in Egypt. Add 1820 years and we have the year 3570. Yes, there you are, Tarrant. And if you can discover the precise age of the amulet you will be able to estimate the exact age of your governess."

"It must have been a mighty strong influence to last over three incarnations, Doctor," said the millionaire, irreverently. "Where do you suppose she spent the last two—and how?"

"Expiating her crime," Doctor Immanuel answered. "Doubtless as a thief and outcast—*faugh*, don't let us pursue that matter, Tarrant. She's won through all of that, poor girl. You're going to keep and help her, Tarrant, aren't you?"

And Tarrant promised.

THE REVELATIONS OF AN AMBASSADOR-AT-LARGE
Transcribed from the private papers of an Englishman who for a time was an unofficial diplomat in the most secret service of the British Government

THE GOLDEN DEATH
Fiction Magazine (11 July 1915)

I shall begin this narration by revealing a fact which, by all the rules of story telling, should be kept for the culminating surprise. Yet perhaps the gossip of the Brussels boulevards is more or less public property, and it is known that the late King Leopold of Belgium did not really die from the effects of an operation alleged to have been performed upon him in his seventy-fifth year.

"Le roi perdu"—the lost king—his subjects used to call him. For days at a time he would disappear from the ken of his subjects and ministers, leaving affairs of state to settle themselves, while he lurked in one or other of his numerous retiring places, absorbed in his hobby, which had already become a master passion.

The many-sided character of the old man has been much dwelt on. It is true he was neither a good husband nor a good father; it is true he sought pleasures which, comparatively venial in youth, are not regarded with condonation in a grandfather. But he had one passion mightier than all which came to dominate him to the exclusion of every other. That was avarice.

In a way it had proved the strongest asset of his realm. Certainly under Leopold Belgium had prospered as never before. He administered her affairs with prudence; but then he was damned in the eyes of all decent men by the atrocities in the Congo Free State, where his agents hunted down and murdered or enslaved the helpless natives, in order that Leopold might line his pockets with the proceeds of the rubber extorted by forced labor from the villagers.

The sudden and mysterious illness then, the story of the old man's death, was a polite fiction, destined to pave the way to King Albert's succession to the Belgian throne. Leopold had become an impossibility. Faced with an ultimatum, and promised the security of his incomes, the old king signed his abdication willingly enough, and retired into obscurity.

Now, whether his crafty mind was breaking down, or whether, below the surface of civilization, there lay a strain of medievalism it is not for me to say, but Leopold, in retirement, became possessed by exactly the same desires which have haunted so many rulers of old days. He sought, in fact, two things, one of which, at least, once everywhere believed in, became regarded as a myth when modern science was born, and again seemed possible at the opening of the twentieth century, when the transmutation of the elements was proved to be not beyond the bounds of feasibility.

One was the elixir of life. The other was the philosopher's stone, or its modern equivalent, which turns all metals into gold.

To have perpetual youth and gold beyond computation became the dreams of an old man of seventy-five.

I was not at that time in the employ of the British government. I had, in fact, been compelled to resign my ambassadorship owing to a certain indiscretion, and I had completed a certain investigation for the foreign office. Yet, being in touch with the secret affairs of nations, I knew the facts of Leopold's retirement. I knew that he was living quietly in Cornwall, where, under the name of Leopold de Lys, he had purchased a small property in a lonely region bordering upon the sea, a manor which had owned the royalties accruing from numerous lead mines, now abandoned.

The lead mines of Cornwall are nearly worked out now, but they were formerly the richest in the world. The galleries were driven far under the sea until a point was reached where engineering science could no longer cope with the problem except at a cost which made the further working of these mines impracticable. Far underneath the waves which leap above the old submerged kingdom of Lyonesse lie lead deposits richer than any in the world, but never to be worked so long as lead remains one of the cheaper metals.

It was in the spring of 1913 that I received a communication from the foreign office asking me to call at a certain hour upon a certain day on a matter of importance. The letter was signed by one of the permanent staff.

As I had been vainly seeking for some time to obtain an interview, in the hope of securing another diplomatic appointment, I naturally concluded that my petitions had at last been heard. And my hopes ran high when, calling at the appointed time, I was shown up into Sir Edward Grey's office.

He was seated beside the fire in a big leather armchair, and with him, engaged in earnest conversation, was a man whom I had never met before. He looked like a church dignitary, in mufti.

"I am glad to see you, Mr. X—" said Sir Edward, rising and giving me a cordial handshake. "Permit me to introduce to you Mr. Graves, one of the Woolwich arsenal directors."

My hopes of a regular appointment were dashed to the ground by Sir Edward's ensuing remark.

"We are face to face with a very perplexing problem, Mr. X—" he said, "and you alone of all the men I know are capable of assisting in its solution. You are, of course, acquainted with a certain fact relative to the late king of the Belgians, which must not be permitted to become public property."

"I am aware that a Heer de Lys has purchased a villa and small manorial right in Cornwall," I answered.

"Excellently put," replied Sir Edward, smiling. "Well, and now you remember the wreck of the Cornish tramp Hesper upon Shoal Island last week?"

I assented. The Hesper had been wrecked on a rocky ledge in a high gale, and the crew very bravely rescued by a torpedo-boat destroyer.

"Only a small part of her cargo was saved," continued Sir Edward, "but there is reason to believe that the whole cargo consisted of one identical substance. In fact, Mr. X—, we recovered a very fine quality of quicksilver. Now, of course, quicksilver does exist in Cornwall in small quantities, and, in fact, wherever lead is found. But if that cargo came out of Cornwall, then somebody has found the finest quicksilver mine in the world. The tramp ship sailed from Polwyn, where Heer de Lys has his estate. She was bound for Hamburg."

"You see, Mr. X—" explained Mr. Graves, "quicksilver is of great value in the manufacture of a certain high grade of explosive. In fact, without its use we cannot positively produce an explosive of that character which will be safe. The British and certain foreign governments have probably the identical ex-plosive, though each discovered it separately. We get our quicksilver from Spain. So do they. Now, in the event of—well, of war—it is essential that an unlimited supply of quicksilver should not be stored in Hamburg."

"So, Mr. X—, we want you to go to Polwyn and find whether our friend the Heer de Lys is interested in the shipment of quicksilver, and where he gets it," said the foreign minister.

I accepted the commission and went to Polwyn in the guise of a health seeker. I saw Leopold's villa from the train as we rolled into the station, which is the terminus of the line. It was a pretty little stucco place with extensive gardens, such as the queer old man had always delighted in. The town itself, straggling up a steep hill, with its one street paved with cobblestones, was about a mile distant. I secured lodgings in the cottage of an ancient widow, representing myself to be a business man in need of rest after a long period of overwork. Polwyn delighted me. I felt that I could spend a couple of weeks there very comfortably. The only drawback to my under-taking was that it was impossible to make the acquaintance of the ex-ruler, since he had known me very well when I was stationed at the Brussels court.

On the morning after my arrival I was up early and, descending the steep street, strolled along the beach, where the fishermen were mending their nets and stringing them between their schooners.

I managed to get into conversation with one ancient fellow, who was kind enough to enliven me with the family histories of the local magnates. After a while I brought him round to the discussion of the occupant of the villa.

"That's Mr. de Lys, you mean," said the old man. "Frenchman he is, or Dutchman, or somewhere between the two. He's a bad 'un, zur—leastways, that's Polwyn gossip. Carries on at all hours of the night, he does, drinking and piano playing—Sundays, too—with a parcel of folks from foreign parts, men and women, sir. We don't think much of him in Polwyn."

His voice dropped, and he looked timidly at me. "They do zay, zur, as how he's sold hisself to the devil," he whispered, with the countryman's fear of ridicule. But, seeing that I showed no disposition to laugh at him, he continued:

"Aye, he walks in the old lead quarries at night, zur. Tom Bower zeen him when he come in on the morning tide last week. Walking out of the quarries at sunrise, zur, with a foreign-looking gentleman in a green hat."

"Perhaps the old gentleman went for a walk because he couldn't sleep," I suggested.

"No, zur. What for would any decent man in Polwyn want to walk where I wouldn't go for all the gold in the Bank of England? There's evil things in the old quarries, zur— evil things that travels night—"

He stopped short and I could elicit nothing more from him. Evidently the old fellow regretted his communicativeness. But as the days passed I received corroboration of the old fisherman's statement from other sources. Everyone in Polwyn firmly believed that Heer de Lys had sold himself to the Evil One. He scandalized the pious neighborhood by Sundays which were, in the broadest sense, continental. There were rumors, too, of a strange ship that came secretly to an anchorage at a point where the quarries ran into the sea. "Contraband," one man suggested; but there is no coast guard station at Polwyn, and with the disinclination of the English countryman to meddle in his neighbor's affairs, nobody took steps to communicate with the authorities.

The quarries ran under the waves at a point about two miles north of Polwyn, a desolate, uninhabited tract of land, a waste of heather-clad hills running sharply down to the beach. At the high-water mark a sort of ramshackle bridge connected the land tunnel with the gallery that had been driven under the sea. A flight of worn concrete steps led down, and

one could enter the gallery without difficulty, even at high tide.

I chose a Sunday for my exploration, having first satisfied myself that Heer de Lys was entertaining his friends at the villa. I approached as near as I could along the road. I could hear sounds of distant laughter and the voices of women. Evidently the ex-king had not forgotten the gayeties of life in his enforced exile. Leaving the road, I crept around the edge of one of those hawthorn hedges that are so prominent a feature of our English landscape, until I was in a position to look across the garden into the windows.

It was not an act of which I was in any way proud. Yet I was consumed with anxiety to assure myself that the ex-monarch was likely to be engaged with his friends for a considerable period. And, just as I settled myself into position a burst of ringing laughter near at hand sent me ducking down behind the hedge.

Heer de Lys was giving a garden party. There were two women and three men, and they were chattering away in French with the utmost vivacity. And now my patience was rewarded, for not twenty paces away I saw a man with a green alpine hat on his knee.

I knew him immediately, though it was five years since I had set eyes on him. His name was Bethman, and he was accounted the most famous chemist in Hamburg—all Germany, for that matter. He had invented new dyeing processes which had enriched the fatherland to the extent of many millions of marks and had created industries employing thousands of workmen. He bore me no good will, for I had been instrumental in blocking a certain patent of his which infringed the rights of a fellow countryman.

I wondered what purpose he had in coming to Polwyn, but it seemed obvious that De Lys had sent for him to report upon the quicksilver discoveries.

Yet, if quicksilver was being mined in Polywyn, where were the miners?

The answer to that question could only be obtained by searching the mine.

I hurried back to the outlet of the quarries, where I had hidden a lantern, and, about five o'clock in the afternoon, I entered the tunnel beneath the sea.

It was not a pleasing sensation, that plunge into the darkness, my only light shed by the lantern, which cast a flickering glow on the dripping rock walls of the tunnel; but I estimated that it would be possible to investigate and return well before twilight. On I went until the glimmer of daylight behind me had faded and the sea's murmur disappeared. The stillness was eerie. The beating of my heart was the only sound I heard. At intervals I stopped to examine the wet rocks. Long veins of lead ran here and there between slate strata. There was no sign of quicksilver.

Presently the tunnel branched, and coming to a standstill, I examined the passages. There was no clue to the right road. I turned to the right and wandered till the passage again divided. Halting again, I was astonished to see that it was nearly six o'clock.

There was still another fork in the way in front of me, and now I came to the conclusion that, with such a multitude of passages, I should be compelled to adopt other methods. Clearly some clue to the way was essential to my success. Besides, I was afraid of returning late, and possibly of meeting the ex-king and his companion. Unarmed as I was, and knowing the unscrupulous nature of both men, that prospect was not a pleasing one.

I retraced my steps until I came to the branch again. I thought the tunnel looked wider and higher than before. I held up the lantern. There were three forks! I must have passed the proper route on the return journey and wandered into the recesses of the quarries.

It was now half-past six. I turned again; presently I saw two more divisions before me. And I realized to my horror that I was completely lost. I had no notion now which was the north. I might wander for days in those recesses without discovering the route.

I think panic is excusable—it is certainly human under such conditions. For hours I must have run to and fro, hoping against hope to find the way, till suddenly my lantern flared up and went out, leaving me in total darkness.

I do not know how long I crouched in the darkness. Had I still had the instinct to fly it would have been impossible, for the passages wound their course irregularly, and at intervals huge rocks of jagged slate projected, formidable obstacles to strike against in the darkness. It may have been an hour or two afterward that I was startled to see a tiny flickering light in the distance—not where I imagined the course of the tunnel to run but to the right of me, where the wall should have been.

As I half raised myself, not daring to trust my eyes, the light came nearer, and I heard the grating sound of a lantern deposited on the rock ground. Then I saw two figures emerge from the darkness and stand facing each other.

One was Herr Bethman. I knew him again; I even fancied that I could see the green of the hat which he had pushed back over his ears. And the other—there was no mistaking that tall, lean figure with the long, square-cut beard. It was Leopold.

Inch by inch I edged forward. Now it seemed to me as though my lantern had gone out just as I reached an open space, a sort of little amphitheater among the passages. In front of me one of the mighty bowlders projected, half concealing the two men as they moved. Noiselessly I made my way upon my hands and knees until I was safely concealed behind it.

"Now, sir, I will answer all your questions," I heard Bethman say. "The quicksilver could not be resolved in Hamburg. I tried both shipments carefully. I have come to the conclusion that it is impossible to halt the process at the quicksilver. The entire transmutation must be done in a single operation. Hence I brought the apparatus with me."

He stooped, and now I saw that between the two men was a complicated mechanism, weighing, I judged, perhaps a hundredweight. It had evidently been placed in the mine some time before, since it was set on a flat slab of stone that formed a natural table in the side of the tunnel. Bethman struck a match and ignited an alcohol flame, which burned steadily, sending the shadows of the pair in hard relief against the wall.

"This apparatus, of course, is merely for testing my theory," continued Bethman, rising and facing the ex-king. "But if tonight's experiment succeeds, it will be a simple enough matter to bring a complete mechanical outfit here and carry on the entire operation in this place for months, if necessary. We are perfectly secure against interlopers. The theory is—"

"Yes, yes, the theory!" wheezed the old man, clapping the chemist upon the shoulder. "First the theory and then the practice. That is as it should be. Go on! Go on!"

"When I was here a month ago," said Bethman placidly, "I succeeded in converting the lead you gave me as far as quicksilver. To produce gold was beyond our powers. I thought then that in my laboratory in Hamburg I could continue the process and bring it to a successful issue. But the quicksilver had 'set,' as we term it—in other words, the atoms had had time to become stable and group themselves so firmly as to defy further transformation. Well—I am on the track now, sire, and I feel confident that I can show you the color of gold tonight."

The alcohol flame was leaping now, and I saw Bethman stoop and begin to blow the tremulous blue light with a pair of bellows. Metal glowed red above it. I felt the warmth in my face.

"It is simply a matter of hastening the decomposition of radium," continued Bethman, seating himself upon a ledge of rock. "Not only does radium decompose most rapidly of all the known elements, but, in doing so, it possesses the power to disintegrate the atoms of those elements of lower atomic weight—lead for example.

"Soddy and Rayleigh have made exhaustive studies on this subject, which have not all been given to the world so far. Take an atom of radium, for example, and watch its transformations.

"In 3.86 days, it has become what we call radium emanation. Three minutes later this has split into helium, carrying two unit charges of electricity, and what is known as Radium A. In twenty-six minutes Radium A becomes Radium B. In nineteen minutes more it is Radium C. Seventeen years later it has become converted into Radium D. And there is where our process enters, for we do in seventeen seconds what nature requires seventeen years to complete.

"Five days later nature gives us Radium E. In one hundred and forty days more Radium F. And after an incredible lapse of time—twenty thousand years or so, perhaps, we have Radium G—which is lead.

"All the lead in these quarries is the product of radium. But you must not suppose that this was once a pure radium mine, for radium itself is a comparatively evanescent phase of what was ionium, and, before that, uranium.

"I shall trouble you a little further, sire, since you have requested an explanation. We have now converted our radium, with an atomic weight of about 226, into lead, with an atomic weight of 206. The next of the elements in order is thallium, with an atomic weight of 204. Then comes mercury, or quicksilver, with an atomic weight of 200. Each conversion is accompanied by the explosion of certain alpha particles, which lower the atomic weight by about four units.

"Now, mercury having an atomic weight of 200, and gold, one of about 197—the weights are never exact—it follows that a single further transmutation, the loss of four more units, will give us gold in place of quicksilver."

The old man, who sat staring at Bethman, as though fascinated by his explanation, slid his arm through the chemist's and, turning him so that they were face to face, looked eagerly into his eyes.

"And then?" he croaked. "Then? *Then?* THEN?"

"Why, we shall be richer than men have ever been before," cried Bethman, in tones of false jollity. "We shall be richer than ever Midas was. We shall not be millionaires, but billionaires. We will bring workmen here to quarry the lead out of these walls, and we will make gold of it. It shall be just as your majesty has said. We will buy back our kingdom, and we will soon own all Europe. We will acquire everything that money can buy—pictures and books and palaces, horses and colonies and women's love and live royally."

"Yes," croaked the old king. "How long, Bethman? For a few years or—forever?"

"Oh, that!—" began Bethman, shrugging his shoulders. Suddenly his face changed, and I knew by an infallible instinct that he was setting out to promise what he could never perform.

"Your majesty," he said, "I am convinced that the secret of eternal youth lies in the power of radium. That the same force which transmutes the base lead into glorious gold can also transform our worn-out bodies into new ones. I am on the track of that secret also. I—"

"O God be thanked!" the age man blasphemed. "You must work on that scheme quickly, Bethman. I am very old and frail now. I have only a few more years before me. The black specter of death is ever at my side. The thought of annihilation is terrible. O, Bethman, promise me, in God's name, that you can make me a youth again, so that I can enjoy my darling gold and have immortality."

Bethman took the old man by the shoulders and whispered in his ear. I could not hear his words, but I saw Leopold smile, and his long, gray beard went nodding upon his breast as he sat chuckling in senile joy.

The heat was now intense; the metal work was fiery red. The chemist arose and began to use the bellows vigorously. I saw the red change to white.

"Now bring me a bar of lead!" he shouted, and the old man lifted one from some place beside the wall and carried it to the crucible.

"Drop it in!" ordered Bethman briskly. "Your majesty, our experiment approaches its finale. Have no fear. You have seen the radium, at 2,000 degrees change lead into mercury. This heat is infinitely less. It requires rather a steady application to loosen the tenacious helium atom. It needs—"

I saw him uncork a phial as he spoke. He raised it to the level of the shimmering, molten mass of metal within the retort and seemed to let a few drops fall. And with a roar like that of a thousand guns the crucible burst into fragments.

My ear drums quivered under the shock. It flung me from where I crouched far into the tunnel, and a fine spray of lead hissed round me. I saw it strike the wall and become instantly transformed into a plaster-like substance that formed one with the slate. I saw a molten stream sweep past me. I heard Bethman cry loudly once; and then, with another roar, the tunnel roof collapsed behind me, and a surge of water swept me bodily onward.

But in that last instant of despair I saw a sight which, for sheer horror, has never been surpassed.

In the single moment between the explosion and the quenching of the lantern I saw Leopold. He stood just as he had been standing the instant before, his tall figure slightly stooped that he might not strike his head against the tunnel roof, his head turned on his shoulders toward his companion.

But the man of flesh and blood had become a statue of gold.

A golden statue, but the lineaments exactly the same; the beard of golden threads, the wrinkles on the avaricious old face of gold,

gold hands and feet, gold tissue where the clothes had been. The man had become gold as surely as petrified wood becomes stone.

I am sure that it was no mere gold film that covered him. The tremendous impact of the liberated ions had gone through flesh and bone, had charged the atomic tissues. I shall see that sight all my life. Bethman dead at his feet, and the old man become that which he had loved more than all else in life.

It was only an instant's vision. Then I was flying wildly before the deluge of the sweeping sea. I tore on blindly, feeling those clammy waters about my knees, my waist—till suddenly they left me and I sank fainting upon the shore under the stars.

THE WOLF TRAP
Fiction Magazine (27 August 1916)

On the verge of the snow line, where the pine growth ceased suddenly, as though shorn away by some Titan's razor, a cabin perched, hard by the cataract that issued from the glacier. The woman stood at the door, shielding her eyes against the western sun and looking into the valley below, where the thin trail ran like a sinuous string from cliff to canyon.

Presently she perceived something that detached itself from the long, dust-whitened street of the town and began to ascend the foothills of Giant's Peak. To valley folks, standing where she stood, this would have been but a moving speck; to her it was a man on horseback. The woman turned and looked back into the hut.

"Milly!" she called.

A girl came from within and stood before her mother in an attitude of obedience, resting her bare feet upon the sill of the door for warmth. The wind caught her frayed and tattered skirts and swirled them round her ankles.

"Wemmer's left his house," the mother said, eyeing her child with famished tenderness. "Where are your shoes?"

"I cain't wear 'em; they hurts me."

"You've got to wear 'em!" her mother answered sharply, her words punctuated with explosive coughing. "Put 'em on before he comes. And your store dress."

"I don't want to dress fine," answered the girl, sullenly. "Not for Wemmer. You taught me to hate him, an' now you veer round an' say the feud's forgotten. I want Jed—"

Her voice broke; but the mother's eyes dropped before the searching gaze of her daughter's tear-filled ones.

"Jed's done with," the elder woman cried, harshly. "Listen, child, 'tis for your sake we've got to make peace with Wemmer. We've got to keep our home from that gray wolf who's coming to steal in. Twice he's offered us peace, and we've refused him. But never did he claim our home before. But the land's his by law, and law runs up to the top of the peak these days. Go in and dress yourself."

The girl turned back into the cabin, moving sullenly. Her mother did not follow her with her eyes, but remained gazing down into the lowlands, eager and gaunt and fierce, as a wolf that yearns toward the lamb-fold.

She focused her eyes through the arch of her hand. Wemmer had disappeared; his horse had crossed the foothills and was hidden among the pines. In little more than an hour he would arrive.

When Olaf Afgaard, her husband, and she had settled there, nearly a score of years before, they had trapped a timber wolf inside the log hut one night as it crept stealthily toward the cradle. Thinking of Wemmer now, Hilda Afgaard pictured him as the same stealthy and silent beast, grayer about the chops and snout, but none the less fierce and relentless. He had taken her man; but he should never take the child. She would fix her eyes on his, no longer dissembling, and hands round his thick throat—no! She had forgotten. That was for Jed to do. Jed must do that! He would—her plans had not miscarried.

She had laid them too cunningly to be frustrated now. Not for a vengeance less God inspired would she have feigned submission to Wemmer, have used her only child as the decoy to lure him to the mountain heights, where his life should atone for the life he had taken in the same place, beside the frozen stream, in the same snows under that unchanged sky.

Some fifteen years had passed since Wemmer, now owner of the town that bore his name, and of the rich Giant gold mine, had lured Olaf Afgaard to the edge of the glacier on Giant's Peak and plunged the knife into his side. It was cupidity that had incited Wemmer to the commission of the crime. The men had been comrades, prospecting among the peaks for gold. When the spring suns had thawed the slopes, they had ascended together to seek the ores that Olaf had located late the preceding fall. Wemmer, greedy for an undivided ownership in the rich prize, had planned and executed his comrade's murder. When he returned alone, stammering out his fabricated tale of disaster, the wife listened—half under-standingly, half numbed, wholly bereft; suddenly she espied his empty belt.

Hate flashed in her eyes. "Where is your knife?" she cried.

Wemmer began stammering anew. She sprang for his throat then, and fell, stunned by his fist.

Piece by piece the mother and child had reconstructed the tragedy during the long winter evenings, linking up a thousand insignificant incidents until they assumed their part in the chain of evidence. The men had set out toward the heights together, where the snows still lingered under the cliffs and across treacherous crevasses. Olaf had poised himself—Hilda found the tracks of his

snowshoes—upon the glacier's edge; and swiftly Wemmer had plunged the steel into his side and the body went toppling over to its grave in the glacier, 200 feet below, where it ran like a ribbon of clouded blue beneath its inaccessible barriers. It turned and twisted in its slow course until the dwindling cliffs reared themselves again at the canyon's edge in an impermeable rampart; and there, warmed by the sun's rays, its steel-like substance shivered into a myriad of ice splinters and flung itself forth to fall, a cataract of foam, upon the slopes below. And year by year, by inches and feet—ten feet, perhaps, during the whole mutation of the seasons this snow ice current moved irresistibly onward by its momentum, carrying upon its frozen breast its plundered freight, the rocks and debris of the hills, until in the end, hundreds of years hence, it would toss them to the cataract to strew the slopes of the hills.

When Hilda Afgaard accused Wemmer the few settlers pitied her as one whose loss had crazed her. So she withdrew to the heights and dwelt there, waiting. But the years passed and justice lingered. It was not until her daughter's beauty suddenly became disclosed to her that the thought came of using Milly to bait the trap. Wemmer had spoken with the girl on those infrequent intervals when she passed his mansion on her way into the town. He had recalled his friendship with her father, deplored Hilda's enmity. One day the mother learned his designs through some innocent words that the girl let fall. She spent that night in a delirium of hatred; with dawn she conceived her new scheme of revenge. That day she went to Wemmer and humbled herself to him. Wemmer was magnanimous.

"Your girl should go to school," he said, eyeing her shiftily. "If I should take her into the mill she could board in the town and study evenings. It isn't fair to her to keep her up on the peak."

"I reckon she won't stay there long," said Hilda craftily. "Jed and she aim to get married soon."

Wemmer bit his trembling lip and a mask came over his face.

"And what'll you do, Mrs. Afgaard?" he asked. "He's a shiftless fellow of worthless stock. They don't shake off that Southern laziness when they come West."

"I'm going South," said Hilda. "My brother's got a farm in Texas and it'll cure my cough to get down there for a spell."

"But our farm?" said Wemmer, and sprung his trap. It was his farm and his land, he told her, and only by grace of him had she occupied it those years. The title was registered at the State capital. But, out of regard for his dead partner—

The threat had broken her spirit. Nothing was settled, but Hilda went home with a memory of Wemmer's sneering face, gradually unmasked again, of his offer of $300 for her poor acres. These words were but the opening wedge. Afterward he grew bolder. The price of the farm was but the price of the child. The wolf had bared his fangs; he who had killed her man now demanded the uttermost—Milly!

Day by day Hilda planned and schemed. If she should lure him to the heights, how could one woman accomplish vengeance? Wemmer had the strength of the mountaineer inspite of years of evil living. They had bloated him and wrecked his nerves, but they had not robbed him of his strength. And meanwhile Jed, slow-speaking, smiling, shiftless, threatened to disrupt her plan when he came courting Milly and spent his evenings in the cabin beside the cataract.

It was not until a trifling incident revealed to her the terrible, volcanic passions that lay hidden beneath Jed's soft exterior that the end of the plan came to Hilda. Now all was clear. Jed should kill Wemmer.

She bought Milly fine clothes. She forbade Milly to encourage Jed's courtship, knowing that the child would repeat her words to him. While she still held Wemmer off with feigned reluctance she set to work cunningly on Jed. A chance word and a trifling hint, and before long Jed was convinced that in Wemmer, a man who had wrested from him half of his own poor squatter's farm, he had a dangerous rival who would balk at no means for the accomplishment of his designs.

And Wemmer came and went unharmed. He found Jed there and abashed him with his patronage; his blood was fired by the mountain girl's innocent beauty. That night he came to terms with Hilda. He would pay $500 and she was to go South. Milly should come to town. Next week he would ride and escort her down. The wolf was creeping upon his prey.

Hilda Afgaard passed back into the cabin again. It was a crude log hut, such as the first settlers had built before the advent of the iron rails had made the frontier mining camp a town and brought the means for harnessing the water power of the stream. She went to the old chest, a bridal gift to her in those faraway days before she set sail with her young husband, Olaf, from Norway, that they might seek their future in the unknown wilderness. Stooping, she drew forth something that she had hoarded there for many a day. It was an ancient knife, keen once and wide of blade, which had been put to service in many a fight with mountain lion and bear. Its blade was completely coated with red rust, which had half eaten through the crumbling steel; but the heft, of hardwood, had well resisted the disintegrating force of the elements, and it bore, still legible upon the wood, the W of Wemmer's name. Hilda had found it on the third summer after her husband's death. That and the rope were all, for the glacier had kept the secret of her husband's murder. Wemmer had told her that the rope broke; but Hilda found it twelve feet over the canyon's edge, and cut cleanly, not frayed. She pressed the knife to her lips fiercely—not the heft, but the blade; then, hearing her daughter's footsteps, thrust it back into the chest again. Upon an afterthought she caught it up and hid it in the bosom of her gown. Then she turned to face her daughter, resplendent and awkward in her new clothes.

"Half an hour and he'll be here," she said. "I'll saddle Sim and ride to meet him." She kissed the girl, went out to the shack, where the pony champed at his corn, placed a worn saddle upon his back, and leaping into it guided Sim down the hill by the halter.

She did not dare look back at the girl in the doorway. Even now, but for the memory of that gray timber wolf, her courage had failed her. For Olaf's sake she must be brave—for his and for their child's. She must rouse Jed to the murder point, so that he would strike home.

Once out of sight of the cabin, under the cliffs, Hilda pulled in the beast, dismounted and running to the canyon's edge peered down through the pines. Far underneath a rider was urging his panting horse up the steep slopes. Wemmer's steed was jaded; he could not arrive for a half hour or more. Remounting, she drove her heels into the pony's flanks and rode at full speed in an opposite direction round the flank of the peak to where Jed's cabin stood, two miles away. The pony arrived with a foam-flecked halter.

Jed came out lazily to meet her, coat off, shirt unfastened at the throat, wiping his brow with his damp hand.

"Good ev'nin', Mrs. Afgaard," he drawled, surprise in his eyes. "I was reckoning—why, Mrs. Afgaard, what's the matter?"

She sprang from the pony's back and stumbled toward him, arms outstretched, face twitching in well-simulated terror. "Wemmer!" she gasped, and clung for support to the door lintel.

Jed leaped at her. "What's he done?" he shouted. "Out with it quick!"

"He came to the house," she cried. "He says it's his house and his land. And he drove me out. Struck me and drove me out, but—but—but—"

"Milly?" cried Jed. "Where is she?"

"She's in the house. He drove me out and struck me. But he kept her there. He thinks we're alone and helpless. Jed, help us. Save her from that gray wolf and kill him, kill him!"

Jed sprang for the pony's halter. He dug his hand into the creature's mane and prepared to vault into the saddle. But Hilda caught at him.

"No, Jed! On foot!" she cried. "It's quicker and safer, for we can climb straight up the crags before Sim could make the path through the pines." She dragged him from the saddle with almost superhuman strength. "Come!" she cried, and drew him after her.

Jed hesitated one instant only. All his faculties were benumbed, save for the single instinct of murder, and he was as clay in the woman's hands. A moment later they were running together over the slope. The precipice of tumbled rocks confronted them. As they surmounted it the red rim of the setting sun seemed to elevate itself for an instant above the streaky clouds in the west; it dipped down through them and disappeared; darkness spread fanwise over the sky from the fading embers of the clouds and the gleaming rind of the crescent moon rode out of the east. They struggled upward, panting, bruising their limbs against the outcropping bowlders. As they reached the top of the precipitous ascent and halted for an instant in the shelter of a fringe of pines, Hilda hissed into Jed's ear:

"What'll you do? What'll you do?"

"Kill him!" he sobbed.

"Wait," she gasped. "Take this."

She drew the knife from her bosom; but Jed was running ahead, outdistancing her. Now she saw the white cap of the peak in front of her, the waterfall roared in her ears, and rounding the bend she saw the black timbers of the hut, a horse cropping the sparse grass that grew by the door, and Jed running far ahead toward the entrance. She saw him disappear; then his cry rang across the slope and Wemmer's bellowing acceptance. Next moment the men came struggling through the doorway linked in each other's arms. They did not see her as she ran toward them, for their fight was the furious death grip of grizzlies and panthers, when they meet in mating time.

She passed them and crept through the door. Milly lay upon the floor, unconscious. She had fallen in a faint and lay perfectly motionless. Hilda cast a fleeting glance at her to ascertain that she still breathed and drew the rope from the chest. Then, creeping to the door, she stood there, poising it in her hand.

Wemmer had his antagonist by the throat and he was slowly forcing his head backward. Jed's knees trembled; he sobbed and threw up his arms with a spasmodic movement. Just then the rope descended over Wemmer's bull neck, tightened and caught him in its coil. As Jed released himself from the powerful arms of his enemy and stared about him in bewilderment, he saw the woman start up the mountain, drawing Wemmer behind her. He heard the breath hiss between Wemmer's purple lips; the rope was strangling him.

The woman seemed deaf to Jed's cries and pleadings. He ran beside her, expostulating, demanding that his be the vengeance. But she did not cease until they stood beside the glacier's edge. Then she unclasped the coil and allowed Wemmer to recover consciousness.

The waterfall roared in their ears. Illuminated by the rays of the moon, the shining ice particles, detaching themselves from the glacier floss, leaped toward the rocky barrier and hurled themselves over toward the valley below. They stood upon the very brink and waited.

Presently Wemmer groaned and opened his eyes. He sat up, clutching at his purple throat. Then the woman drew the knife from her breast and handed it to Jed.

"Aye, look on it," she said to the millionaire. "It's fifteen springs since you killed my man, thrusting it into his side as he stood unsuspecting upon the edge of the stream here, in this spot. This is the knife—look on it. This is the rope you cut—do you remember it? This is the place—I piled those stones that you and I should know it when you came to die. Kill him, Jed!" she screamed. "I have waited too long."

Wemmer's lips opened and a voice, unrecognizable as his own, cried from his swollen throat.

"I did not kill him!" he screamed. "I swear it is not true. It is a crazed woman's delusion. May I die as he died if ever I injured him." He turned his glassy eyes out toward the waterfall and looked down, shuddering, at the line of sharp, needlelike rocks that barred the end of the glacier. Suddenly he stiffened and a look of awful fear came over his face. The others followed his gaze.

On the edge of the glacier, wedged immovably among the sharp apices of the rocks, was the body of a man—Olaf's, but Olaf as he had been those fifteen years before, in all the vigor of his undiminished youth. His blue eyes were fixed in an unseeing stare upon his murderer, his yellow hair tossed and whirled and spun in the eddying current, and in his side was the open, gaping wound of the knife.

The glacier, which had preserved its captive through those long changes of years, secreting him in the dark bosom of its prison, had yielded up its secret in the end.

There was a moment's silence—absolute, dying with the thunder of the waterfall, so that the roar of the cataract seemed hushed and stilled. Then a babble of laughter came from Wemmer's throat.

When they could not hush him they drew the rope from his neck and set him free. They led him down the slope, and all the while he laughed, babbling incoherent words. He did not know them, and he stared at the hut, pointing with an inquisitive and childlike finger. Vengeance had overtaken him, but it was not Hilda's.

www.ingramcontent.com/pod-product-compliance
Lightning Source LLC
LaVergne TN
LVHW081314060426
835509LV00015B/1512